Y0-ABJ-213

HOW TO CATCH
TROPHY FRESHWATER GAMEFISH

AN OUTDOOR LIFE BOOK

HOW TO CATCH TROPHY FRESHWATER GAMEFISH

David Richey

Photos by

David and Kay Richey

Drawings by

Douglas Allen

Lloyd Birmingham

Foreword by

Ben East

OUTDOOR LIFE

CROWN PUBLISHERS, INC.
New York

Published by Book Division,
Times Mirror Magazines, Inc.

Library of Congress Catalog Card Number: 79–3976
ISBN: 0–517–538369

Manufactured in the United States of America

TO

My Wife Kay

CONTENTS

FOREWORD

by BEN EAST

I know no outdoorsman better qualified than David Richey to write a book on trophy fishing.

I have been a full-time outdoor writer for fifty-two years. During all of that time the profession has been plagued by armchair writers, men who did not do the things they wrote about and whose stories and articles on hunting and fishing lacked accuracy and the flavor of authenticity because of that failure. That is the last charge that can be made about Dave Richey. When he talks of taking trophy bass or tells the reader how to get the best of tackle-busting steelhead, he speaks from more firsthand experience than most sportsmen accumulate in a lifetime.

Dave and I are good friends, but we differ on one minor point. He prefers fishing to any other outdoor activity on this continent. Fishing is good, but I have always put hunting at the top of my list because it lets me walk and see what is on the other side of the next hill. However, if I were to turn seriously to trophy fishing tomorrow (somewhat unlikely at the age of eighty, which I have attained) the man I would go to for advice is Dave Richey.

He has been following that sport since he was sixteen. His score on steelhead alone stands at just under 4,000 (most of them returned to the river), a figure very few fishermen can approach, and not a few of them were taken by techniques and tricks that he himself originated. He knows as much about northern pike, muskies, walleyes, salmon, and panfish, and the knowledge has been acquired the same way, in days spent on creeks, rivers, and lakes over most of this continent. Especially he knows how to bring in the big ones.

He travels close to 40,000 miles a year on fishing adventures of one kind or another, and there is not much connected with freshwater angling that is not stored away in his memory—and set down between the covers of this book.

I have never known a fisherman who did not enjoy catching fish of trophy size. All fishing is fun (Robert Traver said in one of his books that trout fishing is so much fun it ought to be done in bed), but fishing successfully for lunkers carries a thrill and satisfaction all its own.

I still remember the look of delight on the face of Bill Rae, the talented editor of *Outdoor Life* with and for whom I worked for more than twenty years, on a day on Spedneck Lake in northern Maine, when he brought to the boat a 4-pound package of dynamite of the kind commonly called smallmouth bass. A 4-pound smallmouth sets no records, but that was the best fish of our trip, it had given a great account of itself, and the whole story was reflected in Bill's expression.

Then there was another day when I took a young fly fisherman out on a tiny Michigan lake only a mile from my home. There was not more than a couple of acres of water in that bog lake, and neither of us expected big fish. We made a fair catch of modest-sized largemouths and were ready to leave, when something dimpled the water in the shadow of an overhanging clump of loosestrife on the marshy shore. Bob laid a fly under the loosestrife, the water exploded, and when the battle was over he had a 5-pound bass in the boat.

Bob rarely showed open enthusiasm. He was even a bit cynical about all simple pleasures save fishing. But right then he looked and behaved exactly like a kid on Christmas morning.

"I didn't know there was a bass that big in a lake that small anywhere in the country," he yelped.

For my own part, I have had my share of lunker fishing and enjoyed every minute of it. There were the big squaretails, overgrown speckled trout, in the almost unfished lakes of the roadless bush of Algoma, north of Sault Ste. Marie, Ontario, many years ago. They measured up to 22 inches long, and the biggest weighed above 4 pounds. And their ability as fighters matched their size.

Then there were the trout, also squaretails, in the lower pools of the small rivers that come down out of the remote wilderness of northern Quebec, along the eastern coast of James Bay. They were not as big as their counterparts in the lakes farther south, no more than 18 inches. But on a light fly rod that is a goodly lot of speckled trout, and these had never seen an artificial fly. I have known no more exciting fishing in my lifetime.

I recall one occasion when I caught no fish of trophy size, but I will never forget the fishing. That was a pack trip to a high lake in the mountains of Montana, for golden trout. It was about the time the beautiful Grace Kelly became Princess Grace of Monaco. On my way to rendezvous with the Montana game warden who had arranged the trip, I stopped at a gas station. The attendant noted my Michigan license and asked where I was headed. When I told him he gave me a wide grin.

"Mister, if Grace Kelly was a fish she'd be a golden trout," he said firmly. That just about told the whole story.

Fishing of any kind is among the happiest of human pursuits. Successful fishing for big fish is best of all. This is a book that tells the reader where, when, and how to go about it, whatever kind of fish he may prefer.

It is also a readable book, a job of how-to writing that is interesting as well as informative. The author himself said of it, in a recent letter to me, "I'm in love with fishing, always have been and always will be. I have tried here to convey that feeling to others, and turn on anglers everywhere to the fun and excitement of taking a big fish by proven methods."

His book is one that beginner and veteran alike will enjoy and profit from.

—BEN EAST

ACKNOWLEDGMENTS

A book of this scope could never have been accomplished without the help of many people who, over the years, shared their knowledge with me, and countless individuals, companies, and state and federal agencies who lent assistance in the form of advice, photos, and products.

I am especially indebted to my wife Kay for her endless hours at the typewriter, taking photos, and researching a mountain of material. For a variety of help I thank Nancy Kerby, George Richey, Lawrence Richey, Andy and Leonard Thomas, Jim Tallon, Jack Duffy, Emil Dean, Dr. Ned Hether, Stan Lievense, Gary Marshall, Doug Knight, Ed Murphy, Ernie Dolinsky, Don Ronn, J. P. Elsliger, Art Dengler, Ben East, Don Podraza, Erwin Bauer, Jim Zumbo, Ed Eppinger, Dan D. Gapen, Ray Brown, Win Bestwick, Tom Corbett, Pat Madigan, Graeme Paxton, Burt Pelkey, Lea Lawrence, Jim Little, Tommye Copeland, Gerald Swartout, Charles Lunn, John McKenzie, Richard P. Smith, Pete Czura, Randy Colvin, Bob Ryan, Ray Gilbert, Tom Gronback, Phil LeBeau, Walt Sandberg, Greg Meadows, and Jim Murray.

Also, I am grateful to the Michigan Department of Commerce Travel Bureau, the Michigan Department of Natural Resources, the Pennsylvania Fish Commission, Evinrude Motors, Lund American, Normark Corporation, the Ontario Ministry of Industry and Tourism, Lou J. Eppinger Manufacturing Company, Sheldons Inc., Gapen Lures, Air Canada, Quebec Air, Vexilar, Minolta Corporation, Garcia Corporation, Burke Fishing Lures, Vlchek Tackle Boxes, Heddon Inc., Uncle Josh Company, Ale-e Fly, Michigan Squid and Michigan Rattlure, Mustad Company, Alpine Designs, Everson's Lodge, Wood's Bay Lodge, Branson's Lodge, Tunulik

River Camp, Luhr Jensen & Sons, and Bay de Noc Lure Company. And the following people: Max Donovan, Ed Apelgren, Jim Freisser, George Young, Homer LeBlanc, Rich Millhouse, Donny Nichols, Charley Hamelin, Stan Bowles, Cory Kilvert, and Arnold DeMerchant.

I also wish to express thanks to the following magazines, which originally published stories and/or photographs in which some of these techniques were first described by me: *Outdoor Life, Outdoor Life's Fishing the Midwest, Sports Afield, Sports Afield Fishing Annual, Field & Stream, Fishing Facts, Motorboat, Fishing World,* and *Fur Fish Game.*

If I've forgotten anyone or any company in this listing, I am sorry—and grateful in spite of my forgetfulness.

INTRODUCTION

Down through the centuries of angling it has become common knowledge that ordinary techniques used to take most fish simply won't tempt the larger specimens. It takes something a little special or different to get a trophy-sized fish charged up to strike. I've had the good fortune to fish all over the North American continent, and many years ago I decided I'd rather catch one big fish—a trophy— than a dozen smaller ones. Through the years I jotted down new techniques which produced big fish for me or my friends. I felt there would be interest some day to make a book on big-fish tactics a valuable addition to any angler's library.

I got my first clue to the burning interest among anglers in catching big fish when salmon were planted in the Great Lakes a decade ago. Midwestern fishermen abandoned other species for a chance at salmon weighing 15 to 35 pounds. They showed the same enthusiasm for steelhead and lake trout when these fish were planted in their region. Then many states began stocking tiger muskies, and the tempo increased. Anglers everywhere got the urge to lock horns with trophy gamefish.

What do we mean when we speak of a trophy fish? Is it simply a fish of a size suitable for mounting? Not necessarily. A trophy fish, as I use the term in this book, means a fish that is considerably bigger than the average fish of the same species in the same body of water. To use a familiar fishing term, it's a lunker.

Certainly, many anglers keep outsize fish and have them mounted by a taxidermist. The appendix contains a section that explains how to care for your catch and how to find the right taxidermist to do the job. But hooking a wallhanger may not be the goal of every angler. Many may be content with the experience of battling a mighty gamefish—and taking home nothing more than the memory of the struggle.

Whatever your aim, this book will tell you how to catch big fish. Armed with the techniques set forth in this book, you'll be able to approach a lake or stream with confidence. Nevertheless, it takes a special breed of fisherman to excel at trophy fishing.

The trophy fisherman is a person attuned to the outdoors and to the ways of his fish. Chances are he's interested in only one species and will fish at every opportunity for a trophy. Most trophy fishermen have one thing in common—the ability to concentrate totally on their sport. The angler who sits on the lake and guzzles beer or carries along a battery-operated television or radio isn't a trophy fisherman, because he doesn't have his complete attention riveted on outwitting his quarry. A trophy angler could be compared with a hunter seeking nothing but the largest buck in his region. His entire being is focused on the hunt. A fisherman must focus his attention in the same way; anything less than total devotion and concentration will not produce the desired results.

This compilation of trophy-fishing methods is the culmination of thirty years of trial-and-error fishing. I'm not a razzle-dazzle fisherman cranked up to take trophy fish every day, but then no one is. I'm an average fisherman with a deep love for my sport and the fish I pursue, and I bomb out as often as the next guy. But I know that I can catch trophy fish if given enough time, the proper weather, and a knowledge of the area. If you can provide the concentration and motivation, this book will arm you with the best tricks and techniques for every important gamefish that swims in North American waters. If just one of these tricks puts a trophy on the end of your line, I'll feel justified in having written this book.

DAVID RICHEY
Buckley, Michigan

I

BASS

I

LARGEMOUTH BASS

My trophy largemouth bass, an 11½-pounder, fell to dogged persistence. I'd spotted a huge bass spawning in Florida's Lake Okeechobee and had tried casting to it from a small boat. Every time I'd work within casting distance, it would flee to deep water. It seemed impossible to get a boat close enough to cast.

I finally decided to try wading in hopes I could work inside and drop a few casts near the spawning bed before the fish spooked.

A friend at a nearby bait shop stopped me before I left. "If you want to catch that bass, wade in very slow and stop every few feet. Make your first cast just past the spawning bed and work it through without hesitation. Your best chance to take that hawg will be on your initial cast. It had better be good," he said.

I motored to within 200 yards of the fish, dropped the anchor, and slipped over the side. As I closed to within 100 yards I began wading at a snail's pace. It seemed to take thirty minutes to close the final 50 yards.

As I eased into casting position and checked the knot on my black Johnson Silver Minnow for the tenth time I dropped my rod tip back and shot the first cast directly on target, 15 yards away. Reeling rapidly, I began darting the lure over the spawning bed. A broad back bulged the water under the lure and followed it 10 feet before striking.

I set the hook, and that huge largemouth boiled out of the water like a rocket lifting off a launching pad. The fish exploded across the water with his tail lashing back and forth. He crashed back down and tried to turn back to the bed.

I leaned on the bass with all the power built into my baitcasting rod. My thumb was clamped solidly to the reel arbor and I wasn't prepared to give an inch. If the fish made it into the emergent vegetation, he'd be gone and I'd have nothing to show for my encounter except a scorched thumb.

The fish came to an abrupt halt within 3 feet of the reeds, and that was the turning point. I continued to pressure the fish, and he responded in another majestic leap, a jump that covered nearly 10 feet, with flared gills and a back-and-forth twisting head.

We settled down to a slugging match. The fish kept trying to take me into the weeds and I kept trying to stay out of them. After ten minutes of heavy infighting I led him to my waiting net—I didn't trust myself to land him by hand. He offered a brief last-minute flurry before rolling up on his side.

I slipped the net under him and lifted 11½ pounds of milt-heavy male into the meshes, my largest bigmouth ever.

The largemouth bass generates more angling interest around the country than any other gamefish. Anglers from the Deep South are in love with this gamefish, as are Western fishermen and sportsmen from the East and Midwest. Largemouths are universally accepted as providing the most sport from some of the biggest fish found on this continent.

The largemouth's accessibility to sportsmen contributes much to the appeal of this gamefish, and the fishing industry has geared itself up to add as much pleasure to the sport of bassing as possible. New gear comes out every year just as spring rains bring green leaves. Lures come and go, but the bass remains, forever a challenge to sportsmen of this country.

The largemouth bass is a prolific critter, found native throughout much of the continental United States and in other countries as well. Transplanting of fish has introduced largemouths into vast areas of the country where bass never swam before. Most notable among these stockings were in the water-supply systems in and around San Diego, California. Florida-strain fish were introduced there a number of years ago and are now growing fat and sassy. They now threaten to displace the world-record fish, weighing 22 pounds 4 ounces, taken from Georgia's Montgomery Lake in 1932 by George Perry. Some California fish have already topped the 20-pound mark, and Western anglers are vowing they will soon set a new record. Only time will tell.

Washington is another state which shows excellent promise with largemouth bass. Although the fish are clearly not as large as Florida or California bass, the anglers are regularly taking 8-pound fish, and this places them in the trophy class in their range.

Bass fishing has developed the reputation of being commercialized. Bass boats, bass clubs, and bass tournaments have sprung up like mushrooms after a rain, and the sport has suffered severe growing pains. Although many bass "pros" catch lunker bass, on their own time, very few jumbo fish are taken during tournaments, since contest rules emphasize total pounds rather than single large fish, although most tournaments also give out large cash prizes for the biggest bass.

This means that many of the tricks used by tournament fishermen won't be discussed in this book, simply because their methods were developed mostly to produce large numbers of bass, while the trophy techniques are intended to produce small numbers of big bass. There isn't a method I know that ensures large numbers of large bass, and most anglers realize this basic fact. But there are methods that consistently produce trophy-size fish.

Many beginning anglers have great difficulty telling a largemouth and smallmouth bass apart. The difference is quite simple. The largemouth is basically green to blackish in color with a broad dark horizontal band running from head to tail along the lateral line. Largemouths get their name from the mouth. Draw a vertical line down through the middle of the eye, and if the upper maxillary (jaw) hinge extends back past the middle of the eye, it's a largemouth. One other clue is available that gives additional help. The spiny portion of a largemouth's dorsal fin will be nearly separated from the rearmost soft section of this fin. Largemouths also lack small scales on the lower portion of this soft spineless section of the dorsal fin, while scales are found here on smallmouths. But the quickest clue is the position of the upper jaw in relation to the middle of the eye.

FISHING SHINERS

One of the hottest current methods of taking trophy largemouths is to fish large golden shiners near weedbeds or patches of hyacinth. This sport is widely practiced in Florida, and it's not uncommon to catch bass weighing from 10 to 14 pounds.

The most important ingredient in this technique is the golden shiner. Guides fish exclusively for shiners, which measure up to 12 inches in length. They are caught on small pieces of worm and kept alive in aerated liveboxes for later use. Weak or belly-up shiners are discarded; the guides are looking for strong, healthy fish capable of swimming beneath floating weed mats.

A large treble hook is inserted in the shiner's mouth, and the huge baitfish is lob-cast alongside openings in aquatic vegetation. The angler gives the shiner plenty of slack line and allows it to swim under the cover. A good shiner knows safety lies in working back into the weeds or hyacinths, and that's where it heads. Of course, big largemouths use the weed mats as cover, since they provide both food and comfort from the hot sun. Temperatures may be 15° to 20° cooler beneath the floating vegetation than elsewhere in the lake.

The shiner is sorely troubled by the hook in its mouth, and this changes the cadence of its swimming, which sends out sound signals to nearby bass. A largemouth may hover near an underwater opening and allow the struggling shiner to swim to it, or it might explode from the weeds in active pursuit of the baitfish.

Many proficient fishermen can tell by the feel of the golden shiner whether the baitfish senses a big bass nearby. The swimming tempo will change as the shiner tries to hide or swims frantically away from a pursuing fish.

I once practiced this sport on Florida's Lake Apopka near Winter Garden. The shiner had been eased into the water near the weeds and immediately headed for cover. Line kept slipping off my Ambassadeur 6000 as the 10-inch golden slowly worked 10 yards back into the cover.

The line started spurting off my reel as the shiner saw a bass. The baitfish hesitated briefly, apparently trying to decide what to do and how to get away, and then spurted off in a new direction in a frenzied burst of speed. The pursuit was on as the largemouth closed the distance.

A large boil suddenly quivered the middle of the hyacinth patch, and the heavy mat shuddered as the bass made contact. My line stopped briefly after the largemouth grabbed the golden shiner and then started angling back deeper into the weeds. I allowed line to peel off slowly until it stopped again. I gave the largemouth a good minute to turn the shiner and swallow it before setting the hook.

Large stringers of weeds and hyacinths draped off my line as I pounded the hooks home. That bass responded in classic fashion; he smashed upward through the weeds, luckily clearing my line in the process, and smashed down again with the tail of my shiner sticking from his mouth.

We wrestled around for the better part of ten minutes as he tried to work his way back into the maze of tangled weeds. I finally gained the upper hand and lipped an 11-pound bass into the boat.

Shiner fishing isn't for everyone; it takes a dedicated angler with time on his side to connect by this method. Some fishermen try the sport once and go back to something that has more action although it seldom produces big fish as consistently. This technique necessitates a generous supply of shiners and the willingness to sit quietly and allow the bait to do its job, but it pays off with wallhangers of unbelievable size.

PLASTIC WORMS

One of the fastest-growing means of taking trophy largemouth is with plastic worms. Since the invention of this lure about twenty years ago, many changes have been made which are all designed to make the lure more appealing to bass.

Several methods exist for hooking plastic worms for bass fishing. They are all based on the so-called "Texas rig," which features a sliding tunnel sinker ahead of the plastic worm and hook. The hook point is inserted straight down through the end of the worm, out just ahead of the collar region, turned sideways, and buried in the body of the worm. This allows the worm to hang straight on the hook with the major portion of the body and tail trailing straight out behind.

This rigging allows the worm to wiggle seductively as it is eased over ledges, stickups, dropoffs, or underwater debris. Burke's Hook Worm is a new innovation; the very shape of this plastic worm causes it to give off an action that largemouths find difficult to pass up. The short plastic projections make it virtually weedproof.

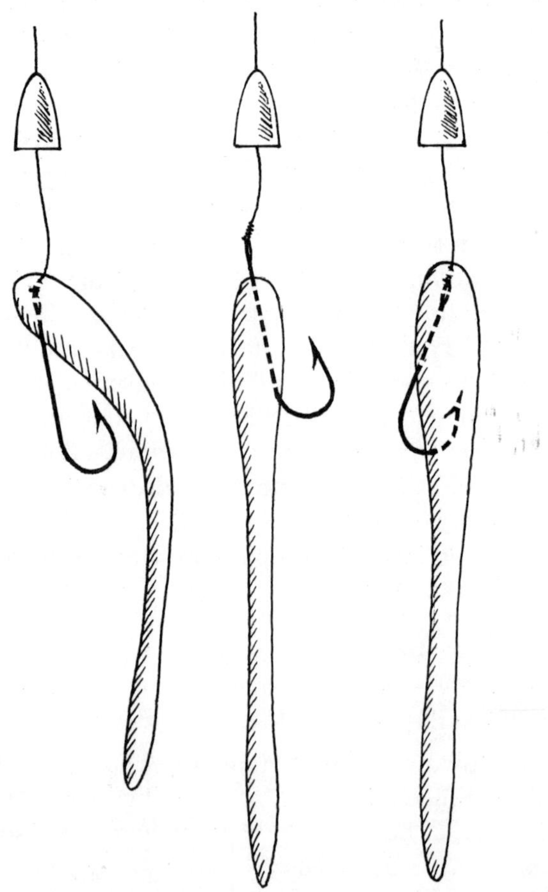

The basic Texas rig which allows the worm to hang straight on the hook with the body trailing behind.

Plastic worms are often used in conjunction with leadhead jigs, which decrease sinking time and allow the angler to work his bait into bassy waters much quicker.

It's been said that as much as 90 percent of the largemouth bass taken in tournaments or by everyday trophy-bass fishermen are taken on the plastic worm. Anglers interested in securing a mounting-size fish should concentrate on learning this technique.

One of the most difficult things to learn is a sense of feel. It takes the delicate touch of a brain surgeon or safecracker to detect the pickup by a bass or to "feel" the plastic worm over underwater branches. Some anglers learn quickly, while others never master this type of fishing because they haven't geared their brain to a change in sensitive vibrations or other signals which travel up the line.

Trophy fishing is a matter of attitude, a willingness to devote one's total attention and will to the fishing at hand. It requires complete concentration and a "sense" of what is going on underwater. Long hours of practice are needed to develop this undivided brand of thinking, and nowhere is this dedication needed more than with worm fishermen.

Many anglers denounce plastic worm fishing, since it's done at a snail's pace. Cast out, allow the worm to sink to bottom, and g-e-n-t-l-y *ease* it back with frequent pauses. My first exposure to this sport on Texas' Sam Rayburn Reservoir prompted me to think it had to be the most boring method of fishing possible. My mentor advised me to take five minutes to fish out each cast. Time dragged by on tired feet most of the morning as cast after cast was made and literally fished right up to the boat. It was difficult to keep my attention from wandering.

I slowly began to get a feel for what the worm was doing. I'd feel it slither up and over a submerged tree branch and then fall off the other side. I'd feel the tiny tick ripple up the line indicating the worm and lead tunnel sinker had encountered a solid obstacle. I'd ever so slowly raise my rod tip and creep the worm over and allow it to tumble down the other side. Once I thought I had a strike but came up with a bit of bark on my hook from a tree trunk.

My time had been allocated to cover a bass tournament, so I was stuck for several days. I made up my mind to master this brand of fishing before the hot June sun baked what few brains I had out of my head.

About noon the clear blue sky took on a look of impending storm; large clouds scudded across the sky and a faint breeze came up. I'd been casting to stickups and had just eased my worm for the hundredth time over an underwater tree branch when my bait took on a different feeling. I couldn't feel it strike bottom—it just went dead.

I lowered my rod tip, pointed it at the imaginary largemouth, waited just an instant, and cranked back hard to set the hook. My jaw dropped open a yard, I'm sure, as an 8-pound largemouth scrambled out of the water as if he were learning to fly and tail-walked briefly before heading down again. My guide was screaming to pressure the fish, so I leaned hard on the rod and prevented the bass from heading back into the tangle.

Two jumps later and a little boatside flurry and my bass came to the net, with ample proof that slow cautious fishing of a plastic worm is an excellent method of taking big bass. That first worm-caught bass seemed to open the door for me, because I followed quickly with two more lunkers in the 6-pound class.

Someone once said that your first love affair, your first whitetail buck, and your first worm-caught largemouth bass over 6 pounds are the most difficult conquests of your life, and I believe it to be true. Once you've mastered worm fishing you've conquered one of the most difficult yet satisfying sports in the world of trophy fishing. Every big bass after the first takes on a special significance and is only slightly easier than the last.

There are times early in the season when largemouth are in shallow water and a slip sinker isn't needed. At these times I prefer allowing the plastic worm to sink of its own weight. This gives the worm an undulating action difficult to attain when weight is used. Many largemouths will strike as the worm sinks in 6 to 10 feet of water.

It's important to keep a sharp eye on the line. A more rapid sink than normal or a twitching of the line is often the only clue you'll have to a strike. Once it reaches bottom, and it's one of my favorite tricks for bedding bass, twitch it along slowly. Since the worm is unweighted it will dart back and forth from side to side instead of up and down as it does when a slip sinker makes it nose-heavy. I tease it into a spawning area, and many times a protective old male will intercept it midway to bottom in an attempt to keep it away from the spawning redd. Dark colors such as black, purple, or grape have been most productive for me for weightless fishing.

Many times bass will be feeding near the surface if the water is relatively cool. In northern areas like Michigan and Ohio I've had phenomenal success using an unweighted plastic worm over the surface or near shallow weedbeds and emerging lily pads. With the hook buried inside the worm the rig becomes virtually weedless, and with a little practice and fairly light line you can snake it through brush and weeds without hanging up. These areas provide super fishing just after the spring spawn.

While most anglers agree that a brief hesitation between pickup and strike is needed when fishing deep with plastic worms, the opposite is true when fishing shallow water or on the surface with unweighted worms. If you're peeling the worm across the surface or fishing shallow-water spawning beds, the strike should be made on contact; otherwise the largemouth will frequently drop the worm.

Some anglers weight their own hooks by soldering a thin strip of lead to the hook shank. I've found that the action of a worm as it sinks with a weighted hook is vastly different than it is when the

Bill Dance tosses out a Texas rigged plastic worm while fishing on an impoundment. Success with a worm requires a sense of "feel."

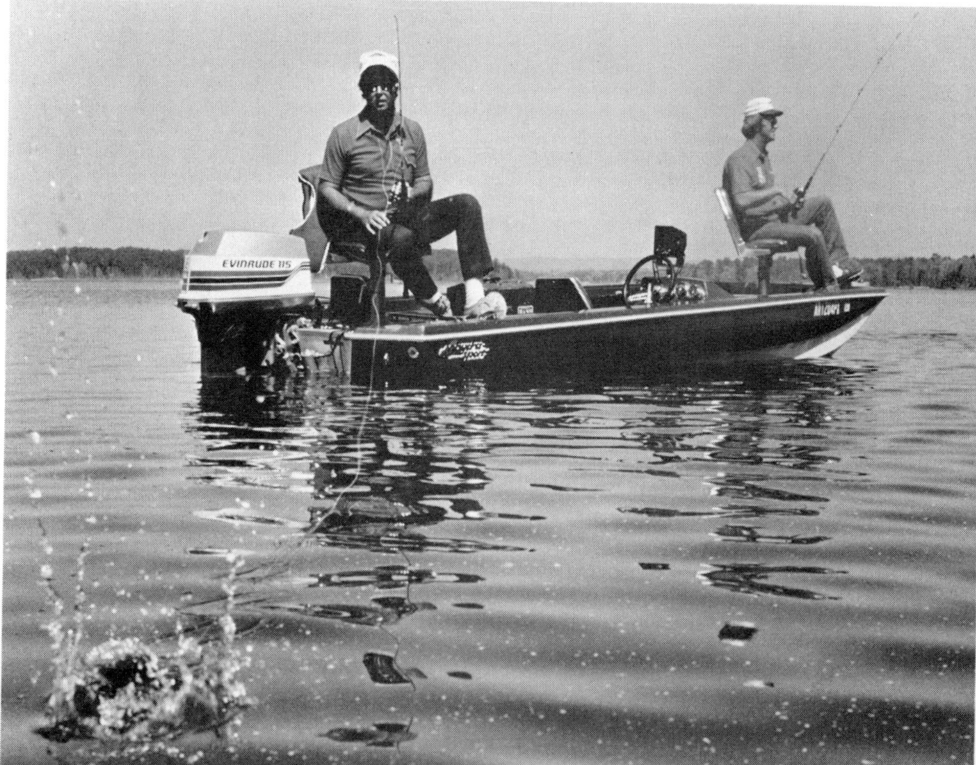

worm is pulled down with a slip sinker. This is definitely worth experimenting with in each area. Some regions or lakes are better suited to one type of rigging than another, although a slip sinker is always best in water 15 feet or deeper.

Several deep-water tricks have evolved with plastic worms. One of my favorites, since it eases my impatience to fish faster, is to lift my rod tip up and down to ease the worm over obstructions. I'll lift my rod tip slowly, ease it over the obstruction, and lower the rod tip as it falls. As soon as it settles in a new spot I repeat the up-and-down procedure with my rod tip. This keeps the worm moving continuously.

Another trick is to keep a tight line as the worm sinks to bottom. Many times a lunker bass will watch the worm sink and attack it before it reaches bottom. A sideways twitch of the line or a noticeable lack of line sinking is often your first indication of a pickup.

Plastic-worm fishing isn't the cureall for a bass angler's bad luck, but it is an excellent method of taking big fish when other techniques fail.

An important thing to remember about largemouth bass is that they hate direct sunlight. I've fished with deep-diving lures and plastic-worm rigs in 30 feet of water, and a friend pointed out to me long ago that the best success usually comes when the dark side of any structure is fished. I've dredged trophy largemouths from river channels flowing through reservoirs, where roadways were submerged, from ditches along old roadways, and have even caught a couple of big bass from exhumed graves which were emptied as a reservoir filled with water. Bass like it dark and relatively cool, and this is an important point to remember with lunkers.

NIGHT FISHING

Night fishing complements the above. Many waters are bombarded daily with water skiers, hotrodders in high-speed boats, and swimmers plying the edges of a lake. Once the sun goes down, the lake takes on an entirely different look, and bass become somewhat easier to catch. I've had some of my best midsummer success on lakes by fishing after sundown and after the lake traffic ceases.

I've read extensively on bass fishing in national magazines and books on the sport and have seldom found any mention of night fishing. In some states it's not legal, but in many it is. Those states with enough common sense to allow night fishing have done the trophy basser a big favor.

With quiet water conditions a big bass can work into the shallows to forage for smaller gamefish, crayfish, and other goodies. Although many anglers feel that topwater lures are best for largemouths after dark because of the explosive strikes they produce, I'm about to knock that theory into a cocked hat.

You can mark down in your little black book that I said that a night fisherman will do much better on largemouths with an underwater or even a bottom-crawling lure than with a surface plug. I get a kick out of the savage display of power when a bucketmouth blasts a topwater lure, but it happens too infrequently with big bass to be my cup of tea. I'd rather fish deep and hang up on bottom occasionally and catch some big bass than toss lures toward shoreline structures until my casting arm falls off in hopes of enticing one fish to strike.

One of my favorite underwater lures for midsummer night bass fishing is Heddon's River Runt. With a steady retrieve this lure will dive to a depth of 6 or 8 feet, which is just right for most situations. Another good choice, also a Heddon product, is the Deep Diving River Runt. I've taken many a jumbo bass after dark on both lures.

We've all heard the old saw about using black lures on black nights for bass. The theory goes that a bass can see it silhouetted against the evening sky. This may be true, because it's been proved that bass can see colors, but after dark? I doubt it!

Instead, I subscribe to the theory that more largemouth bass will strike after dark to underwater sounds or vibrations. The color is basically immaterial. I've taken bass on almost every color underwater plug manufactured, but these lures all had one thing in common—they vibrated and sent out vibrations or sound signals which allowed the bass to home in for a strike. Wiggling plugs like the two named above are classic examples of lures which give off sound waves due to their action.

If you stop to think about it, noise is usually what causes largemouths to strike topwater plugs after dark. Gurgle a Jitterbug along the surface or make a Hula Popper talk on top and this causes big bass to head for the sounds of something they apparently feel is a fish or some small creature in trouble. It sounds like an easy meal to a bass. You must incorporate the same thinking into nighttime underwater fishing. Select any one of a hundred subsurface lures which wiggle and give off vibrations and your catch of after-dark bass will increase.

Many night bass fishermen toss lures at floating swimming rafts, docks, weedbeds near shore, or the shoreline itself, and they catch the odd bass. Spend enough time doing anything on the water in bass country and you'll probably catch a fish or two.

My thought on this type of fishing is to hit a lick on the above-mentioned locations but spend most of your time casting parallel to shore and along the dropoffs or deep-water edges of weedbeds. Bass prowl both areas constantly once the sun goes down because baitfish are just as plentiful here as in the shallows. A big bass is vulnerable in skinny water and he knows it, so many of the larger fish will be prowling water from 6 to 10 feet deep. This makes them ripe for fishing with underwater lures.

I prefer to use a lure which works well at almost any retrieval speed. Cast out and allow the lure to sink (if it is a sinker) before starting your retrieve. If the lure needs to be reeled in to make it dive, begin the retrieve immediately. Strikes on this sort of plug have been known to sprain wrists.

An often-overlooked method of night fishing involves the use of plastic worms. I'd concentrate on the same types of water described for underwater lures and rig out the worm in the same basic fashion but leave the hook point exposed.

Cast the worm out and start weaving it over the tops of weedbeds or along a smooth bottom. A swimming beach is one of my favorite locations for nighttime worm fishing. Set the hook immediately on the strike.

SPOONPLUGGING

Many years ago Buck Perry developed a method called spoon-plugging which was based on his knowledge of bass and their relation to structure. He developed a lure called a Spoonplug which would dive to specified depths during a fast troll. Many anglers scoffed at the idea of fast trolling for largemouths until they saw the stringers of fish Perry brought in.

Spoonplugs are now manufactured in a variety of sizes and colors to suit a variety of depths. Select the depth of water you'll be fishing and tie on a Spoonplug of the proper size and begin fishing.

One of the best night-fishing techniques for big bass is to bounce a River Runt, or similar deep-running plug, down a dropoff.

This method allows an angler to strain the water quickly with a lure of proven ability. I've seen limits of largemouths that would make your eyeballs hang out taken from so-called "overfished" lakes. For some reason this metal spoon has a knack of producing trophy bass from all waters.

TROLLING

One method of trolling deep for bass that has been overlooked by many anglers involves the use of lures such as the Bomber or Water Dog. These lures, when trolled 60 or 70 feet behind a slow-moving boat, are deadly on big largemouths. All too often anglers overlook the need to fish deep and thereby remove any chance they may have had of taking lunker largemouths.

I prefer to troll along stairstep ledges or flat stretches of bottom with Bombers. The yellow model has always been my favorite. I let out line until I can feel the lip of the lure bouncing off bottom. Then I know I'm at the proper level.

One eye should be glued to a sonar unit to keep the boat traveling over the proper depth. My first introduction to this method came

Lea Lawrence plays a high-jumping largemouth on Tennessee's Dale Hallow Reservoir (above), brings it boatside and lands the 8-pounder (below).

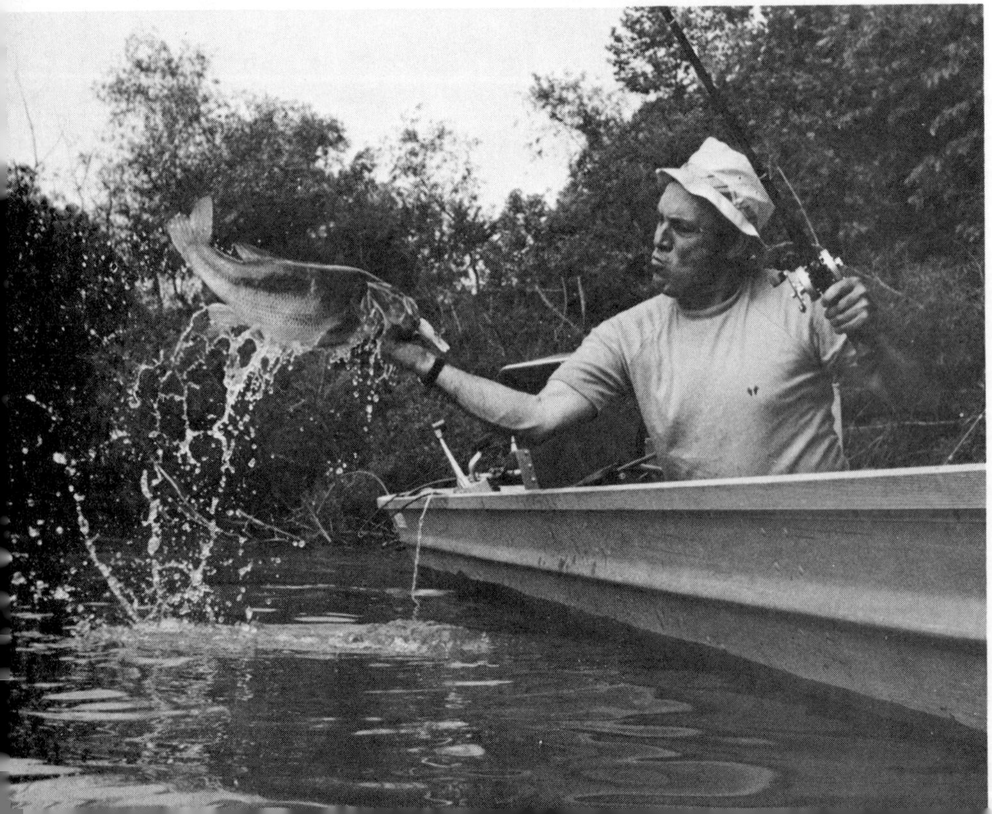

from a fisherman, now long dead, who fished Michigan's Lake Fenton. The lake was overfished and crowded with cottages, speed-boaters, and water skiers. Tom didn't care, because his stock answer was, "Any bass living in 25 feet of water couldn't care less about what goes on on the surface." This basic fact, coupled with his interpretation of the bottom soundings, allowed him to take limit catches almost at will of 5-to-7-pound largemouths. He performed this feat so frequently that other anglers began following him around. No one knew what his lure was or how deep he was fishing. He credited his sonar unit and his choice of lures with much of his success.

The important thing to remember about deep-water trolling is that you must select a lure capable of going to these depths and staying there. Tom's choice of lure color was invariably white, yellow, or black. He figured, as I do, that lure color at that depth isn't nearly as important as the action and vibrations these wiggling lures give off. His success indicates that these assumptions were true.

DOODLESOCKING

During my travels I've found that bass often hole up in areas where deepwater trolling isn't possible. One time an assignment took me to Toledo Bend Reservoir on the Texas-Louisiana border during the heat of midsummer. Bass were rather lethargic, and the surface water was approaching 90 degrees. Any bass being taken were coming from depths of 20 feet or more or beneath floating mats of weeds.

After my photographic chores were over I rented a boat for a day or two of fishing. The boat owner told me that doodlesocking was the only way to go. I'd never heard of this fishing method and was determined to learn it and give it a try.

He explained that doodlesocking was a vertical jigging technique used alongside stickups and other emergent brush. He pawed through my tacklebox and pulled out a Dardevle and told me to give it a try. He explained the up-and-down motions thoroughly. They were very similar to jigging elsewhere, except that I wasn't used to working a lure the size of the Dardevle.

After receiving instructions on where to find a cover near the boat ramp, I headed out armed with new knowledge but rather dubious about success. I tied the bow of the boat to a dead tree trunk jutting out of the water and spooled the lure down through the branches. Once I felt it was near bottom I began jerking the rod tip up with a violent 6-inch lift. Then I'd allow the spoon to tumble back down.

I tried three or four spots in vain, and my skeptical nature was getting the best of me. But I decided to give it one more try. I eased up to another tree, lashed the boat, and began doodlesocking again. I'd made two upward jigs when something heavy grabbed the spoon as it sank and tried to wrench it away from me. I jarred the rod tip upward to set the hook and a big bass began wrestling below me in an attempt to wind my line through the submerged branches.

I remember the boat owner's advice about hooking fish. "If you hook one, keep his head up and dredge him up out of the tangle

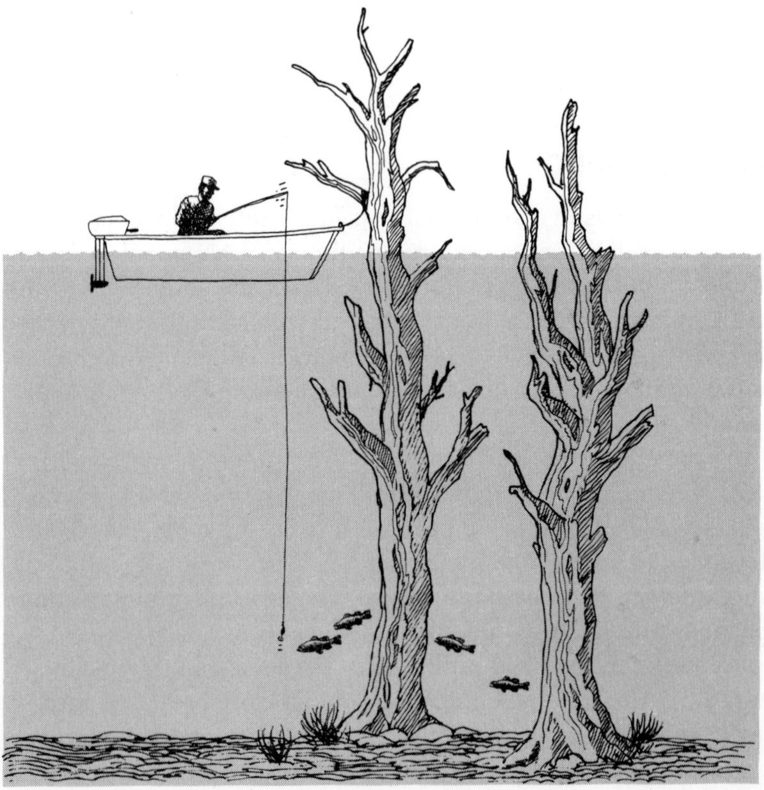

Doodlesocking is another effective technique for hooking trophy-size largemouths. The idea is to jig a shiny spoon along side a stickup or emergent brush.

before he knows he's hooked. Let him get his head twisted around a branch and you've lost him,'' he said.

I heeded his advice and leaned heavily on the rod while my hands twirled like a dervish, and I literally forced him to the surface. He exploded once near the boat and tried again to head for bottom and safety. I kept up the heavy-handed pressure, and slowly the fight went out of the fish and he soon allowed me to bring him to the boat.

He wasn't a trophy, but a 6-pounder hooked in the tangles of a drowned tree can provide a thrilling battle. My new technique later produced another bass slightly smaller, and I was pleased to have mastered a new fishing technique.

Almost any shiny spoon will work while doodlesocking. The key to success is continually jigging. The dark side of a tree is much more productive than working on the side closest to the sun.

Bass fishing is possibly America's number-one sport, and I've had the good fortune of having fished with some of the masters and picked their brains. The above techniques are among the best I know to deliver a brand of trophy largemouth bass fishing that cannot be equaled.

2

SMALLMOUTH BASS

The smallmouth bass is one of North America's most promising gamefish, and it's a shame he hasn't created as large a stir as his close cousin the largemouth. Bronzebacks are a fish of cold clear waters, equally at home in lake or river and generally found in wild scenic areas.

Smallies are common throughout the Great Lakes drainage, in many portions of Canada, as well as select lakes and reservoirs in the mid-South. The smallmouth is a direct opposite of the large-mouth in choice of terrain. You'll seldom find bigmouths in streams, especially rippling streams, while smallmouths prefer rocks, reeds, gravel shoals, and fast water. They reside in waters cold enough to freeze the fins off most largemouths, and this cool water is the thing that often makes a smallie respond to the sting of a hook with frequent jumps and headlong runs. Catch a fighting-mad smallmouth and you may overpower him, but he'll come to the net with fire in his eye.

These fish are found with a variety of body colorations, which are often attributed to the water, mineral content, and diet. The typical smallmouth bass derives its name from the fact that the lower jaw does not extend back past the eye like that of a largemouth. The dorsal fin has a shallow notch in the top center. Smallmouths have a brassy or bronze color, although I've seen some fish from Ontario which were almost coal black.

A distinguishing characteristic of the smallmouth bass is a row of vertical dark bars along the sides. In many waters the eye of the smallie is red at all times, and fiery red after a prolonged battle with the angler. A smallmouth could be compared to a stick of dynamite with a short, sputtering fuse.

Spring months are a peak period in which to catch trophy smallmouths. Spring, however, means different things in different locations. A good time to catch spring bass in Tennessee might be May, while in the northern reaches of Ontario, spring might mean the end of June or even July. The spring months mean spawning time for the smallies, and this often brings some of the best fishing of the year.

Last spring I fished Little Bay De Noc near Gladstone, Mich., during the first part of June. Smallmouths were just going on their beds. It was easy fishing, and the best success came from working rocky shoals in waders. I'd poke along slowly, fan out casts in front of me and on both sides with a Burke Wig-Wag Minno, and work the edges of all protruding boulders. I found the pearl or silver flake to be far superior to any other color or lure for that type of fishing.

The important thing was to use light line, cast far ahead of my shadow, and tease this lure along bottom and on all sides of the boulders. On that trip I shot a cast alongside a boulder lying in 5 feet of water with another 2 feet standing above water. The lure struck the water and began sinking. I saw a flash of bronze separate itself from the boulder and attack the descending lure. On impact I set the hook and a streamlined smallmouth arched out of the water, corkscrewed around, and toppled back, almost on top of the rock.

That fish went wild. He sailed in and out of the water repeatedly before finally tiring and allowing me to lip him out for a brief moment of admiration. The lure had had no apparent action, but the 4-pound smallie had resented the intrusion and struck out of spite and plain ugliness.

As the day wore on I found that no particular action was needed to trigger strikes from the pre-spawning bass. They were on the prod and would strike anything within reach.

Such actions aren't always the case. Many times a smallmouth can be covered from every possible angle and with every known technique and still not strike. But most of the time the angler can work out a method that produces. Smallmouths are often more wary than largemouths, and tricks that work for one usually won't work for the other.

Anglers used to fishing for largemouths with relatively large baits will take few smallmouths. Smallies like small baits or lures, and will seldom strike larger offerings regardless of how skillfully they are presented. Offer a bronzeback a smaller version, at the right depth and with proper action, and you're likely to have a battle on your hands.

Another thing about smallmouths is that a lure which is nailing fish today will be as flat as day-old beer tomorrow. This points out the need for a well-balanced choice of lures for this fish.

Although many anglers think of smallmouth bass as a fish of Canada, they are also taken from other widely scattered areas. The world-record fish, a colossal 11-pound 15-ounce monster, was taken from Dale Hollow Reservoir near Byrdstown, Tenn. A photo of that huge smallie now hangs at Star Point Resort, a famous location for smallmouth fishermen, on that reservoir.

CASTING TECHNIQUES

Trophy fish in large reservoirs are often taken by locating rocky ledges and stairstep dropoffs and working the area with jigs. Yellow or white jigs or spinner baits should be cast near the top of the dropoff, worked slowly to the edge of the ledge, and then allowed to drop downward on slack line. As the lure falls onto the next ledge below, a smallmouth might dart out and strike. If that ledge is unproductive, work it gently to the edge and allow it to fall off again, onto the one below. Work as much of the dropoffs as possible in this manner. Once you've combed each ledge, lift anchor and move down the shoreline slightly, reanchor, and begin the procedure over again. Smallies have a tendency to lie up in certain areas along certain ledges and it takes hard fishing to find them, but this is one of the most productive methods available for big fish.

Southern impoundments are home to native salamanders known as spring lizards. These critters attract smallmouth bass like a prime T-bone attracts a hungry fisherman after a day on the water. Several schools of thought exist on how to hook the lizard, but the majority of fishermen believe it should be hooked either through both lips or through the skin near a back leg.

I prefer hooking mine through the skin near a back leg and casting it out. A small split shot will usually aid in sinking the salamander; it's best to allow it to sink to bottom. A stop-and-go retrieve seems best for this type of fishing, since this is often the way the lizard behaves in the water. Work it on bottom or along ledges with frequent pauses. If a smallmouth strikes, give him slack line while he chomps down on the bait and then set the hook as hard as your line will stand.

Many companies such as Uncle Josh make porkrind lizards which are far sturdier than the real thing and much easier come by. Some fishermen are squeamish about handling and hooking live salamanders. An imitation is best for their purposes.

Some northern lakes have an abundance of crayfish, and this makes one of the finest baits possible for smallmouths. I've heard that the soft-shell phase (peelers) is best, but I don't believe it makes any difference to the bass, and soft-shells are more difficult to obtain. I collect crayfish by building a small trap from wire screen, setting it on the bottom of a lake, and placing a chunk of liver or other meat inside. The crayfish crawl in and gorge themselves on the meat. Frequent checking of the trap will ensure a plentiful supply of this bait with a minimum expenditure of time and energy.

Hook the crayfish through the tail with a No. 2 or No. 4 hook with one or two split shot about 6 inches up the line. Cast it out in prime smallmouth water. Crayfish are fairly delicate and often whip off on the cast unless a soft lob cast is made. The bait should be inched along the bottom with frequent pauses. Smallmouths strike this bait hard and are often well hooked on the take.

Crayfish are considered a wonder bait when used around old pilings or the slab docks found in many northern areas where timber was once floated downstream to the mill. These underwater

Crayfish should be hooked through the tail, fished with one or two split shot about 6 inches up the line. One of the best methods is to crawl the bait over an underwater dock or similar smallmouth lair.

lairs hold fantastic numbers of bronzebacks, and a crayfish crawled over a slab dock is one of the fastest ways I know to get an explosive smallmouth on your line.

Nightcrawlers and crawler harnesses are favorite rigs for smallies, especially in the Great Lakes waters. Many portions of Lake Michigan and Lake Huron, and Lake Erie as well, contain smallmouth bass in numbers. Either the harness or a single-hooked nightcrawler produces well as the angler casts to protruding rocks and gravel shoals. The single-hooked crawler should be hooked once through the collar with a No. 4 long-shank hook and cast out. The retrieve should be slow so that the crawler strings out behind the hook and wiggles seductively in the water.

Although I've taken plenty of smallies with the single-hooked

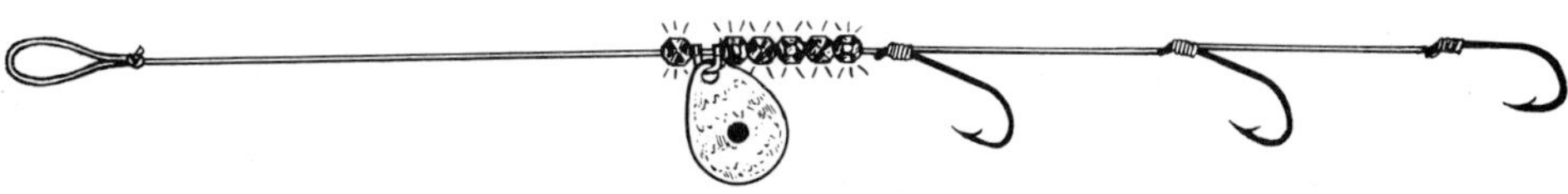

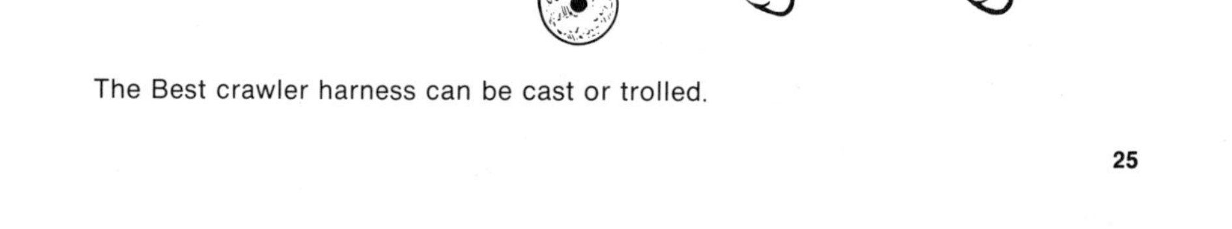

The Best crawler harness can be cast or trolled.

crawler I've taken larger fish using the Best crawler harness. This can either be cast or trolled through prime areas with equally productive results. I prefer either a red- or yellow-bladed crawler harness. It should be retrieved or trolled slow enough so the blades spin and give off a flash. A too-fast troll or retrieve is generally nonproductive.

A trick I mastered long ago was to plop the crawler down on top of a rock in the water. Smallmouths often lie in the shadow of a big boulder, and they can hear or sense something splatting down nearby. If you drop the crawler or harness rig on top of a rock, allow it to lie motionless for a couple seconds and then ease it slowly into the water like something alive slithering off the rock. If a smallie is lying beneath the rock he'll unload on the bait as if he hadn't eaten in a week.

As much as I enjoy wading and casting to suspected smallmouth locations, I much prefer wind drifting along a gravel shoal and casting ahead of the boat. By standing in the boat and using polarized sunglasses I can often spot fish near rocks before they see me.

For this type of fishing I've found it difficult to beat light mono and Burke Jig-a-Do streamers. The brown or green colors work best. This lure is built like a streamer with two single hooks joined together, and its action comes from a built-in plastic scoop on the head. I make my cast, hold the rod tip low, and reel just fast enough to make the lure wiggle. As it dances a jig past a rocky shoal, almost every bass will come out for a look. I've seen times on Ontario lakes when three or four smallmouths in the 2-to-4-pound range converged on the lure at once. It has to be one of the hottest lures in existence for smallies.

The Burke Jig-a-Do streamer is a productive smallmouth lure.

Stan Lievense landed this lunker smallmouth bass on a remote lake in Michigan's Upper Peninsula. It smacked a Jig-a-Do streamer.

I've used a raft of lures for Canadian smallmouths, but one of the finest is the jig. Two types, both made by Gapen, have produced hundreds of trophy smallies for me. I like the brown or yellow Ugly Bug or a yellow ¼-ounce Pinky jig. Although I use jigs in both rivers and lakes, the lure really shines when used in some of the swift rivers of Ontario and Quebec.

I like to take up a position below a waterfall or near a stretch of fast water. Bronzebacks will often choose a feeding spot near the head of fast water. A jig in fast water must be kept moving, and smallies seem to sense that deliberation over a lure may mean a lost meal. Cast near rocks or logs breaking the current flow, tease the jig into the pocket of quieter water found behind the obstruction, and swim it through with occasional up-and-down jigs. If a smallmouth is holding in that location the chances are excellent he'll launch an attack before the current carries the lure away.

Another trick I learned about Canadian smallmouths is to locate a deepwater point or rocky shelf where the water drops off quickly into 10 to 15 feet. If the bottom is strewn with small rocks or boulders, so much the better.

This technique works well from shore and is one of my favorites during a shore lunch break. Rig up a deep-diving River Runt, Bomber, or similar diving lure and cast out into deep water. Crank the reel hard to obtain the maximum depth and allow the lure to bounce up the edge of the dropoff toward your feet. Many times a smallmouth will arrow up off bottom and grab the lure near the edge of the dropoff. This technique works very well for the larger smallmouths which are often taken from deeper water.

Years ago a Canadian guide showed me his method of taking smallmouth bass. He maintained that islands, particularly rocky islands, attracted smallies during warm weather. A minor current flow is set up by the breeze blowing between two islands and the fish often stack up in 8 or 10 feet of water between the parcels of land.

Two anglers work a perfect smallmouth hotspot—a rocky point with a dropoff. Best technique is to bounce a diving plug off the rocks and dredge the bottom.

He'd use a sinking lure of any type and attach a foot-long leader to the trailing hook and then tie on a small ⅛-ounce yellow jig. He'd cast this unwieldy contraption out and get the plug working with twitches of his rod tip. As the plug darted back and forth it would jerk the jig along in the same manner. On two different occasions I watched him fight a pair of 3-pound smallmouths at once, but was never fortunate enough to see him land a double. Each time he managed to land one of the fish, the one hooked on the trailing jig. I'm not sure whether a smallie thinks this rig is two small fish or what, but the trick works often enough to be tried whenever other tactics fail.

Many lakes harboring smallmouths are rimmed with reeds which grow from sandy or slightly rocky bottoms. This emergent vegetation is often found in 5 or 6 feet of water. Reeds are difficult to fish with conventional lures, but bronzebacks like the cover and the abundant food found nearby.

I solved the problem of reedbed fishing one time by using a small silver Johnson minnow, a weedless lure. I attached a 4-inch leader to the hook and tied on a No. 6 single hook as a trailer. A 4-inch blue, black, or purple worm was attached to the lure and the other end to the trailing hook. When this was worked through the reeds with a continuous up-and-down jigging movement of my rod tip I found it to be an effective producer of trophy smallmouths in relatively shallow water.

The lure had to be continually lifted and eased around or over the reeds, but very seldom would the exposed trailing hook hang up—it just followed where the weedless spoon went. Many of the smallies I've taken with this method were hooked on the trailing hook.

TROLLING

I've never been a big fan of trolling for smallmouths because I delight in casting and feeling the strike from a fish on a relatively short line. The usual response is a startling jump when smallies are hooked close to the boat or shore.

A trolled lure generally goes deep and is usually at least 40 or 50 feet behind the boat. Although it can be very productive, it's just not my favorite method. But it can deliver big fish.

Down Tennessee way, anglers have a knack for taking trophy smallmouths. Deep trolling is one of their favorite methods. They like to use Bombers and bounce the plug off rock ledges and rubble-strewn bottoms, both in the lake and near rivers flowing into the reservoir. Smallies concentrate in these locations, and this technique works well during the hot summer months.

One of the finest trolling baits ever developed is the Rapala. It has a distinct minnowlike swim, it looks like a minnow, and it attracts smallmouth bass like a magnet. The most important thing to remember about this lure is that it can't be tied to the line with a conventional knot—only a loop knot will work. The loop knot will allow the lure to shimmy back and forth with a side-to-side wiggle, while a regular fishing knot will tether it too tightly and reduce this shimmy to a fraction of what it should be.

If smallmouths are known to be in fairly shallow water (under 6 feet), no weight is needed to take the Rapala down. At normal trolling or retrieving speeds it will dive to a depth of about a foot. A bronzeback will come this far off bottom to strike a lure dancing over his head.

When smallies are in deeper water I prefer to add one or two No. 4 split shot about 18 inches above the lure when trolling, or I resort to the Countdown model. I prefer the floating model, however, and don't hesitate to add weight to take it down. Just don't make the mistake of crimping split shot on too close to the lure, because it will upset the delicate balance and reduce your chances of taking fish.

I first tried trolling with Rapalas on Kabetogama Lake in northern Minnesota near International Falls. My host and I had originally begun trolling for walleyes, and after taking our limit we began casting for smallmouth bass. The fish weren't hitting well to cast lures, although I tried several methods which had produced elsewhere. No dice.

Out of desperation I loop-knotted on a Rapala and added two split shot above the lure and began trolling. One small walleye struck and was released as we continued on to a cove my guide said contained smallies.

We rounded the point and suddenly my rod tip arced and a bronzeback cleared the water in red-eyed fury, his tail slashing back and forth, gills extended, head thrashing. My rod was pounding against my hand as the fish exploded again with droplets of water spraying in all directions.

I tamed the fish after a short but hectic battle and led him to the boat, where we netted him. I removed the plug and added 3 pounds of prime bronzeback to the growing stringer.

Many times smallmouths school together, and they often pick a point as a schooling location. We turned the boat around and made another pass around the point, and this time my partner had to grab his rod before it bounced over the side. The same explosive leap and head shake and the same determined battle resulted before I could do the honors with the net. This action continued until we both had landed our legal limit of smallmouths; and every fish weighed a minimum of 3 pounds. Two fish crowded 5 pounds.

After we had taken our limit we trolled through the area once with a Rapala minus the split shot and didn't have a strike. If we'd taken a fish it would have been returned, but it was clear that the split shot made the difference that day.

NIGHT FISHING

There is a time when trolling with split shot ahead of a Rapala isn't needed. One of my favorite times to take jumbo smallies, fish up to and over 5 pounds, is after dark and preferably on a moonlit night.

These fish are spooky, like big walleyes, once the sun goes down and a bright moon comes up, but I've learned to troll a 5-inch surface Rapala 75 yards behind a slow-moving boat. Color is not critical—I've caught big fish on all colors—but silver seems to produce best at night.

I try to work my lure close to emergent vegetation, over slab docks, near pilings, or across a rocky shoal. Smallies will often come into knee-deep water after dark to feed, and a surface Rapala shuddering along a foot under the surface is an invitation to a fight.

A bronzeback seems to go beserk when hooked after dark. I've had them jump repeatedly without seeming to spend over a second in the water between jumps. Many fish have jumped from six to ten times before succumbing to rod pressure. This is the kind of action sportsmen can find after dark if they are willing to give up television.

I give the rod tip several short forward jerks while trolling to help activate the lure. Many times smallies will strike while I'm jerking, and this doubles the force of the strike. This method of fishing is guaranteed to spice up your life.

SHINERS 'N SPINNERS

Some inland lakes are so clear that smallies seem reluctant to strike lures. These same lakes are often so glutted with forage fish or crayfish that the bass seldom need to forage for food. The fishing is often poor unless you stumble on a trick as I did in northern Wisconsin two years ago.

I'd been casting lures with little luck while an old-timer at the other end of the lake seemed to be enjoying tremendous success. Every ten or fifteen minutes he'd tie into a smallmouth. After taking his limit he began heading for the boat ramp. I beat him there and was standing patiently nearby when he pulled up to shore.

I laid on my most pleasant voice coupled with a hangdog look as I bemoaned my luck. We traded pleasantries as I admired his fish. He was kind and offered to share his catch with me, but I insisted I'd rather catch my own. After sharing a cup of coffee he said he'd tell me how he did it.

"I live-trap minnows from a creek near home and keep them alive for the trip to the lake. I've found live minnows to be best." He then brought out a tacklebox chock full of small Junebug spinners and a large box of No. 4 long-shank single hooks. He explained his hookup to me like a patient parent explaining the facts of life to a youngster.

"Use only gold spinner blades. Attach the eye of the hook to the spinner and insert the point of the hook through the eyes of a 2-inch shiner or sucker," he said. When he cast this combination he'd allow it to settle near bottom and then begin a slow retrieve combined with an occasional upward jerk of his rod tip.

The bass were accustomed to feeding on similar-sized minnows, but they'd never been exposed to the flashing spinner blades, he said. They would follow the spinner, spot the trailing minnow, which seemed to wobble as if it were injured, and then they would strike. Easy as pie, he told me.

After thanking me for the coffee he returned the favor by giving me two of his spinners and a dozen minnows. He told me that he seldom used this technique on the same lake more than once a year, but he pointed out the place where he'd been fishing.

I jumped into my boat and sped out to the hotspot as fast as my oars would carry me and then coasted into position and anchored

Spinner rig with a shiner for bait.

quietly. I rigged up exactly as he showed me and began casting. I tried to imitate his retrieve, and halfway back to the boat a smallmouth intercepted the rig and struck with a furious yank. He danced around the boat for several minutes before I could put him on my empty stringer.

Twenty minutes later another 4-pounder nailed the spinner-

Pete Czura of Nebraska plays a jumping smallmouth bass on Ontario's Lingham Lake. *Ontario Ministry of Industry & Tourism.*

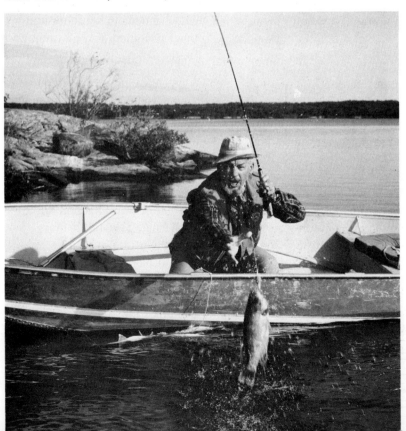

minnow combination and gave a similar fight. I stayed with the spot until I too had a limit of big smallmouths.

As I eased the boat up to the ramp just before dark, another fisherman stopped by to inquire how I'd done. I showed him my stringer of bass and he could hardly believe it. Remembering the generosity of the previous gentleman, I gave him the balance of my bait and one of the spinners. Darkness was falling over the lake as he headed for a bronzeback bonanza. I hope there were a few left for him.

FLY FISHING

I've had exciting fishing a few times with smallmouths on fly rods. My favorite flies are streamers or flies similar to the Muddler Minnow. I prefer fishing from a canoe as I drift downstream. One time I was working a stretch of the Delaware River and ghosting downstream in my canoe. I lay up against a large rock and lengthened line to drop a Muddler into a hole just downstream from a big oak which had toppled into the river. It looked fishy to me, and that was a good enough reason to try several casts.

I lengthened line and dropped the fly under the branches and watched it begin drifting downstream. I twitched it a few times and watched a big boil develop under the fly. An old-timer had once told me that whenever a big smallmouth starts after a fly, keep the fly moving in the current, and the fish will continue after it.

The fly darted through the edge of an eddy, swirled once, and straightened out downstream as I drew slightly on the line. The Muddler jiggled again in the current, and that proved to be too much for the fish. He inhaled the fly and swirled sideways to head for home. I set the hook and was amazed as that river fish slashed the water to a bubbly froth in an attempt to throw the fly. He darted upstream toward the hole, reversed directions and headed downstream, and capped his little run with a head-over-tail leap.

My tippet was light, so I didn't dare pressure him too much, but I moved just downstream from him so he'd have to fight both the current and the rod. Within a minute he turned belly up and came to hand, where I held 3 pounds of streamlined and compact smallmouth underwater long enough to unhook him. As I released pressure on his bottom jaw and twisted the fly out, he swirled and disappeared back to the bottom of the hole.

I've taken many fly-rod smallmouths before that time and many since, but that fish exemplified what anglers should know about river fish. It had been holding forth in a little pocket near protective tree branches. Other excellent locations are under overhanging banks or near boulders in the middle of the river.

River fish will seldom pass up a fly providing it is presented in a manner that mimics an insect floating on the surface. Keep your offering looking like either a surface insect or a struggling minnow and chances are good a smallmouth will take your rig.

If after reading this chapter you have come to the conclusion that I like to catch smallmouth bass, you're right. The fish swims around with a chip on his shoulder. He's always ready for a scrap, and he'll take on all comers. Approach him right and you might wind up with a trophy smallmouth.

3

SPOTTED BASS

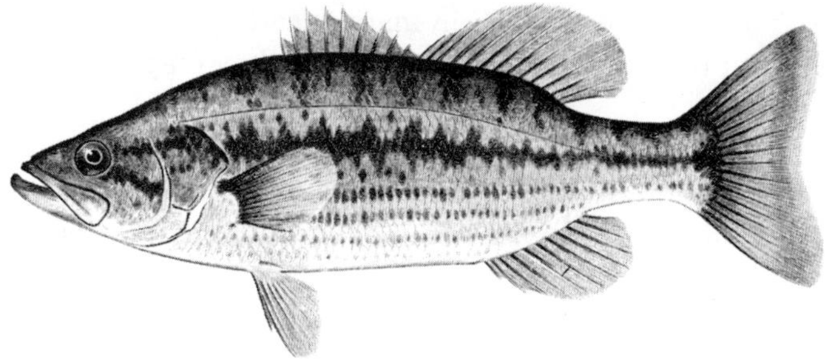

The spotted bass is a relatively unknown fish which is neither largemouth nor smallmouth but is a distinct subspecies common to many portions of the South. It was first discovered in Kentucky, and anglers from that state were quick to tack "Kentucky spotted bass" on the fish.

Since its classification the spotted bass has been discovered in Ohio, Tennessee, Kentucky, Missouri, Louisiana, Arkansas, Alabama, Mississippi, and quite possibly in Florida. Many larger reservoirs in Nebraska, Oklahoma, Texas, and Kansas also contain populations of this fish.

Spotted bass are usually an olive green along the back with dark diamond-shaped blotches or markings. A string of short dark blotches show up along the lateral line, and below that line the scales have dark bases that form lengthwise rows of smaller spots, which probably originally gave the fish his name. The mouth of a spotted bass does not extend back past the eye like a largemouth's. In most areas the maximum size for this bass is about 5 pounds.

This gamefish frequents a variety of waters throughout its range. In southern Ohio, possibly the northernmost reaches of the species, they are often found in sluggish, turbid streams with little current flow. In other areas, most notably in some Southern reservoirs, the spotted bass will frequent rocky ledges, sharp dropoffs, or clear streams. They have been known to go to depths of 100 feet, while neither largemouth nor smallmouth will descend that far.

Many Southern anglers have complained bitterly about the absence of spotted bass during summer months. The foregoing paragraph partially explains this phenomenon; the fish aren't in their usual haunts during warm weather because they've descended to greater depths seeking cooler water and more food. I've talked with several Tennessee anglers who have had to fish for spotted bass at depths of 40 to 50 feet during July and August. This midsummer disappearance has been noted in many locations, but many anglers simply give up on the fish until fall, when they reappear in shallower water.

One of the best methods of catching spotted bass involves a slow downstream float on some of Louisiana's rivers. One man eases a canoe or johnboat along while the angler in the bow casts small spoons or plugs near shoreline obstructions or log jams or works his lures through deep holes. A rapid retrieve seems to be more productive than any other. Use lures which are activated by a speedy retrieve.

Spotted bass feed heavily on crayfish and spend most of their time feeding on the bottom of a lake or stream or somewhere below the surface. There are periods of activity on the surface when anglers do well on bass bugs or streamers, but this, unhappily, is infrequent.

One point anglers should keep in mind is they should normally fish at greater depths for spotted bass than for largemouths and smallmouths. Being schooling fish they are not spread throughout a lake but are highly concentrated in small areas in most lakes.

Spring and fall months are usually the best time to catch any number of spotted bass, since they will often school near a tributary mouth or along rocky ledges where the bottom drops swiftly off in a series of banks or underwater ledges. High ridges slanting out to a sharply pointed area which then falls off into deep water make a good spot to look for this bass. Many veterans insist on locating bottom conditions featuring shale, crumbled rock, or other rubble that also attracts crayfish and minnows, which form the basis of the spotted bass's diet.

Areas of this type are best fished with deep-diving plugs, plastic worms rigged Texas-style, or safety-pin spinner baits. Remember to use a fairly rapid retrieve with everything except the plastic worm.

During the spring of the year, spotted bass often nose up into streams emptying into large lakes or man-made reservoirs. At this time may come some of the best spotted bass fishing of the year, because the fish will often strike anything smaller than they are. The roiliness or turbidity of the water seems to overcome their natural caution. If the water is extremely high and muddy I prefer using small lures which give off a heavy sound wave. Heddon's Sonic is a good choice, since it sinks deep, wiggles like a shimmy dancer, and also gives off vibrations which attract spotted bass.

Many streams may be much clearer and offer a brand of sport similar to river fishing for smallmouths. They seem to prefer much the same water and will respond equally well to small spoons, tiny underwater plugs, Mepps spinners, or flashing streamers tied with a generous amount of tinsel.

During cold weather, look for spotted bass to take up residence in large, deep pools in the lower reaches of streams where they are found. It takes a well-presented cast and a good lure worked along bottom to entice these fish into striking, but you can expect a solid jolt and a strong stubborn fight from every one you catch.

One of the best methods I've found for taking midsummer spotted bass was shown me on Tennessee's Dale Hollow Reservoir. That year August was a scorcher and spots were holding deep. We anchored over deep water where our sonar unit indicated the bottom consisted of rubble at 55 feet.

The air was still, so we didn't have to anchor. We simply stopped in the middle of the lake and began bouncing white jigs up and down near bottom. Every so often we'd bounce the lures directly off the rubble and then raise them about 6 inches.

The jigging went on for almost an hour. We were slowly being baked by the sun when my buddy, Mitch Egan, felt a jolt ripple up the line and down through his rod and into his hand. A fish had socked the jig way down deep. "He's on and I don't know what it is but it feels heavy. It's a big fish," he said.

Mitch's rod bowed dangerously as he battled the unseen fish. At first he thought it might be a walleye and then thought it was a smallmouth, but I'd advised him that very few smallmouths were taken at that depth, even in midsummer.

The fight lasted nearly five minutes before a 4-pound spotted bass rolled on his side near the boat and was netted. We continued jigging deep and caught four more fish, all slightly smaller than Mitch's trophy. Since that time we've taken several other spotted bass with a deepwater jigging technique.

I later talked with another fisherman who specializes in catching the spotted bass throughout its range. He said, "The same jigging technique works even better if a small pinhead minnow is hooked on the jig." I haven't had a chance to try this technique but I'm sure it will work.

The hottest technique I've found for spots is to hook a crayfish through the tail and fish it over piles of rubble when the fish are close to shore. Cast the crayfish out and work it back very slowly to the boat or shore. A too-fast retrieve will not work and will likely tear the crayfish from the hook. The crab should be fished as slowly as a plastic worm, or even slower. When a spotted bass grabs the crayfish, give him an instant of slack line before setting the hook and he'll have the crab deep in his mouth.

Spotted bass have made a definite contribution to American bass fishing, and I, for one, am very happy to have made the acquaintance of this superb gamefish.

II

TROUT

4

RAINBOW AND STEELHEAD

The rainbow of North America and its seagoing or lake-run cousin the steelhead provide anglers with countless hours of enjoyment each year. These fish are savage strikers, make long runs in both lakes and rivers, and jump exceptionally well when hooked.

The consistent taking of any large rainbow or steelhead is comparable to shooting a large whitetail buck every fall. It can be done, but only with persistence and a thorough knowledge of techniques.

Although the rainbow and steelhead are one and the same fish, the rainbow is considered a "stay-at-home" species while the steelhead is a migrant that has access to the sea. Steelhead migrate downstream and into the Pacific Ocean or one of the Great Lakes and then feed voraciously for two to four years. Near the end of its life cycle the steelhead homes in on the river of its birth and ascends the stream during fall, winter, or spring to spawn. Both rainbows and steelhead spawn in spring, although some research indicates some fish to be fall spawners as well.

The rainbow derives its name from body coloration. The broad band running along the lateral line and extending forward onto the cheeks and gill cover may vary from fish to fish but is usually a combination of pink, crimson, lavender, or even the color of orange-pineapple ice cream. The upper portion of the back and sides will be a greenish color with a liberal sprinkling of black spots extending onto the dorsal, adipose, and tail fins. Male fish have the highest degree of color, particularly at spawning time. They also develop a pronounced hooked lower jaw and a brighter slash of red along the lateral line.

Steelhead fresh from the ocean or Great Lakes are often silvery in color. The belly is nearly white in females, while males tend to be slightly darker. The caudal, dorsal, and adipose fins are dotted with black spots. A faint pink stripe may show along the lateral line or may be absent. The upper portion of the body is greenish, which makes the fish nearly impossible to see in rivers until they assume the more noticeable coloration of a rainbow. The mouths of rainbows and steelhead are white, which can serve as a guideline where this trout's range overlaps that of coho or Chinook salmon. The inside of a salmon's mouth is dark, or the gum line is shaded with gray.

Rainbows and steelhead like fast water; the heavier the flow and the more gravel-bottomed a river is, the better they like it. They like highly oxygenated waters and normally seek out springs in a lake or fast-water riffles in a stream. This is particularly true during midsummer months when the water level is low.

Trying to take steelhead from rivers can be exasperating unless you know a few tricks. I consider the steelhead one of the gamest fish that swims, and I've pursued them throughout their North American range, from the big-fish rivers of British Columbia down to brush-choked streams draining into the Great Lakes.

A steelhead, once he leaves the vast expanse of the Pacific or one of the Great Lakes, is a wary adversary. In his former environment he had little to fear, but in a river situation the fish is susceptible to predation from man, bears, birds, and other animals. Therefore, the fish seeks out cover, comfort, and feeding stations, in that order.

Cover can mean many things on different rivers. It could be a deep hole or smooth run along a riverbank where the current has sluiced out an 8- or 10-foot-deep channel; it could be under a stream-improvement project in a sparkling headwater creek; it could be in a comfort cushion of quiet water behind a great boulder on one of our Western streams. A steelhead will seek out any type of cover where heavy current can be avoided.

Comfort is a big thing. Steelhead are like people and wish to be as comfortable as possible. This means that cover and comfort routinely run hand in hand. Any type of cover that shields the fish from overhead predation and still blocks the flow of current will provide comfort. Water temperature contributes to the fish's comfort. If the water is bitter cold from an icy runoff or a cold rain, the fish tend to be sluggish and seldom strike well. A water temperature of at least 44° F. is essential for hitting the peak fishing action. Steelhead will strike in colder water but it becomes a chancy situation at best.

Feeding stations vary from season to season. Early-season steelhead while on their spawning runs will seldom bite well. Any strikes seem to be more to protect a spawning redd or eliminate other fish eggs or intruding lures and baits than to satisfy hunger pangs. Pre-spawning or spawning steelhead seldom have anything in the stomach; in many cases the stomach is shrunken and really not capable of holding much food. This is a biological change which occurs when most trout or salmon commence spawning.

FLY FISHING

Some of the finest steelhead fishing I've had has been during the peak of salmon runs. Steelies normally take up a feeding station directly downstream from a pod of spawning coho or Chinook. This enables them to feed actively on free-drifting eggs as they float downstream. I've found an orange or red fly such as the Orange P.M. Special to be admirably suited to imitate this bonanza of fish eggs.

The steelhead will normally hold downstream within 20 yards of other spawning fish. Deep pockets, small runs, and under overhanging brush are good spots to drop your fly in smaller streams. In larger rivers, the fish will still hold at about the same approximate distance but may not seek out any cover other than the deeper water over their heads.

The fly should bounce slowly downstream with the current in

Steelhead often take up feeding stations downstream of spawning salmon and feed on the drifting eggs. An orange or red fly drifted into their stations will usually fool them.

the same manner as drifting eggs. The take is normally soft, and the downstream drift will usually stop for an instant before the fish drops it and the fly continues along its way. Strikes must be made quickly, as steelhead seldom hold a fly for any length of time. I learned long ago to strike whenever the fly hesitates for an instant. Many times a steelhead will be mouthing the imitation.

This technique has been particularly useful on Michigan's Platte River. The fish will dart back and forth capturing eggs every time a salmon releases a cloud of spawn. I try to stand slightly downstream and across and throw my fly upstream far enough so it will be scraping bottom when it reaches the steelhead. The fly will hesitate momentarily and I'll set the hook hard on the take. Fall steelhead will often be down into my backing before I can get moving. They are full of fight and difficult to tame on light tippets.

Fly fishing is the fun way to take steelhead, but in many areas of the West the rivers are wide, deep, and very swift. This necessitates the use of a lead-core shooting head of a weight balanced to the fly rod. The standard cast is made quartering across and downstream. A lead-core line will sink readily and pull the fly down to the bottom. Many anglers prefer to have the fly swing across and downstream on a tight line.

One time, many years ago, a veteran steelheader on the storied Rogue River gave me a lesson in taking fish. He had watched my feeble attempts to cover fish and apparently felt sorry for me. "Try twitching the line every few seconds with your line hand as it straightens out downstream," he said.

I fished down through the pool and practiced the twitch and within a half-hour a steelhead came to the fly hard and rushed off downstream on a run that left me breathless. The fish capped that 50-yard sprint with a powerful headlong jump that made me hurt. Fifteen minutes later I slid the big hen's belly up on the bank, gently removed the hook, and held her motionless until she regained enough strength to move off by herself. That fish was 14 pounds of pure dynamite and proved the worth of the line-twitch method while fly fishing.

Precious few anglers realize how productive a nymph can be for steelhead—especially during cold-water periods. This technique was demonstrated to me on Ontario's Agawa River one year when the spring warmth forgot to come. Steelhead were holding in the bottom of pools and seemed reluctant to strike. I'd worked down through the best holding water, switched flies every ten minutes, and tried everything I knew to entice the visible fish to strike.

I sat down for a smoke and watched a pool which contained upwards of twenty fresh-run steelhead from Lake Superior. Another angler worked upstream toward me and stopped for a chat, and I gave him permission to work the pool. "There's no fish in it that will strike," I said. "They've refused everything in my fly boxes."

This fisherman was using lighter tackle than I was, and his tippet seemed about 2-pound test. He knotted on a No. 8 nymph pattern and waded into the shallows. He lengthened line and dropped a dainty cast upstream near the edge of the pool. The line worked downstream with an occasional mend and suddenly I saw him strike. I'd been watching closely and hadn't seen a fish move. His rod bent nearly double under the weight of an enraged steelhead.

The battle raged downstream for twenty minutes before he slid his net under a mint-silver steelhead just hours out of the big lake. He walked upstream and told me it was his fourth fish of the day but the only one he had kept.

He informed me that during cold-water periods a nymph pattern is often more productive than any other fly. Gray, brown, tan, yellow, and black nymphs produce best when fished right along the bottom. They must drift downstream with the current. I'd watched him slowly strip in line as the nymph scratched the bottom of the river during its downstream journey, but I hadn't seen the take.

"Strikes are very difficult to recognize because the fish takes the nymph very daintily and rejects it immediately. I watch the fly-line-

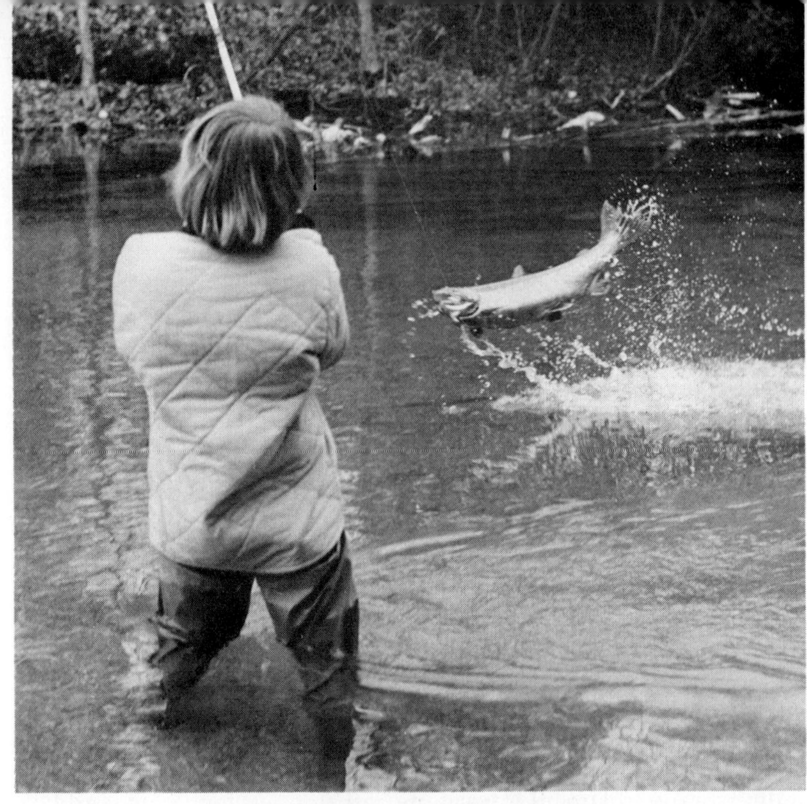

Richard Smith plays a jumping steelhead that struck a fly drifted deep through a run (above), then unhooks and admires his 12-pound trophy (below).

to-leader connection and whenever it twitches, I set the hook. Almost every fish will be lip-hooked and provide the most spectacular battle of all," he said.

Since that time I've tried nymph fishing whenever conditions warrant it and have found it to be a super way of taking trophy steelhead when other methods fail.

Many Midwestern steelhead streams, particularly in Michigan, are shallow, narrow, and brush-choked. A fly can be deadly only if the fisherman can get it down to the fish. In many instances the angler has only a yard-square area in which to drop his fly, and the steelies are often holding beneath the brush.

Several years ago my brother George and I decided to work out a method of fishing flies in such spots. We finally spooled level 15-pound monofilament on our fly reels, tied on a fly, and crimped on one, two, or three (depending on the water depth and speed) split shot to provide the weight needed to cast the fly accurately.

We found that the traditional means of fly fishing resulted in the fly or split shot banging off our heads or ears. So, we learned that an underhanded lob or swing cast was in order. The shot allowed us to place the fly much closer to steelhead, and it sank more readily than standard sinking fly lines. We were able to work out four or five casts to a nearby area while a standard fisherman was lucky to get one good cast into the area out of every ten tries.

This method enabled us to systematically place our flies in the best areas with a minimum amount of lost time. We were able to bounce the flies downstream and into the holes and hook fish consistently.

We did notice that strikes with this method were difficult to detect. Steelhead seem to mouth the fly only for a second and then drop it as quickly as they picked it up. The key to hooking fish with this short-range "mono" fishing method is to strike whenever the split shot and fly hesitate for an instant. An angler capable of taking fish on bait would find little problem catching steelhead with this method.

BAITFISHING

Baitfishing is another method that produces large numbers of steelhead, and it has nearly as many variations as fly fishing. Bait is especially productive during the fall, winter, and early-spring months. Without a doubt it is the leading producer of fish along West Coast streams.

Spawn bags, chunks of raw steelhead or salmon roe, nightcrawlers, single salmon eggs, wigglers (larvae of the mayfly), and small minnows are productive, although most fishermen prefer raw spawn or spawn bags. Anglers using the other types of bait are few and far between.

The baitfisherman must be a reader of water; he must know where steelhead or rainbows hold and how best to cast so his bait will work down to the fish in a proper manner. One trick I learned long ago is to hold two or three loose coils of line in your hand and feed it into the drifting bait whenever the stream bottom drops off. A sharp break in depth along a river bottom will cause the bait to drift over the heads of fish instead of being down on bottom where it belongs.

One of the first tricks I learned about baitfishing for steelhead is that the bait *must* bounce along on bottom. If it drifts 6 inches to a foot off bottom, you'll obtain very few strikes. The bait must also be bouncing downstream at the same speed as the current. A too-fast or too-slow drift is just as ineffectual as one where the bait swings over the tops of fish.

Baitfishing calls for the sensitive touch of a professional safecracker. Many times steelhead will merely tap the bait softly once or twice as it drifts past them. The only solution is to set the hook whenever the drifting bait doesn't feel right. The majority of the time you'll come up with leaves or a bit of debris, but you'll occasionally barb a trophy fish.

One of the easiest methods of taking trophy fish is to watch where others fish. Learn where they fish and then try to do 'em one better. I've discovered that all streams have an easy side and a difficult side to fish from. Most anglers fish from the easy side because they get a better (they think) drift that way. An old buddy of mine, George Yontz, now gone to better steelhead waters, once told me that anyone can catch fish from the easy side but damn few anglers will trouble themselves to try from the opposite side of the stream.

He then proceeded to show me how to fish a pool from the opposite side. "Not many people know it, and I've never shown anyone else, but the steelhead hold just ahead of where the water begins to shelve up above that riffle. Fish it from the easy side and the swirling currents lift the bait over their heads. Fish it from this side, like this, and the bait bounces naturally along bottom and right to the fish."

His first cast plunked into the same area that I normally cast to from the opposite side. The rod tip telegraphed the tapping of the lead weight along the bottom, and I soon saw the unmistakable tapping strike of a fish. George set the hook and a silvery fish vaulted into the air in a series of somersaults. Several minutes later, after a rough-and-tumble scrap, he led the fish to my waiting net.

"See how effective it is?" he said.

Any steelhead fisherman can probably think of many areas that could be fished from the "wrong" side of the river. This little trick is one overlooked by too many anglers.

Minnows can be particularly effective when fished during a spawning run (where legal). I tie up a minnow harness with two No. 4 or No. 6 hooks about 1½ inches apart. Place the top hook through both lips and out the top of the minnow's head and hook the bottom hook back near the tail. One or two small split shot will aid in sinking the minnow in swift currents.

Locate an area where steelhead or rainbows are actively spawning and cast the minnow across and downstream and swim it through the spawning bed. This may not be legal or accepted in some states, but it is legal in many and is a tremendous way to take home that trophy you've always wanted.

I've found it pays to jerk or twitch the minnow as it passes either in front of fish on a spawning redd or through a deep pool or run. This gives the minnow action and increases the chance of a strike. While soft baits like spawn bags or salmon eggs elicit only a dainty strike much of the time, a minnow provides the angler with a wrist-wrenching sock. It is necessary to work the minnow close to bottom for maximum effectiveness.

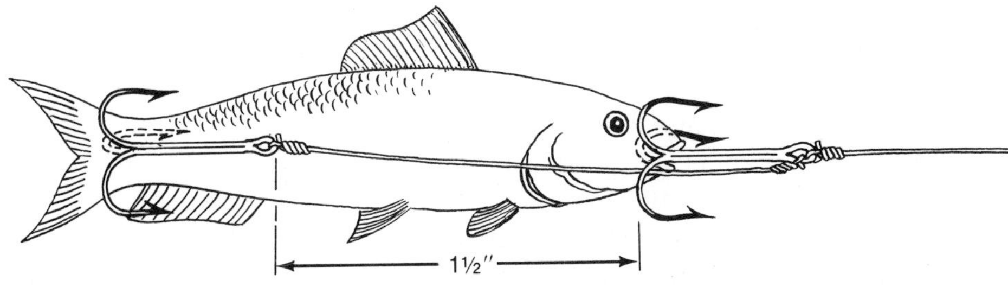

Minnow rig for fishing rainbows or steelhead in a river.

Many West Coast or Midwest fishermen use Okie Drifters with great effectiveness, but I've learned that a small addition of raw spawn to the hooks increases this lure's ability to produce fish. Two or three single salmon eggs or a kernel of raw roe is like adding chocolate topping to a dish of ice cream. The Okie is fished in the same manner as other live bait and is bounced downstream into holding water at the same speed as the current.

LURE FISHING

One of the most effective lures I've used is the Cherry Drifter. This balsa lure with a flashing blade combines the attraction of sound and flash with the appearance of free-drifting steelhead or salmon eggs. This lure is a favorite of mine when water conditions are high and dirty and the visibility nearly zero. Steelhead seem to home in on the flash and strike hard.

Another technique that has proved effective wherever big rainbows are found is to cast upstream with a No. 4 or No. 5 Mepps Aglia spinner. In dirty water I've found a silver-bladed lure is best, while in clear water a brass, copper, or black spinner is better.

This method has astounded me while fishing from the banks of many rivers. If a deep-water run is located along the riverbank I'll cast directly upstream and within a foot or so of the bank. Allow the spinner to sink until it's bouncing bottom and then retrieve it slightly faster than the current. This brings the spinner near the surface, while a too-slow retrieve will tangle in underwater debris. The fisherman who totals up the cost of lost spinners will seldom catch fish with this method, since you lose quite a few. But it takes fish from deep rivers that might otherwise not be taken.

BOAT FISHING

Three methods of boat-fishing rivers are productive for steelhead. The Western method of running HotShots ahead of a riverboat is one of the best methods of taking steelhead from large rivers like the Rogue. One or two anglers sit facing downstream while the boatman rows steadily upstream against the current. The current naturally overcomes the rowing movement, but the downstream drift by boat is slow and enables the fishermen to place their

HotShots about 10 or 20 yards below the boat. The upstream movement of the boat against the current allows the lures to wiggle in the most productive locations. A pull on one oar or the other will enable the guide to work the lures on both sides of boulders or other likely spots. Many riverboats are powered by jet engines and the guide often works down through a spot, motors back upstream, and then covers the area again.

Guide Emil Dean of Kaleva, Mich., fishes two large streams in that state, the Big Manistee and St. Joseph rivers. He has a large 22-foot johnboat with a jet engine. His method of fishing is particularly effective for large steelies and is called the dropback technique.

He anchors his boat directly upstream from a known holding spot, and he'll use either an X-5, U-20, or T-4 Flatfish or a medium-sized Tadpolly. The Flatfish is used during low water or in areas with little current, while the Tadpolly requires a heavier current flow to bring out its seductive wiggle.

Emil uses 20-pound braided Dacron line with a small swivel and 6 feet of level 15-pound monofilament down to the lure. He uses a Garcia baitcasting reel and throws the reel into freespool. He initially releases about 20 feet of line and places his thumb on the reel arbor, halting the downstream travel of the lure. This causes the lure to dive near bottom and wiggle frantically in the current.

After the lure has shimmied in place for up to thirty seconds he'll lift his thumb and release 3 more feet of line before stopping the lure's travel. This makes the plug dig toward bottom in a new location. Every thirty seconds he'll release 3 more feet of line and let the lure wiggle in a new spot.

In this manner he can fish a long drift of 75 or 100 yards without moving the boat. The strikes steelhead give on this method are ferocious; I once saw a rod yanked right over the stern by an angry fish. More than one fisherman has gone home with a sore wrist caused by a trophy steelie ripping away at the lure. An exciting feature about this method is that it produces very few small fish. Many steelhead of 10 to 15 pounds are taken, and the occasional 20-pounder. This is the stuff of which steelhead dreams are made.

Another boat-fishing technique I learned long ago was to anchor the craft in midstream directly across from a good-looking run. This method calls for spinning tackle with a sensitive rod tip. The best lure I've found is Heddon's Tiny Deep Diving River Runt Spook in yellow coachdog, red with white, or perch scale.

This fisherman used the tricks outlined in this chapter to take a 15-pound steelhead on a trolled Flatfish.

This lure has a long metal lip which enables it to dive quickly near bottom and wiggle like a dog with fleas. I prefer to stand and cast and aim my lure so it strikes the river about 10 feet above where I feel steelhead are holding.

Keep the rod tip low and reel just fast enough to bring out the wiggle. The lure will head for bottom like a flat stone, and the large lip will prevent it from fouling on underwater debris. Maintain a steady retrieve and work the lure through all parts of a pool or run. One area in which this lure shows its expertise is when fishing around submerged brushpiles or trees which have toppled into the river. Steelhead often hold in or near this debris. The lure dances through the brush like a weedless lure and triggers many strikes.

The strike is often a mere stopping of the lure's downstream travel. It will seldom stop when it encounters a stick or log, so I've learned to set the hooks whenever I feel a sudden halt to the lure's motion. Many times a steelie will be hanging onto this darting lure and a sharp upward setting of the rod tip will anchor the tiny treble hooks.

I've also found that steelhead will follow this lure as it works downstream and strike as it begins to swing around and straighten below the boat. Experiment with direct upstream casts as well as the across-and-upstream method—both work.

TROLLING

One trophy fishing technique common to the Midwest but not practiced along the West Coast is trolling. Many streams in Michigan flow into Lake Michigan, and many have small inland lakes just upstream from where they enter the Great Lakes. These inland lakes are superb for both spring and fall trolling, since the steelies tend to congregate in the smaller and warmer bodies of water before ascending the streams.

Trolling is a deadly method of tangling with a 15-pound-or-better steelhead. We use small boats with a very small outboard motor such as a 5- or 7½-horsepower Evinrude. The objective is to troll down to a rowing speed. A fast-trolled lure seldom produces.

We use either X-4 or X-5 Flatfish in red, red with black spots, silver with pink spots, or all silver. We troll lures about 50 or 60 yards behind the boat; two lines are the maximum which can be used without a costly tangle.

We normally use rodholders and angle the rod tips far out over each gunwale. This helps prevent tangled lines on turns. The rod tips will gently nod from the action of the lures at slow speeds. If they pull steadily toward the stern the lure has generally picked up some type of floating debris.

Short quick turns to port or starboard frequently trigger strikes, as does a quick speedup or slowdown of the trolling speed. Another trick is to lift the rod tip high over your head to make the lure swim harder. A following steelhead will often strike whenever we add these tricks to our trolling repertoire.

Excellent areas to troll are in front of tributary streams flowing into the small inland lakes, near outflowing rivers, along any sharp dropoff, or near a rivermouth where it flows into the Great Lakes. Steelhead hold in these areas for days and even weeks before moving upstream. They often can be located by a rolling boil or the clean jump of migrating fish.

A lightly set drag is important, because strikes are determined and savage. I had a rod tip broken once by an angry 18-pound steelhead that ripped my Flatfish. The fish boiled to the surface, ran swiftly toward the boat, and jumped just behind my motor. I was afraid the fish was gone as I hastily reeled in slack line, but when I tightened into the fish, it went berserk. That steelie catapulted from the water, did a series of twists and shakes like a beginning belly dancer, and flopped back with a mighty splash. That's when my rod tip parted.

It took twenty minutes of careful handling to persuade the fish he should come to dinner with me. He finally rolled on his side in submission and was netted. As I slid him gently on the floor of my boat the hooks dropped from a tiny sliver of skin on his upper lip. Another ten seconds of wild jumps or bulldogging runs and I'd have lost him.

Rainbows are widespread throughout the country and are stocked heavily in many lakes; they grow fast in the food-rich environment of a lake system. Many anglers consider them rather difficult to catch.

NIGHT FISHING FOR RAINBOWS

One day a buddy of mine asked me, "Have you ever taken rainbows at night—under the soft glow of a Coleman lantern?" The idea generated dark thoughts of idle fishing while sitting amid a horde of mosquitoes and other insects.

"No, I haven't, and it doesn't sound like much fun to me. I like to take big rainbows, and I've never taken many after dark, especially from an inland lake," I told him, as I shuddered at the thought of the prospect.

He wheedled and cajoled and finally I consented to give it a try—on one condition, if I could bring my fly rod along and try casting poppers for bass. The idea of sitting half the night on a dark lake and drowning bait sounded only one notch better than watching the grass grow.

We hit the lake at dusk and launched our boat. Larry flipped on his Lowrance Fish Lo-K-Tor and we began scanning the depths along an underwater ledge. It was apparent he'd done this before, and the thought of scientific fishing intrigued me slightly. After ten minutes we anchored quietly off a point jutting out into the lake.

The broad red reading on the sonar unit indicated a hard bottom near the dropoff—good rainbow water. It was about 18 feet deep.

"Now it's time to rig up," he said, and I reached for my rod. "Not yet," he hollered. "First we have to rig the lanterns." Two double-mantle Coleman lanterns were fastened to the gunwales, one on each side of the boat. They cast a broad flat glow over the water.

He then reached into a cardboard box and retrieved a can of whole-kernel corn and a pint of large-curd cottage cheese. "Dinner time?" I quipped. He merely shook his head sadly at my apparent ignorance and began ladling the corn and cottage cheese over the side, a little at a time.

After we fed the fish what seemed like an excessive amount of "chum," as he so aptly called it, we sat back for several minutes. My patience was being severely tested. "When do we begin fishing?" I asked.

"Patience, my friend, patience. We're waiting for the small fish to find the food. When the minnows show up we'll begin fishing," he said as he glanced over the side. "There's some," he yelped as he reached for his rod. "When the minnows show up the rainbows aren't far behind."

He passed me a jar of single salmon eggs and we added two to a hook. A single BB split shot provided all the weight needed to take the bait down to bottom. I cast 30 feet from the boat and the bait slowly sank. I kept an eye glued to the descending line and suddenly it began sinking at a faster rate. I reeled up tight and set the hook, into what I didn't know.

The fish yanked line off my reel with a steady run that ended with a splashy jump that bathed the rainbow in moonlight. I tried to work the fish back, but my 6-pound mono wasn't up to it. It became a tug of war outside the far edge of the lantern glow. "He's taking my line," I hollered as Larry chuckled from the stern.

The rainbow finally got turned around my way and I began retrieving line. The harsh sound of a buzzing drag announced a fish on by Larry. Five minutes later I slid my fish into the net and humbly admired the sleek lines of my 4-pound rainbow. Larry's 3½-pounder was next.

"Ready to quit yet? This is pretty boring fishing," he chided. I answered his question by baiting up again and promptly hooked into a tailwalking dandy. By the time the night was over we had a handpicked limit of ten rainbows and every fish was over 2 pounds.

We ramped the boat out and put our fish on ice. It was just before we pulled out for the trip home that I remembered I'd never cast a popping bug for largemouth bass. Somehow it didn't seem to matter.

RIVERMOUTHS

One of the most productive methods of taking steelhead and domesticated rainbows is practiced by Jack Duffy of Midland, Mich. This young man is addicted to these fish—he fishes at every opportunity, which is at least twice a week during spring and fall months. The number of fish he catches is astronomical. I've seen him catch and release fifteen fish daily for several days running, and he's taken as many as thirty-one steelhead in one ten-hour day. He seldom keeps fish but just enjoys catching and releasing them. He's taken many three or four times, which points out that steelhead aren't nearly as smart as many fishermen give them credit for.

He fishes various rivermouths along Lake Michigan and Lake Huron, and his technique works wherever it's tried. Jack is a bait-fisherman, and one of the best, but he abhors river fishing. He likes the quiet and solitude of boat-fishing a secluded rivermouth where his only competition are sea gulls.

Duffy also prefers light line and uses either 4- or 6-pound test. His method of rigging terminal tackle is part of his secret. He'll tie one end of his line to a barrel swivel after running the line through a ¼-, ⅓-, or ½-ounce slip or egg sinker. The sinker rests above his swivel. Below the swivel he'll tie in a 6- or 8-inch length of 4-pound-test leader and a No. 12 or No. 14 short-shank gold egg hook.

Marble-size spawn bags are used for bait. But here is where he differs from other rivermouth fishermen. He adds a white miniature marshmallow to the hook and slides it up the line just past the eye. He'll then lightly hook the spawn bag and slide the marshmallow back down onto the hook with the bait. The marshmallow will lift the spawn bag off bottom where cruising steelhead can spot it.

He chooses his spot to anchor off the rivermouth in much the same manner as a man studies the plans for his dream house. I've seen him study the river current, the wind direction, and the wave action of the lake for ten minutes before deciding where to anchor. He's determining which way the current is flowing, and I've seen him anchor in 3 feet of water over a sandy bottom and catch steelhead beneath the boat. He likes to fish *in* the flow of current as it works down the beach or out into the lake. One day he'll be fishing near shore and the next day he may be anchored in 10 feet of water. The current flow is the important thing, and it can change several times during the day as the wind and waves switch direction.

Once he's selected his anchoring location he fishes with two rods at once, both rigged the same way. It's a lazy man's way of fishing because he'll cast out into the current flow and lay his rods down with the drag set very light. Many times he looks as if he's asleep, but he's got both eyes glued to those rod tips.

These fish strike one of two ways. They will either literally rip the bait with a savage rush and line will peel off the reel with a shriek, or the rod tip will gently nod up and down as the fish mouths the bait and marshmallow.

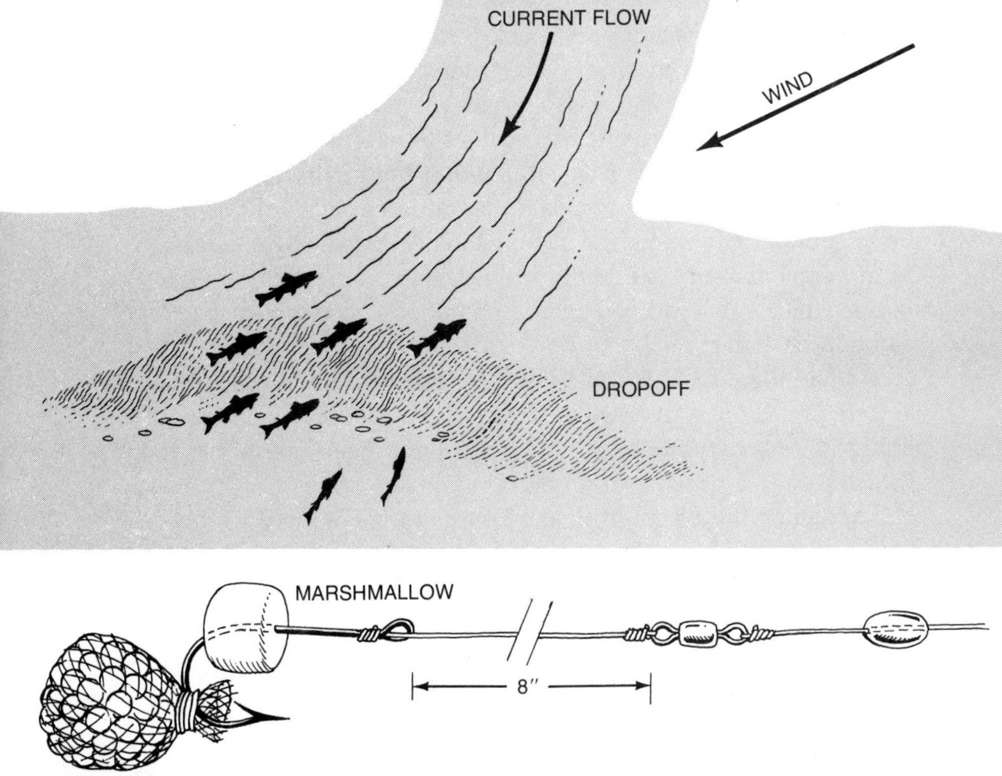

Jack Duffy's rig for fishing rivermouths.

The hard strike requires nothing more than tightening up and the fish is generally on. The soft strike necessitates lowering the rod tip to give the fish slack line and then setting the hook gently as it comes tight. I've seen Duffy have two steelhead on at once several times, and that is a double handful of excitement.

One time Jack and I were fishing—he with two bait lines and I was casting with lures. I hooked a rampaging 10-pounder that ran away from the boat. Duffy grabbed one line and started to reel it in when a fish grabbed his bait. As he fought to tame the high-jumping fish I heard the other reel sing as a steelie grabbed it. We had a tripleheader going.

Jack tried to keep the lines light on both his rods and wasn't very successful at it. I kept the pressure on my fish and he slowly wore down, but my partner was cussing as both fish crossed lines.

Jack allowed his fish to stay away from the boat until I managed to net my prize. It was unceremoniously dumped in the bottom of the boat and I grabbed one of the bait rods. The line slanted across the bow and I could see it under Jack's line. As I tightened into the fish it began tailwalking across the surface with angry shakes of its head.

We both bore down on our fish with as much pressure as the 4-pound leader would take. Jack's 8-pounder tired first, and he led it to the net. Once it was in the boat I committed a cardinal sin—I offered Jack's rod back to him and he took it. As we switched the rod from one man to the other, a little slack must have formed in the line and the fish jumped again and got off. It looked to be another 8-pounder.

We'd had three fish on and should have landed all of them, but we were proud of the two we'd boated. We went on that day to hook at least twenty steelhead and boated our legal limit of ten fish.

Steelhead and rainbows aren't all that difficult to catch, provided you know how they react in rivers, lakes, or the Pacific Ocean. The methods described here have allowed me to catch at least 4,000 steelhead from all areas of the United States and Canada, including both the West Coast and the Great Lakes.

These methods have worked for me and will work for you.

5

BROWN TROUT

A wealth of copy has been written about how to catch brown trout. Invariably the author tells how shy, retiring, and cunning this species is, and reams have been written on how stealthy approaches are necessary. I'll go off that well-traveled path just a little and say that trophy browns are no more shy or cunning than any other trophy-sized fish. They just require a proper approach to any given situation.

Browns were badly maligned at the turn of the century. Many states halted propagation and stocking of this European import because they said it had cannibalistic tendencies, especially on native brook trout. Almost all trophy fish are cannibals and grow large because minnows or smaller fish constitute a major portion of their diet. It's a basic truth that big browns never attain their size by eating just insects. They require meat and plenty of it. A brown is no different from other species except he'll often make a glutton of himself if enough forage is available. I've seen brown trout from the Great Lakes that look like footballs from gluttonous feeding on alewives. I once caught a 12½-pound fish which taped 23½ inches; it regurgitated seven husky alewives as it was netted.

At one time brown trout were classified as Loch Leven or VonBehr trout. These nicknames came about because one strain of browns was imported from Loch Leven, Scotland, while the other was imported from Germany. To this day the nomenclature persists in scattered portions of the country, but to most people, they are browns.

The brown trout assumes many and varied colorations. I've seen deeply bronze-hued males taken from streams or open water, and I've taken large numbers of silvery fish with distinctive X marks on their sides from inland lakes, streams, and the Great Lakes. The fish seems to develop distinctive colorations from each inhabited body of water. They have one of the widest ranges of body colorations found on any freshwater gamefish.

The basic coloration on browns shows an olive-green or olive-brown back with a golden-yellow or bronze belly. The upper sides are liberally dotted with bright-red spots. Some fish have wide bluish rings encircling the red lateral dots. The upper flanks are sprinkled with many black or dark-brownish spots, and these same spots are found on the dorsal fin and occasionally on the upper portion of the tail. The fins are unspotted along the belly and are often a yellowish green, although I've seen some fish with greenish-brown fins. The adipose fin is often dotted with red or brown spots. Some areas boast brown trout with white-edged fins similar to those of the brook trout.

Browns are fall spawners, and this usually takes place from September to December, depending on latitude. The resulting fry are hatched in fifty to sixty days. The lifespan of a brown is anywhere from less than a year in streams with tremendous fishing pressure to ten or more years for trophy fish that finally fall to a well-placed cast or die of old age.

Contrary to popular opinion, the largest browns are not necessarily the oldest fish. Wherever food is plentiful and little angling pressure exists, a brown can attain respectable weight in two years. Some Great Lakes or inland-lake fish may weigh upward of 10 pounds by the time they are two or three years of age. As a rule these fast-growing trout seldom live past the ripe old age of six years, and many spawn the first time and die when they are three or four years of age. But they might be tackle-busting fish of 15 pounds by that time.

Taking trophy browns on anything approaching a consistent basis requires fishing skill, a healthy pinch of luck, and an excellent knowledge of browns' habits and their habitat in rivers or lakes. Browns are usually a nonmigratory species, although anadromous runs occur from inland lakes up tributary streams, and from the Great Lakes and into spawning streams, and a strain of seagoing brown trout makes runs into sweetwater streams in various states such as Massachusetts and Delaware, and occasionally into various rivers flowing into the North Atlantic provinces of Nova Scotia and Labrador.

The easiest method of narrowing down the search for stream browns, the true trophy fish, is to find a pool or run that doesn't hold small fish. The cannibalistic tendencies of large resident fish drive smaller trout away. Although a pool or run may contain a large fish, big fish aren't found in an entire stretch of river; lunker browns will hold forth in just one small stretch of a pool or run and seldom move out except under cover of darkness.

One time I was prowling Michigan's Sturgeon River, in the Lower Peninsula, and the midsummer run of browns was coming upstream out of Burt Lake. I eased stealthily along the bank and studied deep pools and slicks for signs of fish. After two hours of looking I eased my head over a bank and located a school of browns—every fish weighing at least 6 pounds and one lunker that would go 12 or 13 pounds. They were holding position just downstream from a sweeper that had toppled into the water. It created a quiet cushion of pocket water just below.

A bluejay flew over the stream, and the shadow spooked the fish into a nearby pool. Ten minutes later, their fright over, the fish moved back behind the sweeper and held in the pocket of quiet water. Ten fish were packed into an area slightly more than a yard square.

I eased downstream, placed a cedar tree between me and the fish, and quickly cast a small Rapala upstream past the sweeper. It rode the current downstream and swept around the sweeper, and I gave it a jerk and fast retrieve to pull it under. The lure shimmied past the browns, and the last fish peeled out of the pack and nailed the plug with a savage smash.

I set the hook and leaned heavily into the fish to get him positioned below the others before he began fighting. I didn't want to spook the others in the school. The brown turned downstream, boring for the bottom, and then splashed to the surface in a lather of spray. He started downstream as I left the protective cover of my cedar tree and started to follow. The fish tried once to work back upstream, but I foiled the attempt by hurrying below and applying more pressure.

A 20-yard run and another brief flurry of topwater excitement followed before I was able to turn the fish toward my waiting net. A minute later I slid the 7-pound brown safely into the net and carried it onto the bank. I managed to take two more browns from the school before it spooked and disappeared into the bowels of the hole.

This anecdote points up the importance of initially locating trophy browns instead of merely fishing down through a stretch of water in hopes of taking big fish. Generally, browns are solitary fish and drive away any smaller trout once they've staked out a home turf.

Anadromous runs of browns often ascend a river in loose schools totaling up to twenty fish—all trophies. You'll seldom see lake or saltwater browns moving upstream by themselves; they are usually accompanied by at least eight or ten similar-sized fish.

I've seen runs of browns coming up streams tributary to Lake Michigan that number fifty or more, but they often take up a holding position directly behind spawning coho or Chinook salmon. In this feeding position they feed heavily on free-drifting eggs. This type of river situation is common on only a few rivers and isn't representative of brown trout fishing on a national scale. The same methods apply here as with steelhead in the same situation, as discussed in the previous chapter.

FLY FISHING

One of the most pleasurable methods of taking trophy browns is fly fishing during the so-called caddis or salmon fly hatches. The caddis hatch is common during June on many Eastern and Midwestern streams while the salmon fly emergence takes place on Western streams. One of my favorites is the Madison River in southwestern Montana. Many other mountain-meadow streams have heavy hatches of salmon flies.

The best hatches occur at dusk or after dark, and I've spent many midnight hours on Michigan's Au Sable River as caddis flies *(Hexogenia limbata)* hovered over the stream. This fishing is characterized by extremely heavy hatches; the whirring insects alight on streamside bushes, cover your head, crawl down your neck. And they drive large browns mad.

When a hatch is in full force, brown trout often lose all sense of caution and feed avidly throughout the river. They may set up feeding stations where insects are consumed at a regular pace. Many veteran fishermen time the dainty slurp of a rising brown and cast their imitation just a second or two before the fish is due to rise again. This places the imitation directly over his window of vision at the right time and a strike is made.

Night fly fishing for rising browns during a caddis or salmon fly hatch calls for better than average wading ability, good night vision without aid of a light (it puts fish down), and enough expertise to place the fly consistently where you want with a minimum of false casting.

Caddis or salmon fly imitations are designed to represent the insect, both in size and color. Both insects are large, and flies are tied on No. 4 to No. 8 hooks.

Night-feeding browns are discriminating feeders and are finely attuned to foreign noises such as those made by a wading fisherman. Many anglers walk the banks until a good fish is located. They then wade slowly and quietly into the river and take up a casting position within 40 feet of the steadily rising fish. If the fish is rising regularly, they time each rise and the interval in between, and cover the trout on subsequent rises. Many times the hatch is so heavy that a brown will rise and suck a natural off the surface alongside the imitiation.

Delicate presentation is needed, and the angler must learn to drop the fly daintily to the surface just upstream from the fish. Browns are basically leader-shy, and a 9-to-12-foot leader tapered down to 4X or 5X is often necessary to tempt fish into striking.

Once the cast has been made and the fly passes over the rising fish I prefer to allow the fly line to straighten out downstream and to one side of the fish before lifting it from the water. If the cast is made from one side of the trout it won't be spooked when the line is lifted out to make another cast. Care should be taken that the fly line doesn't float down over the brown's lie.

This basic method of fishing large hatches is useful on both Eastern and Western trout streams. The important thing to remem-

These husky browns were taken from a western river during a caddis-fly hatch. When a hatch is in full force, brown trout often lose all sense of caution.

ber is that night fishing limits the trout's ability to spot imitations and each cast must be on the money. Anglers willing to practice casting will find this method can produce startling results with big browns once the sun goes down.

Night fishing holds a special fascination for me; it's a time when brown trout may feed without caution, and it's proved to be one of the best times of day to take a trophy brown. After-dark hours are not for everyone, since many anglers aren't comfortable about wading water they can't see into. For this reason I've always advocated fishing down through a stretch during daylight hours to learn where obstructions lie and to obtain a feel for the water. I always pick out conspicuous landmarks which will be visible against the night sky. In this manner I've been able to fish a stretch of river up to a half-mile in length without having to leave the water.

I enjoy fly fishing, and another tactic that has paid off is to toss large white marabou streamers or Muddler Minnows to quiet-water pools. Select a pool known to harbor respectable browns and one that allows plenty of room for a backcast while standing on the bank or in the water. Wading skill isn't necessary for this method, but room to cast is, and only a few pools on any river will meet the requirement.

A floating fly line is used, and I prefer a level 6-pound leader. The most productive technique I've found is to cast the fly quartering across and downstream, similar to wet-fly fishing. A pool with a heavy surface current running through the middle will call for line mending. So I look for an area that is slow and deep without varying eddy currents.

The fly is cast across and slightly downstream and allowed to swing around and straighten out below. I've had success by allowing the fly to float on a dead drift or by imparting a slight twitch of the fly line with the line hand. Either technique works, but many strikes occur as the fly line straightens out below you in the current. The fish will lay into the submerged fly hard. This is when the fun begins.

A constant twitching of the line will activate the feathers on marabou flies, and this pulsating, breathing action makes a streamer look alive. I've had browns up to 8 pounds slam a fly two or three times as it swings across in the current before they are hooked.

If a fish strikes and misses, allow the streamer to continue on and give it another twitch. Many times a brown will follow up his attack with another slashing strike.

Many inland lakes have large hatches of caddis flies every summer, and vast windrows of nymphs struggle to the surface and are blown against nearby shorelines. At this time nymph fishing can be a pleasant way to work a lake, but it is both time-consuming and frustrating. It takes long hours of fishing to locate feeding browns, but once located they can be taken with a sinking fly line, a long leader tapered to 5X, and a nymph pattern which closely imitates the nymphs found in the lake.

I've never taken large numbers of husky browns with this technique, but I've caught enough to know it works best on calm days or evenings during peak hatching periods. Some of the 4- to 8-pound browns I've taken have been gorged with nymphs.

I prefer fishing from a drifting canoe or small aluminum boat. I'll normally fish in 10 to 15 feet of water, lay out a 60-foot cast, and allow the fly line to sink near bottom before gently inching the line and fly upward with short inch-long twitches. This will cause the nymph to swim upward in a struggling motion like a real insect heading for the surface.

A brown will usually take the imitation and swirl away and become hooked firmly in the corner of the jaw.

I've used this same technique on several weedy Western waters like Henry's Lake in eastern Idaho. Fish in that lake feed heavily on freshwater shrimp, and the same technique with a shrimp pattern can be deadly.

A slightly different technique has been perfected on Michigan's Little Bay De Noc near Gladstone. A small wet fly named the Silver Streak is used and tied on a No. 12 to No. 16 hook. The fly has a red tail, silver tinsel body, and wing and throat of gray, brown, or black bucktail or calf tail. The basic fishing difference is that a floating line is used with a 2-pound tippet.

During October, browns work in close to shore to spawn and make a last-minute feeding spree, and anglers cast to porpoising fish in 4 to 6 feet of water. They time the rolls and determine the direction the fish are heading and lay the fly in front of the trout.

The take is solid but not savage, and setting the hook with a fine tippet calls for a mere tightening of the line. A hooked brown will often make a 50-yard run straight out into the bay before sounding or throwing itself into the air. I've witnessed and been involved in several battles with these fish that have lasted the better part of thirty minutes. The average size is about 8 pounds of pure dynamite, although some fish up to 20 pounds are taken yearly.

SPINNING

Years ago when I first became interested in taking trophy browns after dark I decided that big fish want big meals and began using 5-inch Rapalas. A medium-action spinning outfit with 8-pound monofilament was my choice of weapons. I'd select a stretch of river that could be waded and I'd cast quartering across and downstream and allow the lure to swing across on a tight line. I would make a dozen casts before moving downstream another 10 feet. With this cautious, stop-and-go technique it took several hours to fish through a quarter-mile stretch. But pinpoint casting accuracy was needed, and it required time to peg casts under overhanging willows or alongside logs, or to cover fish audibly rising in midstream.

Each cast would be directed to a likely-looking area, and the entire water had to be covered with at least one cast, and more to better-looking spots. I learned that browns may totally ignore the first three or four casts and then lay into the next one with reckless abandon. Irritation, perhaps, was the major reason why the last of several consecutive casts produced a strike. It pays to fish an area thoroughly, and I've often gone back to an area after having had a missed strike and firmly hooked and landed a big brown on my second trip.

One time I eased downstream, casting to the available cover, and a huge boil enveloped my lure. The fish missed with his hasty strike. I waited ten minutes for the trout to calm down and began casting again. After thirty minutes of persistent casting I decided I'd put him down for the night.

I worked downstream and picked up two browns, a 6-pounder and a gorgeous deep-bodied 9-pound male with a great hooked jaw. Dawn was just an hour away and I considered quitting, but the thought stuck with me that I might possibly tempt the fish I'd risen earlier.

Backtracking, I paused at the pool where I'd had the earlier strike and began casting. I decided to offer the fish a different retrieve. This time I cranked hard on my reel handle and switched the rod tip back and forth several times and then eased up and allowed the Rapala to bob back toward the surface. As I started reeling hard again the lure stopped as if it had buried itself in a tangle of underwater debris.

I slammed the rod tip back to make sure and the lure didn't budge. Mad, I pounded the tip back again and was rewarded with a slight underwater movement. I tightened the line and leaned hard on my rod and a big brown rolled to the surface, slapped the water with a tail as broad as this page is tall, and then bored off downstream with his back out of the water. I followed downstream as best I could and caught up to the fish after a 50-yard sprint along the darkened river.

The brown worked up near my waders, saw me at the last instant, and plowed back upstream toward his home pool. Twice we went up and down the river before he finally rode the current downstream, thoroughly tired out. I beached him just as the sun rose on the eastern horizon. I slid two fingers under his gill plate and gently lifted 12½ pounds of trophy trout onto the grass. He was a gorgeous fish with spots as large as a dime. I had no need for another fish since I'd kept the two earlier fish, so I released him back to the river. A slight change-of-pace retrieve gave that fish something he'd never seen before and couldn't resist.

One of the most interesting techniques I've seen was shown to me by an unlettered mountain man from Tennessee. He talked with a slow drawl and told me that he matched the hatch for big trout from the Little Tennessee River. Differing from his fly-tossing compatriots, this man created his own "hatch" with nightcrawlers. "Worms are best for big meat-hungry browns," he said.

He knew the whereabouts of every trophy brown within 10 miles of his home near the river. His theory was that browns feed heavily on worms or nightcrawlers which drift downstream after a rainstorm.

His methods were delightfully simple and extraordinarily effective. He'd work 50 yards upstream from a suspected trout lie and begin easing large clumps of black earth into the water. As he sifted dirt upon the waters he'd also sow a few garden hackle. Within ten minutes the water in the nearby hole would be alive with the rolling actions of a gigantic brown as it intercepted every crawler that drifted down in the muddying water.

Once this mountain dweller decided the fish had fed free long enough, he'd ease downstream along the bank, nestle behind a screening bush, and flip an unweighted nightcrawler up to the head of the pool and allow it to drift downstream. The brown had been trained like Pavlov's dog and would nose up to the wriggling crawler and suck it in without hesitation. The angler's only deference to modern-day fishing was the use of a quality spinning reel and sound 8-pound mono.

The drag would scream as the fish tore the pool apart, but this old gentleman would play the trout with all the skill of a world-traveled veteran. After thirty minutes of back-alley scrapping he'd slide the tired old warrior onto the beach and his trout fishing was over until he decided to go again. He didn't take many fish, but every trout he caught from the Little T weighed from 10 to 20 pounds, and many were as long as your leg.

Many anglers find baitfishing repulsive, but there is no denying that some baits work well on big browns. I'm mindful of the time I tried minnow fishing on a small pond that contained native brown trout. The pond looked like a bass fisherman's paradise, with stick-ups poking through the surface. The bottom was laced with dead logs from timbering days and carpeted with a fine growth of weeds. Brown trout would lie in the logs or weeds and ambush anything that entered the area.

Max Donovan, my brown trout mentor, told me that he'd taken many fish on minnows from this pond. One night we pushed off from shore with two dozen 2-inch shiner minnows swimming happily in a minnow bucket. Max handed me my rod as I rowed onto the pond and began threading our way through the ghostly trees bathed in moonlight.

He'd tied two No. 8 treble hooks to the line, 1½ inches apart. "Hook one point of the top treble through the minnow's chin and out the top of its head, and then insert one point of the aft hook near its tail," he said.

Once this was done he then instructed me to squeeze the minnow until the air bladder burst, which would cause it to sink slowly in the water and also release some of its scent.

Max has an alternate method of sewing a minnow. It's a bit more time consuming, but the minnow looks more normal. You need a thin 5- or 6-inch surgical needle. Here's how to do it:

Tie an 18-inch leader of 6- or 8-pound mono to the tail hook with a clinch knot and thread the other end through the needle's eye. Insert the point of the needle into the minnow's side (or vent), just forward of the tail, push it through the stomach cavity and out the mouth. Pull the leader tight, pulling the shank of the treble hook inside the minnow. This leaves the hook points exposed, ready for short-striking browns. Then push the needle through the top lip and out the chin, sewing the lips together. (See illus., page 73.)

Max and I add a second treble hook under the chin. The leader is simply passed through the hook-eye, without tying it on, and the end attached to a small barrel swivel to prevent line twist while casting.

We cast methodically toward shore, allowed the minnows to sink about 2 feet, and slowly eased them back to the boat. This hookup caused the baitfish to undulate slowly in the water. Frequent pauses allowed it to sink near the weed tops. I'd been casting for ten minutes when the minnow suddenly stopped. I could feel a trout chewing on the other end. "Give him a little slack line," Max's voice boomed from the darkness. I instinctively pointed the rod tip at the fish and offered slack line until I felt a sudden surge of power as the fish swallowed the bait and headed for home.

I set the hook, although the brown was hooked deep, and we waltzed around that eerie pond for ten minutes before I worked a tired 5-pound brown to the net. "Not bad for a beginner," Max said as he lifted the trout into the boat.

Wherever legal, minnows are an ideal bait for pond or lake fishing. Some states have regulations governing the use of any minnows, dead or alive, in trout waters. This technique is a killer on big browns, especially after dark on quiet waters. It calls for light line and the ability to plunk a minnow down quietly. A slow retrieve brings out all the action needed to produce big trout.

Another minnow-fishing technique involves using the same terminal rigging, but a sharp knife is used to cut fine slashes along the side of the baitfish. This allows scent to dissipate from the minnow but keeps it more buoyant. A floating minnow is especially suitable when fishing in extremely weedy lakes or ponds.

I've found that a steady retrieve works best with minnows, but a slight jerk-pause will also pay off with more sophisticated browns. The jerk-and-pause method will cause the minnow to dart and weave like an injured baitfish. Strikes must be restrained until the angler feels the full weight of the fish. Many times a big trout will slash at the bait or grab it and attempt to carry it back to his lair before turning it around for swallowing. At the first hint of a strike, point the rod tip at the fish, giving slack line, or open the bail of the spinning reel. Once the fish takes up the slack and comes heavily to the hook, a slight set will generally anchor the hooks. Strangely enough, many browns will be taken on the tail hook.

Many years ago I spent several weeks fishing Montana waters and discovered a method that takes big browns below the huge power dams on some of the larger rivers. The dams disgorge vast amounts of chewed-up fish as they are swept through the turbines with the water. As this discharge water comes out below the dam,

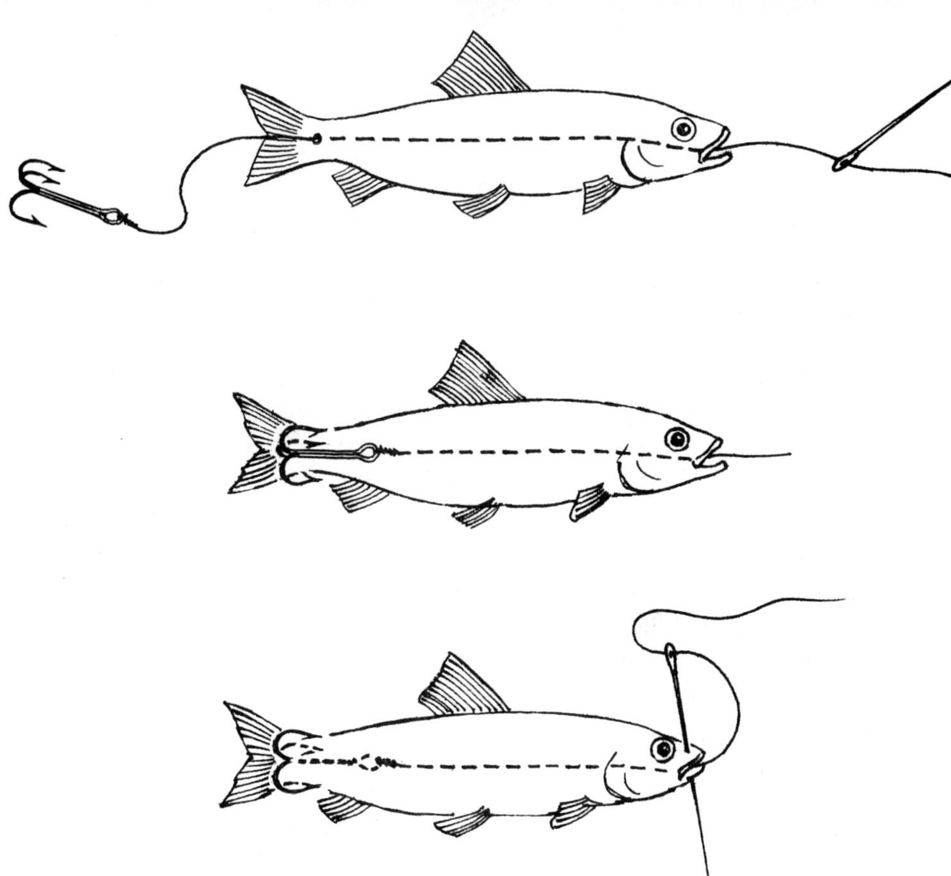

Method of sewing on a minnow for casting or trolling. Courtesy *Fishing Facts*.

large brown trout wait nearby to feed on whatever the current drifts down to them.

This large water is found below some dams such as Fort Peck on the Missouri River. The use of a boat is necessary to adequately cover the best water. A transient fisherman named Pete Jones told me about his success with big browns. Formerly from Utah, and fishing his way through the West, Pete had spent nearly a week trying to entice big fish from the waters below Fort Peck without success.

He finally decided to fish those big browns in the same manner he'd fish walleyes: on the bottom with jigs. He'd cut a chunk of flesh from a trash fish taken from the reservoir and attach an inch-wide sliver of meat to a Gapen Pinky jig. The meat would waver in the current as the jig was worked downstream. It also gave off scent, which added to its effectiveness.

He'd cast either directly upstream or across and upstream and allow the jig and fish flesh to hit bottom, and then he'd bounce it slowly downstream with short vertical lifts of his rod tip. He'd reel quickly to take up slack line and lift again. This method didn't produce an abundance of trophy browns from the Missouri, but I watched him catch four fish over 8 pounds in three days. He lost one lunker which would have weighed at least 15 pounds. Every fish struck as the jig settled to bottom between jigs, and each brown felt as if it was mouthing the lure. The hook setting was merely a forceful extension of the jigging motion. Whenever he felt a fish grab the jig he'd simply jig harder to force the single hook into the brown's jaw.

I've since tried this jigging trick below other dams around the country, and it pays off as it did below Fort Peck Dam. I tried it last year below Bull Shoals Dam on the White River near Mountain Home, Ark., and was rewarded with a fine 6-pound brown. I hooked another fish, presumably a brown, which was on for fifteen minutes. I never saw it but I think it would have weighed 10 to 12 pounds. It finally wound my line around another fisherman's anchor line and broke off.

Fishing a jig baited with a chunk of fish flesh below a dam. The jig is cast upstream or across and bounced along the bottom.

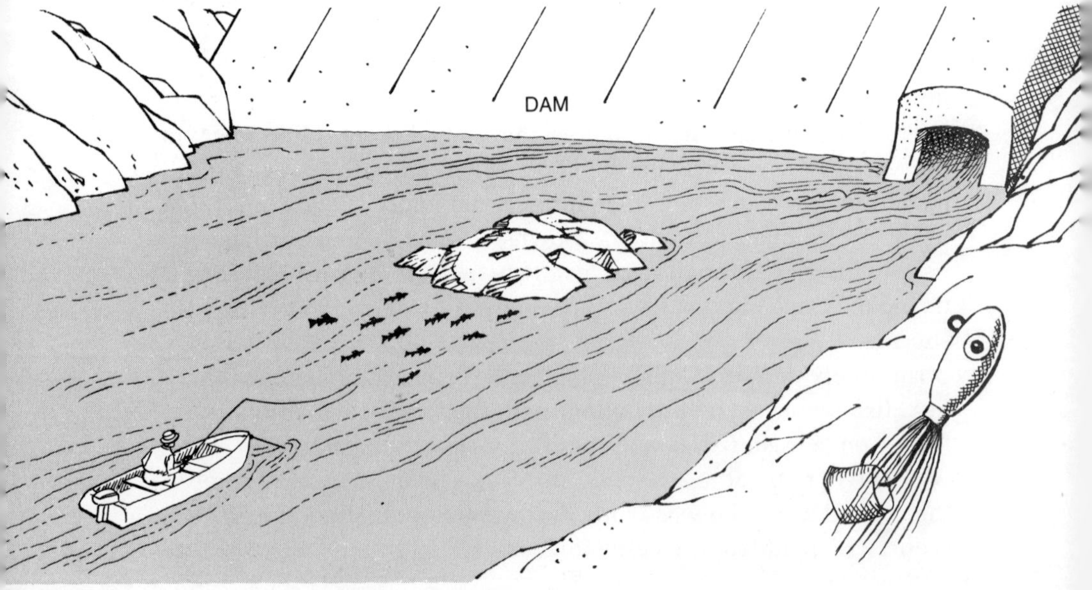

The fish that day hadn't struck the normal jigging-type retrieve. I'd tried it unsuccessfully, so I began experimenting with various lure retrieves. I finally tumbled on the fact that if I reeled slowly as the jig worked downstream, without a vertical jigging motion, the browns would strike like caged tigers. Last fall I tried the same trick below Michigan's Tippy Dam on the Big Manistee River and all I could catch was coho salmon. So, jig fishing pays off at times and falls on its face at others, but such is the case with almost all fishing methods.

TROLLING

In the early 1970s large numbers of brown trout were planted in the Great Lakes, most notably in Lake Michigan and Lake Huron. A few large browns are also taken from Lake Superior as well as Lake Erie and Lake Ontario. But the stronghold of this open-water fishery revolves around select locations in northern Michigan and Wisconsin. Numerous methods have been developed which have been instrumental in allowing fishermen to catch and land trophy brown trout since these plantings began.

Jack Duffy, a serious young fisherman from Midland, Mich., broke the ground on a Great Lakes brown trout fishing program. He began fishing for browns years before it became common knowledge that lunker trout were available. Through trial and error he settled on a technique that has allowed him to catch as many as thirty-one trophy browns in one day—all 6 pounds or better. His current Michigan state-record fish, a potbellied brown, weighed 31½ pounds.

Duffy likes to troll and does so from a small aluminum boat powered by an 18-horsepower Evinrude. He uses light-action spinning outfits stocked with 6-pound monofilament. "Light lines are needed to overcome the natural wariness of these fish in crystal-clear water," he says.

Flatfish in sizes X-5 and U-20 are used in either silver plate or pearl, and Duffy insists on trolling them 125 to 150 yards behind his slow-moving boat. He prefers fishing close to shore during May and June and slightly farther out during July. As he trolls he looks for rolling fish while steering a zigzag pattern. If the fish are in very shallow water, over rocky shoals, he'll fish with a Sugar Spoon and a slightly faster trolling speed. The important thing is to troll at speeds which will bring out the maximum lure action.

Many times spring browns will be found in 6 to 10 feet of water as they haze minnows into shallow water to feed. Duffy prefers to troll along the outside edge of the fish to prevent spooking them. He sets his drags very light, and each strike results in a fish peeling out 50 yards of line.

Another trolling trick that works with light line is to gun the motor occasionally. This causes the lure to increase its wiggle, and it often turns fish on. The short burst of speed should be maintained for about 10 feet and then a quick slowdown to the original slow trolling speed. This works particularly well on a turn to port or starboard.

Dawn seems to be the best time to fish, although big Great Lakes browns will hit all day occasionally. The most important thing is to be able to locate fish, and this may sometimes take the better part of the morning. But once located, the fish strike well if the lure is far enough behind the boat.

Another interesting aspect comes to mind about taking trophy browns from Great Lakes waters. Shortly after ice-out, which occurs anywhere from March to mid-April, browns move inshore to feed actively on smelt, which are preparing to scoot up spawning streams. I've seen large numbers of smelt being systematically cut to shreds by schools of hungry brown trout. This massacre will continue, barring sudden severe changes in weather or wind direction, for upwards of a month. At this time the fish are not as large as during early summer months, but the majority of trout taken will average between 3 and 6 pounds, still a trophy trout for many people.

WADING SHORELINE

I prefer to either wade the shoreline and fan-cast small Devle Dogs, Krocodiles, or Little Cleos in a circular pattern around me. Browns are often in water as shallow as 4 feet, so movements must be kept slow and quiet. A rapid retrieve seems to produce best, since it doesn't give the fish time to inspect the lure thoroughly.

At other times the fish will be feeding in slightly deeper water

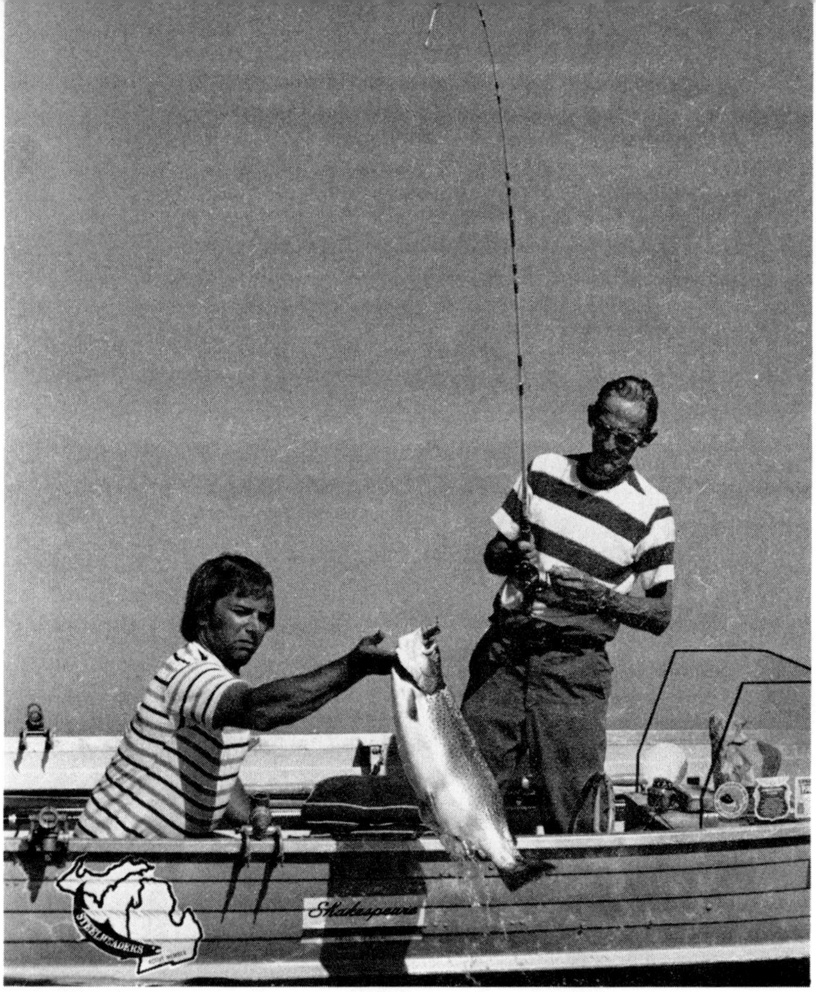

Jack Duffy (left) swings a silvery 12-pound brown trout into the boat for Lawrence Richey, the author's father.

and out of casting range of waders. Then I'll launch a small boat and drift or row out to the fish and anchor within casting distance. The same lures and retrieve work well, although I'll often allow the lure to sink 2 or 3 feet before starting it back.

My Vlchek tackle box is loaded with accessories that often turn browns on. One trick I've used to great advantage is to apply small strips of silver, gold, green, or blue Luhr Jensen Prism-Tape to the backs of my lures. This gives off added flash and often turns the trick when fish are reluctant to strike or after two or three fish have been taken from one school.

Browns are often moving during this period, so it's necessary to switch locations as soon as the fish do. Many times a move of 100 yards is enough to get back into fish. An observant angler can usually spot boils on the surface or rolling and jumping fish in the new area.

Rivermouths, rocky shoals, sharp dropoffs near shore, and along the edges of sandbars are good places to look for Great Lakes browns in late spring or early summer. The wind is important: If the breeze blows offshore for a day or more the warm surface water is blown out into the lake and the fish will often be up tight on the beach. If the breeze flows onshore it piles warm surface water close to shore and the fish will be found farther out. Savvy fishermen have learned to play wind direction to their advantage.

One of the most overlooked methods of brown fishing takes place on countless inland lakes or man-made reservoirs around the country. By June, in most areas, enough sunshine and warm

Jack Duffy works his way along the Lake Michigan shoreline with a limit catch of brown trout. The smallest fish weighed 6 pounds, the largest, 18.

weather have been present to warm the surface waters and establish a definite thermocline. Browns prefer a water temperature of about 60° F., and they tend to follow this narrow band of cool lake water as it sinks. Many times during June, July, and August I've had to troll in 20 to 30 feet of water to catch trout. This type of fishing involves knowledge of a brown's feeding habits, his temperature preferences, and the type of cover and bottom terrain utilized during midsummer months.

It's important to realize that most brown trout in inland lakes are bottom-oriented fish. They are normally found close to bottom and near the 60° level. They also prefer sharp points dropping off into deep water, submerged weedbeds or sandbars far from shore, stair-step ledges of bottom contours dropping off into deep water, and around rocky reefs. Combine a 60° bottom temperature and one of these distinctive features and you're on your way to more and bigger trout.

As important as the above knowledge is, it's also extremely important to be able to fish effectively at those depths. This means a sonar unit is needed to pinpoint changes in bottom structure and to allow the fisherman to comb these areas with his lure or baits.

I've not found anything better than live minnows for taking trophy browns from inland lakes or reservoirs. Two-inch shiner or perch (where legal) minnows are the preferred baits. It's best to use minnows native to the waters being fished.

An 18-inch leader of 10-pound monofilament is used, and one end is tied to a No. 8 treble hook. Use a 2-inch stainless-steel surgical needle to insert the point of the needle either through the anus or just ahead of the minnow's caudal (tail) fin. Thread the standing end of the leader through the needle and push it through the minnow and out the mouth. Pull the leader through and force the shank of the treble hook up into the anus or in the small hole by the tail. The shank must be buried inside the baitfish.

Trolling attractors such as Luhr Jensen's MainTrain or Beer Can cowbells are my choice for tolling in lunker browns from deep water. The preferred finishes on these cowbells are silver for dark, overcast days; brass or half brass, half silver for bright days. Copper, chartreuse, or blue PrismTape cowbells seem to work equally well during any sky-cover conditions.

The leader and minnow are tied onto the tail end of the cowbell. If you'll be fishing at depths under 20 feet I suggest adding from ½ ounce to 1½ ounces of bell sinker directly to the rudder of the cowbell. At depths over 20 feet I prefer using a three-way swivel 12 inches ahead of the cowbell and attaching heavier weights to the bottom portion of the swivel. This keeps the weight away from the flashing attractor blades.

Slow trolling speeds are necessary to bring out the pulsating throb of the cowbell's blades. I prefer using an Ambassadeur 6000 baitcasting reel stocked with 20-pound braided Dacron. At a slow trolling speed, release line cautiously until you feel the lead weight bump bottom. Take the reel out of freespool and continue trolling at the proper depth indicated by water temperature. If the lead weight doesn't bump bottom occasionally, you're fishing too high and must release more line. If the weight continually drags, you have too much line out and must reel in. The hotspot area is within a foot or two of bottom.

The bottom of many lakes or reservoirs is constantly changing, and the alert troller must do the same. This means keeping one eye on the sonar unit and the other on the fishing line. If the bottom contour begins shallowing up, move out slightly toward deeper water. If you are trying to follow a 20-foot bank, for example, and the depth is going down, you'll have to steer a slightly shallower course. This means the angler must learn to anticipate bottom-contour changes and steer the boat accordingly.

One time I was trolling massive Quabbin Reservoir near Ware, Mass., and was concentrating my efforts along a 25-foot bank near the midlake islands. I'd lowered my cowbell and minnow near bottom and slowly made the changes necessary to keep my bait and attractor throbbing near bottom. One line was out and a beautiful June sun was baking the area. I sat lost in daydreams when suddenly my starboard rod began thrashing back and forth and huge chunks of line were ripped from the reel. I grabbed the bucking rod and watched a large brown vault into the air and twist back and forth as the cowbells glittered and danced around his head, and then he fell back in a tower of spray.

When trolling with two rods the idea is to keep moving until the free line is in. Since I was fishing only one rod I didn't have this problem to contend with. I stopped the boat with one hand and tended to the matter at hand.

This fish had been badly suckered by an undulating bait near bottom and resented the fact. He crashed through the surface twice more before he began swimming small circles beneath the boat. I was then able to lead him to the net. One scoop with the net and my first trophy brown, a 7½-pounder, came to the boat from an Eastern reservoir. I've also taken big browns from other inland lakes and reservoirs all through the Great Lakes states and from some of the larger Southern reservoirs. Twenty minutes later I added a 6-pounder to my stringer and I'd learned this basic trolling technique is good for browns anywhere they are found.

ICEFISHING

Fishermen living in the northern tier of states can expect to catch some trophy browns during winter months, but they must learn basic icefishing tricks. Browns often congregate off mouths of rivers during winter months, since these areas also attract baitfish.

Two methods produce. Tip-up fishing is a slow, steady producer of good fish. But I much prefer jigging. It produces flashy strikes and steadier action.

Tip-ups are baited with 2- or 3-inch shiner minnows. The angler must experiment with various depths until it's determined which level the browns are using. Winter trout move around a great deal, since food is scarce and they must hustle for meals. I'll generally set tip-ups at about 10 feet and work up or down until I begin hooking fish.

Once a brown nails a minnow, and the tip-up flag rises, you must allow the fish to run until he stops and swallows the minnow. Once the second run begins, set the hooks and enjoy a good fight.

Jigging is more spectacular because browns often sock lures hard and you have the opportunity to feel the strike, which isn't possible with tip-ups. Several lures work well for browns, but my favorites are Swedish Pimples, Do-Jiggers, small Devle Dogs, jigging Rapalas, and small Little Cleos. It pays to experiment with colors, but I've found silver-blue combinations to be best, followed closely by silver-red or silver-green. Occasionally chartreuse with red spots will turn the trick.

The lure is lowered to a depth of about 6 to 10 feet initially and jigged slowly up and down with very brief pauses. The majority of the strikes will occur as the lure is being raised at the beginning of another jigging stroke. Fish do strike as the lure flutters back down, and this can be a very deceptive take and hard to feel. Most strikes are forceful enough that the angler has little trouble telling he's got a fish on.

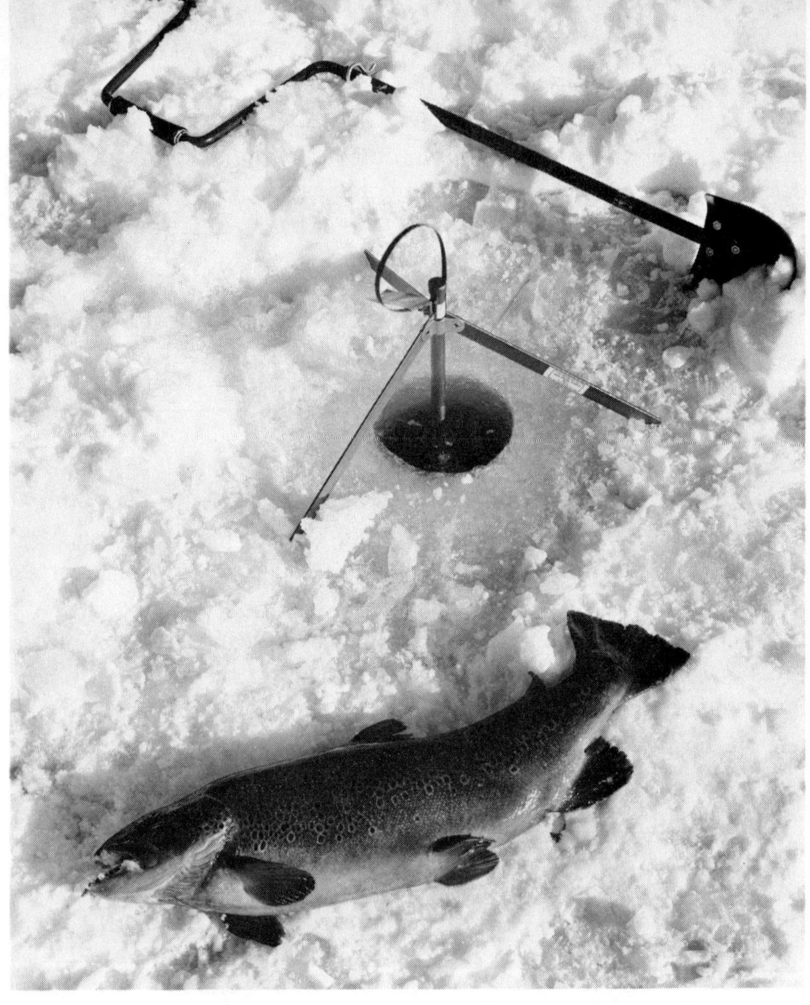

Icefishing with tip-ups is a good method of catching winter brown trout.
Michigan Travel Bureau.

If shallow depths do not produce, never hesitate to slowly probe deeper waters. I've taken browns from 25 feet of water during winter months, although this is highly unusual.

Brown trout are not all that difficult to catch, provided one goes about his business in a systematic manner. It calls for plenty of legwork and selecting one of the foregoing techniques and possibly modifying it to meet the prevailing conditions. Over the years I've taken nearly 1,000 trophy browns up to 18 pounds with the methods listed above. To me, a brown must weigh 5 pounds before it's classified as a trophy.

Try these techniques in your area and you may be surprised at the results.

6

BROOK TROUT

The taking of a trophy brook trout is one of fishing's toughest goals. These fish are not plentiful anywhere except in more remote areas of Canada, and few waters harbor trophy specimens, although big specks are still taken from such rivers as the Albany, God's River, Minipi River, and other well-known streams. Most of the largest brookies left to be caught are in hard-to-reach spruce-rimmed ponds and lakes nestled far back in the Canadian bush. Here brookies are holding on against encroaching civilization and an angler can still take big fish. Not consistently, mind you, but occasionally, and the lunkers come to those anglers willing to sacrifice time, money, and physical comfort in some cases for their sport.

A big brook trout is one of nature's most beautiful creations. His beauty matches that of his surroundings. One look at the gorgeous bright-red or yellow spots along the lateral line, the ermine-white piping along the leading edges of the lower fins, the broad square tail, minute vermiculations along the bronze-and-green back, and a blush of red, orange, gold, or purple along the belly is a just reason for spending time in wilderness areas. This is one beautiful fish I hope never disappears from my life. When the brook trout goes, man is on his way too.

As with all other fish, the environment of the species and food supply have much to do with body coloration. Some brookies taken from tannin-dyed streams are very dark with vivid spots, while specks taken from larger lakes and deep water are often silvery, with indistinct spots along the lateral lines.

Brook trout have the reputation of being stupid and easy to catch, but this doesn't apply to larger trophy fish. They can be as difficult and wary a fish as anything I've sought. Once I fished a lake on private club water leased from the Quebec government and watched a steady parade of huge brookies, every fish a 6-pounder or better, swim past my anchored boat. I'd cast far ahead of the fish in much the same manner as one leads a tailing bonefish on the Florida flats and then swim my lure past their collective noses. Each time they ignored my lure, although I made hasty lure switches in a vain attempt to tempt one into striking. None did, and my respect for this native trout, actually a char, increased almost to the point of awe.

I've spent the better part of twenty years chasing brook trout all over Canada and have taken a goodly number of fish up to 7½ pounds. Of all these gorgeous fish I've taken, I've kept only one specimen, my largest, to adorn my office wall and to remind me there are wild places still.

I maintain that if fishermen are willing to concentrate their efforts on small or large Canadian bush lakes, especially in Quebec and Ontario, they can locate larger concentrations of big specks than by fishing much-touted streams that afford spectacular fishing occasionally but often fall far short of their reputation on a day-to-day basis.

Most bush lakes are deep, cold bodies of water where specks live without fear of predation. This deep water affords protection and a plentiful food supply and seldom suffers the oxygen depletion that causes winterkill.

Float-plane pilots and flying-service personnel are often the likeliest people to know of untapped lakes where brookies exist. They can usually fly fishermen in to larger lakes, with a canoe and tent, and the anglers can explore nearby areas for brookies. A week-long trip will normally produce good fishing if the lake is chosen carefully.

Another way to locate seldom-fished areas is to contact logging companies in more remote areas of Canada. These companies open new roads into areas yearly and thereby place new waters within reach of discerning fishermen. The only flaw in this is that most logging crews also fish and it doesn't take long for a lake to be fished out or polluted by logging debris or human garbage. Such timbering operations have been both a boon and curse to brook trout fishing throughout much of Canada.

One year, while passing through Quebec on a magazine assignment, I was following a logging truck. It turned off on a logging

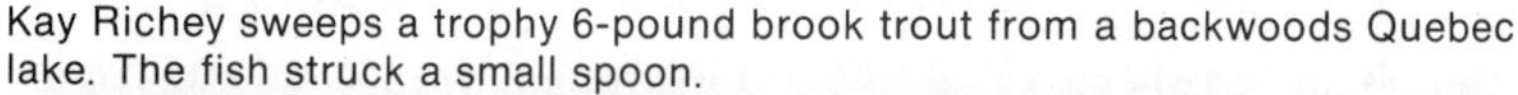

Kay Richey sweeps a trophy 6-pound brook trout from a backwoods Quebec lake. The fish struck a small spoon.

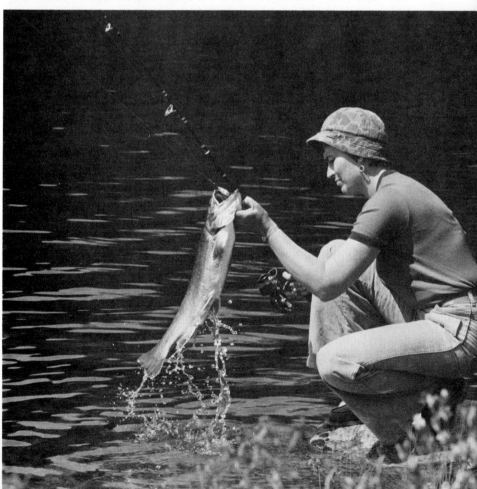

trail to the north and stopped briefly. I stopped and chatted in pidgin English and French with the crew and determined that there was a chain of small lakes near the cutting operation. They consented to let me follow them and spend the day fishing.

The road snaked through cedar swamps, crossed small trickles of water, and ended at the logging operation. Partway down the logging trail I saw sunlight glinting off a pond in the bush. I pulled off the trail and into thick cedars which shut off much of the sunlight. I parked, grabbed rod and tackle after hoisting on hipboots, and walked the quarter-mile to the pond, a 10-acre body of water nestled in a sea of spruce.

I eased down the steep slope and waded gingerly into knee-deep water. My first cast with a small spoon dropped next to a spruce toppled into the water. I spotted the flash of white-edged fins as a brookie struck hard without hesitation.

The speck fought gamely and deep, with the savage bulldogging runs common to this species. Several minutes later I eased the fish to shore and returned 5 pounds of firm, glistening brook trout to the lake. The balance of the day was spent crawling over deadfalls trying to reach a new stretch of water, hooking and releasing trout up to 6 pounds. I kept one badly hooked 5-pounder for my supper and breakfast the next day.

I returned to that pond two years later and found that other men had found the brookies and had left behind their inevitable pile of debris . . . and they'd caught most of the fish. Within a period of three years the pond was fished out. Such is man's progress, unfortunately.

This doesn't have to be the case, since many lakes and ponds can be hiked into. As inevitable as progress is, good fishing still exists in many areas if fishermen are willing to look for it. It's inevitable that good-looking lakes or ponds will fail to produce a single trophy-size speck while other lakes, in the same area, may hold nothing but jumbo fish. One learns to be philosophical about brook trout fishing.

I'm firmly convinced that many Canadian lakes hold brook trout of world-record size. I know of two lakes, one in Ontario and the other in Quebec, that are teeming with oversized specks. The largest fish landed on hook and line from the Quebec lake weighed 11 pounds 4 ounces, but fishermen have hooked and lost larger specimens. The Quebec Department of Fish and Game test-netted the lake and took out fish weighing up to 13½ pounds. I refuse to name the lakes, since the mere mention of their names would induce a steady flow of fishermen and a steady decline of the brookie populations. Much of the fun lies in finding your own areas and learning how to catch fish.

Several basic facts apply to fishing Canadian brook trout lakes. Big specks do not feed ravenously on a daily basis as do other trout. I've seen times when anglers would go two or three days at a time on trophy lakes without a strike and then catch a limit within an hour the following day. This sudden change of feeding activity can take place any time of day, and the only recourse is to fish hard, all the time.

I've discovered that the best time of year to fish for trophy brook trout is either the two-week period immediately after ice-out or during late fall as the trout work into the shallow spawning areas. In most areas the season is closed during this late-season period, so anglers are advised to concentrate their efforts during the spring after ice leaves the water. This is where a friendship with a flying service can be valuable; they can phone and advise you of current weather conditions, or ice-out, and a spur-of-the-moment trip is often necessary to hit the best fishing.

ICE-OUT FISHING

I've flown in on trips where the plane's skis swished down amid floating chunks of late ice. At this period brookies will usually be in shallow water and close to shore—and very hungry. It might take a day or two to locate the best spots, but this is the optimum time to catch trophy fish.

Ice-out usually concentrates brookies near creek mouths where high runoff water gushes into the lake. Deepwater areas near the mouth can be a good location to begin fishing. I'll usually fish it for an hour or two and move off and return again later in the day. Brookies frequent these areas because the creek water washes food into the lake.

Abrupt dropoffs near shore are hotspots for spring feeding activity. Big fish hold in deep water and move into the shallows to feed. Other spring hotspots are long tapering points dropping off into deep water, particularly if large rocks or boulders provide cover.

Large trees which have toppled into the water also afford protection for brookies. Never pass up steep, boulder-studded shorelines or large stretches of rubble-covered bottom.

Shallow-water specks are notoriously spooky. A canoe is the best method of covering the water, since it can be eased silently along and it doesn't scare the fish as a boat does. A small anchor lowered gently to the bottom will allow you to fish without chasing the trout from the area. A motorboat, if used, should be shut off and rowed into casting position to minimize noise.

Wind drifting is one of the best methods to use when fish are feeding in shallow water. I prefer to motor or row upwind and then drift down with the prevailing breeze and direct my casts to dropoffs, fallen trees, or protruding boulders. Cast ahead of the boat so the lure works through good water before the boat. Brookies show a tendency to avoid striking once the boat has gone over them.

Retrieval speed is critically important. Every lure has a certain speed that brings out its best action, and most fishermen stick to this one speed. Brook trout are suckers for a change in lure speed or action. I experiment with sinking times, jerk-pause retrieves, and fast or slow reeling until I hit on something that produces a strike.

Many Canadian lakes are as dark as strong tea, while others are gin-clear and you can see a rock in 20 feet of water. The choice of lure color and lure type is something I've worked on for twenty years. I've narrowed down my choice of colors to solid copper for dark water and chartreuse with red spots or yellow with red spots for clear-water lakes. These colors have produced the bulk of my trophy brookies.

Small lures are generally more productive than larger ones, and ¼- to ⅓-ounce spoons such as the smaller Krocodiles or Dardevles fit the bill very well. They have a built-in wobble that seems to excite specks and are still flexible and balanced well enough to enable fishermen to experiment with different retrieves. As these lures sink they achieve a fluttering action that has taken many big brookies for me. The fish often strike as the lure flutters downward and before the retrieve begins.

Small Rapalas produce well in lakes where brookies feed heavily on forage fish. The silver-gray color has produced best for me, although I've had good action twice on the orange-red model when I've cast near treetops and retrieved just fast enough to bring out the action. These strikes are usually ferocious and often come from some of the largest trout.

Trolling with Rapalas produces well, provided the angler uses line no heavier than 6-pound-test. I prefer to run Rapalas about 75 yards behind the boat and weave in and out of the shallows so the lure will occasionally work through water the boat hasn't covered. A slight back-and-forth chugging motion intensifies the lure's action and can be the turning point between getting a fish on or going without action.

Fly fishing is a seldom-practiced sport on brook trout lakes and ponds but it can be extremely effective on bodies of water containing freshwater shrimp. Some lakes I've fished are glutted with these small shrimp. Almost any nymph pattern which is approximately the same size, shape, and color as the shrimp will take fish.

A sinking fly line should be used with a 6-pound level leader. Tapered leaders aren't necessary, since delicate presentation of a tiny fly doesn't contribute much to the overall success of the method.

Favorite areas for shrimp-feeding brookies are near any aquatic vegetation such as reeds, moss, or weeds. Early spring finds big specks nosing out shrimp from the shallows near submerged trees or near rocks and boulders.

Many of my fly-caught brookies are taken in 5 to 10 feet of water by wading along and casting ahead and to both sides. Lakes with steep dropoffs close to shore are best fished from a canoe or boat where the flies can be worked in along the dropoff.

Pay close attention to any cover such as boulders or treetops and cast parallel to the dropoff. Allow the nymph to sink slowly before easing it back in inch-long pulls.

Strikes on slow-sinking or moving nymphs are delicate, and I use a red Leader Link between my fly line and the leader to telegraph these soft takes.

SUMMER FISHING

Many fishermen are unable to fish during spring months for one reason or another. For them, it's a summer trip or nothing. Brook trout can be caught during hot summer months, but it involves more prospecting and longer fishing hours, since the fish can be scattered anywhere. They will usually be in deeper water soaking up the comfort of 55–58° F. water.

A trick I learned was to fish near underwater springs during summer months. Cooler water bubbling from the bottom spells comfort to specks and more productive fishing if you approach the situation correctly.

Brookies often hover directly over significant underwater structures near bottom and close to their preferred water temperature. This becomes even more pronounced if a steady food supply is located nearby and the fish have deep water to which they can retreat for protection.

One of the best methods of taking midsummer brookies from deep water is to use the cowbell rig described in the brown trout chapter. I simplify this rigging somewhat and use a pair of No. 3 or No. 4 Mepps spinners hooked in tandem by a split ring. The treble hooks are removed from one spinner, both lures are joined head to tail by the split ring, and a 12-inch leader runs back to a single hook on which a nightcrawler has been placed. If weight is needed, use a three-way swivel 12 inches ahead of the spinners and troll it slowly near bottom. The flashing spinner blades attract fish in deep water, and they home in on the scent of the crawler. It's a deadly combination.

A slow chugging back-and-forth sweep of the rod tip will cause the spinner-worm combination to dance excitedly near bottom. Brookies often strike as the rod tip is lowered back down.

Jigging with Swedish Pimples near bottom from a wind-drifting boat can be an excellent method of locating schools of lunker specks. I'll motor upwind, cut the engine, and lower my Pimple near bottom and begin jigging with 2-inch pulls on my rod tip. The fish generally strike as the jig drops back toward bottom.

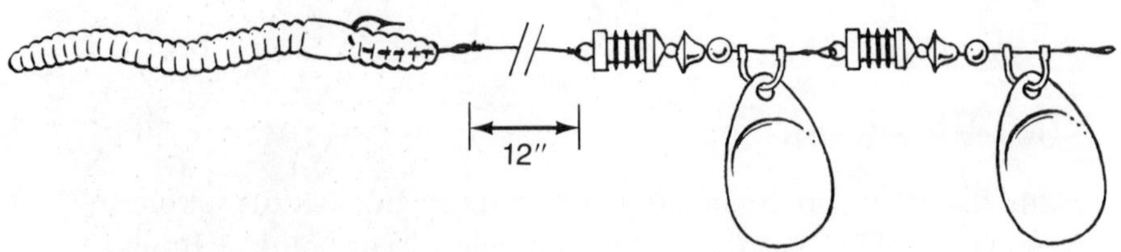

Trolling rig made with Mepps spinners.

Brookies are notorious minnow eaters, and I'll often sweeten the lure with a tiny piece of fish meat or the ventral fin from another brook trout. The white leading edge of the brookie's fin shows up well in deep water, and its wavering action on the hook seems to attract feeding fish or will convert nonfeeders into a more positive feeding attitude. Keep the lure working within inches of bottom at all times.

Another jigging method that produces big fish is casting a ¼- or ½-ounce Pinky or Ugly Bug jig from an anchored or drifting boat. Allow the jig to settle to bottom and inch it back slowly to the boat

Tom Corbett caught this 6-pounder while trolling with cowbells and a Flatfish.

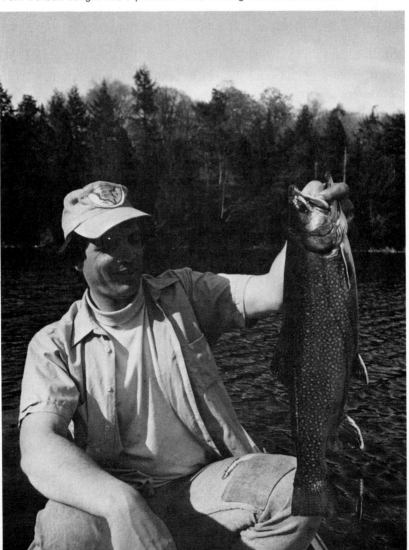

in a series of short hippety-hops with frequent pauses. Whenever the jig stops, set the hook hard, because big specks just grab on and seldom strike with force. A small minnow, nightcrawler, or 4-inch plastic worm attached to the jig greatly adds to its effectiveness.

Some of the more remote and rocky stretches of Lake Superior and Lake Michigan have very small runs of "coasters," a famous anadromous species of brook trout. Coasters are the fisherman's fiery sunset or gorgeous sunrise; they are decked out in a vivid array of color such as brilliant reds, pinks, and oranges. In addition to their beauty they attain weights seldom seen in other wild brook trout. I've taken only a few because they seem to be dwindling in numbers, although every coaster I've seen or caught has weighed at least 4 pounds, and two scaled over 8.

The best areas seem to be along the north shore of Lake Superior in the Ontario trackless wilderness. A major road, Highway 17, works west from Sault Ste. Marie and skips past some of the better areas. I used to fish off the mouths of streams near Batchawana Bay and near some of the smaller streams east of Wawa. A boat is necessary to work into some of these better areas. Small spoons or spinners fished near large boulders has always been the most productive method.

Some coasters are still caught along Wisconsin's Door Peninsula in the vicinity of Cave Point, Jacksonport, and Bailey's Harbor. The fish seem most plentiful in late summer and early fall.

7

LAKE TROUT

The lake trout is king of the clan. It grows to the largest sizes, puts up a long struggle, and is most admired for the awesome waters it is found in. In farflung places where lakers reside, a 30-pounder impresses no one; it takes lunkers of 35 to 50 pounds before a jaded angler lifts an eye. You see, fishermen are accustomed to catching big lakers, and little ones are often cussed in the same manner that anglers once knocked small pike.

But all things are relative. A trophy lake trout from Branson's Lodge on Great Bear Lake is one thing, while an 8- or 10-pound laker from another area may still be a trophy fish. A trophy is a big fish from the body of water being fished, although it could be small when compared with fish from a different area.

Lake trout are found from far eastern Canada, through the central provinces, through many of the Great Lakes states and in particular in Lake Michigan, Lake Huron, and Lake Superior, and have been transplanted into some of the deeper lakes of the West.

The stronghold for big lake trout has and probably always will be in some of the largest lakes of the Northwest Territories. This vast land, containing few people and fewer fishing lodges, remains the Shangri-la for lake trout fishermen. Most notable in this barren land with deep cold-water lakes is Great Bear Lake. It reminds me of a large aquarium filled with alcohol-clear water where fishermen can see bottom and big lakers swimming in 40 feet of water. It also holds the world record for a rod-caught lake trout, a 65-pound fish.

Throughout its range the lake trout is subject to as many color changes as the brown trout but retains one feature found on no other trout—a deeply forked tail. This is a trademark of lakers and one which easily identifies them to anglers. The basic coloration is a grayish green, blue, or brown along the back with a pale-blue, white, or slightly pink belly. I've seen many cases where lake trout may feature different colors from various portions of the same lake.

The back often has vermiculations like those of brook trout; these can be either very pronounced, weak, or nearly absent in other fish. The sides normally have fairly pronounced yellow, cream-colored, or slightly pink spots, and they cover the body, gill covers, jaws, head, and adipose, dorsal, and caudal fins. The lower fins are similarly spotted, and the leading edges are occasionally heavily edged with white similar to a brook trout. I've seen some lakers with this edging missing while on other fish it's readily apparent. Lakers often tend to be much darker in shallower dark water and almost silvery from deep water and clear lakes.

Lake trout are fall spawners, with a very short peak period of spawning activity. Much of the spawn is completed within two weeks; they seem to require less time for this activity than other trouts. Spawning normally takes place during October and November, although it can occur much earlier at more northerly latitudes.

Someone much wiser than I once said, "The hardest thing about catching lake trout is finding them." This pretty well sums up the sport. Lake trout are easy to catch once they've been located. They seem to compete for a lure, and I've sometimes been able to pull my lure away from one fish and allow another to take it. Competition is keen among lakers, and this accounts for their falling prey to fishermen.

Two basic types of trophy fishing occur for lakers—the easy type of fishing enjoyed by anglers wealthy enough to fly in to remote lakes where the largest specimens are taken, and the type of fishing found in the continental United States where forktails are planted in inland lakes or the Great Lakes. We'll first discuss methods needed to take jumbos from far northern lakes.

NORTHERN LAKERS

Last summer is a classic example. My wife, Kay, and I flew via Air Canada from Chicago to Edmonton, Alberta, and then north by chartered Siddeley-Hawker to Echo Bay (formally Port Radium) on Great Bear Lake. Our destination was Branson's Lodge and our quarry was big lake trout, fish much larger than those taken from Lake Michigan near our home.

When we arrived on Great Bear we were awed by immense ice floes which jammed many bays. Enough ice was floating on the lake itself to prohibit boat travel. It was July 1 and spring was just coming to the Northwest Territories.

Ernie Dolinsky, the owner of Branson's Lodge, had little choice but to fly us and other guests to and from other bays which were ice-free. The main portion of the lake was impossible to fish, but the smaller bays had been free of ice for nearly two weeks and the water temperature was about right, 48°F near shore.

It has been said that Great Bear's big lake trout never go deep, and this is somewhat true. The main lake seldom warms up as much as some of the shallower bays, so anglers must learn to fish the water temperature. The big trout were in shallow bays because the water was much warmer and more food was available. This is a factor many fishermen, and guides, overlook in that country. The biggest lakers will be found in the warmest water, at least early in the season.

I'd been to Great Bear two years earlier, but it was Kay's first trip. Charley Hamelin had been my guide during the first trip and was again chosen to take us fishing.

We flew from the lodge to Conjuror Bay and immediately began trolling. We started out with two proven lures—the familiar red-and-white-striped Dardevle and an L-9 silver Flatfish. Both lures work within 10 feet of the surface, and we knew this was where the lakers should be. A rocky shoreline with a jumble of boulders near shore was our first choice. It proved good, because we saw large numbers of small whitefish and grayling leaping from the water in an attempt to escape a big laker below.

The outboard was throttled back to the slow speeds I like for lake trout and we trolled back and forth through the area. Small fish were jumping on both sides of the boat as my rod tip snapped down from the piledriver force of a big laker's strike. I jabbed the hooks home and hung on desperately as the fish sounded for bottom.

Kay reeled her line in while I pumped and reeled in an attempt to lift the fish off bottom. After ten minutes of arm-straining tug of war I could see the big laker ghosting up through the clear water; it was twisting and rolling in the line and its white belly gave off a pearly glow. Bubbles began coming to the surface, but it took another ten minutes to play the fish into submission. Charley held the net motionless and I led the trout to the boat. A big splash and a 24-pounder came into the boat. We quickly unhooked the fish and returned it to the lake.

That fish had been taken because we were observant and had noticed small fish jumping from the water. Only one thing makes them behave in that manner—a big lake trout feeding below.

The taking of *big* lake trout from bodies of water like Great Bear is mostly luck, but a certain amount of skill enters the picture. I've seen some fishermen who cannot consistently catch lake trout from this huge inland sea. I've personally taken some out near the lodge to show them how to fish. Many guides are not good fishermen; they troll much too fast for lakers, and the anglers simply get a

Small baitfish jumping on the surface usually signal the presence of big lake trout feeding below.

good boat ride. Slow speeds are more important to success than any other factor I know.

Although large Dardevles are often touted as the best northern lake trout lure, I've found some others that are just as good. Large spinners like the Lucky Strike produced big lakers for my wife, while I couldn't catch a thing on the same lure. This large-bladed spinner with red golf tees for a body and a single treble hook doesn't go very deep, and at slow trolling speeds the blade revolves and throbs like something alive. Kay found that an occasional jigging movement back and forth adds more action to the lure and produces strong strikes.

Too many anglers insist on using weight on their lines to take lures deep. This is a mistake, since most of the fish are within 10 or 15 feet of the surface at all times. As we trolled we watched the water near the boat and could see big lakers cruising away from us in depths of less than 10 feet. Kay saw one huge lake trout that was over 60 inches in length. We guessed its weight at 70 or more pounds—a sure world record. The wake it kicked up as it sped off to deep water looked like someone had dropped a cow off a bridge.

Another common mistake among fishermen is to use a wire leader. Lakers do not have sharp teeth and can't cut the line. One of the best fishermen I know, Greg Meadows of California, fishes Great Bear lake trout with 6-pound monofilament and a buggywhip rod. Every year he takes lake trout up to 30 pounds on this wispy line. This points out the fallacy of wire leaders for lake trout. Leaders inhibit the action of the lure and decrease the number of strikes.

This area of northern Canada is known as the land of the midnight sun, and it's true during summer months (July and August). An angler can wear himself out fishing lake trout. I'll often fish sixteen hours a day. I've found that certain periods of the day are good while other periods are less productive. I like to fish from about 8:00 a.m. until noon and again from 7:00 p.m. to midnight. The fish seem to be more responsive during those periods.

I've taken large numbers of lakers at all times of the day and night, and Greg Meadows and I once fished twenty-four hours straight and caught fish around the clock. But periods of diminished light intensity seem more productive for near-shore fishing; I'd assume the lowered light conditions allow the bigger lake trout to move inshore to feed on whitefish, smaller lake trout, and gray-

Greg Meadows grunts as he lifts a 24-pound lake trout into the boat on Great Bear Lake. He uses 6-pound mono and a lightweight rod.

ling. This is when I've seen the most activity from forage fish leaping into the air from attacking trout.

Large spinners seem to produce exceptional results from lake trout. Years ago I hit on the theory of taking two Mepps Musky Killers and removing the hooks from one spinner and attaching it to the head of a similar lure. This gives two large flashing blades and slightly more bulk, which allows it to sink to about 10 feet at slow trolling speeds.

A back-and-forth chugging motion causes the two spinners to fold slightly in the center at the split ring and changes the beat of the blades. Lake trout often strike when the lure is dropped back after being chugged. The strike feels as though you've hooked an immovable boulder.

Jigging is an overlooked technique that works well. Last year Charley Hamelin introduced me to deep-water jigging. "The fish aren't as large as the ones we take trolling," he said, "but we'll take lots of fish. It's a good way to take trout for shore lunches." He's a savvy guide, and when he speaks I listen and follow his advice.

Kay selected a large Gapen Pinky jig and knotted it to her line with a loop knot while I lowered my double spinner rig over the side. The water was 60 feet deep and my lure was halfway to the bottom when I could no longer feel it drop. I quickly reeled up the slack and set the hooks into a nice dinner-sized lake trout. Kay had lowered her jig near bottom and it was doing a slow dance off the bottom rubble when her rod tip suddenly jerked down from the slash of a good strike. We had a doubleheader going.

Each fish seemed determined to stay as near bottom as possible, but neither trout was over 10 pounds and we could quickly pressure them toward the surface. Both fish were netted and released. We continued to have strikes almost every time we lowered our lures. Charley fished with us, at our insistence, and he caught and kept our shore lunch. We hooked and landed over twenty lakers in less than an hour and finally quit jigging when a bigger trout smashed my spinner combination and made off with my lure.

The important thing about northern lake trout fishing is to be flexible, experiment with lures and fishing methods, and never get locked into day-after-day trolling. The trout are plentiful and they'll strike almost anything presented in a logical manner. Anglers that limit their fishing to one technique are losing out on a wonderful opportunity to try other methods and catch more fish.

One of the more pleasurable methods of taking trophy lake trout from northern lakes is to find a shallow bay with water no deeper than 15 feet. Lakers will be fully exposed to view; I've seen schools numbering over a hundred fish ranging in size from 6 to 20 pounds, and every fish competes for a lure.

I carry a light-action spinning outfit stocked with 10-pound mono for these happy occasions. A medium-sized Dardevle is attached to a snap swivel and I'll pick out the fish I wish to catch and cast just ahead of him. I've seen 20-pound lakers peel away from the school and follow a lure 30 yards back to the boat before striking at the last moment. This type of fishing calls for nothing more than reasonably accurate casting so a particular trout can be fished for. All too often, however, a smaller laker will beat a big fish to the lure, and then all fish scatter before regrouping in another portion of the bay.

One afternoon Greg Meadows and I fished like this and caught over sixty lake trout before we tired of the sport. We pinched the barbs down on our lures to facilitate easy removal without lifting the trout into the boat. Our largest was a streamlined 21-pound fish, which was released.

FISHING THE GREAT LAKES, ETC.

Lake trout fishing in smaller inland lakes or the Great Lakes is an entirely different story. These trout are in shallow water for a brief period during spring and fall and in deep water the rest of the time. Locating the fish becomes the fisherman's biggest problem.

Spring and fall fishing is normally done in depths of 25 feet or less, while fishing at 60 to 150 feet is common at other times. Lakers are normally a bottom-oriented fish and will be found feeding or resting near rubble, rocks, hard-packed sand, or great boulders 10 feet tall.

One of the deadliest methods of taking big lake trout during spring or fall is to fish with cowbells and lures or Herring Dodgers and flies. One of my favorite combinations is a chrome or chartreuse Jensen Dodger with a green Michigan Squid fly. This combination, when bounced along bottom, has produced more big lake trout up to 15 pounds than all others combined.

Lake trout aren't nomadic fish like salmon, but they move from one area to another, and lakers found in one region today may be a mile away tomorrow. This means that trolling will enable you to place lures and/or attractors within striking distance of more fish than any other technique.

Many anglers prefer using wire line and heavy tackle for forktails, although the same lures or baits are used. Wire-line fishing is effective, since it has little stretch and the wire sinks the lures without aid of weights. But it becomes boring and very tedious to constantly sweep the rod tip up and lower it again in the traditional chugging motion. Nevertheless this chugging technique is deadly on big lake trout and shouldn't be discounted.

A wealth of lures work well for big lakers. Some of my favorites are Spring Spoons, Sugar Spoons, Krocadiles, Tadpollys, HotShots, FirePlugs, small J-Plugs, Michigan Squids, the Barber Fly, Michigan Rattlure, Ale-E-fly, and others. I'll generally fish any of these lures behind a Jensen Herring Dodger or Main Train Cowbell. One important factor is to avoid using Dodgers of different sizes if more than one line is used, because it requires a certain speed for each Dodger-fly combination to bring out the proper action.

Some of the finest spring fishing will occur whenever lakers are in 6 to 10 feet of water. At this time no weight is needed and attractors should not be used because the increased flash will spook wary fish from the shallows.

I'll usually use a lightweight spinning outfit like my Mitchell 300 reel with 8-pound line and knot on a green Tiny Tad (Tadpolly) and troll slowly in a zigzag course. The lure should be trolled about 50 yards behind the boat with frequent sharp turns. This bait will dig down 10 feet and bounce along over the rocks. As the boat turns, the lure will make sudden changes of direction and produce jarring strikes.

Lakers are notorious for following a lure and tapping at it several times before becoming hooked. Art Dengler, an old lake trout fishing buddy of mine, once told me that lakers can be teased into striking. If you feel one of those tapping strikes, pull the lure away from him. The trout will often follow, tap the lure again, and miss. Keep pulling it away from him, and sooner or later he'll become so obsessed with it he'll hook himself. Since Art gave me that advice

Two deadly trolling rigs for lakers: (top) a Herring Dodger and Green Michigan Squid Fly; (bottom) a string of cowbells and a deep-running lure.

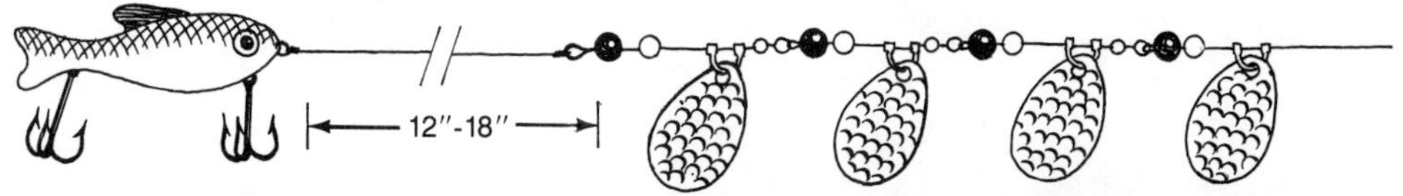

I've taken countless lakers by teasing it away from them until they strike hard enough to hook themselves. I've often had lake trout follow for 200 yards, pecking at the bait, until they are hooked. It's an exciting feeling!

Another aspect of lake trout fishing that many overlook is weather. Lakers are dirty-weather fish—the rougher the water, the better these trout often strike. Of course, it can become too rough to fish, but I've often taken more trout with 3-foot seas than at any other time. Fair weather with plenty of sun may be fine for sunbathing but it generally produces poor lake trout fishing.

Some of the best shallow-water trout fishing comes during the dirtiest weather of the year—in November. The waves take on a dull-gray look to match the sky as lakers move in on shallow shoals to spawn. The males generally come first and simply fan silt off rubble for the females to drop eggs on. This inshore movement often follows a two-day onshore blow which washes the bottom clean of silt.

Many fishermen work shallow shoals or reefs in the northern portions of Lake Michigan and Lake Huron during early November, and they catch large numbers of trophy fish. After-dark hours seem best as the angler casts small spoons into the face of howling winds. Many times lake trout will be in 3 to 6 feet of water, within easy casting distance of wader fishermen, and the action can be unbelievable. Darkness seems to calm fish down, and this is doubly true of lake trout. This is one of the best techniques I know for taking nice fish.

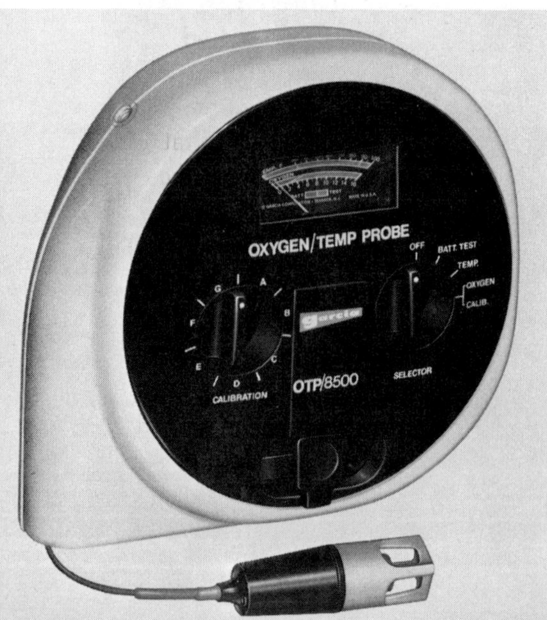

Many anglers use an oxygen temperature probe during midsummer to locate the band of 50° water temperature lakers prefer.

Midsummer fishing calls for a drastic change in fishing techniques. Lakers are often taken at depths of 60 or more feet as warm winds and sunshine warm the surface of the lake and drive cool water deeper. Many fishermen rely on an electronic water thermometer like Garcia's OTP (oxygen temperature probe) to locate the narrow band of 50° F. water lakers prefer. Once this temperature is found it still becomes necessary to keep your lures at this particular depth, and downriggers, a classic fishing invention designed to solve the problems of fishing at greater depths, become a household word among Midwestern and Great Lakes fishermen.

DOWNRIGGERS

Downriggers are large manual or electric reels stocked with 125-pound-test wire line that attach to either the stern or gunwale of a fishing boat. I used four Jensen Auto-Trac downriggers on my Boston whaler last year. The wire downrigger line is attached to an 8-to-12-pound lead weight called a cannonball. A line release system is attached either to the cannonball or to the wire line just above this downrigger weight.

Lures are selected and run from 8 to 25 feet behind the boat, and the fishing line is attached to the downrigger's release system. The cannonball is lowered to the required depth and locked in place. This holds the lures at the proper depth. Once a fish strikes, the line pulls away from the release system, and the angler has his fish on an unweighted line. The cannonball is raised during the struggle, and as soon as the laker is landed, the line is attached again to the release system and lowered to the fish zone.

Downriggers have completely revolutionized the sport of deep-water lake trout fishing. The method has become so popular that only a handful of anglers still fish with the old wire-line rigs once common for lake trout.

By proper depth spacing of the cannonballs an angler can spread four lines over a 10- or 15-foot range, and this will place all lures within striking distance of most lake trout. Careful attention must be paid to bottom contours, because downrigger weights can hang up on underwater rubble or boulders and break the wire line and create havoc with equipment. Uneven bottom conditions necessitate constant raising and lowering to keep the lures riding either just off bottom or within the proper temperature zone.

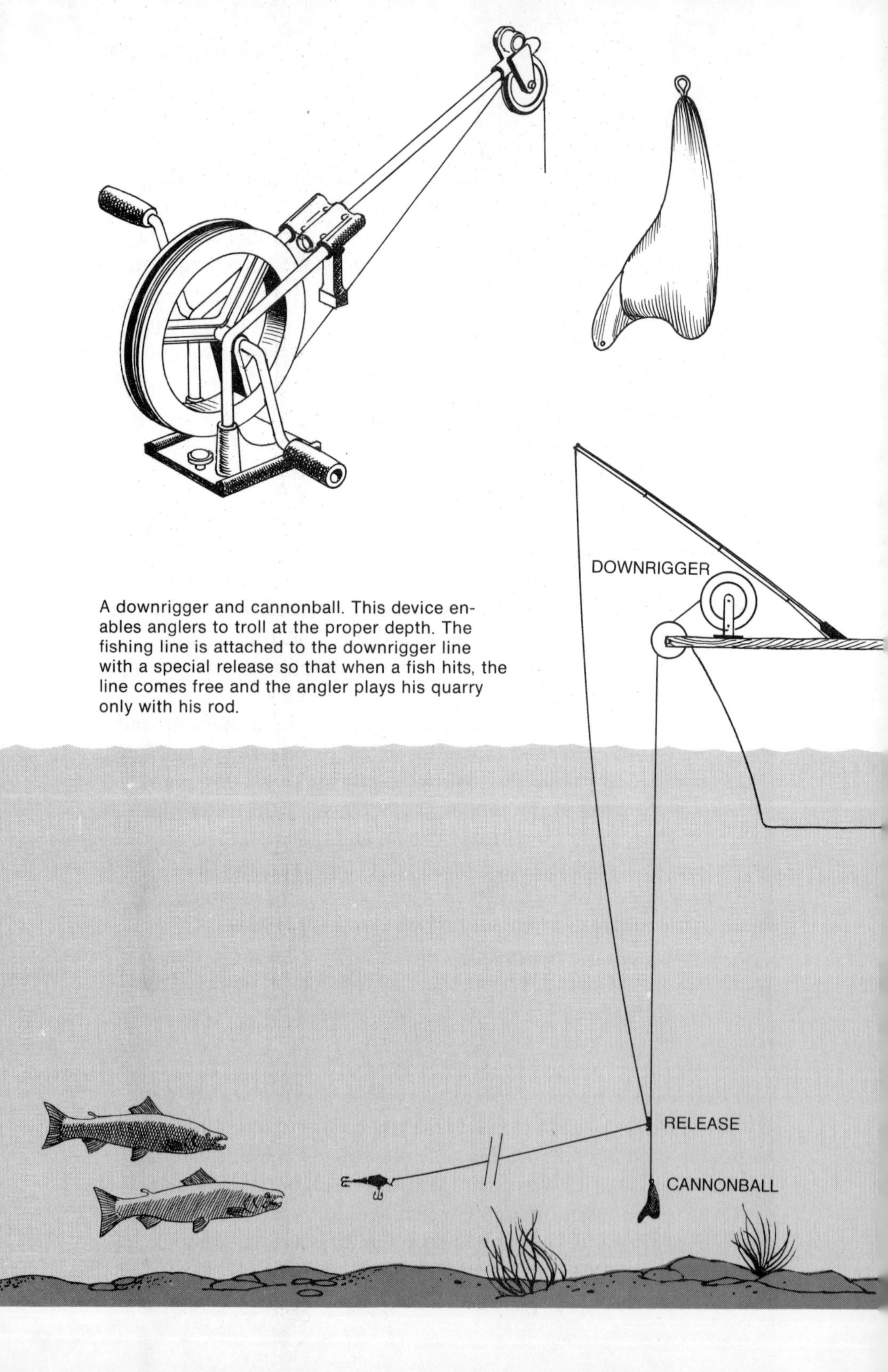

A downrigger and cannonball. This device enables anglers to troll at the proper depth. The fishing line is attached to the downrigger line with a special release so that when a fish hits, the line comes free and the angler plays his quarry only with his rod.

I stated earlier that lake trout often follow lures for long distances without being hooked. This phenomenon can be seen on the sophisticated chart recording graphs being used by many fishermen. A laker will be seen trailing along near the cannonball and lure but won't strike.

Many fishermen have learned that lakers can still be teased with downrigger-hooked lures by quickly cranking the cannonball up and down three or four times for 6 or 8 feet. As the cannonball is raised the lure will literally leap away from the following lake trout. As it is lowered back down it will again pull away from the forktail. Two or three repetitions will often turn a follower into a fighter—on the end of your line.

Constant experimentation with downrigger fishing has proved to me that lake trout will often come up for a trolled lure but will seldom, if ever, go down to strike a lure trailing a cannonball. If

Captain Emil Dean shows a greedy lake trout from Lake Michigan. The fish struck two spoons at once off two different downriggers and was hooked and fought on two rods—a million-to-one shot.

lake trout marks are seen on a chart recording graph, set the cannonballs and lures just above the fish in a staggered manner. Lakers like to attack from below, and lures passing just over their heads are more effective than cannonballs and lures passing through their midst.

Frequent bursts of speed and quick slowdowns to normal trolling speed are good techniques for the lake trout fisherman. Sudden sharp turns to port or starboard will also trigger strikes from following lake trout, and both techniques seem to produce trophy fish when other methods fail. These are musts for trollers and should be added to any fisherman's repertoire of tactics when action slows down.

RIVER FISHING

Rivermouth fishing can be a fantastic means of taking lake trout on light tackle. Frequently, during the fall spawning period, rivermouths will become a gathering point for big fish. Some streams, like Michigan's St. Joseph and Leland rivers, receive runs of anadromous lake trout. Large numbers of lakers collect off the mouths within a week or ten days of the upstream surge, and they provide an exciting brand of fishing until they either move off to spawn or ascend the streams.

The same techniques which take steelhead or brown trout off rivermouths will work for lake trout. The only difference I've found is that night fishing is much more productive than fishing during daylight hours.

Some streams like the Leland River are closed to protect spawning lake trout from fishermen. I've been in various portions of Canada during the tail end of the season and found lakers nosing up streams. When the season is open these areas can offer an angler one of the easiest methods of taking trophy lakers. They feed heavily on salmon or trout eggs, and I've caught fifteen lakers up to 17 pounds in a matter of three hours by rolling single salmon eggs slowly downstream along the bottom. As the bait dropped into the rivermouth hole a big lake trout would delicately mouth it and I'd set the hook and hang on as the fish fought a head-down bulldogging battle.

Many Canadian rivers have lake trout in them, although these fish seldom approach trophy size. Many river lakers will weigh between 5 and 10 pounds, although it's always possible to tie into a lunker of 15 pounds or more. With a current at its back a big lake trout will provide a fight long remembered.

Lake trout in rivers will often take up holding positions in deep holes or behind boulders and rocks that break up the current flow. Lakers are used to feeding on almost anything edible that is washed downstream. Since they are in a vulnerable position in regard to food almost anything a fisherman wishes to use will be ravaged by stream fish.

My favorite lures are Mepps or Panther Martin spinners. One time I was fishing the Camsell River near where it flows into Great Bear Lake in the Northwest Territories. This water doesn't have too many lakers; pike and grayling are the standard fare. I had taken several grayling and was concentrating on trying to catch a big northern pike. I angled a cast with a No. 4 Mepps behind a large rock in midstream and began bringing it back.

The spinner didn't travel over 6 feet when it stopped abruptly. My first thought was a pike, but the line then angled downstream in a heavy run as I tripped along jumping over large rocks.

I caught up with the rampaging fish 100 yards downstream and we fought it out. After a drawn-out battle of fifteen minutes the fish began to tire and rose to the surface, where I saw it for the first time. It was a laker of nearly 20 pounds and had probably been feeding behind that boulder for years.

The fish slowly ceased making headstrong runs and started coming to the shore. I kept the pressure up and was finally able to fit its head into my wide-mouthed net. We quickly hung it off pocket scales and it pulled the peg down to 17½ pounds, a trophy lake trout from a stream.

ICEFISHING

Icefishing is a means of taking lake trout once winter lays her iron hand over the water. If lake trout go deep during summer months, they must submarine during the winter, because the majority of hardwater fishing is done at depths of 120 feet or more. The areas where lakers are found are invariably windswept and bitterly cold during winter months, and this brand of fishing is only for the hardy. The action can be fast-paced enough to warm one's blood, however.

Tip-up fishing is one of the best methods, provided an angler has access to a semi-secret bait—the smelt. Smelt possess a good strong odor and have become one of the most successful baits to be used in the Great Lakes area. Fishermen in Canada and other areas of the United States often use suckers or large shiners for lake trout, but the smelt reigns supreme wherever it shares the same waters as lakers.

Live smelt are the best and are lightly hooked under the dorsal fin with a No. 8 or No. 10 treble hook and lowered near bottom. The bulk of the lake trout taken during winter months will be within inches of the lake's floor. Large tip-ups with a minimum of 250 yards of line are used for this exciting brand of fishing.

Once the laker takes the live smelt he'll usually run for 20 to 75 yards to swallow the bait. The angler must stand by and watch line melt off his tip-up reel and wait for the fish to stop, turn the minnow for easier swallowing, and begin his second run. As the second run begins the angler allows the line to come tight; then he'll set the hook and the action begins. Landing a 10-to-15-pound laker through 2 feet of ice is a heady challenge that few anglers can ignore.

In many areas anglers do not have access to live smelt, but frozen smelt work almost as well. A fisherman needs to buy one of the large wide-bend Swedish hooks designed to be inserted in the fish's anus, through the body, and out the top of the head. With careful insertion and positioning the minnow will hang in a horizontal position on the hook. The bait is lowered near bottom, and the fisherman should stand nearby, since the hook must be set immediately on the take if the angler is going to hook the fish. This type of hook, the Mustad 7724, has revolutionized baitfishing with dead minnows. Some anglers carry small nails in their pockets to insert in the minnow's mouth if the bait hangs in a head-up position on the hook. A head-down position can be corrected by moving the hook point farther back on the minnow's body.

Jigging is the most enjoyable means of taking big lakers through the ice. Many anglers prefer using short jigging rods, but I like a 2-foot rod with an Ambassadeur 5000 reel stocked with 15-pound mono. A fish hooked on this outfit can be played in a conventional manner, while lakers hooked on wooden jigging rods must be hurried to the hole by sheer force. My method is more sporting and a great deal more fun, since the action is prolonged.

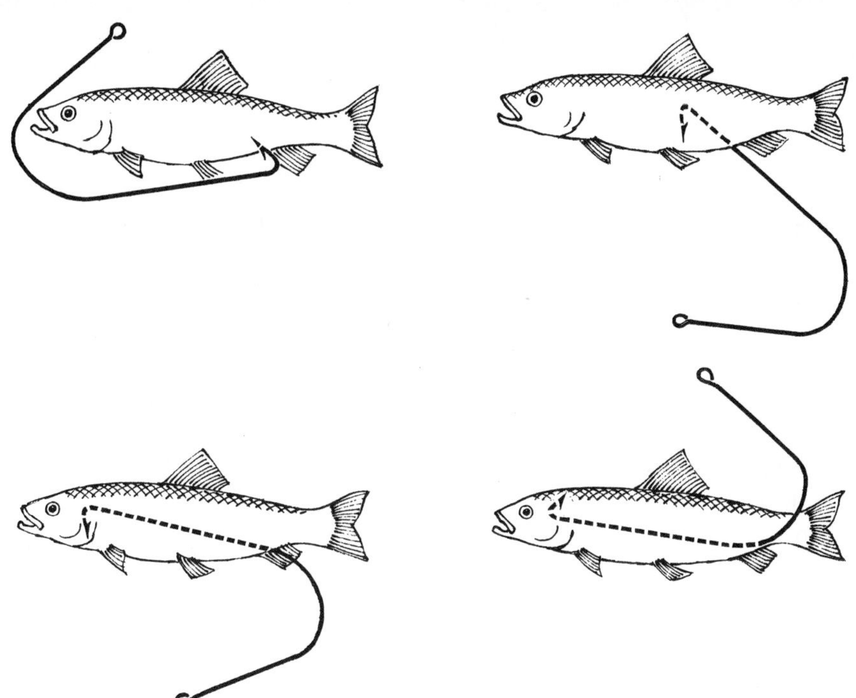

How to rig a minnow on a wide-bend hook for icefishing.

An icefisherman swings a nice laker from a hole on Lake Huron.

Several lures work well for jigging at this depth. The No. 6 or No. 7 Swedish Pimple in all-white is my best producer. I've also taken a fair number of fish on jigging Rapalas, LuJons, Do-Jiggers, Dardevles, Barracuda jigs, and a raft of others.

The important thing to remember is that the jig must be near bottom and kept in motion at all times. Lakers simply will not strike a stationary jig. I prefer to jig up and down with 6-inch jerks of my rod tip, with a brief pause between jigs. During the pause the jig will still be moving and many strikes occur during the pause, although most strikes occur as the lure flutters back down on the downstroke.

I've found that sweetening the hooks of a jig with a sliver of smelt or sucker meat gives it an added attraction that few lakers can pass up.

If a fish doesn't strike near bottom, try raising the jig several feet and repeat the jigging technique. It often takes up to a half-hour before lakers strike, since they seem to be on the move constantly during the winter. If the change of depth doesn't pay off I move toward deeper water.

My fishing usually begins at about 120 feet, and I'll progressively work out into 160 feet of water before the day is over unless I find the fish in shallower water. Drilling new holes can be the difference between success and failure in taking lake trout through the ice.

Lake trout are one of my favorite fish simply because of their tremendous power and large size. Like brook trout, big lakers are normally associated with wild places where man is an insignificant figure in an area little impressed with material things. And I hope it is always so.

8

OTHER TROUT

Trout are often considered among the most fun-producing gamefish found on the North American continent. Unfortunately, too many anglers feel the sun rises and sets on brookies, rainbows, browns, and lake trout. By adopting this attitude fishermen overlook the sporting qualities of golden trout, cutthroats, splake, and Dolly Vardens.

I can count among my most prized hours those spent in pursuit of the lesser-known trouts. It's true that much of my fishing time is spent chasing the four favorites, but I'll fish for the other species whenever and wherever the opportunity presents itself—not so much for the sake of catching these fish as for the chance just to fish for them. They are as much a part of the fishing scene as their better-known cousins, but they just haven't had the benefit of as much ink.

Yet, as with any other species, there are methods which have been developed and are best suited to them. Some anglers totally ignore the glamour species and devote all their angling time to pursuit of these gamefish.

We will not discuss little-known or endangered fish such as the

Gila, blueback, aurora, Sunapee, and tiger trout. Some are found in very localized areas, others in only tiny numbers, and others are fully protected by law; they remain untouchable to the average fisherman.

GOLDEN TROUT

This gamefish is acknowledged to be the most beautiful trout found on this continent. Once found only in the headwaters of the Kern River in California, this lovely fish has been planted in numerous high-country lakes in California, Wyoming, Arizona, Montana, New Mexico, Utah, Idaho, and Washington. Other states have made speculative plantings in remote lakes and streams, but the golden is a difficult fish to transplant and survival rates are low.

The terrain of the golden is in mountaintop lakes rimmed by steep talus slopes and alpine fir. Much of the fun of taking goldens is in getting to where they live and enjoying the mountain scenery while fishing. I've been skunked more times by goldens than by any other species, but the letdown is always eased by absorbing the peacefulness and beauty of high-country lakes.

One year I hiked into Grizzly Lake just as the ice was going out. It was a still, clear July day without a riffle on the surface. The hike into the lake through a portion of the Medicine Bow National Forest near Laramie was uneventful. The fishing turned out to be uneventful too, something I've learned to accept from golden trout.

I threw everything in my lightweight tackle box at the fish and managed to catch one obviously demented 10-incher. I'd set my sights on a golden of mounting size—something nearing 2 or 3 pounds. The fish struck a small brass spinner and fought well for its size, but I released it in hopes I'd take a larger fish. The big fish were seen and several made halfhearted passes at my lures, but none struck. The mystique was complete; I'd had my chance and had muffed it, and this seems to be one of the reasons why more people fish goldens one time and never go back. The fish can be frustratingly difficult to catch most of the time and behave like village idiots the next time. All too often, however, the bad trips with no fish outweigh the good trips where fish feed ravenously.

One thing I've found about golden trout is that they seem to prefer flies over hardware or live bait, and the flashier the fly the better the fish seem to like it. I've flailed several lakes with traditional patterns like the Adams, Black Ant, and Royal Coachman, and a variety of wets, dries, and streamers. They pass these offerings up like a pay car passing a tramp. But offer them a gaudy fly bordering on the ludicrous and they'll often strike.

Why? Beats me. These brilliant patterns tied in sizes 10 or 12 imitate nothing the fish is used to feeding on. Perhaps that in itself is the reason; they may be looking for something offering a change of pace. Perhaps the bright colors excite them, like waving a red flag in front of a bull.

I've also noted in trips to various lakes nestled among the peaks that goldens seldom strike near the surface. They like their flies fished deep and slow, and I've taken quite a number of fish by ticking my offerings over boulders near bottom. I always carry a small box of tiny split shot in my backpack on mountain trips for golden trout. I'd as soon leave my fly rod behind as my split shot. These tiny pieces of crimp-on lead can make all the difference.

An interesting aside to this method of taking goldens on flies is that they will often strike well on gaudy patterns for a while and then stop hitting altogether. Whenever this happens I'll switch to a dull pattern and the action usually begins all over again. Some of my favorite dark patterns are Muddlers, Skunks, and dark marabous.

I've taken goldens on small spinners tipped with a piece of nightcrawler on happy occasions. I fish them deep and slow like flies, and they produce occasionally.

Much of the secret of taking golden trout is to find lakes with fishable populations. These lakes are often rimmed with rock, snow, or ice, and at elevations above 10,000 feet. Goldens thrive best in lakes where no competition exists with other trout. A lake

Four beautiful golden trout taken from a wilderness lake in Wyoming. Goldens seem to prefer flies to hardware or bait. *Erwin Bauer photo.*

with brookies or rainbows may contain goldens for a few years, but the competition is too keen and these brilliant carmine-sided trout disappear.

Names of golden lakes can be obtained from various conservation agencies. The next course is to obtain topographical maps which point the way to a chancy goldmine of fishing activity. Horseback or shank's mare are the two ways to reach golden country, and these ankle-twisting trips are not for persons suffering from heart or respiratory problems or prone to leg cramps. Overnight or three-day trips are best; anglers should avoid the up-and-back trips made in one day, since they are often too tired to devote full attention to the fishing and scenery.

CUTTHROAT

This sporty gamefish is found throughout the western United States and can be taken from lakes, streams, and also some of the larger rivers flowing into the Pacific Ocean as sea-run fish. Many subspecies exist.

Cutthroats are a beautiful gamefish with a slightly forked tail and a red slashing under each lower jaw. They are found with a variety of body markings, but the most prominent is the crimson slash on the bottom jaw. Fish from the Yellowstone area are a yellowish green with large sparse dark spots on the rear portion of the body. The Snake River cutthroat is more heavily spotted with smaller dots marking the body. Sea-run fish are a greenish blue with small black spots on the head, body, tail, and fins and a silvery flank similar to a steelhead.

Cutts seldom jump when hooked, although sea-run fish are more prone to break the water than fish from inland lakes or streams. Wherever they are found, the cutthroat is a well-accepted gamefish in the West.

My first meeting with cutthroats came about 1950 when I traveled to Yellowstone National Park with my parents. My brother and I were budding teenagers and charged up with enthusiasm to fish for cutthroats.

Our first campsite was near the famous Fishing Bridge at Yellowstone Lake. After pitching our rig we sidled down to the shore, where several anglers were sitting with rods propped in Y-shaped crotches stuck in the mud. We'd been there only a couple minutes when one angler rared back, set the hook, and my brother George and I stood breathless as the fisherman battled a big cutt.

The fish was promptly netted after a short but spirited struggle and stringered along with several other fish in the 4- to 5-pound class, and they resumed fishing. Just minutes later another fish was hooked and landed and the fishermen quit. "You can have our spot," they said. "Just cast about 30 feet from shore and fish on bottom. There are still plenty of cutts down there."

We rigged up our spinning reels (some of the earliest models were Airex half-bails such as we had) and began fishing on bottom with worms as we'd been told. Several minutes later we were rewarded with a tugging on the other end, and after a brief, scrappy battle we managed to land our first cutthroat. Within an hour we had four beautiful fish for our dinner, and thus began my love affair with this fish.

Since that time I've chased cutthroats throughout the West, and caught my share sometimes and been thoroughly skunked on other occasions. Many fishermen take cutthroats for granted; they seem to be accorded the same mentality as brook trout have. This thinking by ill-informed anglers can lead to very poor fishing. Cutts are more sophisticated than many give them credit for, but they can be caught by several different methods. Worms fished on bottom still catch naive cutthroat, but it pays to have other tricks in your fishing bag.

Most of my fishing for this species takes place during August, since this is when business often calls for me to tour the West from my Michigan home. The streams are generally much lower than during spring months and moderately clear, although not as clear as during low-water fall months.

I like to wade certain portions of streams or hire a float-trip guide for a day's run down a river. The best fishing is often found near the edges of the riverbank. Small fast-sinking spinners or spoons worked deep near these edges can produce dynamite fishing.

Some good cutts have fallen to the double-hook minnow fishing technique described for brown trout fishing in ponds. One hook is inserted through the head and another near the tail, and the minnow is allowed to "swim" through deep holes. A slight jig-twitch type of retrieve has produced best for me. Deeper pools necessitate the use of split shot about 6 inches above the minnow.

If the water is slightly high and colored from runoff I'd suggest a small spinner and minnow or nightcrawler combination. The added flash of a tiny silver spinner ahead of the bait can make a big difference.

Some of the best cutthroat fishing comes from high mountain lakes just as the ice goes off. Quiet bays or coves often lose their ice first, and this ice-out period triggers a feeding frenzy that must be seen to be appreciated. Some of the largest cutts of the year are taken at ice-out with yellow and black painted spoons. This seems to be a hot color combination. The lures should be fished fast with frequent jerks. Sight feeding seems to play an inmportant part in the cutt's life at ice-out, and this retrieve works best.

Once the fish end this early-season feeding period they tend to go deep, and trolling with cowbells and lures or minnows is the best method of taking big ones.

Sea-run cutts are another story. They ascend streams similar to salmon or steelhead, and late summer or early fall are the best times to fish. Anadromous cutthroat spend from one to three or four years in salt water after having been born in a stream and then migrating to sea. They fatten up on the abundant forage of the ocean and return to spawn at maturity. Many anglers never realize these fish are available, since only a handful of streams harbor sea-runs.

Harvest trout, as sea-runs are often called, are best taken with bait early in their run. Bait fishermen use everything—single salmon eggs, spawn bags, nightcrawlers, or pieces of white meat cut from small suckers or other fish. Sizable baits attract more cutts than a meager offering. Many fishermen completely cover their No. 6 hook with meat or other bait.

Once the run of harvest trout is on, anglers often line the banks of rivers such as Washington's Columbia. They cast their bait out and allow it to lie on bottom. As schools of sea-runs move through the area, rod tips nod from the gentle strikes, and the fish is hooked.

Another more pleasurable method of taking cutts is to cast small wobbling spoons such as the Krocodile or Little Cleo or small plugs like the Lazy Ike or Tiny Tadpolly into deep holes. The last time I fished Washington's Naselle River I was pitching a Tiny Tad upstream and cranking hard to take it near bottom where I could feel it ticking over the rocks. The lure bounced several times and stopped fast—a big sea-run cutt had picked up the lure. I set the hooks and was amazed at the strength and quickness of the 4-pounder. It dashed back and forth, upstream one minute and down the next, and made great swirls in midstream before tiring and coming to the net.

The next fish came from alongside a log jam where the current swept in at the top, swirled heavily around the logs, and then quickened its pace before leaving the close confines of the pool. I'd been fishing a wobbling spoon deep through the hole and under the logjam when the spoon stopped briefly and was followed by a heavy strike as the fish turned and headed downstream.

The harvest trout had set the hooks on the strike, and I followed it downstream until the fish ran out the spool. We then tussled for another five minutes before a gleaming side showed through the clear water. My first guess was a steelhead, but it hadn't jumped. It turned out to be another cutthroat, a fresh-run 5-pounder, gleaming and sleek from the sea.

I've learned that slow deep pools are often good places to look for schools of harvest trout. These fish are ripe for picking with a fly rod, and this method takes as many trophy sea-runs as any other and provides the most fun.

A sinking line with a tapered 9-foot leader has proved to be best in most cases. Several patterns are good. Some of my favorites are the Royal Coachman, Kalama Special, and an assortment of bucktails and streamers. A good selection is important, since sea-runs can be picky about patterns.

I'll find a good quiet piece of water and cast quartering across and downstream. Some fishermen prefer a dead drift, but I like to give the fly a little action by twitching the fly line with my hand. It causes the fly to dart, and cutts often strike and flail out of the water, all in one smooth motion. I've learned that if a cutt makes a pass at the fly and misses, I should bring it in and change flies. They will seldom come back for a second try, although they may strike if the fly pattern has been changed. If the fish struck a bright pattern and missed, switch and offer him a dull-colored fly, or switch sizes by going larger or smaller.

Sea-run cutthroats provide action comparable to that of summer steelheading, and I know of no other gamefish that tastes as wonderful on the table. Sea-runs are super.

SPLAKE

The splake is a fish resulting from the successful breeding of a male brook trout (Speckled trout is another name) and a female lake trout.

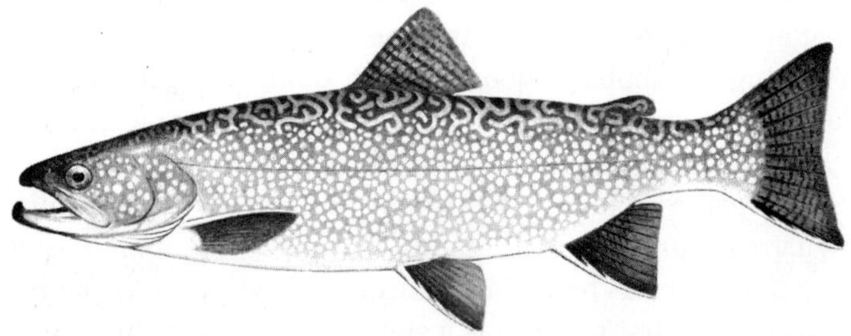

Splake were originally developed by the Ontario Department of Lands and Forests because they grew faster than lake trout and heavier than brook trout. Since the birth of this gamefish, various agencies such as Michigan's Department of Natural Resources have further refined the species by backcrossing both to obtain the more dominant features and characteristics of either brook or lake trout.

The splake is a fertile cross, a hybrid, and capable of spawning.

In general appearance the splake is heavier-looking than the laker and slimmer than the brook trout. The *normal* coloring has yellow body spots similar to lake trout. The red spots of the brookie are usually missing. Backcrossing between splake and brook trout or splake and lake trout creates a widely varied body conformation.

Typical are fish which look like lake trout but have square tails, fish that look like brook trout but possess the laker's forked tail, and fish containing characteristics of either parent. Even fisheries biologists can be confused, especially between splake and lake trout, which often frequent the same waters. The only positive check is to count the pyloric caeca, which differ between splake, lake trout, and brookies.

Splake in a natural state are very rare; most fish are the result of trout-hatchery production. Ontario still has some lakes containing splake, but Michigan is currently leading the way with hatchery production and plantings. Splake are now common in many inland lakes and the Great Lakes. Northern Lake Huron is the present site for the heaviest splake plantings, and 10-pound fish are being taken consistently.

This gamefish behaves much like lake trout, and the same techniques described in the chapter on lakers will take splake.

This hybrid often follows schools of pre-spawning and spawning trout or salmon into shoal water during fall months to feed. One very productive technique involves the use of light line and a spawn bag or single salmon egg impaled on a small hook. Splake bite very gently, and the take is difficult to ascertain. Many anglers have started using small quill bobbers to indicate the delicate take. The bobber is set to suspend the bait on or just off bottom. Whenever the bobber quivers, the hook is set and an angler is often rewarded with a hard-fighting fish.

Icefishing has long been my favorite method of taking big splake. Solid ice cover seems to put splake on the feed, and they move around a wide area in search of forage fish. The one basic difference between fishing splake and lake trout through the ice is that splake are commonly at much shallower depths, often between 15 and 40 feet. The feeding pattern is not bottom-oriented as it is with lakers. I've seen schools of splake move through my ice hole within 6 feet of the ice. Shallow water eases the problem of catching splake.

A lightproof shanty is a splake fisherman's dream come true, for many reasons. First, areas where splake are found are often bitterly

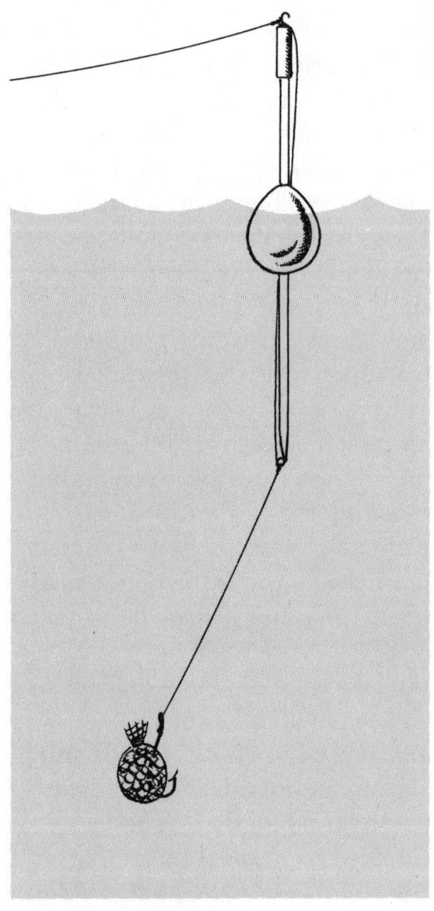

Bobber rig with spawn bag is effective for splake. Quill bobber is best for signaling fish's delicate take.

cold and windswept, and a heated shanty is a definite asset. Second, splake are delicate biters and often lie back a foot from a lure or bait and watch it intently before easing up and softly sucking it in. This strike is difficult to feel but easy to spot from a darkened coop.

An angler can lower a jigging lure or bait down and watch its action and the action of incoming splake. When the fish mouths the offering, the angler can set the hook immediately.

I've found that splake will strike almost anything smaller than themselves. I've taken fish on tip-ups baited with a 2-inch shiner minnow, but this is a slow process with many lost fish. The splake will often peel the bait off the hook before being hooked.

The best method of icefishing is to sit inside the shanty and jig with a small ice rod and a blue-silver Do-Jigger with a single hook.

Cut the tail off a dead shiner and attach it to the hook and jig it slowly up and down with lengthy pauses in between. A splake will spot the darting spoon and work in slowly to investigate. I've seen them watch a spoon-and-tail combination for over a minute before striking. Many strikes come as the spoon hovers motionless; it takes a sharp eye to spot the take. Short 6-inch jigs with the rod tip will provide the proper action, but allow the spoon to remain motionless for at least 10 seconds before jigging again.

Bait seems to be a preferred meal for splake, and I've taken them on small pieces of cut-up smelt, salmon eggs, cornborers, waxworms, and nightcrawlers. It pays to carry several types of bait on splake waters.

I prefer using a small ice bobber when fishing bait for splake. It helps telegraph the soft strike, although often the bobber does nothing but rise a fraction of an inch in the water as the fish takes the bait. A thin spring-steel rod-tip bobber is another means of learning when a splake is at the bait. The paper-thin length of steel will dip down slightly on the strike.

Splake are rapidly becoming one of our great gamefish and I predict the day will come when more anglers will learn just how much fun this hybrid can deliver.

DOLLY VARDEN

The Dolly Varden is a Western fish indigenous to Rocky Mountain states, Alaska, some of the western Canadian provinces, and many streams making up the Pacific Ocean watershed. Said to have been named after a character in a Charles Dickens novel, the Dolly is a colorful fish.

A fall spawner, the bull trout (a nickname) has been cursed with a poor reputation because it feeds on trout or salmon eggs. It's been found that all trout feed on other fish eggs, but now the Dolly is trying to live down its bad reputation.

Fishermen would be hard pressed to hold egg-eating against this beautiful trout. From salt water it is silvery, but in cold mountain streams it often has bright-orange or red spots on the sides. Lake fish often possess yellow spots only on the back.

Several years ago I made a trip to the Flathead River in northwestern Montana for a go at bull trout. The best time to catch fish ranging up to 20 pounds is during the fall spawning run, which

usually begins in June or July and ends in September or October when the fish return to big lakes such as Flathead.

My September trip found many larger holes full of large dark fish which looked like sunken logs. I'd been told that large red and white Dardevles were among the best of lures provided they were cast upstream, allowed to sink, and retrieved in a wobbling manner along bottom.

We had been fishing for two hours before I hooked my first Dolly. I'd been casting to a slow deep pool flanked by a fast stretch of water. Dolly Vardens prefer this type of water. My spoon was midway through the pool when it suddenly stopped as if I'd snagged bottom. I jerked on the rod and a fish jerked back. Line sizzled off my spinning reel as the fish bucked into the air with a jump that threw water halfway across the river. Plunging back, the fish bulldogged for bottom briefly before twisting downstream around a gravel bar. I followed the fish along the gravel bar and closed the gap to 20 feet.

Far below me in the depths of the hole the bull trout surged back and forth in an effort to throw the spoon. The battle raged for ten minutes before I could slide a 10-pounder onto the bar.

We spent the rest of the day catching and releasing heavy Dolly Vardens. Almost every pool was full of fish eager to strike once the early-morning fog burned away.

Business took me away for three days, but I returned for another engagement with bulls. The fish had finished spawning while I was gone, and my next trip was a total washout. This is often the case.

Many Western anglers specialize in catching Dolly Vardens, and they agree that heavy medicine for these fish includes large plugs or spoons, jumbo streamers suitable for salt water fishing, and bait fished near bottom. The important thing is to keep your offering moving with the current among the rocks and stones.

Spoons should be in the 4-to-6-inch class, and the Rok't Devle in red and white or yellow with five red diamonds is a good choice. Large plugs like the J-Plug, Flatfish, Magnum Tadpolly, or other salmon-type lures are fine provided they are white and red or orange and red, the two most productive colors.

Bull trout are meat eaters, and many fishermen use dead suckers or sculpins and hook them with a two-hook arrangement, head and tail, and drift them deep under brushpiles, undercut banks, below waterfalls, behind boulders, or through deep pools. Some fishermen use raw beef and a No. 2 treble hook and fish it exactly like other bait. The Dolly Varden is impartial to the offering as long as it's large and meaty-looking.

Fishing with lures or bait should be done as slowly as possible. A fast retrieve is not productive, since these fish seldom chase after their meals. They would rather have it come to them with the current. Spawning fish seldom feed but will strike out of irritation or reflex.

Some large bull trout are taken by trolling many of the larger inland lakes of the Rockies. I've fished Montana's Swan and Flathead lakes several times and Hungry Horse Reservoir one time, as well as several of the smaller lakes nestled in the mountains.

Dolly Vardens are hard-fighting fish when taken on reasonably light tackle. I never use over 12-pound mono and often go as light as 8-pound test, and I've had bull trout battle me to a standstill. Tangle with one of these fish in a rushing river and you'll possibly wind up with bull trout fever. They have a knack of getting under your skin and making you wish you could fish them every day.

III

PIKE, WALLEYE, SAUGER

9

NORTHERN PIKE

Northern pike have managed in the last ten years to gain a reputation among anglers as a hard-fighting, heavyweight gamefish. No longer are they scornfully tossed aside. There once was a time when fishermen looked down their noses at pike of any size and hated to hook one.

Now, northern pike, especially trophy fish, are well up on the list of any angler looking for a thrilling battle from a fish that slashes heavily at a lure, often jumps when hooked in cold water, and tastes mighty fine on the table once the tiny Y-bones are removed.

Pike are circumpolar in distribution. They are found from northern subarctic lakes rimmed by spruce to southern lakes where their chief competition for food comes from largemouth bass. They are the mainstay of tourism for many Canadian and Great Lakes areas and are plentiful enough in trophy sizes to enable any fisherman to take his share—if he knows his business.

The northern pike is virtually the same fish wherever he's found. There is very little variation in color—certainly much less than shown by many members of the trout and salmon families. Pike are rather long, slender, and rapierlike in shape, with a large flat head. The jaws are studded with sharp teeth capable of holding any smaller fish or small birds and mammals unfortunate enough to land in the water.

The dorsal area of northern pike is dark green and shades to lighter green along the sides. The belly is often white or beige. Small bean-shaped yellow spots are located along the lateral line, both above and below, which gives the fish a light-on-dark appearance. The fins are usually a reddish orange with large dark spots. Five or less mandibular pores (small sensory openings) are located on the under side of the lower jaw. This helps distinguish the pike from the muskie, which has six or more.

Down through the years the pike has assumed a mythical reputation, in part because of its manner of living. In the Middle Ages the "waterwolf" was assumed to be a devil being, created only to eat small children or farm animals that dared go near the water.

The pike feeds voraciously on other fish only slightly smaller than itself. This feeding habit of trying to consume anything which is alive and smaller endears northern pike to trophy-seeking anglers. Almost any lure or bait will bring a response from big pike, and this is one reason why northerns are one of the easiest trophy fish to take.

My personal record weighed 29 pounds and was taken from Manitoba's High Rock Lake, a wide island-studded area in the sprawling Churchill River. That trip was exciting because it delivered a brand of fishing excitement few anglers have experienced. During four days of fishing, two partners and I landed over twenty pike that scaled from 18 to 29 pounds. Many of the fish were over 20 pounds, and that is a trophy pike anywhere.

Ice-out had taken place two weeks earlier, and the giant northern pike were supposed to be ravenously hungry. We found just the opposite during the first part of our trip; we had all we could do to land enough dinner-sized walleyes to make a meal. A just-caught walleye was to figure dramatically in our locating the monster northerns.

We were wind-drifting down the lake and casting spoons to the shoreline, to weedbeds which were emerging, and along the drop-off. We'd taken one walleye, which was placed on the stringer—it would be our lunch. We neared a tiny bay, nothing more than a pond with a trickle of creek water entering at one end. As we approached the mouth of the bay a terrible ruckus occurred alongside the boat.

Stan Bowles, owner of the outpost camp and Athapap Lodge on Lake Athapapuskow at Cranberry Portage, hollered, "Look at that pike!" Cory Kilvert, a longtime Manitoba lodge owner, looked, and his jaw dropped open. "Its one of the biggest pike I've seen in thirty years of fishing this country."

A bruiser of a pike, which looked well over 20 pounds, was doing its best to twist the tethered walleye off the stringer. It would let go, back off a few feet, and dart in for another slashing attack on the hapless fish.

The next time it backed away, Stan fired a Dardevle at the fish. The jumbo northern socked the spoon instantly and the fight was on, although Stan had a difficult time controlling his fish. All this time the wind was blowing us deeper into the tiny pocket of water off the main arm of the lake.

We saw a flurry of activity farther back in the bay as Stan's fish jumped and lathered the water near the boat. We finally slid the meshes around his pike, and it weighed just over 21 pounds. Elsewhere in the bay small suckers and other baitfish were skittering from the water in an effort to escape the relentless attack of marauding northerns.

We'd found the pike, and every fish was huge. We threw spoons, jigs, Creek Chub Pikie Minnows, and almost everything else from our well-stocked tackle box, but the fish wouldn't hit, although they continued to chase the smaller fish. We'd see an angry swirl on the surface and a small sucker would disappear in the boil. Tails and dorsal fins broke the water as big pike wolfed down the small baitfish. We were witnessing a massacre.

Cory decided to try skittering his lure rapidly across the surface. He began his retrieve before the spoon hit the water and ripped it fast over the pike. Small suckers darted into the air, apparently thinking it was another pike attacking from above. The Dardevle suddenly stopped with a jolt. Cory set the hooks and line peeled off his reel as the fish jerked away. The water was shallow and this was a circus for him as the fish splashed into the air, fell back with a belly smacker, and immediately jumped again. It took ten minutes of bare-knuckle fighting before we could land the northern. It scaled 24 pounds, right on the nose.

Dale Staimbrook nets a trophy pike for Ray Gilbert on Savant Lake, Ontario.

My turn came next as I practiced Cory's "skittering" fast retrieve. The spoon stopped as if it were snagged on bottom. We'd made enough retrieves to know that bottom was clean; besides, a huge back had creased the water behind my lure and quickly closed on it before the lure stopped. I knew it was a pike, and a big one.

I set the hooks and nothing happened for an instant, so I slammed the hooks home again. That did it! The pike surged out through the mouth of the bay like a wartime hero heading home. He wanted out of that bay as much as I wanted to keep him there. I could no more hold him back than I could harness a wild horse.

We followed, and the battle raged back and forth for a long while. The other pike had jumped in shallow water, but this fish stayed deep before coming to the surface near the end of the fight. He then twisted like a snake on a hot rock and vaulted into the air, his wide toothy jaws spread with an evil grin. That jump took most of the fight from him, but it was still far from over. We slammed back and forth for another ten minutes as I tried to keep him from going under the boat and hanging my line up on the keel.

He finally rolled on his side in total submission and was promptly landed. I knew he was huge, but it wasn't until the hand-held scales settled on 29 pounds that we knew just how large he actually was. I'll never forget the excitement I felt when I gazed upon that huge pike and realized I'd really taken a trophy.

We took many other trophy pike from that little bay during the day but kept only two fish, mine and a 22-pounder for Stan. It was the final consensus that the pike had finished spawning and were famished. The suckers were just beginning their runs, and the shallow bay was choked with forage fish. The pike had congregated like a wolf pack surrounding a sick caribou and systematically cut the baitfish to shreds. Our top-of-the-water retrieve that skipped along was an exact imitation of the frightened behavior of the small suckers. By accident we'd stumbled on a sure-fire way to take trophy northerns from shallow water early in the spring.

One time years ago I was doing a story for *Outdoor Life* on the big pike of Kasagami Lake, 50 air miles southeast of Moosonee, Ontario, which is at the bottom end of James Bay. This is trackless country, home of the moose, an occasional caribou or polar bear, and the timber wolf. We would hear wolves howling every night.

Kasagami is a beautiful but shallow subarctic lake, rimmed by birch and stunted spruce and dotted with islands large enough to contain a small town. It's full of big pike, but it took us several days to find them.

One day, after several hours of listless action, we had a heavy rolling strike. The fish missed the spoon and wouldn't be tempted to strike again. I told the guide, "I guess the pike went to sleep."

"I'll wake him up, by damn," the ancient Cree said, in one of his

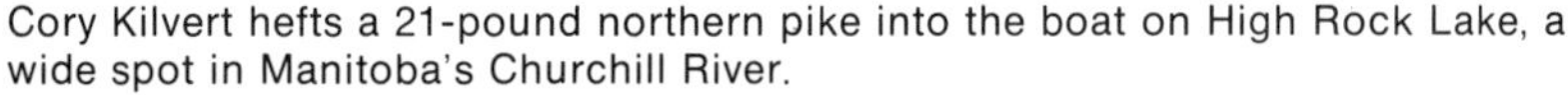

Cory Kilvert hefts a 21-pound northern pike into the boat on High Rock Lake, a wide spot in Manitoba's Churchill River.

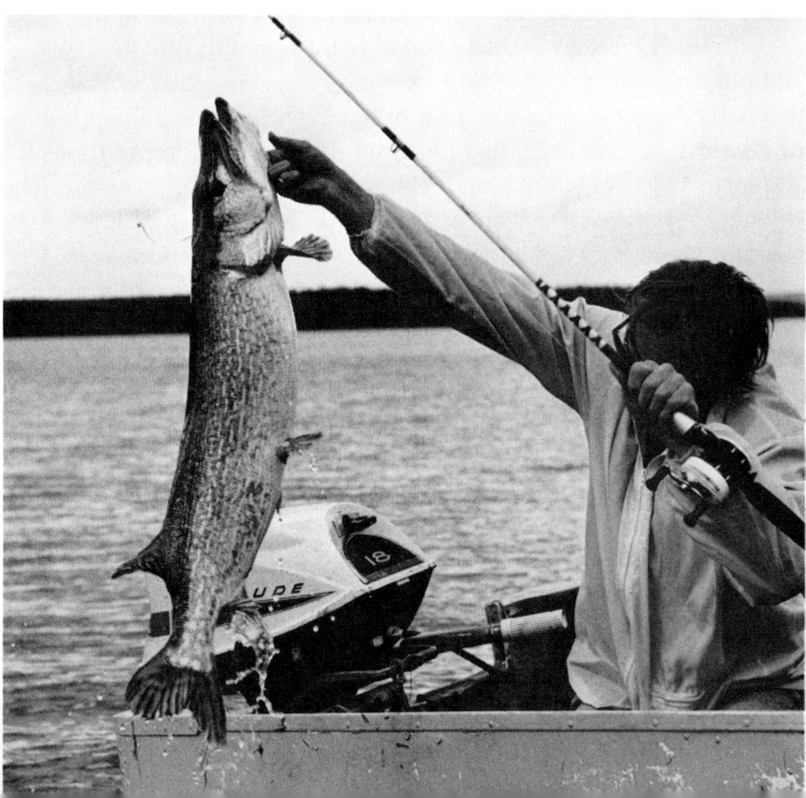

longest speeches during our seven-day stay. He motored up into the weedbed harboring the pike and raised the prop half out of the water and revved hell out of the outboard. Spray flew in all directions as he churned water and weeds into a greenish froth. He continued back and forth through the weedbed in this manner for five minutes before taking us back out into open water.

"He's awake now," the Cree said, in what had to be a classic understatement. I figured the fish should be halfway to Moosonee by then. "Cast!" he ordered.

My buddy and I began casting, more in deference to our guide's flat demand than in any hope of catching fish. Ray had made his second cast as I finished my first. His spoon stopped abruptly as it wobbled under the floating bits of prop-chewed weeds. He set the hook out of pure reflex and a northern pike tried his best to yank him into the lake.

The fight lasted ten minutes while our guide broke his stoic composure and grinned for the first time. "See?" he asked. I saw but didn't believe. Ray stubbornly fought the fish to a standstill, and we landed the 19-pounder by hand; the guide didn't have a net.

The weed-churning trick worked one other day when the fish stopped striking. Through a one-hour conversation with the guide during which he answered yes or no, I learned that this old Indian trick was used whenever they needed fish to eat and the pike wouldn't respond to more traditional methods. He allowed as how the noise causes them to stir around, out of self-defense, I suppose. But it works and is a trick that has produced for me at other times and places when pike develop lockjaw.

By nature I'm a caster, a spot caster, and I take pleasure in dropping a lure near some type of pike cover and obtaining a strike. I get charged up when an apparently good-looking piece of structure yields a savage strike and a trophy pike.

One trick I learned through experience is that casting produces best during late spring, early summer, and again in the fall, always during periods of cooler water. During midsummer heat, pike are often sluggish and seek deeper water in search of food and slightly cooler water.

A trophy pike fisherman could develop muscular arms by continuous casting and still not have anything to show for it except exercise. It pays to know when and where to cast.

I'm mindful of a trip my parents, brother, and I made when I was fourteen to Ontario's Batchawana River. We didn't know much about fishing and especially pike fishing. I lucked out (that is the proper phrase) and landed a 19½-pound 42-inch northern on 6-pound line by casting off the dock our first day in camp. No wire leader, no experience, and no skill—just luck. Well, I thought pike fishing was easy and 19-pounders commonplace. It took three more days of steady fishing before I decided that Dame Fortune had blessed me with a stupid fish.

We tried trolling and casting at the same time and caught a few small fish while working the Batchawana River, but it was slow going. My father told me, "Try casting near some of those fallen trees that have toppled into the river. You might get a pike from under one of them."

My brother George and I started pegging erratic casts near the fallen trees. It strikes me now that Dad spent as much time retrieving wayward spoons from tree branches as he did running the boat.

George made an accurate cast at one point and began working his spoon back to the boat. A pike charged out from under a fallen spruce and hammered the lure. He rared back on his rod tip hard enough to anchor a 6/0 hook into a 150-pound tarpon. Luckily the line held, and the pike darted back and forth for several minutes under the boat before George tired him enough to lead him to the net. Dad scooped him up and 15 pounds of writhing pike fell to the floor. George was so excited you'd have thought he was a six-year-old on Christmas Eve waiting up for Santa Claus.

Our trolling success had been dismal at best, so we concentrated on casting to toppled trees, ledges of rock that had fallen into the river, the deepwater edges of weedbeds, and around the tips of points and islands. Our trophy-pike score continued to soar. At the tender fishing age of fourteen we'd discovered that luck helps at times but it's more important to substitute skill and knowledge for large pike.

We didn't take any fish larger than my lucky 19-pounder, but we boated seemingly a ton (at least twenty fish) from 15 to 18 pounds. This was twenty-five years ago but the occasion remains vivid in my fishing bank of memories. It was extremely good fishing at the time, and still remains excellent sport in this jet-age era we're toiling through.

Those facts we learned years ago still hold true for jumbo northerns. These fish lie in ambush and dart out from under cover to garner their meals. Slanting a well-placed cast alongside this type of cover and taking a jumbo northern pike is still high and exciting fishing.

One year I was fishing Michigan's Houghton Lake, a massive body of water 17 feet deep at its deepest spot. It is subject to huge waves during storms and is also one of the weediest lakes I've had the pleasure of fishing.

The weedbeds grow to within inches of the surface, and even a weedless lure would get fouled up. I told my tale of woe—too many weeds and not enough pike—to a local bait-shop owner. "There's only one way to fish Houghton Lake for pike when the weeds are at their peak. Whenever I want northerns I'll use a 5-inch floating Rapala. It has to be fished slow so it barely moves. Reel it at normal speeds and it will dive down a foot or so and all you'll catch will be more weeds. Fish it like a surface plug for bass and you'll catch pike," he told me. His advice accomplished three things: It allowed me to catch pike I wouldn't have taken otherwise; it alerted me to a whole new concept of fishing in weeds; and it got the shopkeeper deep into my wallet, as I bought four of the big floaters.

The first few casts were reeled much too fast and I found myself bringing in long trailers of weeds. I slowed the retrieve to a bare crawl and began getting explosive surface strikes. The key was to keep the lure moving just enough so it would start to dive and then I'd allow it to bob to the surface. The pike mauled the lures for three days before I lost my last fish-catching Rapala. I now carry a double handful for such occasions and they have proved useful on many lakes.

I'd like to make a statement now that will probably draw fire from many anglers. *I don't and won't use a wire leader when fishing for big pike with artificial lures.* Wire leaders rob many lures, if not all of them, of their built-in fish-catching ability. Sure, many big pike are taken yearly by fishermen who attach a big wire leader ahead of the lure. But they would probably catch many more if they were to tie the line directly to the lure or to a snap swivel.

LURES VS. BAIT

Studies made several years ago in Michigan, Wisconsin, and a few other states should provide a clue to pike fishermen about their choice of lures. It showed that more pike are taken on spoons, plugs, and spinners than on live bait. If I had to go into pike country with only three lures, they would be the Dardevle, Rapala, and leadhead jig.

Bait is fine for them that wants it, but keeping minnows alive during a fishing trip is more hassle than I care to have. I'd rather troll than fish minnows and I'd rather cast than troll, so you can see where my priorities are.

Lures are the proven producers over much of the pike's range. Just as there are probably a hundred lures capable of taking pike, there are also as many ways of fishing these lures. Northern pike are moody fish, but during any four-hour daylight period on good water the fish will usually go on a brief feeding spree. Be on the water at that period and you'll probably catch fish, if your lure is working properly.

Few fishermen ever experiment with different lure retrieval speeds or rod-tip actions with their favorite lures. Some lures will work only at certain speeds, but they are precious few. The red-and-white Dardevle is a time-honored pike lure, but many anglers fish it only one way—with a steady retrieve. By falling into a rut they rob themselves of the pleasure of finding a new retrieve or action that works. I know of at least five different retrieves that work well with Dardevles, from jigging and hopping slow retrieve to the high-speed method that worked so well on Manitoba's High Rock Lake.

I've taken jumbo northerns by reeling steadily for several feet and then allowing the lure to flutter back down. Resume the retrieve and let it wobble downward again. This technique has taken some of my largest northern pike.

Another technique that works well is to reel steadily and then raise the rod tip sharply in a vertical motion. This causes the lure to swim upward in the water. Lower the rod tip and reel in the slack line before beginning the retrieve. Another upward lift of the rod tip is followed by a sharp downward flutter as slack line is taken up. Pike often grab the lure as it drops down, and as you take up the slack line they'll be heading back to their lair. These fish will usually be hooked in the corner of the jaw.

Jigs are fun lures to fish pike with because they are heavy enough to cast and sink rapidly. The jig is commonly accepted as a walleye or smallmouth bass lure but few anglers try them on big northerns, and they thus miss out on a golden opportunity to take fish. The jig isn't worth the lead it's made from if it is fished in weedy areas. The angler will spend all his time removing lettuce from the lure.

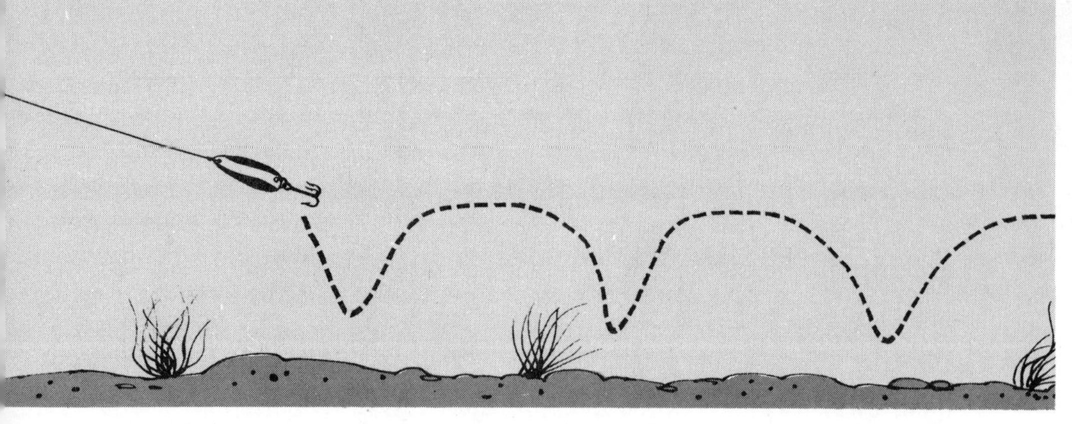

Two effective retrieves for pike. The flutter-down (above) is achieved by intermittently cranking and stopping the reel handle; the flutter-up (below) by raising and lowering the rod tip during the retrieve.

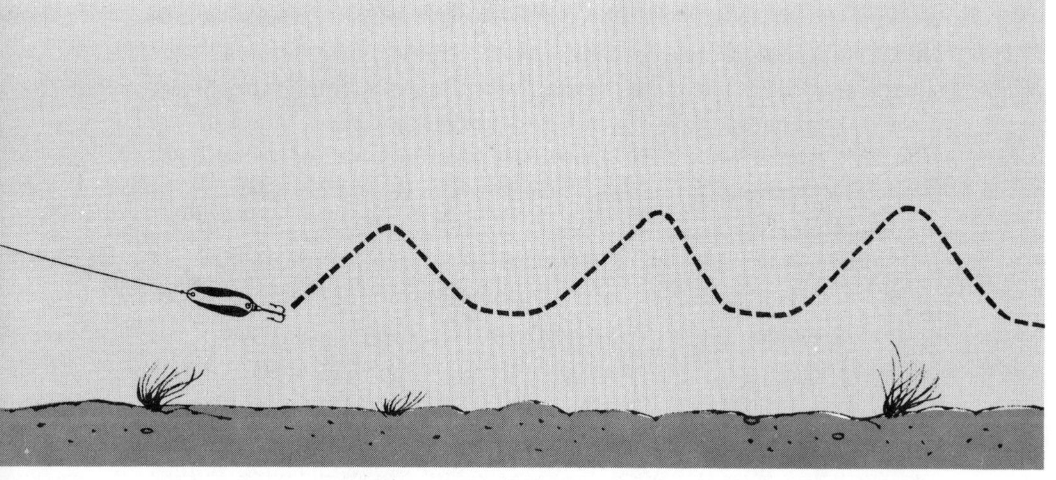

Instead, I prefer fishing jigs in deepwater bays or off rocky ledges in good pike waters. The bucktail jig or Hairy Worm (an ugly-looking jig with short plastic worm tail) may be unattractive to me but northerns latch onto it as though the call were out for their last supper.

Jig fishing for northerns calls for a little luck. I've found they often inhale the lure and are hooked deeply, but occasionally you'll lose a fish when sharp teeth shred the line. Long frequent pauses between jigs are more apt to hook fish deep than a continuous bottom-creeping up-and-down jigging motion. If the lure is kept in motion by reeling and alternately raising and lowering the rod tip, most fish will be hooked in the jaw, fewer lures are lost, and tempers are less apt to flare when a big fish gets away.

Another trick I've used to tempt northern pike is to add a white Uncle Josh porkrind to the jig. The wavering action of the pig skin combined with the up-and-down jig movement is a deadly killer for jumbo northerns.

As strange as it sounds, I've taken a couple trophy pike on a jig retrieved steadily through the water. I was sure both times the jig had weeds or other debris fouled on it and I was hurrying it to the boat to remove the crud. Then a pike nailed the jig hard and the fight was on. I've tried it many times since and only once has it produced a jarring strike. But that's the way trophy fishing goes; you may discover a trick that works some of the time, most of the time, or only occasionally.

NIGHT FISHING

Few fishermen are aware that northern pike *occasionally* feed at night. I've hit on this happy circumstance only three times in my years of chasing pike, but it does happen.

One time my brother George and I were working a largemouth bass lake after dark. The bass were uncooperative, although we fished in every area we'd taken fish from before. We stopped fishing, moored our boat, and began casting off the dock. I was getting tired of rowing (have you ever noticed how some unlucky fisherman always gets to row?) and we were both nearly exhausted, I from rowing and George from casting. We'd been on the lake for six hours without a strike.

George was fishing a black-and-white sinking River Runt while I cast with a Jitterbug. On his second cast he hooked a fish that slammed from the water, too far from shore to learn its identity, but we thought it was a bass. "It's really a big fish," George ventured, between tightly pursed lips. The fish was hauling line from his reel as though the drag hadn't been set.

We tottered around the end of the dock for fifteen minutes as the fish stayed just out of eyesight. George would gain line only to lose it to another rush that caused his reel to howl in anguish. It jumped again, the second time a sloppy last-ditch effort to throw the lure.

He led it toward the dock and I leaned over to slide the net under the fish. When that flat head and evil grin followed by a greenish body hove into view, I almost fell off the dock. "It's a big pike and he's barely hooked," I said as the net slid around the fish. The hooks fell out as I lifted it onto the dock and then ran with it toward the yard light.

The northern was 39 inches long and weighed 16 pounds. A 6-inch sucker was regurgitated as I laid the pike on the grass. We'd heard that pike seldom strike at night, but this fish proved that for every rule, there is an exception.

TROLLING

As I mentioned earlier, I dislike trolling for northern pike. But I do know that at certain times trolling is about the only way to make the jumbo pike connection.

Midsummer is a case in point: As the waters warm (this is more true of southerly waters) the fish will follow the forage minnows, and this may take them as deep as 15 or 20 feet. Trolling at these depths is difficult but not impossible.

The best areas are in river channels or along the deepwater edges of weedbeds. I never troll more than two lines, regardless of how many anglers are in the boat. Position one fisherman in the bow to watch for changes in the weedline or for shallow spots or to keep one eye fixed on a sonar unit.

I prefer using 1 or 2 ounces of weight in the form of a keel sinker about 3 feet ahead of the lure. One of my favorite lures is the Rapala (floater), and another is a Creek Chub Jointed Pikie.

Release 40 or 50 feet of line at a normal trolling speed. The weight will allow you to fish fairly close to the boat and still maintain the proper depth. It's not necessary to get right down to bottom, because big pike will rise off bottom or part the weedbeds to make their attack.

Both lures will work at normal trolling speeds, but one technique I've found that increases their effectiveness is to pull the rod tip forward and then drop it back. This causes a slight speed-up in lure speed and wiggle. It then returns to its normal action as the rod tip is dropped back down.

One thing I've discovered when big pike are hooked by deep-water trolling is that the lure suddenly stops—I mean, right now! There usually isn't a slashing strike followed by a heavy pulling; it feels as if you've hooked bottom, and more than once I've been fooled into thinking the lure was fouled on a log or other form of underwater debris. I can't remember the number of times I've backed up until I was directly over the lure and started pulling upward in hopes of freeing my lure. All of a sudden the fish would realize he's hooked and shoot off for friendlier waters.

The thing I like about this method of fishing is that very few "hammerhandles" are taken. It's usually big fish or nothing, and I like the former rather than the latter.

One time I was making a canoe float trip down a Michigan river and decided at the last moment to take along a rod and reel. It was mid-May and pike season had just opened, and I hoped to latch on to a big northern. A buddy of mine told me that the winter before he'd taken several large fish from the area I'd be floating.

After obtaining directions on where his fish had been taken I shoved off and began a leisurely float. I'd toss small spinners in likely areas, but it was an hour before I drifted into the winter fish-holding area.

A small drain, little more than a farmer's ditch, entered the river at that point. The current was moving slower than summertime molasses, so I dropped my anchor, a red fireplace brick, over the side on a 6-foot line and stopped to make several casts. A large hole formed where the current from the drain entered and it looked fishy.

I tossed a No. 3 Mepps bucktail into the hole, allowed it to sink near bottom, and began moving it back just fast enough to make the spinner blade turn over. I felt something peck at my lure, although it didn't strike hard, so I assumed it was the spinner hitting something on bottom.

Three more casts covered the pool when a northern struck like a caged tiger. That fish ripped the pool apart on the strike and swam almost on shore as I set the hooks. It was an unnecessary gesture, because the fish had buried the barbs on the strike.

We slam-banged back and forth through the 20-yard pool for several minutes. The fish didn't jump or offer any aerial acrobatics common to colder-water pike, but the wrestling match was equal to the best topwater fight I've ever had.

I was using 6-pound mono and it took some doing to subdue that rambunctious pike. It ran upstream, rode the current back down into the pool, and then darted downstream on a short run.

As he tired I began pumping him toward the canoe. I hadn't thought of hooking really big fish, so my net was back in the car. When the pike rolled on his side next to the boat, I waited my chance and pounced on him like a cat playing tag with a mouse. I

A fisherman puts an eye hold on a pike that will not be released. This method of landing the fish is only used if it is going to be kept for mounting or food.

locked my fingers across the back of the head and over both gill covers and hoisted him unceremoniously into the canoe.

I managed to extract my spinner without being chewed on and admired the fish for a few seconds and then lowered him back to the stream.

"He" turned out to be a husky female, a ripe late-spawning fish heavy with roe. I held her by the tail underwater until she swam off under her own power. I estimated her weight at nearly 15 pounds, an exciting spring fish.

This anecdote points out an important point. Northern pike normally spawn in a tiny tributary, but they generally do so much earlier in the year. As they move up to spawn, pike will gather in deep holes near running water. This fish was probably hoping for a rain which would raise the water level in the drain so she could head upstream farther. Meanwhile she lay in the deep hole and launched an attack on anything that swam by. Fishing as early in the season as possible is one of the best ways I know to take exceptionally large pike. The females are distended and pot-gutted from a heavy weight of roe, while some truly jumbo males accompany the females.

In many states the northern pike spawning run is over by the time the season opens. But where legal, early-spring fishing is an odds-on favorite for catching trophy fish.

ICEFISHING

Icefishing in snowbound areas means either spearing or fishing with tip-ups baited with minnows. Spearing is judged by many to be an unsportsmanlike method of taking fish, but the odds are more in favor of the fish, not the fisherman.

Pike spearing is done from a dark fish shanty. The majority of the spearing coops are about 5 or 6 feet square with a 36-inch hole cut through the shanty floor and the ice. Snow is packed around the edges of the shanty to prevent light from leaking in around the bottom.

Once your eyes have become accustomed to the darkness, the bottom of the lake will begin to take shape. Most spearers try to position their coops in 10 to 15 feet of water. The important thing is to position the shanty along a dropoff or edge of a weedbed, areas often frequented by winter-hungry northerns.

Spearers suspend a large 10- or 12-inch sucker about 6 or 8 feet below the shanty hole. The actions of this large baitfish are often an indication of nearby pike. The sucker may swim lazily in circles if danger isn't present. But allow a northern pike to swim into view of the sucker and it changes its behavior immediately. It will dart crazily off to one side, swim right up into the spearing hole, or try to take refuge under the heavy mantle of ice.

Pike may swim into view and play with the sucker like a kitten with a yarn ball. When a pike makes up his mind to attack, he'll do so with the speed of heat lightning. A spearer stands his best chance to sink the tines in the fish before it makes its move.

The four- or five-tine spear is lowered directly over the fish and dropped. It is not thrown but simply dropped straight down onto the pike. I've speared several times and found that judging where to drop the spear (due to light refraction) is difficult, and many more pike escape than are speared. It's a novel way of fishing and does produce a whopper occasionally.

Tip-up fishing is my favorite winter means of taking pike. Many fishermen select a 6-inch sucker or shiner minnow and hook it through the skin under the dorsal fin and allow it to swim freely. Over the years I've taken many fish in this manner, but several years ago I chanced on a method as productive and much less costly.

During the spring smelt run I'll hand-pick six dozen smelt in the

6-inch class. These are kept frozen until needed, usually about January in my area.

Smelt are an oily, smelly fish and attract all types of gamefish, including pike. I'll attach a No. 14 treble hook to the smelt, usually just under the dorsal fin, and lower it directly to the bottom. For some reason I haven't been able to discover, pike will seldom grab a dead shiner or sucker but will inhale a dead smelt off bottom. Perhaps it has something to do with the odor.

The tip-up is set in proper fashion and the angler sits back to await a strike. It doesn't take too long in most cases. I usually stagger my tip-ups near the mouth of a spawning river that pike run in springtime.

When the flag goes up the fisherman races to his tip-up and stares in fascination as the spool of line slowly unwinds. The pike is moving off with the smelt before swallowing it, and one must wait until the fish stops. It will turn the smelt head first and down goes dinner. As the second run begins, allow the tip-up line to come tight in your hands and set the hook.

If it's a big pike you can count on a lengthy under-the-ice struggle before the fish is ready for landing. I carry a three-prong gaff which is lowered into my ice hole as the fish tires. When the pike is led over the gaff, a quick upward pull will sink one of the prongs into the fish and he is pulled from the hole.

If live suckers or shiners are used for bait the icefisherman often has false strikes or "wind bites." This can be eliminated by placing the back side of the tip-up opposite the flag mechanism facing into the wind. It serves as a shield and you'll have fewer false alarms.

Some minnows are sluggish or inactive during winter months. Lower them into an ice hole and they do nothing. Pike like either dead smelt on bottom or lively minnows off bottom. A trick my brother showed me involves cutting off one lobe of a minnow's tail. This upsets the minnow's balance and it has to struggle more to remain upright in the water. The jerking and thrashing of the minnow trying to keep itself upright will give off underwater troubled-fish sounds that pike home in on.

Northern pike are indeed one of this continent's greatest gamefish. They now generate more angler interest than ever before. And that is good, because this is a prized trophy fish that anyone should be proud of catching.

10

MUSKELLUNGE

Muskies are maniacs. Pure and simple, they are crazy, nuts, impossible to live with, and like a good woman, impossible to live without. They are unpredictable, belligerent, given to moods of inactivity, and also capable of causing a muskie fever in sportsmen that approaches epidemic proportions.

The muskellunge is the largest member of the pike family, and there are three distinct subspecies. They often attain weights of 30 or more pounds, although the average size taken would be closer to 10 or 15 pounds. The world-record muskellunge was taken from the St. Lawrence River and weighed 69 pounds 15 ounces.

Muskies travel by a raft of aliases, but the three subspecies are the Great Lakes or spotted muskie; the Ohio or Chautauqua (northern) muskie; and the tiger muskellunge, a cross between the northern pike and northern muskellunge.

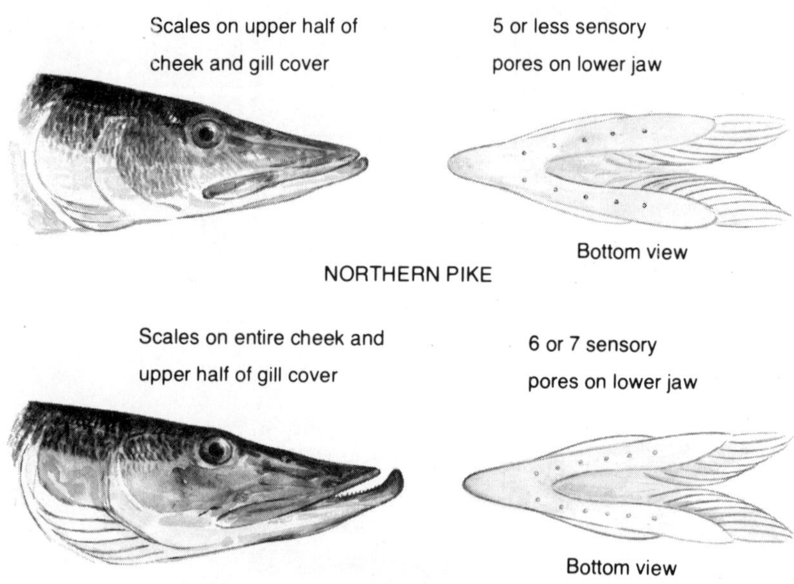

How to identify the species of the pike family.

Many fishermen confuse the muskellunge with northern pike, but there are many differences between the two. The fish are similar in shape, but the body colorations are vastly different. A northern has what looks like a light-on-dark coloration (yellowish spots on a greenish body), while the muskie usually has a dark-on-light coloration. A case in point is the Great Lakes muskie; it is light-colored along the sides but decked out with large dark spots. The tiger muskie has dark vertical stripes (like a tiger) on a light background. The Ohio or northern muskie is more of a solid, light-grayish color. These are the basic colorations, although muskies will often have bars along the sides.

The muskellunge can be distinguished from other pikes by a lack of scales on the lower half of the gill cover and cheek. It also has six to nine sensory pores on the lower jaw, along the bottom. The head is also scaled and shaped much like a duck's bill. The fins are frequently reddish, and the anal fins are set far back on the body. The caudal fin is pointed, while a pike has round tail fins.

The original range of the muskie was confined to the Great Lakes area, through the Ohio River drainage, the Tennessee River system, the St. Lawrence River between New York and Ontario, Michigan, Wisconsin, Minnesota, Kentucky, Tennessee, West Virginia, Pennsylvania, New York, Ohio, and Ontario. Research and plantings which began in the 1950s have since spread this tremendous gamefish to other states, such as North Carolina, Iowa, Missouri, Indiana, Illinois, Delaware, and Alabama. Fishing in the Southern states, with the exception of Tennessee and Kentucky, is a losing proposition at this time. The fish are widely scattered and not large.

The best muskie fishing still remains throughout its original range, although Tennessee is producing some excellent fishing in reservoirs, where lake muskie were planted to provide a trophy fishery.

The muskellunge—any one of the three subspecies— is likely to be the largest gamefish freshwater anglers ever encounter. A muskie experience is like an encounter with a raging brown bear along an Alaskan salmon-spawning stream—it will provide memories that time will never erase.

Muskie fishing could be classified as hunting. These fish are never overly plentiful in any location, and it reminds me of trying to hunt a wary trophy whitetail—one of the most difficult animals to obtain on the face of the earth. Muskellunge are much the same; they are around but as difficult to catch as a big buck is to shoot. They have made fools out of more fishermen than any other species I know, but anglers go back for more, like a punchy fighter getting back up off the floor after taking a mandatory eight-count. Muskie addicts seem to thrive on the masochistic punishment they dish out to themselves. Fishing for this species does that to anglers. Presidents, governors of muskie-producing states, and ordinary fishermen all fall under the spell of this trophy gamefish.

Muskie fishing isn't for the angler who expects to fill a boat with fish. Some anglers have fished for muskies for many years and never caught a legal-size fish. On the other hand, muskie experts often catch and release big fish simply because they know how, where, and when to fish. This is important, because some months, some areas, and some times of day are generally better than others.

I remember one time when I traveled to Brevort Lake in Michigan's beautiful Upper Peninsula. I was working on a magazine story at the time and was on a different lake when one of my contacts tracked me down and said the Great Lakes muskies in Brevort were going wild. "Everyone is catching big fish," he said.

It was just after the May 15 muskie opener, and we'd had a very cold and prolonged spring. The water was still chilly and the big fish hadn't spawned. I met up with a foursome from the Detroit area and they showed me two muskies that made my eyes bug out. Both fish were well over 30 pounds, each a plump female full of eggs. It's been proved that the biggest muskies are usually females; males seldom weigh over 20 pounds.

Louis Paolina, on the rod, and Bill Borland team up to land a 35-pound Great Lakes muskie. The fish struck a Rapala and fought for thirty minutes.

These Brevort Lake fish had been taken by trolling a magnum Rapala over 6-foot-deep mudbars. The females were going into the warmer water to spawn. These enterprising fishermen had determined that the fish should be there, if anywhere.

Their fishing technique was amazingly simple. They trolled a floating Rapala about 40 feet behind the boat at a slow speed and gave the rod tip a jerk once in a while. The extra action was enough to drive those big females wild. They would hit, somersault into the air, and smash back down. Heavy with roe, they wouldn't fight very hard, but each battle lasted 20 minutes before the fish would come to the net. The Rapalas were twisted and broken, with the hooks nearly straightened out, but they took fish.

The action continued for three days. The largest fish taken scaled nearly 40 pounds, and other bigger fish were lost. The rest of the lake then warmed to a point and spawning took place in other areas. The same group of anglers returned the following year, to the same location at the same time, and found fishing terrible. We'd had a warmer, earlier spring and the fish had spawned and left before the season opened. So goes muskie fishing.

The muskie is a gamefish that follows lures repeatedly and seldom strikes. One year I fished with Don Podraza of Green Bay, Wis. Don had established a reputation as a muskie wizard. He could produce muskie strikes and follows when other fishermen were wondering where the fish had gone.

Fishing Tomahawk Lake in northern Wisconsin, we would have fifteen or twenty follows for every strike, and this frustrating behavior went on day after day. The muskies followed the lures like bird dogs on a pheasant track. Some fish would pursue the lure to the boat, while others lost interest after a few feet.

THE FIGURE 8

Don showed me the "figure 8," a boatside maneuver that keeps the lure working continuously. It never paid off with a fish, but we had several smashing strikes before losing the fish on a jump. He told me, "Muskies lose interest in a lure whenever it stops moving. This is one reason why veteran muskie fishermen do the figure 8 every time the lure comes to the boat. As long as it is moving there is a chance a fish will strike. If the lure stops and is lifted from the water the fish will slowly sink from sight and you've lost a chance at him."

One time Podraza and I had a 35-pound muskie follow my lure up to the boat, and I began the figure 8. The fish would follow it back and forth but wouldn't strike, although I kept it up for a minute or more. As I continued working my lure I told Don, "Drop your lure next to mine and start working it around your end of the boat. It won't strike my lure but might take a crack at yours."

He dropped his Eddie Bait next to my Suick and began working it back and forth across the surface. The muskie left my lure and began following his. By the time the fish lost interest we had worked it around both sides and ends of the boat. It never struck nor showed other than a passing interest in the lures.

The figure-8 maneuver keeps the lure working continuously. Muskies lose interest in a lure unless it is moving.

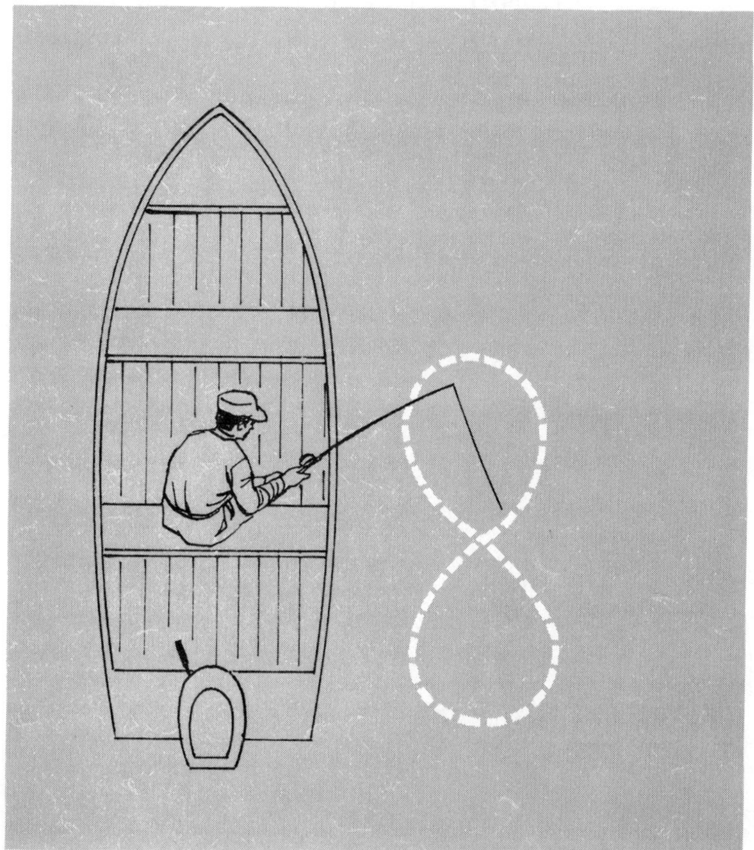

THE CRISS-CROSS

A muskie fisherman I encountered on another Wisconsin trip told me about a technique he's used when fishing with another angler. He called it the "criss-cross" method and it is based on much the same thing that Don and I had tried. Both fishermen cast from the same side of the boat and begin working their jerk baits across the surface. One angler will cast across the other's line. If a muskie begins following one lure and suddenly sees the other plug or spoon coming in from another angle, he may strike if he feels another fish is going to take the lure away from him.

This technique calls for teamwork and casting accuracy between two fishermen accustomed to fishing together. It requires patience and skill to place the lures so they cross near each other at the same time. Hasty casting or inaccuracy will result in tangled lines and no fish.

I've found the best success with the criss-cross method comes when one angler uses a jerk bait like a Suick, Swim Whiz, Eddie Bait, Bobbie Bait, or Rapala while the other fisherman fishes with a large spoon like a Swim Zag or large Dardevle. One should be a surface lure while the other should travel underwater.

The criss-cross maneuver is used to provoke a muskie into striking. The fish follows one lure, apparently sees the other lure as a predator fish about to deprive him of a meal, and strikes the first lure.

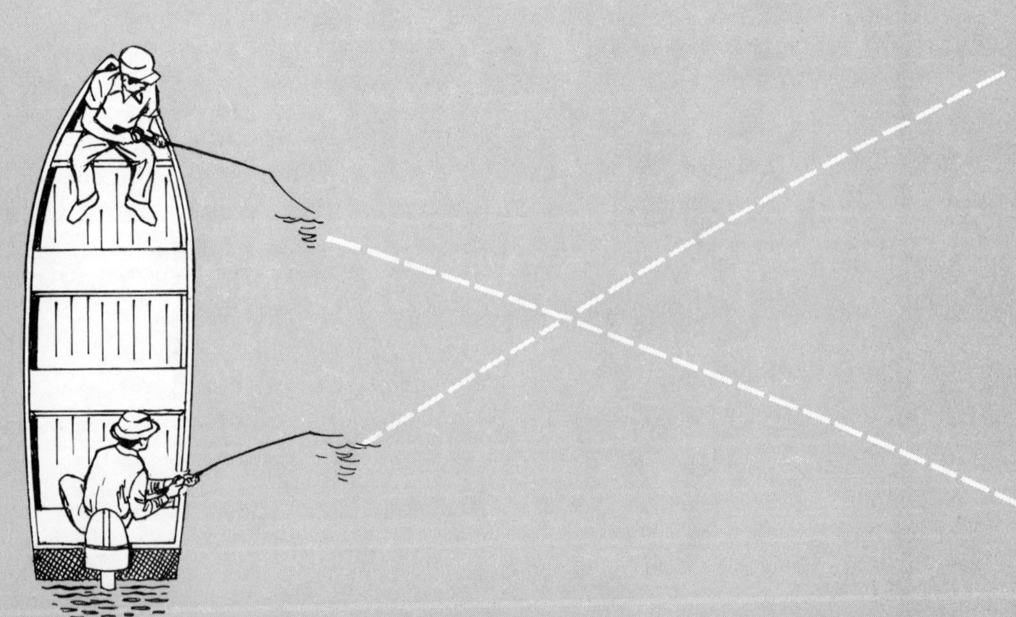

JERK BAITS

Studies have proved that muskie anglers may produce more fish on spinner or crank baits, but large topwater jerk baits garner bigger fish. Fishing a jerk bait reminds me of the old saying about fishermen—"A jerk on one end waiting for a jerk on the other end." After spending three or four days of continuous casting and enduring the physical punishment that your arms and back suffer while fishing these lures, that old chestnut rings more true than we care to believe.

The jerk bait is often 6 or 8 inches long and armed with two or three needle-sharp treble hooks. One time I buried a hook in the palm of my hand while fishing with Don Podraza. I'd had a strike near the boat and set the hook with as much force as I could muster. I missed hooking the fish, but the Suick came flying toward the boat and would have struck Don in the face if I hadn't stopped it with my hand. I worked the hook free and we went back to fishing. This may be a classic case of the masochism I spoke of earlier.

A jerk bait has to be worked with the rod tip, using your arm, wrist, and back muscles. It has no action except that given it by the fisherman. You hold the rod tip low to the water, give it a jerk which will cause the lure to bob and weave like a drunken sailor, and then immediately reel up the slack line. It is brought back to the boat in a series of jerks and retrieves.

Don would fish with a two-jerk movement of his rod tip. He'd give it an initial jerk closely followed by another jerk, and the lure would wobble from right to left, and back again, all the way to the boat. Some fishermen allow the lure to drift almost to the surface and then jerk it under again. This has never produced for me, although it does for some fishermen.

I've seen some fishermen bend the tail fin of a jerk bait up or down in hopes of obtaining the proper action. I usually fish them the way they come from the box, but a battle with a big muskie can bend the fin out of position. It must then be tinkered with to regain the proper action.

It should be pointed out that jerk baits pinpoint more following fish, because the lure can be easily seen and the angler usually has his eyes on it all the time. A long, dark shadow trailing along behind is bound to be a muskie. If the lure stops the fish will sink

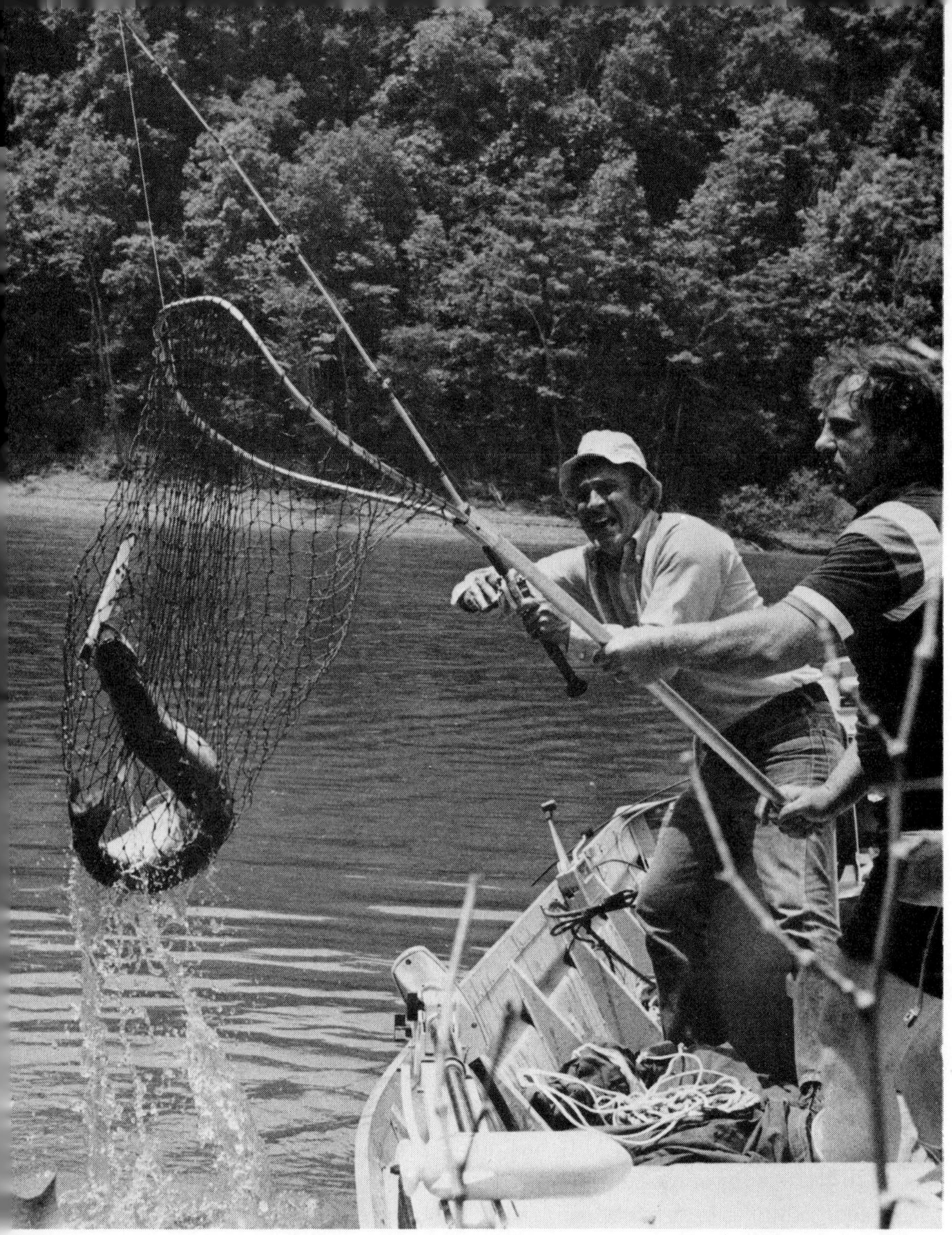

Jim Little nets a huge muskie for Lea Lawrence. The fish struck a Suick, a jerk bait, and jumped several times before it was landed.

from sight and you've lost your best opportunity to hook him. Keep the lure working and never allow it to stop. Sometimes a brief speed-up or slowdown will cause the fish to strike, but it is doubtful.

If the fish follows to the boat and turns away, muskie experts advise either changing lures and colors or leaving and returning an hour or two later. I've switched lures and colors often on following muskies, but it seldom produces. Very little produces with muskies!

I'd much rather pinpoint a muskie hotspot by triangulating the location with three shoreline markings, and then move away for a little while. I've raised the same fish three times each day for two days before it struck and was landed. It was a 22-pound northern muskie from a Wisconsin-Michigan border lake called Lac Vieux Desert. A wait of two hours is plenty of time to rest a following muskie.

It's become an accepted fact among many muskie fishermen that the striking fish are generally those you never see. They arrow up off bottom and smash the lure without betraying their presence until the explosive strike jars your senses. Fishing jerk baits becomes monotonous; the fisherman lapses into occasional daydreams while putting his lure through its paces. They are mentally alert to following fish, but the sudden dynamite strike of a fish from below usually shakes up the most ardent angler.

One time my wife and I were casting jerk and spinner baits in the Iron Creek section of Tennessee's Dale Hollow Reservoir near Byrdstown. We were camping at Star Point Resort and had learned that this area had produced a wealth of big Ohio-strain muskies for other fishermen.

We'd pounded out cast after cast, but the water was murky from the wake of passing houseboats. A muskie could be 6 inches below our lures and we'd never see it.

Kay was using a black Mepps Muskie Killer and I was using a black Suick. My lure plopped down next to some overhanging brush and I began working it back—jerk, reel up the slack, double-jerk, reel, jerk—and then the water erupted like Old Faithful going off. The muskie struck during the middle of a jerk and it felt as though my shoulder would separate; that fish must have struck going away from me as I jerked the lure toward the boat.

I held on as the fish lathered the water to a froth before sailing out in a head-to-tail jump that would have done credit to a 12-inch rainbow taken on a dry fly. It was a classic jump, the sort pictured on the covers of outdoor magazines and calendars. It crashed back into the water like a load of bricks dropped off a bridge.

The muskie spurted off on a short run and became airborne again. He nosed back into the water, and we settled down to an old-fashioned brawl. Twenty minutes of muscle-straining anguish later the fish rolled on his side near the boat and Kay slid the net under him. I helped her lift 30 pounds of trophy muskie into the boat. It took long minutes to work the hooks loose; all three were buried in the bony mouth.

Two hours later Kay tangled with a fighting-mad muskie of 24 pounds and he danced around the lake, more in the air than in the water. She later commented that muskies are mean, and that has to be the understatement of the year.

TROLLING

We learned that trolling is by far the best method of taking Tennessee muskies, but we did take a few fish by applying the northern methods of fishing jerk baits and spinner baits.

Trolling, down Tennessee way, is usually done with a greenish-colored Bomber. The angler trolls along old creekbeds, near drop-offs, and around points, and his lure should be bumping bottom in about 15 feet of water. A slow troll is needed to bring out the best action.

Many sportsmen have learned that a zigzag trolling course is best when pulling one or two lures. By steering in and out along a predetermined course, the fisherman can cover a great deal more productive water than by working a straight course.

Trolling for muskie is frowned upon by casting fishermen because they consider it to be a deadly method. The mere fact of trolling isn't what makes this method deadly, it is the knowledge of the fish and where they are located.

Homer LeBlanc of St. Clair Shores, Mich., is a muskie fisherman and guide who completely understands these fish. He's also a dedicated troller and has invented lures that work extremely well on muskies. His catch of these fish is awesome from Lake St. Clair, which is considered one of the best muskie waters on the North American continent.

LeBlanc feels that muskies are often attracted to the boat and the propeller churning the water. He feels so strongly about this that he'll often troll lures in his prop wash to catch fish. He'll troll a lure off each corner of the stern, about 4 feet back and about 2 feet deep, which places the lures in the bubbly prop wash.

He feels that one of the best times to fish muskies is about an

Kay Richey battles a big muskie with the help of the author on Dale Hollow Reservoir. The fish struck a trolled Swim Whiz lure.

hour before a storm hits, when the barometer is falling rapidly and strong winds and rain are in the offing.

Homer believes in fishing as many rods as the law allows, which in Michigan is two lines per person. If he has four clients on board, he can fish eight lines, with each rod in a separate rodholder. A trolling speed of 4 or 5 mph is sufficient to set the hooks when a muskie strikes.

His trolling setup is shown in the accompanying illustration, but it bears additional clarification. To ease the details of remembering which rod is which, they are hereby numbered 1 through 8.

Number 1 rod: A 10- or 12-foot rod is used on the starboard side and located amidships or as far forward as possible. A 2- or 3-ounce keel sinker is used and approximately 70 feet of line is released. A bucktail spinner is normally used on sunny days. The lengths may be varied from 15 to 30 feet on the number 1 rod if extra weight or a deep-diving lure is used.

Number 2 rod: A 4½- or 5-foot rod is set up amidships on the starboard side, but the rod tip is angled downward and toward the stern. The lure, such as a Swim Whiz, is hooked with a swivel

The LeBlanc trolling system for eight rods.

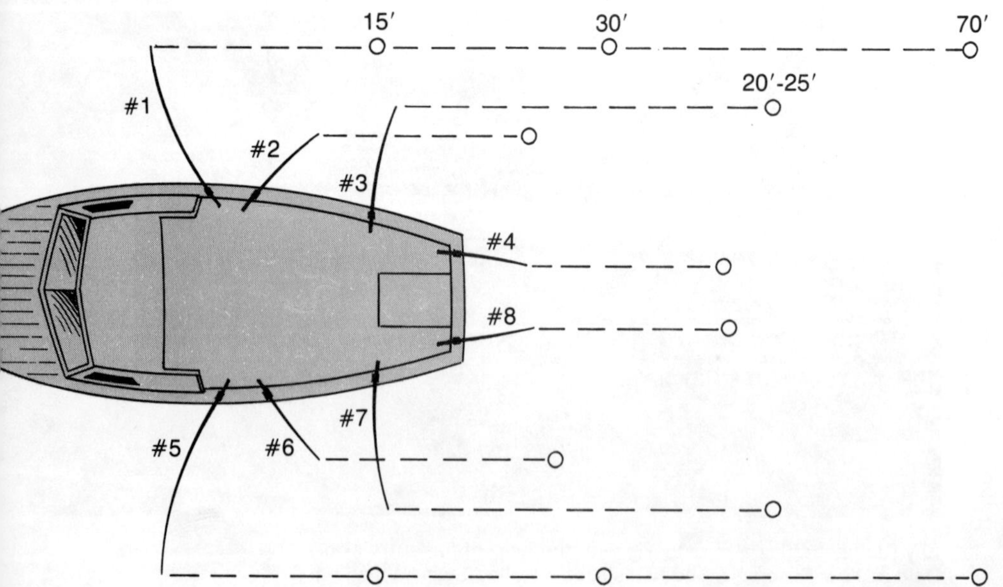

through the deepest-running eye and is trolled 4 feet astern the starboard quarter. Enough weight should be used to hold it down about 2 feet and keep it in the prop wash.

Number 3 rod: A 5- or 5½-footer is positioned near the stern and angled straight out from the gunwale. This lure is pulled down by a 4- or 5-ounce trolling keel sinker and runs about 2 feet below the surface and 20 or 25 feet behind the stern. It will also be in the prop wash.

Number 4 rod: A 5-foot rod is held in a rodholder on the stern and pointed inward slightly toward the motor. Release about 15 feet of line and use a 6- or 8-ounce lead sinker and a deep-running lure. This combination will take the lure down about 5 feet and just below the bubbling water of the prop.

Number 5 rod: This is mounted the same way as number 1 on the port side. These rods can be fished high, at medium depths, or deep. This choice depends on weather conditions, period of day, and other factors. If the fish are hitting deep, rods 1 and 5 should both be fished deeper.

Number 6 rod: This is set up in the same manner as number 2, and the lures should be fished near the boat and 2 or 3 feet down.

Number 7 rod: This is fished the same as number 3.

Number 8 rod: This should be fished the same as number 4. LeBlanc often will set the lures on this rod slightly deeper or farther back.

It should be noted that every rod, with the exception of numbers 1 and 5, are in or very close to the prop wash. LeBlanc has actually had muskies strike the prop of his outboard, so the logic of this trolling method is easily seen.

He advocates taking the boat occasionally in and out of gear. The out-of-gear period allows the lures to settle slightly before the craft starts forward again. Muskies often pick this opportunity to slam one of the lures.

A keen student will note that most of these lures run just under the surface to about 5 feet deep. This is based on LeBlanc's observation that traveling fish are usually found at that 5-foot level.

Another technique Homer has used is to hook two lures in tandem. He'll use a bucktail spinner about 20 inches ahead of another lure on the assumption that a muskie will see both lures at once and will strike one or the other. I've never used this technique, but almost anything is logical with muskellunge.

Some trolling is done at these depths with lures such as a Cisco

Kid, Creek Chub Pike Minnow, or deep-diving Rapalas. But 4 to 6 ounces of lead must be attached at least 12 to 18 inches ahead of the lure, and a slow trolling speed must be used.

A highly productive method called "speed trolling" has been proved in many muskie waters. The name aptly describes the technique. The fast troll doesn't give the fish time to follow and examine the lure; it must either strike or forever lose a chance at a possible meal. The proper speed is 6 to 8 mph.

I've tried speed trolling several times, and it seems particularly effective during fall months when the fish are stocking up lard for the coming winter. September, October, and warm days in November are best because the muskie seems to feed most actively at that time.

Many lures work well with this method, but I'll usually use a single- or double-bladed spinner bait on one rod and a diving crank bait on the other side. The edges of weedbeds produce the most fish because the muskie looks for food in these areas.

Try to keep one lure (usually the spinner bait) almost in contact with the weeds at all times. If the outside edges of the weeds are down 8 to 10 feet you can troll right over the tops without fouling.

The important point in this method is to troll just as fast as possible and still keep the lures in the water. Some crank baits will not work, but many produce outstanding results when fished in this manner. One of my favorites is the Swim Whiz, which is hooked in the back eye. It can be trolled extremely fast and gives off a tight wiggle that attracts big fish.

This technique will often move fish that would otherwise never strike. It is a tactic that should be carried in every muskie fisherman's bag of tricks, especially during the fall months.

JIGGING

One deepwater fishing method which has escaped many anglers is the use of a jig and large minnow. This is jig fishing of the common variety, but much heavier jigs, 1-to-1½-ounce lures, are used. A 3-to-5-inch chub or sucker is hooked under the chin and out the top of its head and fished right down on bottom.

Some muskie fishermen prefer wind-drifting and jigging deep water beneath the boat with this combination. Some days the trophies will strike a normal 6-inch up-and-down jigging motion, while on others they seem to prefer the lure to hippety-hop along bottom, fished in much the same manner as for walleyes.

This method of jig fishing with suckers and chubs works during spring months immediately after the spawning period. Spring fish are often frequenting a gravel or sand bar or along the sides of a long flat, and the jig-minnow rig must be fished on bottom.

Jig fishing with minnows is also very productive late in the fall when the lake has made its turnover. Muskies can be as deep as 35 feet, and the only baits they seem to hit at these depths are those fished as slowly as possible. A wire leader at least 12 inches long should be used with this rig, because muskellunge will often inhale both jig and minnow and are usually hooked quite deeply. They can sever the line when deeply hooked if a leader isn't used.

DOWNRIGGER FISHING

There are times when muskies will suspend off bottom, and another enterprising Michigan muskie guide began experimenting with downriggers. These depth-control rigs were first used for Great Lakes salmon and lake trout, but innovative fishermen have found that muskie fishing is another excellent use for this outfit.

Lures are placed about 6 feet behind the cannonball, and the fishing line is attached to the release system. The lures are lowered to the proper depth (according to the water temperature and position of the fish) and locked into place. Once the muskie strikes the fight will be on a weight-free line.

With downriggers the skipper can work his baits over submerged humps, along the edges of deepwater weedbeds, or at any conceivable depth muskies may be found. It takes only seconds to raise or lower an individual lure, and this can be a definite asset if the fish are moving up or going down in the water. All downrigger lines should be staggered as to depth to allow maximum coverage of the water.

Downrigger fishing works because in many muskie waters the fish are often found at depths of 20 or more feet during summer months. Anglers have learned that taking a muskie from 20 to 40 feet of water is not uncommon and it often produces the largest fish of the year. Fishing at depths such as that can be easily done with downriggers, whereas with conventional tackle, a large amount of lead is needed to take the lure deep enough to be effective.

CRANK BAITS

Crank baits can be a dynamite lure during summer months. These lures, such as the bucktail or tandem spinners and various diving lures, will take fish at other times of the year, but summer seems best. They are usually most productive as a high-speed lure. Fishing crank baits takes skill and some knowledge of the fish and where they are found at certain times of the year.

One of the hottest areas for fishing a spinner bait such as a Mister Twister Tandem Spin would be right in or alongside a good weed growth such as cabbage weed. This weed grows from a firm bottom and is also called muskie weed, red top, and other names. It can grow as deep as 20 feet in clear waters.

Fishing this type of water is best accomplished by two fishermen. One will fish the topwater areas of the weedbed while the other will fish on bottom along the deepwater edges. The deep fisherman can use a Pow-rr Head jig and a 5-inch Reaper worm. Drifting and casting is the preferred method rather than anchoring.

The surface fisherman should plan to "rip" his spinner bait over and through the weeds. It's best to remain in contact with the weeds at all times, although the lure shouldn't settle deep enough to hang up. I've found it best to work the spinner bait so it just tickles the tops or edges of the cabbage. A muskie will slam right up through these weeds and take the spinner. I once caught a 24-pound muskie from Wisconsin's Tomahawk Lake in this manner.

The lure was whipping through the weeds as fast as I could retrieve when huge jaws separated and inhaled the lure. I slammed the rod back hard, four times, to set the hooks. The fish responded by submerging and slashing out through the edge of the cabbage and heading for bottom. We played tug-of-war for fifteen minutes before the fish rose to the surface. My partner dropped his rod into the bottom of the boat to reach for the net, and this spooked the muskie off on another run.

This charge was much shorter and lacked the power of the first run, and the fish slowly angled back toward the surface. It tried a last-minute flurry next to the boat and was netted. We admired it briefly, hooked it on small scales for weighing, and then lowered it back into the water. The muskie darted away and was last seen streaking back into the weedbed.

Although ripping spinner baits through and over weeds can be a productive method, I've taken more summer fish by concentrating on the deepwater edges of these cabbage beds. The fish are often located near bottom and along the edges of the weeds. Here they find comfort, security, and an excellent location from which to attack passing baitfish.

The jig-worm combination should be cast out and retrieved right along bottom and as close to the weeds as possible. An up-and-down or horizontal jigging movement adds to the effectiveness of the lure. The horizontal sweep of the rod tip is sometimes more productive with muskies than the conventional up-and-down method. By jigging horizontally, the lure tends to swim more than hop, and this is particularly effective for big muskies.

Wherever the muskie is found, and regardless of which subspecies is hooked, this fish will shatter your concentration, destroy your ego, and make a shambles of your equipment. At the same time he will also give you enough heart-pounding excitement during one battle to completely hook you on the sport.

11
PICKEREL

The pickerel is the smallest member of the pike family. Although small, it is the eastern and southeastern counterpart of the northern pike, a highly sought-after gamefish found primarily in the northern tier of states.

This diminutive gamefish doesn't grow to earth-shattering sizes like pike or muskellunge, but wherever it is found, the pickerel gives a good account of itself. Georgia now considers this species one of its prized gamefish, and it is considered a highly desirable species.

The pickerel family is composed of three subspecies, although some people disagree. The chain pickerel is probably best known, although both the redfin and grass pickerel have their followers. Although these fish closely resemble one another and all look like small northern pike, they possess minute body-structure and coloration differences.

The chain pickerel has a long concave snout with a fully scaled cheek and gill cover. It has fewer than five sensory pores on the underside of the bottom jaw, and its flanks are a greenish color with many interconnected links, hence its name. It also possesses a black bar in front of and below the eye. The tail is a greenish-gray and is moderately forked.

The chain pickerel is commonly found in the Southern and Eastern states and is most abundant in New Jersey, New York, Rhode Island, Connecticut, Maine, and Massachusetts. However, some of the largest chain pickerel are found in Florida and Georgia waters.

The redfin pickerel has a short convex snout with both cheeks and gill covers fully scaled. It has less than five sensory pores on the underside of the lower jaw. This gamefish, although rarely more than 10 inches in length, is a scrapper on light tackle and tiny lures. The sides are a very light olive color with dark vertical bars. It has dark black bars in front of and below the eyes.

The redfin is found in the Atlantic drainage from Maryland south to Georgia and Florida. It has been found in limited numbers west as far as Alabama.

The grass pickerel has a long concave snout with fully scaled cheeks and gill covers. Like all pickerel, it has fewer than five sensory pores on the bottom jaw. The sides are marked with fifteen to twenty-three thin olive or black wavy bars and a pronounced black bar below the eye.

Grass pickerel are considered to be the westernmost pickerel found in the United States. The subspecies extends from the St. Lawrence River southwest through Lake Ontario and Lake Erie into Pennsylvania, Kentucky, and Tennessee. It is also found in Ohio, Indiana, Michigan, Illinois, Wisconsin, Iowa, Nebraska, Missouri, Arkansas, Louisiana, Alabama, Texas, and Oklahoma. It has been reported that grass pickerel are now found in limited numbers in Washington and Colorado.

Angling techniques for pickerel are much the same wherever this species is found. It's sad, but too few anglers have learned just how sporting this smallest group of the pike family can be. They are often ignored by adults and relegated to providing sport for young beginning fishermen. It's true the fish doesn't grow to jumbo sizes such as those attained by northern pike or muskies, but size is relative in trophy fishing. What represents a trophy to one fisherman is considered a small fish by another angler.

Pickerel habitat is similar to that of panfish: small ponds or lakes containing large amounts of weed growth; small brackish-water ponds near tidewater along the Eastern Seaboard; or wherever suitable cover exists where they can lunch on smaller gamefish after an attack from a nearby hiding spot. Brush-choked streams are popular locations for pickerel in many areas. These gamefish will lurk under or around some type of overhead protection.

Angling techniques are similar to those used for northern pike, except everything is scaled down in keeping with the size of the quarry. Ultralight spinning rods, reels, and lines are recommended to allow the fisherman to enjoy the ultimate excitement from his encounters with these fish.

FLY FISHING

One time I was fishing in Florida for largemouth bass but small pickerel kept taking my spoon. My guide, a crusty cracker gentleman, told me, "Why not switch to a light fly outfit and learn to appreciate the true fighting qualities of pickerel?"

With that he snatched my baitcasting outfit away and reached under the seat and hauled out an outdated fly rod and reel. It looked as if it had wintered too many years under that boat seat, but it cast like a dream. "It's not much," he drawled, "but it's all you need to catch pickerel."

He knotted on a bright-orange-and-red bucktail tied on a No. 4 hook. With a nod toward a nearby weedy area he pinpointed a likely spot for pickerel. "The fly used isn't as important as the technique. Make that fly dance and appear lifelike and you'll have all the action you can handle," he told me.

My first cast, a 30-footer, snaked out and the fly dropped near the edge of the weedbed. I twitched the fly line, shivered the rod tip, and made the fly dart and wiggle like something struggling to stay alive. It was halfway back to the boat when a furious jolt rippled through the rod and down my arm. A hefty pickerel had hammered the fly and was doing his best to dart back to safety.

I hauled back on the rod to turn the fish and the tippet popped. The old-timer was furious. "Dammit, you don't have to set the hook like you're sticking a 10-pound bass. Ease back and gently jab the fly home and then hang on. With care you can land 5-pound fish on that outfit."

He tied another fly on and sculled the boat 100 yards down the lake to another weedbed. "Try it again and be careful this time." I repeated my earlier technique of shivering the fly. I twitched it along as though it was alive and dynamite struck again in the form of a chain-sided pickerel, a 4-pounder.

Remembering the advice, I gently stuck the fish and the pickerel danced across the surface, sulked, broke water again, and put on a lively demonstration. The fight was short, as most pickerel battles are, but it was a dramatic demonstration of the fighting capabilities of this great gamefish.

We landed that pickerel and I admired the sleek sides and wide gaping mouth suitable for catching smaller gamefish. It was released and the rest of the day was spent chasing pickerel in other parts of the lake. I had more fun taking those fish on a fly rod than if I'd landed a big bass. Bass can be taken almost anytime, but I seldom have the opportunity to catch chunky pickerel.

In the Northwest, many anglers catch pickerel with popping bugs, small deerhair bugs, or small frog-colored surface poppers intended for bass. Again, the important thing isn't the type or color of lure but the technique. The popper or surface bug must look and act alive to tempt old chainsides.

SKITTERING

Skittering is an age-old method of taking pickerel. The requirements for this sport are simple: a 12-foot cane pole, a 12-foot length of line testing about 10 pounds, and the lure of your choice.

Fishermen that practice this sport scull along quietly and dabble or "skitter" their lure in likely areas. One of the best lures is a porkrind frog or large white or red V-shaped piece of porkrind. Some anglers have taken pickerel skittering with a single hook and a piece of red cloth.

The lure is lowered to the surface and quickly dragged back and forth in small circles near weedbeds, brush, lily pads, or other likely cover. The important thing is to keep it moving and to cover all available hiding places. If the lure stops, the pickerel will probably lose interest and not strike. There is no special movement pattern that must be followed as long as the angler works each patch of cover completely.

The long cane pole allows the fisherman to swing the lure about

20 feet from the boat and make it dance across the surface. Surface strikes are common, and they can make your neck hackles rise when a big fish nails the lure on a short line.

SPINNING

One of the best lure choices for pickerel fishermen is a small flashing spoon or spinner. I have used tiny Dardevles or No. 2 Mepps spinners effectively. These lures should be fished at a rapid pace to prevent the fish from determining that it is an imitation. I prefer to cast along the edges of weedbeds, allow the spoon or spinner to sink slightly, and begin a fairly rapid retrieve. The built-in action of these lures will do the rest.

One factor little understood by pickerel fishermen is that these fish are best taken by casting parallel to weedbeds or other cover. Like their larger cousins, pickerel will hide back in the weeds and dart out to feed. A lure fished right into the cover will surely tangle and produce few if any fish. Concentrate on the edges of cover or weed lines and you'll take more fish.

Porkrind is an excellent pickerel bait. Its softness and wavering action in the water attracts these fish like aquarium guppies to fish food. One technique that has worked well for pickerel fishermen, at least in the Northeast, is the use of porkrind chunks. The chunks seem more attractive to pickerel than strips.

Cast the pork chunk out and allow it to settle to the bottom. Begin a slow, jerky retrieve along bottom until a pickerel grabs the bait. If the chunk contains only one hook you may have to allow him to swallow it before setting the hook. Some fishermen rely on a second hook, a tail hook, to eliminate this problem. When the fish grabs the chunk, set the barbs instantly and you'll often have him on the back hook. This technique often pays off when all other pickerel-fishing techniques fail.

A pickerel-fishing trick exists that works well in most waters, although it may be illegal in some states. If small bluegills or perch can be used as bait, they make an excellent meal for these small members of the pike family. The small panfish must be dead, because pickerel will seldom swallow these sharp-spined gamefish until they are rendered inactive.

If this sport is legal in your state (check first), hook a small yellow perch or bluegill lightly through the back or through both lips and cast it out into likely pickerel cover. Fish a lip-hooked baitfish in much the same manner as a lure, with short jerky retrieves. The back-hooked panfish should be fished deep, near bottom, and near the edges of weedbeds or other cover.

Pickerel often frequent inshore waters which are extremely shallow. This inshore feeding migration often takes place during late spring as the fish feed on small minnows and gamefish. A Connecticut fisherman once showed me his unique method of taking large chain pickerel at this time.

He'd move along slowly in a lightweight canoe and cast small lures over an overhanging bush, tree limb, or log. He would allow the lure to dangle down into the water and then jiggle it. This often brought about a strike if a chain pickerel was feeding nearby. His only concern was to select limbs or logs which were fairly smooth so that he could slide the lure off the obstruction when a fish struck. His success with this trick paid off with big fish and plenty of action.

The smallest floating Rapalas are deadly for pickerel when the fish are feeding near the surface. A light line is used and the lure cast out and jerked or twitched rapidly across and just under the surface. This technique works very well in all waters.

ICEFISHING

Icefishing is the preferred way for many anglers to take pickerel along the northeast portion of their range. The same techniques work for chain pickerel as for pike, although the bait size must be scaled down to entice these smaller gamefish.

I've never had the good fortune to fish pickerel through the ice, but some of my Eastern buddies have and they report that it is great fun. They use tip-ups baited with tiny treble hooks and small 2-inch shiners, chubs, or suckers. The edges of weedbeds are the preferred place for winter tip-up fishing on small ponds, creeks, or lakes.

Action can come fast and furious when anglers find a body of water teeming with chain pickerel. They strike well during winter months; ice and bitter cold temperatures don't seem to bother them one bit.

Jigging is another icefishing technique that produces some of the largest pickerel of the year. Small glittering spoons are jigged up and down in much the same manner as one would fish for panfish, except the lure is worked faster and with more action. Even during the winter, pickerel are attracted to flash and action-producing lures.

Some icefishermen add a tiny minnow to one of the hooks of the jigging spoon, and this combination of flash and scent from the bait is a combination that cannot be topped for pickerel. One jigging angler told me he increases the number of strikes he obtains by cutting several small slashes in the sides of the baitfish attached to his lure. The slashes release more odor and often stimulate the feeding attitude of chain pickerel.

These gamefish are small, but they are quick-tempered, with the explosiveness of a powder keg. They strike well, and a large pickerel is a prize for any angler, young or old.

12
WALLEYE

The walleye is one of the most highly prized gamefish found on the North American continent. It is also a fine table fish. I can think of few other sport-caught fish capable of generating more interest, except possibly trout and largemouth bass. The walleye is often king wherever he's found.

Old Marble Eye has a rather round and elongated body, a forked tail with the bottom lobe tipped with white, olive-green or brassy sides, and a light-colored belly. The back is marked with six or seven dark bands. Large milky-colored eyes glow like fire at night and enable the fish to see well after dark, when it feeds a great deal.

The spinal rays on the dorsal fin have a dark blotch or streak, which is a telltale sign of the walleye. Its close cousin the sauger does not have this blotch, nor does the sauger have the white tip on the lower lobe of the tail fin. The sauger has rows of dark spots on the first dorsal fin, whereas the walleye only has the one dark splotch of color near its base.

The walleye was once a denizen of more northerly waters. It now has become a cosmopolitan gamefish, with recent stockings in many new waters. This species is easily adaptable to life in inland lakes, reservoirs, and large manmade lakes as well as rivers. It prefers cold clear water with an abundance of forage minnows. Walleyes were once common to most of the Northern states and Canada, but their range now includes Tennessee, Kentucky, Arkansas, Oklahoma, Alabama, Mississippi, North Carolina, Virginia, Arizona, Colorado, Iowa, Montana, and New Mexico.

In addition to being fairly recent arrivals to the above states, walleyes are found throughout the Great Lakes and Midwest states and in New York and Pennsylvania, Ontario, Quebec, Manitoba, Saskatchewan, Alberta, Yukon and Northwest Territories, and Alaska. A few walleyes are taken in British Columbia.

Several factors account for the walleye's popularity in many areas: they are a schooling fish and easy to locate in rivers or lakes; they strike readily on a variety of lures and live baits; they bite well during all periods of the year; and they grow to large sizes.

The walleye isn't a jumping fish or a flashy battler but is a persistent and dogged fighter. Anglers once complained that walleyes didn't scrap as much as other gamefish, but they would catch this fish on tackle heavy enough to subdue a big muskellunge. It was simply a matter of winching them in without any semblance of a struggle. If the walleye is pursued with reasonably light line I know of no angler who has tangled with a trophy that doesn't have good words to say about the experience.

This gamefish lends itself well to trophy fishing, since schools of similar-size fish often congregate in one area. Catch one big fish and the chances are good you'll catch others of similar size. The walleye isn't a trophy fish to be taken lightly; they are wary and easy to spook from a feeding area by too much noise, too much light, and too much fishing activity.

Walleyes are predominantly bottom-oriented. In order to make consistent catches a fisherman must learn to think almost like the gamefish and determine where he'd be if he were a walleye. To do this requires knowledge of their habits and preferences.

Bottom contours and breaks in those contours are prime locations for walleyes. I look for walleyes in lakes to be located near distinctive underwater locations such as humps, points, sandbars, gravel bars, near weedbeds in summer months, near rubble-strewn areas below waterfalls (especially in Canada), near boulders, along steep stony bluffs or cliffs, near sharp granite ledges, or around points or islands. Lakes often develop slight currents around these contour breaks, and a walleye seeks moving water, no matter how slight. Much of the time this species will be hugging bottom and moves up or down only to feed. A normal migration pattern for feeding will usually follow bottom contours.

Walleyes will suspend off bottom when following schools of forage fish. As baitfish move up or down according to temperature preferences, wind direction and velocity, or sunlight, the walleye will move with them. This particular phenomenon normally occurs during summer months when baitfish are more active. This is often the case when walleyes move from the depths and up into the shallows to haze baitfish against the shore and massacre them.

The best places to fish for walleyes in a lake are shown in this drawing. In general, the fish seek bottom structure of one type or another.

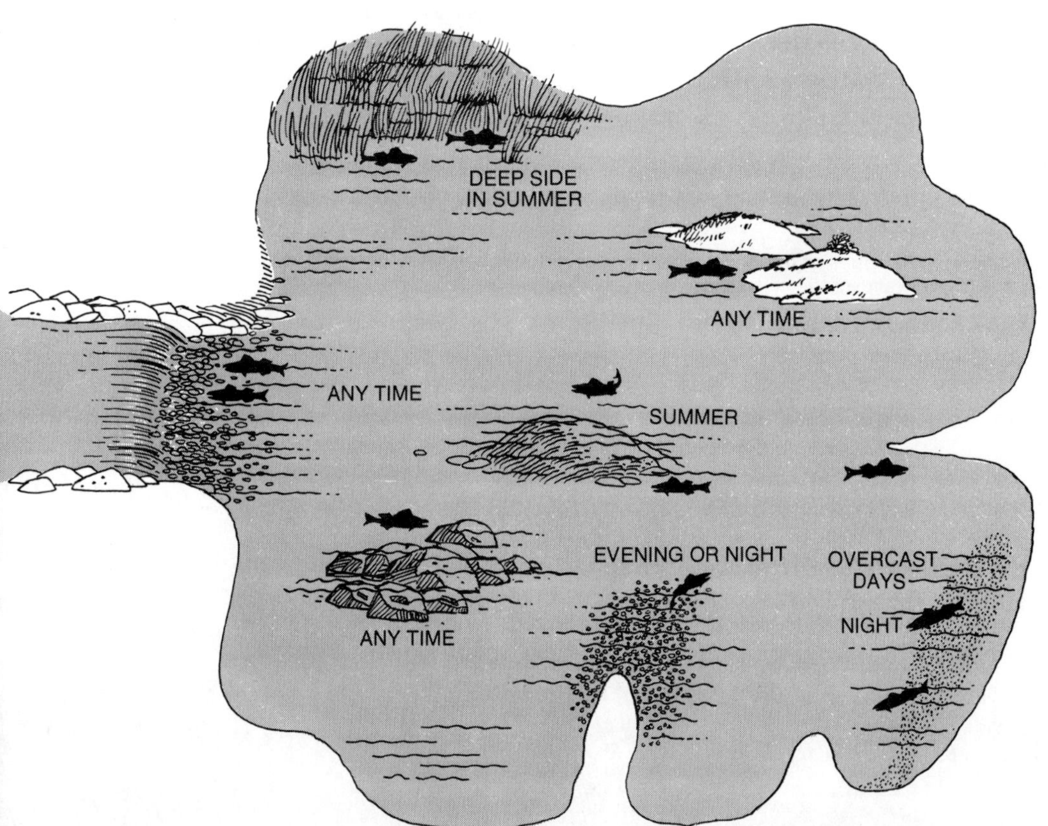

One look at a walleye's large eye will clearly show why this gamefish has developed a reputation as a night or overcast-daylight feeder. Marble Eye is extremely sensitive to direct or intense sunlight. This offers a clue to fishermen; if the sun is full on the water, the best advice is to fish deep. Whenever the sun is obscured by clouds, during rainstorms or evening hours, the walleye will often feed in much shallower water. This is an oversimplification but holds true more often than not.

Summer heat often drives forage fish into the cover of nearby weedbeds. Although fishermen have long associated walleyes with being a hard-bottom-oriented gamefish, they have missed out on some superb fishing by ignoring the weedbed areas. When walleyes begin searching weedbed edges for minnows, you can find fantastic action.

One year I fished at Everson's Lodge on Ontario's Kabinakagami Lake, north of Wawa. The lake was glutted with weeds and it was difficult to locate the fish. I finally decided, with the help of my son David, that small avenues of open water between weedbeds had to be where the fish were concentrated. We made one pass through an opening between two massive weedbeds, bounced jigs off bottom, and we found the fish. In two hours we boated our limit of walleyes ranging up to 5 pounds. Every other weedbed opening held walleyes in large numbers. They were feeding on the abundant minnow supply in those areas.

Avenues of open water between weedbeds are often hotspots for walleyes. They feed on minnows in these areas.

Moving water stimulates a walleye to feed heavily. A stream or river flowing into a lake or impoundment will often have walleyes heading into the current. They know that moving water will often drift food their way, and they never have to expend much effort to feed. Walleyes seldom hold in the full force of the current. Instead they seek obstructions that cushion the flow of current and spill food around the holding spot and directly to them.

Dams or wingdams on large rivers like the Mississippi or Wisconsin's Wolf River offer both current and food. Rocks located near these wingdams offer concealment and excellent feeding opportunities.

The weather can greatly influence walleye fishing. A steady barometer reading for several days can result in excellent fishing. The fish will scatter during the first day or two of a high-pressure center and then regroup when clear weather holds over an area.

A lowering barometer reading on the third day after a high moves into an area can create good fishing conditions until the storm moves in or the barometer starts to rise again. Just before a storm can produce some spectacular fishing, because walleyes apparently can sense the changing pressure and they feed right up to the moment a rain begins falling.

A slight breeze can aid the walleye fisherman because it produces a riffle or chop on the surface that reduces the amount of sunlight entering the water. Windy days generally produce better shallow-water fishing, since the fish move closer to shore to feed.

One further tip should be brought to mind before we begin a discussion of fishing techniques geared to taking trophy walleyes. In walleye country two types of lakes are found—clear water and dark water.

Clear-water lakes are generally larger and more sterile and contain fewer but larger fish. A dark-colored lake is often shallow and usually produces more fish but fewer trophies. The clear lakes are generally much deeper, while dark lakes have shallow heavy weedbeds and muddy bottoms.

Look for walleyes over flat, slow-breaking contours in a clear-water lake. These fish are often found along sharper breaks or humps in dark waters.

Clear-water lakes often have walleye hotspots in shallow water once the sun goes down. Sunken islands, the tops of weedbeds in 6 to 15 feet of water, and bays are good clear-water locations to fish after dark.

Andy Thomas swings a Rapala-caught 10-pound walleye into the boat on Ontario's Georgian Bay, one of the best areas in Canada for trophy walleyes.

Weed lines should command your fishing attention in dark-colored lakes during summer months, when most people have an opportunity to fish. These areas contain an excellent balance of oxygen, cover, and forage. I look for a wide weedbelt to produce more fish than a thin strip of weeds.

NIGHT FISHING

Although many fishermen scoff at the idea, I maintain that some of the largest trophy walleyes are taken at night. A classic example was a trip I made two years ago to Woods Bay Lodge near MacTier on Ontario's Georgian Bay. I asked Ray Brown, the owner, when we could expect the best fishing. "Oh, it's difficult to tell, but it usually begins sometime around 10:00 p.m. and lasts until 2:00 a.m. The fish move in from Georgian Bay about dark, and it takes a while for them to work into these islands. But when they do, we'll catch some trophy fish you won't believe!" His matter-of-fact attitude impressed me.

We trolled large Rapalas just under the surface on long lines. We'd release nearly 100 yards of line and troll slowly and give the rod tips a forward-and-backward jerk every fifteen seconds. This would cause the lure to dart forward before dropping back on the slack line. It imitated the death throes of a large minnow struggling near the surface.

We'd been trolling for about two hours when my lure suddenly stopped. The forward motion of the boat caused line to rip off against the drag. "I'm snagged up!" I grumbled as Ray took the boat out of gear. He stood up and turned on the light. I felt stupid when the snag suddenly started moving away from the boat. It was a walleye and a big one.

The walleye and I waltzed around Georgian Bay for ten minutes before I caught the reddish-orange gleam of its eyes in the soft glow of the flashlight. A white-tipped tail then hove into sight and Ray softly dunked the net around my first Georgian Bay lunker walleye—a fish weighing just over 10 pounds. "Some snag," Ray chuckled under his breath.

An hour later we tangled with another big fish on my wife's line. It struck and turned sharply for deeper water and didn't feel like a snag. Of course, she's much smarter than I am and realized these things immediately. I have to be shown.

She fought that walleye for fifteen minutes before the flashlight picked up the fish swimming tiny circles beneath the boat. It looked much larger than mine at first glance. It surged for bottom in a bulldogging run typical of trophy walleyes but soon ran out of steam, and Kay pumped it back to the boat. One dip of the net and Ray had Kay's big walleye in the bag. It weighed just over 12 pounds.

Others in our party were taking walleyes up to 15 pounds, although the average fish scaled *only* 8 pounds. This area annually produces walleyes up to 18 pounds, which are trophy fish of the highest class.

Another type of night fishing that produces extremely well is casting. Years ago I practiced a sport called "bar hopping"—totally unlike the common variety that some people enjoy. We would hop from sandbar to sandbar and point to point in an attempt to locate feeding walleyes. It can be a very productive method on some nights and totally ineffectual on others. If you miss the fish on every bar or point, you wind up skunked, which is a basic lesson trophy fishermen must learn to contend with.

My brother and I had learned that walleyes often work into shallow water over points, sandbars, or gravel bars after dark to feed on minnows. One night George and I pushed off onto Michigan's Manistee Lake under the milky glow of a full moon. I had my doubts about the walleyes feeding in shallow water, but we began fishing shoreline locations where no lights except that of the moon showed on the water.

We would ease up within 100 yards of the area to be fished, cut my twin 70 Evinrudes, and then slowly coast or paddle into casting position. We never used any lights other than the boat's running lights for navigation. We were afraid the light from a lantern or flashlight would spook the fish.

The boat settled quietly on the still waters of the lake and we sat quietly and listened. After a minute we could hear the faint "plop" sound of a walleye smacking a minnow near shore. It was soon followed by a rippling noise; minnows were jumping from the water in an effort to get away from the relentless attack of the walleyes schooled below. "We've found them!" George giggled as he fired a sinking Heddon River Runt Spook toward the shoreline. I was using a similar lure, a black-and-white model, and my plug dropped within inches of the shoreline.

We began working the lures back just fast enough to bring out the seductive wiggle. George made two turns on his spinning-reel handle before his lure stopped. "Gotcha," he grunted while setting the hook.

I increased my reeling to get my line out of the way and my lure stopped with a jolt. I set the hook and felt the submarine dive of a big walleye. We had a doubleheader going.

I sculled the boat toward open water with one hand so we wouldn't spook the other feeding fish. When the boat was positioned over 20 feet of water, we moved to opposite ends of my Lund boat and began the scrap anew. George's fish stayed faithfully off the stern, while my fish tried dredging a new hole in the bottom of the lake off the bow.

It took nearly fifteen minutes to work each fish up off bottom and into the boat. I kept one ear cocked for sounds of feeding fish while we battled our unseen walleyes. Every once in a while a walleye would scoop a minnow off the surface near shore. They were still feeding.

We finally boated our trophy walleyes. George's fish weighed 13½ pounds and mine 12 pounds. We conked them on the head with an empty Coke bottle, tossed them in the ice cooler, and headed back for another encounter with the fish off the sandbar.

It took two casts each before George pounded the hooks home on another trophy walleye. This fish sizzled off on a tangent for the other end of the lake; it wasn't an explosive run, just a steady line-peeling slow-motion movement of a heavyweight fish.

I pounded another cast toward shore as George's fish began bulldogging. My Runt wiggled back almost to the boat, and a walleye slashed at it under the soft light of my white stern light. I was overanxious and managed to hook the fish for only an instant before it rolled next to the boat and shook off. It looked to be 10 pounds at least.

We followed George's fish for 30 yards, and he began pumping and reeling in an attempt to work the fish up close enough for netting. We wanted to hit the school once more before it left the sandbar. His fish resisted every inch of the way and didn't want to leave the security of the bottom. After another long struggle the walleye gave up the fight and headed for the surface, where I promptly netted it. It looked like a twin to George's earlier fish, except it weighed just a hair over 14 pounds.

I managed to take another fish—a 10-pounder—before the school scattered and the action ended for the night. Our total catch was four fish which weighed nearly 50 pounds. The next night was a repeat, except our largest pulled the scales down to 15 pounds.

Action such as this is the stuff of which fishing dreams are made. Unfortunately, this type of action doesn't happen often unless the angler makes the necessary arrangements to be on the water almost every night and knows where the fish will feed. This takes patience, plenty of nights when you learn the areas but catch no fish, and it takes constant experimentation with lures and action to determine which ones are most productive on that particular body of water. George and I spent nearly two years of frustrating summer evenings fishing Manistee Lake before we learned how to take the fish.

Such fishing isn't consistent; if it were, anglers would soon tire of catching jumbo walleyes nightly without a challenge. And a challenge is what trophy fishing is all about. Without it, one might as well be dunking worms in a farm pond for bullheads, which also can be fun but isn't much of a challenge.

JIG FISHING

Jig fishing is one of the deadliest tactics for taking jumbo walleyes that I've run across. Although jig fishing pays big dividends in walleye waters across the northern tier of states, it is in Ontario, Quebec, and Manitoba that I've learned the rudiments of this art. A garden variety of jig fishing will always take some walleyes, but I've found that certain tricks will up your chances of catching a big fish.

One of my favorite tactics in Canadian waters is to sweeten the jig with the throat latch of another walleye. A tiny V-shaped piece of meat is located in the throat skin near the gills. It attaches to the lower gill covers and to the throat area. Catch a small walleye, a shore-lunch fish, remove this piece of meat, and hook it through the apex of the throat latch so both tiny legs of meat dangle back behind the lure as it bounces across the bottom.

This gives the flesh a wavering action similar to porkrind except it retains the flavor and scent qualities of fresh walleye meat. I've found that the combination of Gapen Pinky jig (preferably yellow) and a throat latch will usually catch some of the largest walleyes in the area.

The jig and throat latch should be fished slowly with 6-inch hops over the bottom. The up-and-down motion plus the scent and action of this piece of fish flesh is a triple-barreled combination that is irresistible to walleyes. They will usually strike just as the lure lifts upward off bottom or just as it settles. I've taken many fish that apparently grabbed it as it settled and when I began the next jigging movement, they were hanging on tightly. The strikes are soft and difficult to detect, but if the jig is kept moving you'll hook many fish.

A trick many jig fishermen overlook is the knot they use with monofilament. I prefer 6-pound test when jig fishing and will tie a loop knot that allows the jig a much freer action. It's a small point but extremely important if one is to obtain the maximum amount of efficiency from the lure.

I've also determined that a slow rolling jig maneuver can be deadly with marabou or bucktail jigs. The easiest way to perform this technique is to jig horizontally instead of vertically. The jig will tend to roll over the bottom instead of hop. Simply move the rod tip in a horizontal direction for about 6 to 12 inches, drop the rod tip back, pick up the slack, and roll it horizontally again. This will cause the marabou feathers to pulsate or "breathe" in an attractive manner.

Walleyes can be extremely difficult to locate at certain times, particularly on strange waters. A fish-finding technique that many guides use is to row or motor to the upwind portion of the lake and drift down with the wind at your back.

Lower a jig or jig-and-throat-latch combination over the side until it strikes bottom. Bounce the jig up and down off bottom as you drift slowly and you'll eventually locate the fish. If the walleyes are small, return them to the water and keep drifting. This is one of the best ways I know to locate big fish on strange lakes. Once big walleyes are located, triangulate the location with three shoreline positions and return as often as necessary.

If the fish spook they will generally be found at the same level or slightly deeper and usually within 100 yards. The disturbance created by hooking and fighting fish may cause them to drift away, but they seldom go far. Continue jigging at the same depths until the fish are located again.

The addition of a fathead minnow or other small baitfish can increase the effectiveness of almost any walleye jig. Select fresh

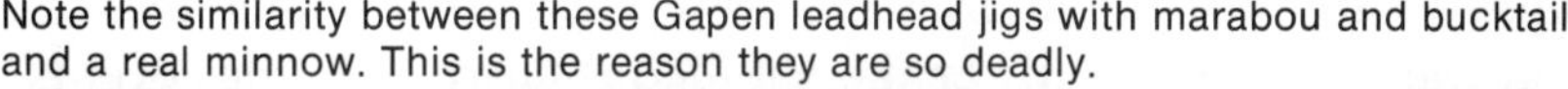
Note the similarity between these Gapen leadhead jigs with marabou and bucktail and a real minnow. This is the reason they are so deadly.

live minnows from the lake being fished, if possible. Insert the point of the hook under the chin and out the top of the head and fish with either the vertical or horizontal jigging motion. The shiner or fathead minnow will kick upward as the lure is jigged and then sink with a wavering action as the jig falls to the floor of the lake. This technique appeals to the walleye's sense of smell and taste and can often make the difference.

Many years ago I decided to combine trolling and jigging to see what it would produce. I selected a weedy lake with large submerged weedbeds at 10-foot depths. It was midsummer and I knew the weeds would be loaded with minnows. The walleyes wouldn't be far away from this loaded smorgasbord table.

I lowered my jig so that it just brushed the tops of the weeds and began a slow troll. A heavier than normal jig (about 1 ounce) was used (I seldom use over a ½-ounce jig when casting). I kept the boat speed to a crawl and continuously jigged up and down directly under the boat.

My partner and I hadn't traveled 100 yards in this manner when he had a strike. He fought the fish out into deep water and finally boated and released a 4-pound walleye. That technique continued to pay off handsomely the rest of the day as we caught and released our limits of 4-to-6-pound fish.

Jig fishing can be tremendous during spring, summer, and fall in rivers. The fish often congregate in large holes or along wingdams to feed. An excellent location for big fish is around any point that extends out into the river. The fish may be on the upstream side of one point and along the downstream portion of the next point. It takes some scouting and trial-and-error fishing to locate these areas, but walleyes will usually be there if food is nearby and the cover is adequate. Look for points with hard-packed sand, gravel, or other rubble nearby. I've taken a few river walleyes over a soft bottom, but very few. Good points to fish are those that extend out and drop off quickly into the stream channel. Long tapering points sometimes produce, but structure and sharp breaklines are necessary to attract the largest number of fish in any river system.

Some states or provinces have open seasons during the walleye spawning runs, and this can be one of the hottest times to land trophy fish. Large spawners are present and they strike well during this period.

A sure-fire combination is a Gapen ¼-ounce leadhead jig tipped with a small shiner minnow. Cast into deep holes or smooth deep runs next to the riverbank and inch the jig and minnow back. Walleyes tend to congregate in holes just upstream or downstream from shallow gravel bars. These gravel areas are the actual spawning sites, but the fish will stack up in holes before spawning begins.

Another technique that produces well for spawning fish is to cast a yellow or perch-scale Deep Diving River Runt Spook into the heads of deep holes or runs. Retrieve just fast enough to bring out the wiggle of the lure. It must be scraping bottom to be effective. I've taken several 10-pound-plus walleyes during spring months while fishing for steelhead with this lure. In Michigan, the walleye season is closed at this time, and the fish must be returned to the water. Many states do have open seasons on Marble Eye during the spring spawning run, and it's one of the hottest times of the year to take trophy fish.

Some rivers are wide and flat with medium depths. Walleyes tend to concentrate in these areas if moving water is present. A successful technique is to cruise slowly upstream with an orange- or yellow-bladed Best nightcrawler harness. It usually requires some weight to take the lure down, but it is good for spawning walleyes.

BACKTROLLING

Backtrolling has come to be one of the hottest methods of taking walleyes in the Midwest, where this method originated. Backtrolling means exactly that—the fisherman trolls in reverse. Boats are outfitted with splashboards on the stern to prevent water from coming in. This method allows more accurate placement of the craft in relationship to the structure being fished.

Another aspect of backtrolling is that the boat's movement is much slower and allows increased lure-presentation time. If walleyes are feeding pickily, this method enables the fisherman to keep his lure or bait in the most productive location longer.

A very popular outfit has evolved for backtrollers—the Lindy rig. This is a slip sinker, swivel, and 12-inch leader with a single hook. The backtroller can use either worms, leeches, or minnows on the hook as bait. Leeches, although ugly cusses, have become one of the leading walleye baits in many areas. They should be hooked through the head like minnows. Worms should be hooked once at one end and allowed to string out behind the hook.

The backtroller lowers his bait and sinker over the side and begins a slow backward troll with the bail of his spinning reel open. One finger holds the line from stripping off while the slip sinker bounces along the bottom. By trolling backward the angler can make tighter turns along contour changes, and it allows his bait to cover proper depths at all times.

When a walleye strikes he'll usually gently tap at the bait, and the fisherman should release slack line. Allow several coils of line to peel off before starting the retrieve. This gives a few moments of slack line and gives the fish time to swallow the bait. By the time the slack is reeled up the fish is usually on and the angler should set the hook.

Backtrolling also works well with lures that deliver the maximum action at slow speeds. I'd suggest small Flatfish, Ping-a-T's, Rapalas, Rebels, or similar lures. Some weight is usually needed to take these lures deep enough to be effective, although the first two mentioned will dive to 8 or 10 feet at slow speeds. Orange, yellow, and red-and-white or yellow-and-white lures work best. They can be painted if not available in suitable colors.

One of the hottest walleye techniques I've used is an old-timer. It produced twenty-five years ago and still catches fish. Slow trolling with a baited nightcrawler harness has always been a sure-fire producer of big fish.

An angler releases a 6-pound walleye in hopes he'll be able to catch it again once it gets larger. Many trophy fishermen release fish that others would keep.

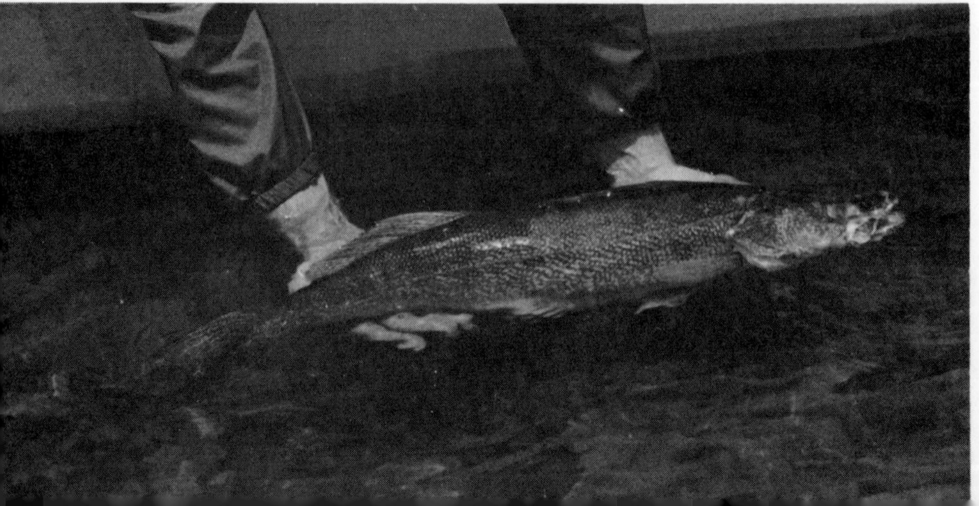

I used to weight the line so that my crawler harness (usually a Best harness in yellow or orange with silver or red spinner blades) would scratch along bottom. It required a slow putt-putt trolling speed, in forward or reverse, to give a walleye enough time to strike. A frequent up-and-down chugging movement of the rod would tease walleyes into a hard strike.

I also learned that walleyes can be teased into grabbing a lure. Many times they will follow along and nip at the bait several times without taking it well enough for a hookup. If I feel a following fish nip at the lure I'd pull it away and then drop it back to the walleye. Do this three or four times and most walleyes will sock it hard. This chugging technique works for many fish but is a little-known producer on walleyes.

FLY FISHING

One time while researching a walleye article for *Outdoor Life* I found some dusty literature which indicated that these fish feed heavily on insect life during May, June, and July, depending on latitude. As mayfly nymphs and adults hatch and emerge on large inland lakes, the walleye is often found nearby taking advantage of the free lunch.

A study made on a northern Michigan lake showed that walleyes gorge themselves on insects whenever a major hatch occurs. Twenty-seven of thirty-four fish stomachs examined during the study showed the fish had been feeding on insect life exclusively.

This fact has alerted a few fly fishermen into making healthy catches on nymph patterns. A fly-rod addict should concentrate on walleye lakes known to possess large numbers of mayflies and to coordinate fishing time with the peak of the hatches.

A sinking fly line, a long leader tapered to 3X, and a nymph pattern which closely imitates the emerging insect should do well. I'd try to obtain the struggling, swimming action of a nymph heading for the surface. Walleyes taken on a fly rod can provide tremendous sport for those fishermen lucky enough to hit a hatch at its peak.

One walleye technique that many fishermen have either ignored or never knew is that strong summer winds will force feeding walleyes into downwind shoal water. A heavy breeze blowing from any quarter will eventually create a strong rolling surf on a shallow lee-shore shoal. This rough water gouges out bottom fauna, creates murky or muddy water, and permits walleyes to feed actively in shallow waters during daylight hours.

My first choice would be shallow rocky reefs or shoals whenever a hard wind blows steadily from one direction for more than twenty-four hours. The rolling action disturbs minute organisms which attract minnows, which, in turn, attract big walleyes.

One day I waded onto a sandbar on Michigan's Burt Lake after watching a strong wind blow for two days. Within an hour I landed a limit of 6-to-9-pound walleyes on floating Rapalas. Three fish were caught between shore and my wading position, a distance of not more than 50 yards. The fish had been feeding in roiled, white-capped water less than a foot deep.

This calls for quiet wading to prevent spooking the feeding fish and deliberate casting. On two different occasions the wind caught my line and lure and blew it far off the target area. Casting light minnow-imitating lures into the teeth of a gale is difficult. Many times it's easier to cast across the wind and retrieve along the edges of the reef or shoal. Always turn and cast toward shore, because the fish may be feeding between you and the shoreline.

Walleyes are a prime food source because of their delicious white flesh and are highly prized by anglers wherever they are found. The combination of good eating and hard underwater fights with big fish has made this species one of my favorites.

13
SAUGER

The sauger is a little-known gamefish which is found only in scattered areas. It looks enough like a walleye to be a cousin, which it is, and sometimes the ranges of the two overlap, causing confusion among anglers. The differences in body coloration and markings has been explained in the chapter on walleye, but certain other points should be made clear.

Saugers are capable of tolerating much more turbid waters than walleyes. They seem able to withstand more pollution and warmer water conditions than their cousin, and this enables them to provide a fishery in areas that cannot support good walleye populations.

The life style of the sauger is similar to that of walleye except it tends to spawn a few days later. This gamefish is known to inhabit only large bodies of water, often much larger than the walleye, and they are known to migrate long distances.

The current range of the sauger is concentrated primarily in the Great Lakes states and the Canadian province of Ontario. Some saugers are found in the Mississippi, Missouri, Tennessee, and Ohio river systems and their tributaries. Although the average sauger taken by fishermen will range from 1 to 3 pounds, some fish nearing the 8-pound class are taken yearly from the Missouri River system. The world record weighed 8 pounds 12 ounces and was caught in Lake Sakakawea in North Dakota.

Sauger fishing is a great deal like walleye fishing, except a few novel twists enter the picture, and unless sauger fishermen realize what these are and learn how to overcome them, they are likely to spend time in prime waters without taking a single fish.

I received my sauger introduction several years ago. I'd heard scattered reports of jumbo sauger—fish weighing 5 to 6 pounds—being taken consistently from two remote Michigan lakes, in the Copper Country of the Upper Peninsula.

Torch Lake and Portage Lake near Houghton are the sites of excellent sauger fishing. The word came down that Bob and Bernice Smith, college students at the nearby university in Houghton, were the undisputed champs at taking these fish. After several hurried phone calls I contacted Bob Smith and he agreed to take my party fishing. I was working on a series of sauger stories for *Outdoor Life, Fishing Facts,* and other magazines. It looked like a golden opportunity to learn more about this gamefish. Until then, my knowledge of this species had been limited and I knew nothing of the techniques needed to catch them. I was clueless, as some of my Canadian friends are wont to point out.

The early September sun was beginning to dip behind a hill overlooking Torch Lake when we met Bob and Bernice. He'd earlier told me that the last two hours before dark, and the two hours at daybreak, are the best times to catch saugers.

"Fishermen believe that saugers will respond to the same techniques as walleyes, and they do, up to a point. They move constantly from deepwater structure shoreward to shallower structures to feed late in the day," he told me. So far it was similar to walleye movements just before dark. I was still in the ballgame, but it didn't last very long.

We trolled for some time before Bob pointed to his sonar unit. A red blip showed we were approaching a steep underwater hump that rose from 20 feet to 8 feet, leveled off for just a few feet, and dropped off again, "This is excellent sauger water. Look sharp, now. We'll probably get a strike," he told me.

Seconds later our Rapalas swam in an undulating manner past the underwater hump and Bob had a jarring strike. "I got him," Bob yelled as he set the hook. "It really feels like a nice fish." His rod tip was bowed over the gunwale and line was ripping off the reel as the sauger headed for deep water.

I had a short pecking strike as I reeled in. I set the hook and missed. "Reel faster—he may still strike," Bob hollered over his shoulder. He later told me that saugers often strike more than once if you speed up the retrieve or pull it away from them.

My hands spun on the reel handle as I cranked furiously. The lure traveled 20 feet and stopped as a fish inhaled the orange-and-yellow plug. A grin spread from ear to ear as I fought my first sauger.

Bob's fish was larger than mine, and I boated my 3-pounder with little difficulty. I then stood back to photograph and enjoy his fight. I get more turned on watching others catch fish than I do if lunkers fall to my lure.

We were interested in getting Bob's fish in as quickly as possible before we lost our daylight and the school of sauger disappeared off the hump. They never stay very long in a place like that.

It took a little longer before I was able to dip Bob's 4½-pounder from the lake. As soon as it fell into the net, he dropped his rod and spun the boat in a circle and we began another trolling pass over the hump. There wasn't a wasted moment as I unhooked his fish and added both saugers to the stringer; we were again trolling in less than thirty seconds.

Bob could see scattered flashes on his sonar unit as we began working the hump again. The lures worked into the edge of the underwater plateau, and I had a savage strike that bent my rod in a bow. I jabbed the hooks home and the fish headed directly for deep water, a characteristic trait of big saugers.

After a lengthy battle with bulldogging rushes similar to a large walleye, my sauger rolled up in a bronze-glow of submission and Bob lifted a 5-pound trophy into the boat.

Bob Smith feels that structure fishing is imperative in order to take sauger consistently. This tends to correspond with information gleaned from a test netting for sauger which was made in an attempt to learn more about their habits. The results of that netting may be shocking to many fishermen who think they're fishing deep.

The tests were compiled on Michigan's Torch Lake and Portage Lake in 1971 by the Department of Natural Resources. It showed that smelt were the principal forage fish and that saugers often descended to unheard-of depths for this species.

Biologists found saugers in test nets ranging from shallow bars of 4 feet down to underwater structures located in 85 feet of water. The *average* depth that saugers were found was 30 to 40 feet, much deeper than many fishermen explore with their lures.

Saugers found in these depths were utilizing deep water as a sanctuary and were not actively feeding. Like the walleye, saugers are often motivated to feed during periods of low light intensity. They would usually make one or two trips daily to inshore areas to feed over shallow bars or reefs where it is more practical to fish. These movements occur during low light periods such as dawn and again in the early evening just before dusk.

The early-morning hours have proved as effective for fishing as those near dusk. Sudden changes in the bottom contour are often hotspots for fishing as long as one central area will serve as a scatterpoint where the migrating saugers will spread out.

A scatterpoint, such as the underwater hump described earlier, is a natural as long as deep water is available on three sides of the structure. Saugers, and most other gamefish as well, hate to get boxed into an area where retreat to deep water is not available.

We found that saugers will move up from the depths, contact the edges of the structure, and then move slowly and cautiously into shallow-water areas to feed.

A good spot to troll is where the bottom contour changes rapidly from 10 to 25 or more feet. Sauger often lie along the sudden breaks of a hard-bottom dropoff and will strike almost any lure that comes along. Sudden dropoffs or any break in the bottom contour near an area of deep water are often prime locations to make contact with these fish.

The sauger seems to possess an adaptability to more polluted waters; in Michigan's Torch Lake, the dropoffs are often made by old landfills from the mining companies. These man-made contours are attractive to migrating fish.

Prime months for saugers are the spring months just after ice-out or September and October. The fall months are often best for big fish because they are feeding heavily in anticipation of winter.

Bernice Smith nets a sauger for her husband Bob (above) while Stan Lievense watches the action on Michigan's Torch Lake. Below, Stan and Bernice admire the 4-pound trophy.

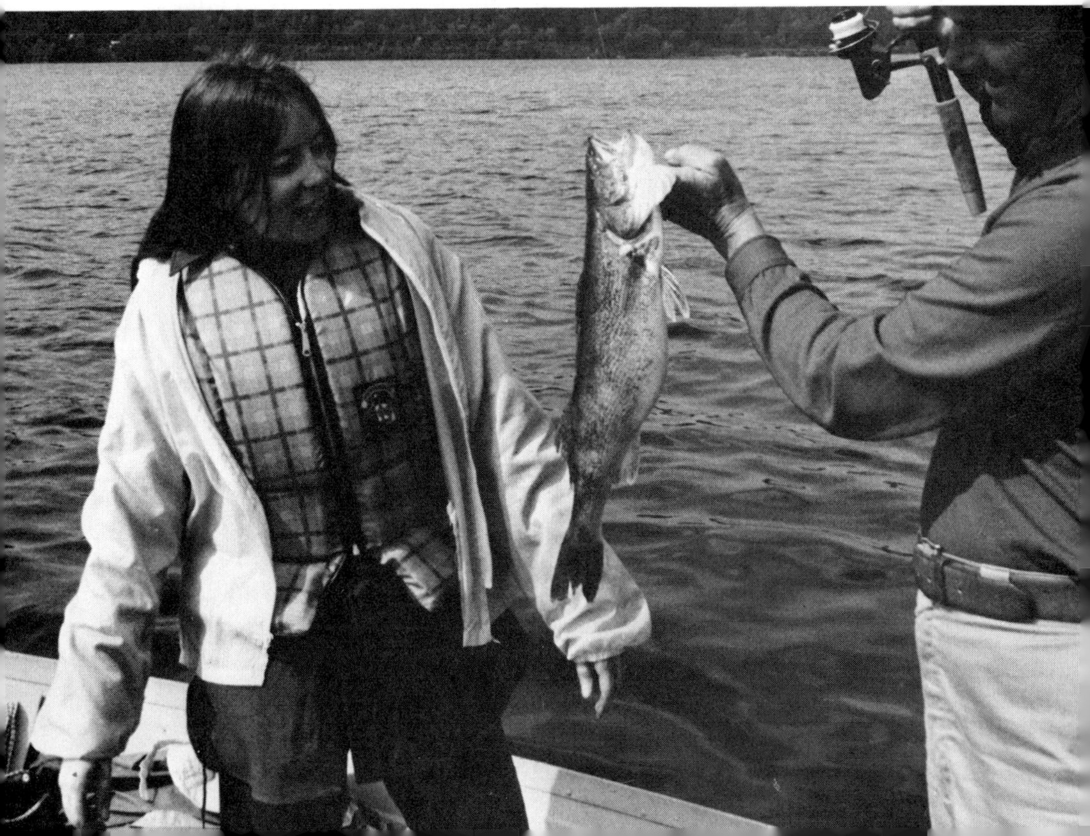

TROLLING

Trolling is the deadliest method of taking saugers, but certain techniques must be followed to obtain the thrill of a trophy fish on your line. Light line should be used because shallow-water saugers, taken during early morning or late afternoon periods, are as leader-shy as a wary old brown trout. Four-to-6-pound test is entirely adequate. Wire leaders should not be used.

Longlining is a fishing technique especially adapted for taking big saugers. A small barrel swivel should be attached 3 feet ahead of the lure to prevent line twist. The lure is slowly released under tension as you troll down the lake. It's best to troll minnow-imitating lures such as a Rapala 75 yards or more behind the boat. This places the lure far back from the disturbance of the motor in shallow water.

By the time the plug wiggles within range of a sauger feeding along a breakline or other structure, the memory of the passing boat has long been forgotten. A zigzag trolling pattern is better than a straight-down-the-lake course, and boat control is necessary to keep the lure working near good cover.

Sauger fishermen will do well to forget what is commonly accepted as being the way to fish for walleyes. A similarity in appearance is about all the two gamefish share; their feeding habits are different and they prefer lures presented in a different manner. Walleyes usually strike a very slow-trolled lure, but saugers demand a much faster troll. The proper speed is about half again the speed used for walleye fishing. A sauger will rise several feet off bottom to strike a lure, whereas walleyes like their meals served on or very near the bottom except when feeding on suspended baitfish. Black-and-silver or orange-and yellow Rapalas in the 5-inch size are two of the most productive lures and colors. The brighter colors seem to produce best on overcast windy days.

Another lure combination that works very well on cloudy days is a minnow harness. A shiner or small sucker is threaded onto the minnow harness and the shank of a No. 6 treble hook is pulled inside the baitfish. Use brass or silver spinner blades about 3 inches ahead of the minnow.

Both lures and minnow harnesses must be activated by the fisherman to achieve jarring strikes. Add a periodic twitch to the line every five or ten seconds and your number of strikes will rise. Bob

Smith would jerk continuously on his rod tip to impart lure action in the form of a darting motion or increased wiggle. Many strikes will occur just after the rod tip is worked in this manner.

If saugers are feeding in relatively shallow water it isn't necessary or desirable to add weight to take lures or baits deeper. Weight will usually kill the action of these lures.

Fishermen should look for areas where deep water lies within a stone's throw of the shoreline. This type of water often has stairstep breaks which sharply drop off to the deepest nearby water. Saugers will lie along these breaks and feed actively. The shallowest breakline (usually about 8 feet) often serves as the feeding site for these fish during prime times. These spots would be my first trolling choice.

Your lures should be well behind the boat and actively working as a trolling pass is made. Saugers apparently can determine that a lure or bait is coming by the underwater vibrations, and if it is properly presented, they'll often strike on the first pass through the area.

The zigzag trolling pattern takes advantage of the sauger's tendency to strike as a lure passes from shallow into deeper water. If the boat curves in and out of shallow-to-deep water as it follows the breakline, the lure will be doing the same thing far behind the boat. I've found in my limited experience at sauger fishing in Michigan, Ohio, North Dakota, and Ontario that strikes will usually come when the lure or bait drops over the edge of the dropoff and starts into deep water.

Many strikes will occur as the lure works from deep water into the shallower areas and then passes over the shallowest breakline.

STILLFISHING

Certain areas on some lakes lend themselves admirably to stillfishing. Two rigs work well for this method of sauger fishing: a leadhead jig tipped with a throat latch, or a piece of white or yellow porkrind. The Lindy walleye rig baited with a 2-inch shiner minnow is another productive outfit.

I enjoy casting with a yellow or white leadhead Pinky jig, and have found a porkrind to be an effective addition to this lure. The key to success is to anchor on top of any area which has deep water on all sides. A barely submerged island is a good example. Allow the anchored boat to drift near the edge of the dropoff and fan-cast the lures to all sides of the dropoff.

Casting leadhead jigs for sauger demands the soft touch of a burglar. Cast far out and allow the jig to settle into 20 to 35 feet of water. It's important that it settle all the way to bottom. Be alert to a soft take as the jig falls, because I've hooked several saugers that struck as the jig settled on the downdrift. A soft switching of the sinking line will be the only clue you'll have to a strike.

After the jig has settled to the bottom, raise the rod tip slowly for just a few inches and reel up the slack as it tumbles back down. Keep inching the jig back to the boat in short gentle lifts of the rod. A sauger will often strike just as it lifts off bottom, and you must set the hook quickly or you'll miss him.

Once the jig reaches the edge of the dropoff beneath the boat, slow the retrieve down and take more time between jigging movements. Saugers are very deliberate about striking when a jig is crawling up the edge of a dropoff. The strike is so soft it is often impossible to detect. I've never had a sauger strike hard on a jig.

The Lindy rig is a super method of catching lunker sauger. A ¼-ounce walking slip sinker is used to take a lip-hooked shiner minnow to the bottom. Use care to prevent knocking any scales off the shiners while hooking them through both lips.

A very small Dylite bobber should be positioned halfway between the slip sinker and the minnow. Cast into deep water and allow ample time for the minnow to reach bottom. The Dylite bobber will keep the minnow floating slightly off bottom and prevent it from hiding beneath stones or other debris. It also holds the bait in a position where prowling sauger can spot it easily.

Inch the minnow back to the boat in very slow movements. Sauger are slow, deliberate feeders in deep water and hasty reeling will offer nothing but exercise. It should take at least five minutes to fish out each cast.

Saugers will grab a lip-hooked minnow slowly and very deliberately. At the first indication of a fish mouthing the minnow, strip off some line and allow the sauger to move off with the bait on a slack line. Feed out slack line in a controlled manner and give the feeding fish time to swallow the minnow. A sauger can be teased into taking the minnow hard by pulling slightly on the line. This makes it feel as if the minnow is fighting to get away. When the sauger pulls hard on the line, set the hook quickly.

The Dylite bobber technique is worth its weight in gold when the time comes to inch the minnow up the edges of steep dropoffs. The minnow will float out away from the dropoff and is easily seen by fish. This particular method has produced many of my sauger. This gamefish takes a more positive feeding attitude when the minnow crawls up a steep dropoff. The strikes are usually more aggressive and forceful.

Some saugers are taken from rivers throughout their range. One of the best times to fish is during their springtime spawning run. The same techniques that take river walleyes will usually take saugers. Jig fishing with a small minnow hooked either through both eyes or through both lips has been a very successful method for me. It should be bounced slowly along bottom in deep pools or runs where sauger concentrations are known to exist.

The sauger is a relatively unknown gamefish, even in waters where it is found. Few anglers fish exclusively for them, and many confuse them with walleyes. I think this is a horrible case of mistaken identity. The sauger is a fine gamefish, and the taking of a trophy specimen is just as difficult and time-consuming as catching lunker bluegills.

He may look like a walleye, but his habits are different and he is a different species. Learn these habits, and where he is located, and you'll come to enjoy this gamefish as much as I have.

Lindy rig for saugers consists of a walking slip sinker, a bobber, and a lip-hooked minnow. The bobber keeps the minnow off the bottom and visible.

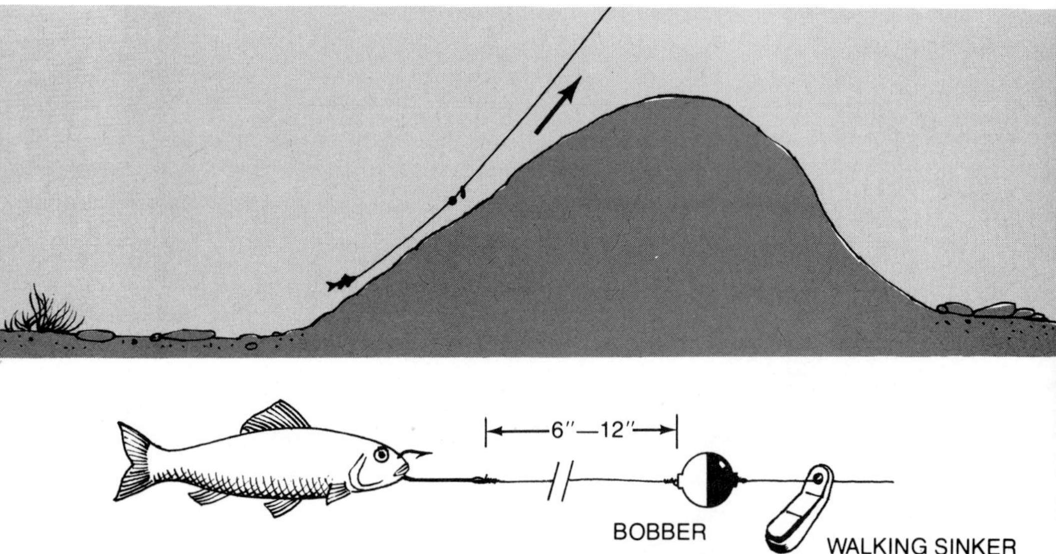

IV

PANFISH

14 BLUEGILLS

Show me a man who has learned how to catch bull bluegills consistently and I'll show you a very popular person, on the water or around home. The bluegill expert is a person far removed from the run-of-the-mill fisherman. Like many experts, he makes his own luck, and doesn't depend on outside help for it, either.

Make no mistake about it: Big trophy-sized bluegills are extremely difficult to catch anytime, and few are the fishermen who can take these fish with any regularity. It's my humble opinion that bulls are the most difficult gamefish of all to catch—certainly far more difficult than a big steelhead or fat brown trout.

Bluegills vary more in coloration than any other sunfish. The basic body colorations range from dark blue to yellow, and some fish may appear almost transparent. The back is usually a dark olive green. The sides are usually marked with six to eight irregular, dark, vertical bars over a purple or iridescent-blue background. Adult fish are marked conspicuously with a broad blue or black gill flap with no red spot. The stomach is often a blaze of colors ranging through yellows and oranges to a golden bronze.

Gills were originally widespread only in the eastern portion of the country but now have been introduced into many states via farm ponds. They adapt readily to any environment containing weedbeds and are favorite gamefish for all kinds of fishermen.

Bluegills are common throughout the South—where they're called bream, pronounced "brim"—and it is there that many of the largest bulls are caught.

One of the first things bluegill fishermen must learn is that bulls are mighty particular fish. A technique that will knock hell out of them one day may be dead the following day. In order to take these fish consistently an angler must possess more tricks than a traveling magician. Many fishermen learn one technique and it may work for one day and never produce again. A classic example follows.

Many years ago I felt I was a topnotch fisherman capable of taking any type of fish at any time. It took the bluegill to knock that theory and my ego into a cocked hat.

One day I'd decided to go bluegill fishing. The water temperature that splendid May day was about 68°, just right for spawning gills. I eased down the shoreline casting small wet flies and took the odd fish, nothing large. As I entered a shallow bayou I saw pockets of dish-shaped spawning beds ahead and numerous big bluegills milling around. I kept my silhouette low and cautiously dropped my fly into the midst of an area honeycombed by spawning redds.

A bull, a really nice 10-inch fish, rushed the fly and beat his brothers to it. He struck, the hook was set, and we danced back and forth with the fish pulling at right angles to the line. He'd lay his thick side against the pull of the rod and it was like trying to move a dump truck.

A spirited tussle took place, and the other bluegills scattered to deep water in the bayou. I finally landed the fish, sat down to smoke a cigarette, and waited for the other gills to return. They came back, one by one and cautiously, and finally began their spawning chores again. When I made my presentation again, a repeat performance occurred and I tucked another 10-inch gill in my creel. By this time I was feeling pretty chipper, and that feeling continued the rest of the day as I landed scores of bluegills ranging from 8 to 10½ inches, all bulls decked out in their finest spawning colors. I kept only six fish, the largest, and returned the others. Each fish was the size of my hand or larger.

The next day I returned for another engagement, but this time brought a friend who had seen my catch from the previous day. He had pounded my back and congratulated me, and my ego and my big head were bursting as he told me what a great fisherman I was. Being a modest gent by nature, I agreed with him.

We sneaked in the back way and found the bayou loaded again with big gills. "Watch this," I told him. "I'll show you how to do it and we'll both clean up." I made my first cast while telling myself it would be a piece of cake, same as yesterday.

The wet fly was the same one I'd used the day before, but on this occasion it sent bluegills streaming from the bayou in mass panic. One cast, just one cast, had spooked every bluegill from the area, and they never returned. My buddy wasn't impressed, because he'd taken a day off work to catch fish that disappeared like a magician's rabbit. "Boy, that was really something," he said, in what later proved to be a memorable putdown. Needless to say, he's never offered to go fishing with me again.

From that point on I've never taken bluegills or any other gamefish for granted. I'm like many fishermen—I have my days when everything goes right and others when I'm skunked in grand fashion. Whenever I feel that I know everything about fishing I only have to remember the day the bluegills put the whammy on me.

The best fishermen are those who remember techniques and learn to apply them to the situation at hand. Almost anyone with normal coordination and skill can produce fish at one time or another, but very few anglers can take trophy gamefish on a regular basis and under a variety of circumstances. And no other form of fishing pleasure will place greater demands on skill and know-how than fishing for big bluegills.

During spring months when bluegills are bedding is the best time to take jumbo gills, especially in the South. Five years ago I got into bedding bluegills on Lake Kissimmee in central Florida during the spawning period. My original intent was to dredge up a trophy largemouth, but it was impossible to overlook the trophy bluegills that day. Large areas were pockmarked with the oval depressions of spawning beds. Each nest was guarded by a jumbo male, and they challenged all comers like a heavyweight trying for a shot at Muhammad Ali.

That day a weighted green nymph tied on a No. 10 hook was the deadly fly. I'd cast out, allow the nymph to sink for a slow four-count, and start it back in a series of twitches caused by jigging my rod tip upward or a slow line twitch with my line hand. Most of the time I didn't need the line twitch, because a bodyguard for the nest would nail the intruder like a bouncer at a private party.

One jumbo bream after another followed. I managed to creel an even dozen of the largest bulls before the area went as dead as yesterday's news. The following day was a washout, a total disaster. I took just one demented gill that day, a puny 6-incher. But I'd learned my lesson not to brag up my prowess and simply switched over to bass.

It must be pointed out here that two of my most productive flies (told with tongue firmly planted in cheek) are red wet flies and green nymphs. They have produced good catches *when* I've been the only person fishing and *when* the bulls are bedding. Never have they produced dramatically under other circumstances. This points out the driving need to arm yourself with as many techniques as possible when approaching trophy bluegills in any location. Simply stated, what produces today will probably account for nothing tomorrow. That's called "Richey's First Rule of Bluegill Fishing."

Fishing for bedding bluegills must be done stealthily. These fish are pugnacious in nature but reasonably small compared to other predatory species found in the same water. A shadow, a sloppy cast, or a lure which has become too familiar will spook them badly. They are extremely wary and often appear afraid of their own shadow in shallow water.

One thing I've learned about bedding bluegills is that the larger ones often spawn in deeper water, as deep as 6 or 8 feet. Smaller gills may spawn in water so shallow their backs crease the surface as they mill around a bed. Males protect the bed like a jealous husband and will strike any accurately presented small lure. Knowledge of areas where big gills spawn is an important requirement, and I've learned that if spawning nests of small bream are located in shallow water, the best place to begin the search for big fish is nearby but in deeper water, often near the edge of a dropoff.

Big bluegills are often less receptive to spawning on bright days than on overcast days. There seems to be a direct correlation between fishing success, water depth, and the amount of available sunshine. Bulls may be slightly shallower on overcast days than when it is bright. This is a point to keep in mind, especially in Southern waters.

One year I was fishing Florida's Puzzle Lake, which is part of the St. Johns River system. Shad were on the docket that day but they forgot to show up. We began fishing for spawning bluegills in some of the off-river bayous. My uncle, Rich Millhouse, and one of his friends told me there was no use fishing right then. It was a flat statement that bore investigation. "Why not?" I countered. "We've been taking fish for the last half-hour and it's only been just the last few minutes that the gills have slacked off."

"Look at those range cows," Rich said. "They are lying down, and when the cows lie down, the fishing goes to pot." I'd never heard of this method of determining whether the fish would or would not bite but decided to see if it held a grain of truth.

An hour later the cows lurched to their feet after chewing their cud. Almost on cue the bluegills began striking actively again. I noticed this held true throughout my Florida fishing visit. It's since gotten to be a joke with me when fish quit biting. I've tried to determine whether it has any basis in fact and have been unsuccessful in that regard. Yet I have noticed it to be true in more cases than not.

Another Florida fisherman named Fort Hartley uses his nose to locate spawning bluegills. Honest! We would be trolling along the edge of the lake and he'd stop abruptly, throw his nose in the air like a Walker foxhound puzzling out a cold track, and then we'd take off again. "Nothing there," he'd say as I sat trying to figure out what he was doing.

Fort pulled this several times before he said, "Here we go. There are bluegills here, and lots of them." The water was murky and I could see nothing that gave any indication that bluegills were within 200 miles of that spot. I noticed a slight odor, something vaguely similar to cucumbers, and wondered if Fort had some sliced cukes in his lunch basket. The fishing had been overwhelmingly unspectacular up to that point. Food sounded like a good idea, certainly better than bluegill fishing with a man who sped all over the lake with his nose in the air.

Fort tossed a tiny sponge-rubber spider with rubber legs out near the shoreline, and a dainty "plop" followed. He fixed me with a pointed glare as if he'd been reading my mind. "See?" I saw, but I didn't believe, until he managed to put several jumbo bream into the cooler. I smelled the first two bluegills and again detected an odor reminiscent of cucumbers. He was sniffing out spawning beds.

That sponge-rubber spider was so deadly that day it should be outlawed. Fort and I caught a fair number of big bream as the spider kicked its wiggly imitation legs in grand fashion. We were forced to retire the water-soaked and bedraggled spider and replace it with small popping bugs. It made little difference what we used. When action paled at one spot and the cucumber smell emanated more from the fishbox than the water, we'd pick up and charge around the lake until Fort's sniffer located another bed. Then we'd be back into jumbo gills in short order.

The above trick has to be seen to be believed. I admit I was skeptical, but I've since made up my mind that there is definitely something to it. I personally cannot pursue spawning bream by smell like a hound baying along a scent, but many Southern people can. And it's a joy to watch them perform.

One of the hottest methods of taking large numbers of big bluegills was shown to me by Max Donovan, a gifted fisherman with an amazing ability to figure out almost any fishing problem. He always caught his gills on a fly rod. The trick was, he'd use two flies, a dark black, gray, or green nymph pattern on the end and a dropper fly off a 3-foot leader attached about 4 feet above the nymph. The dropper fly was usually a brightly colored wet fly of red, orange, yellow, and white or pink. It served two purposes. One was to alert the angler to a soft-biting gill on the nymph, and the other was to serve as an active fish producer itself. If he saw the dropper fly switch, he'd set the hook and invariably come up with a nice gill on the lower fly. Many were the times when he'd hook fish on each fly, and it's a ball when two fish sashay off in different directions.

He'd jiggle this two-fly setup at all times, and it would talk to those fish. His procedure was to cast out, allow the nymph to settle 3 or 4 feet on a slack line, and then jiggle the fly back to the canoe in short inch-long upward movements of his rod tip. Each fly would dance a jig during this rod movement, and more often than not, the nymph would catch the most and biggest fish.

Bluegills have small mouths, so fishermen are advised to use fly patterns on the small side. I never use anything larger than No. 10, and No. 12s or No. 14s are often better. This calls for a leader tapered down to 6X or 7X. Hook a bull bluegill on a light tippet and you'll think you've tangled with a much larger fish before it is landed.

Another time I was fishing in southern Georgia during the bluegill spawning period. After checking around country stores I determined that the premier "brim" fisherman in the area was an aged black gentleman named Moses. I was directed to his home and made my request—I wanted to fish big bluegills.

"Suh, we's go cotch some bulls, sure enough. They's a big slough back yonder, and I knows where dey is." "Do we need bait?" I asked. "If so, I have crickets, worms, and flies."

"Lord God A'mighty, suh, we shore enough don't. Why, alls I fish with for dey bulls is a hank of red flanna'." He waved a piece of an old red flannel shirt at me.

He led the way down an overgrown path to the slough. Quail darted across the path and I was yearning for my Remington 1100 instead of my fly rod. I was convinced it was a wild goose chase, a snipe hunt that would leave me holding an empty bag, a far-out chase for the mythical bull bluegill.

Moses stopped at the water and pointed to a nearby area, the bottom dug out and peppered with light-colored oval spawning beds. The critters had dug so many beds that the bottom looked ready for cultivation. "They's heah, suh. Lots of dem bulls," he said.

He fashioned a V-shaped piece of red flannel about 1½ inches long and attached it to a No. 12 hook. "Jes' lay it on top of dem bulls. Twetch it one tahm and dem bulls dey go crazy for dat red flanna'."

I "twetched" it one time and a big bull slammed into it like a

An effective rig for fishing bluegills consists of a nymph on the end of the leader and a wet fly on a dropper.

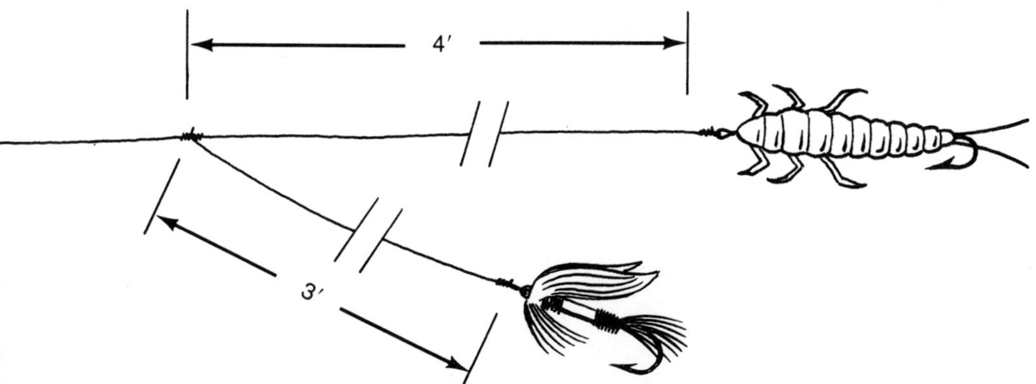

marlin whacking a skipping surface bait. I set the hook and again had the magnificent feeling of a big gill swimming in broad circles, his flat side pulling heavily against my rod.

A minute later I slid the 10-incher onto the bank. "One down, suh, and more to go," Moses intoned near my shoulder. His large eyes were wide in pleasure. He was getting as big a kick from my catching the fish as he would from taking them himself. Moses' trick was paying off.

I caught several more slab-sided gills before Moses began fishing. A true Southern gentleman, he'd given me first crack at his private horde of bull gills. We fished for several hours and between us we half-filled his burlap bag with fine eating fish. When we left the slough Moses had enough fish to feed his large family for several meals. I kept one fish—an 11-incher that now adorns my office wall. Typical of big bulls, it has a pug nose and is hand-size from dorsal fin to belly. A thick slab of a fish, that gill weighed nearly 2 pounds when I caught it. Bluegills of that size are a rarity, and only a handful are taken each year by the millions of anglers that fish bluegill waters.

Another Southern trick I learned, although I detest fishing in this manner, is to use catalpa worms for bait. These horrid creatures must represent dessert to big gills, because they take some of the largest bulls every year from Southern waters.

The trick with catalpa worms is to use the point of the hook and turn them inside out so the gooey stuff is on the outside. They look like a midnight snack for the inmates of hell, but bluegills find them tasty. It makes me half sick just to watch a good old Southern boy wring 'em inside out and place that mess on the hook. It doesn't bother bull gills at all.

The time to fish catalpa worms is as soon as they begin crawling around the trees. Find a catalpa tree near the shoreline and the bluegills will have beat you to it. This is usually shallow-water fishing, and many anglers use a small quill bobber to supply the casting weight. The catalpa-worm-baited hook is cast beneath the overhanging tree and allowed to remain motionless. I've done it only once and found the bobber doesn't remain motionless very long. A bull usually has it as soon as it strikes the water, and when a 1-pound gill makes up his mind to grab something, it gets grabbed, right now.

There are many bluegill fishermen who do not realize that *some* gills will feed at night, and invariably they're the largest fish. Some years ago I went on a bass-fishing spree after dark that lasted most of the summer. The bass seemed to prefer small lures that year. Lures like the smallest Jitterbugs, Hula Poppers, and Tiny River Runts were deadly.

One evening I was fishing alone and heard a racket caused by fish feeding in mid-lake. I thought it might be bass, so quietly rowed within casting distance. I laid my lure out, moved it about 2 feet, and felt a heavy strike. The fish went fairly deep, didn't surface, and it felt like a big bluegill pulling at right angles away from me. I dismissed that thought because of the age-old truism that gills don't feed once the sun goes down.

The fish finally gave up the fight and came to the boat. I was genuinely surprised to note it was a jumbo bluegill—a 10-incher. It had somehow hooked itself on the rear treble, although I still fail to see how it could take that lure in its small mouth. I didn't dwell on the subject too long because other fish were still feeding. I'm an opportunist when the fish are biting.

The boat was again eased within range and I promptly had another hookup. Again the fish felt like a bluegill, as it later proved to be—an exact twin to the first one I'd taken. That bit of action put the fish down for the night, but it had proved that some bluegills will strike after dark and will often attack lures much larger than normal.

I've since run into the same situation one other time. That evening I landed only one bull, but it was an 11-incher, broad and thick and a beautiful fish.

Why the following is true I don't know, but there are days during midsummer when big bluegills are found in the middle of a lake and right on the surface. I've seen this happen several times and can never find any logical reason for this occurrence. There are no fly hatches and the surface water is extremely warm.

The first time it happened I'd been fly fishing the shoreline depths out to about 10 feet. Action was slow, so I began rowing around the lake and casting. Still nothing doing, so I continued rowing and decided to take a shortcut across the lake. My fly line and small nymph were trailing behind in much the same manner as one would troll a spoon.

I was midway across the lake when a fish struck and nearly pulled my rod over the stern. I grabbed it, jabbed the hook home, and was rewarded with the heavy pull of a big bluegill. We fought a spirited battle in mid-lake and I landed a beautiful 9-incher.

PLUGS

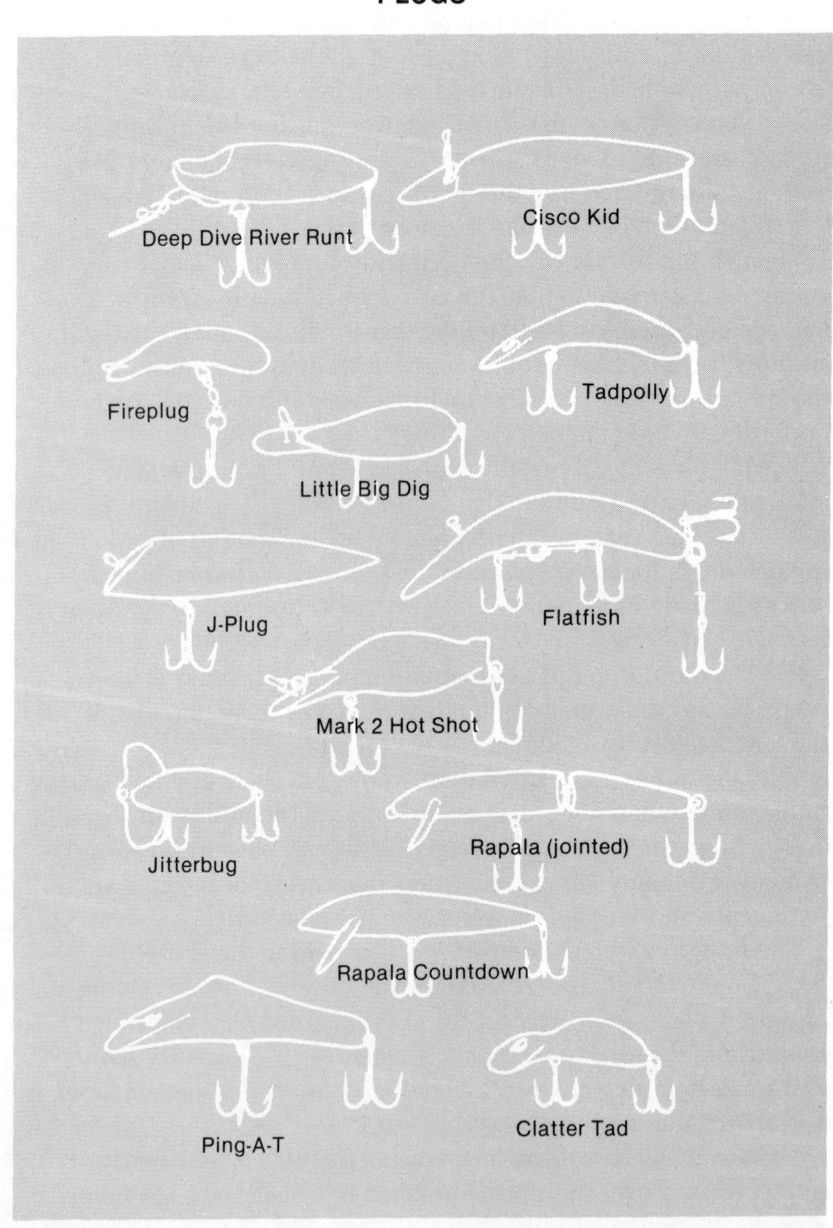

Deep Dive River Runt
Cisco Kid
Fireplug
Tadpolly
Little Big Dig
J-Plug
Flatfish
Mark 2 Hot Shot
Jitterbug
Rapala (jointed)
Rapala Countdown
Ping-A-T
Clatter Tad

JITTERBUG

SPOONS AND SPINNERS

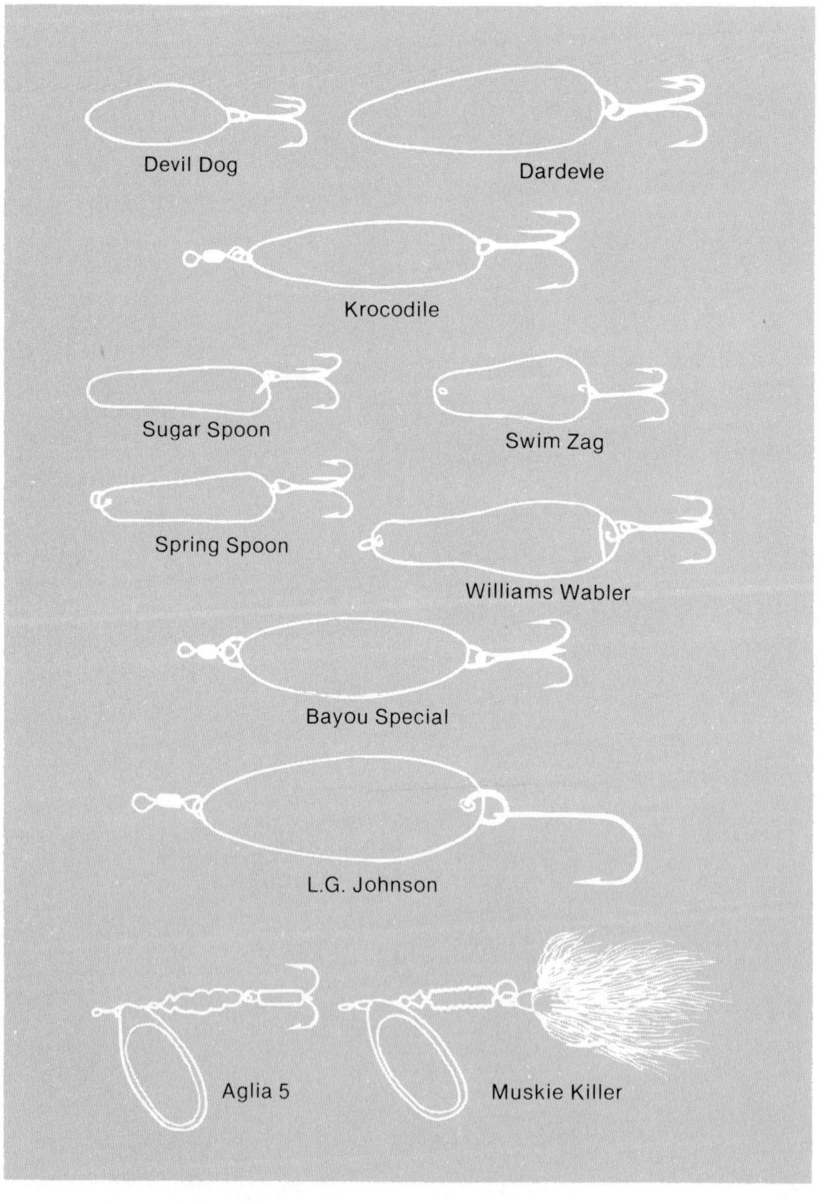

Mepps
AGLIA
5

JIGS

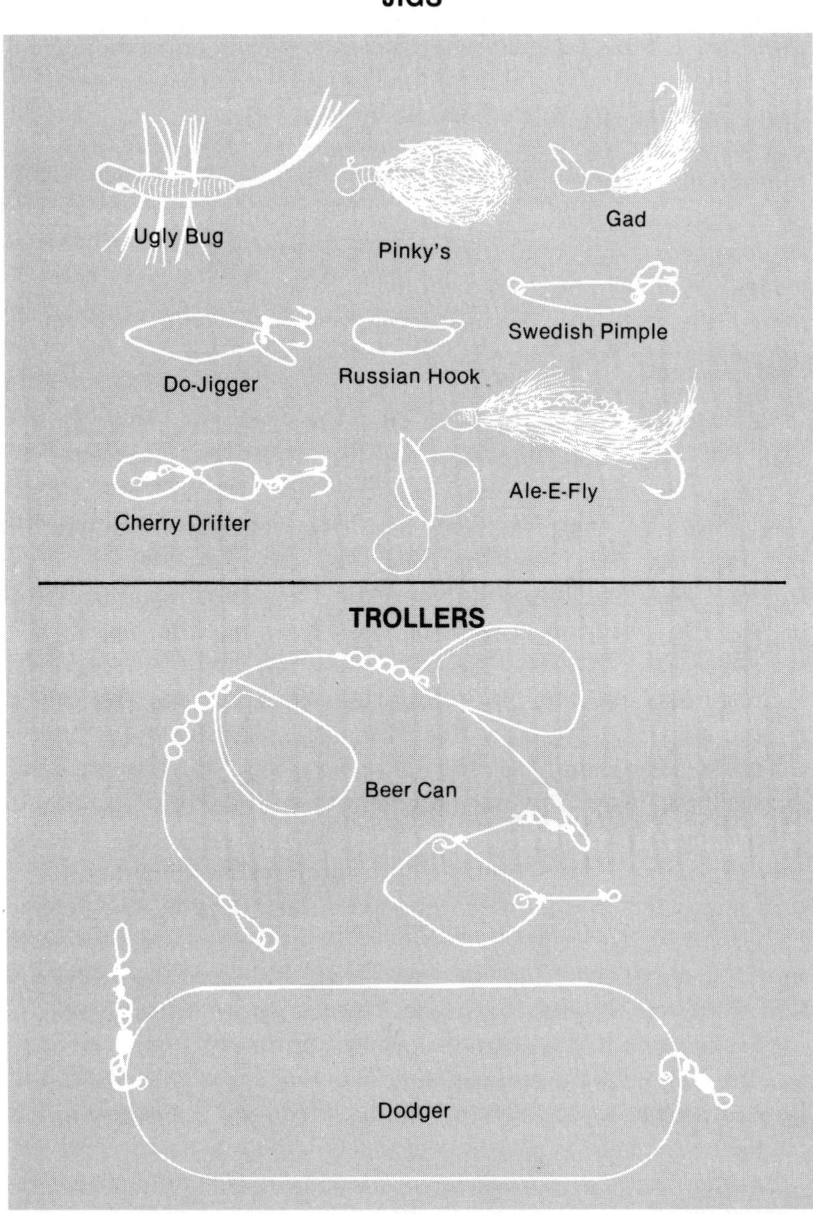
Ugly Bug
Pinky's
Gad
Swedish Pimple
Do-Jigger
Russian Hook
Cherry Drifter
Ale-E-Fly
TROLLERS
Beer Can
Dodger

I rinsed the slime off the nymph (bluegills do not like flies matted down with mucus from other fish) and made another path through the same area. Sure enough, I'd hooked another fish and he was also landed. Repeated casts to the area would not take a fish, but the trolled nymph, as unlikely as it sounds, produced still a third fish. I managed to land five fish in that manner before they quit striking. My smallest was 8 inches and the largest just a hair over 10 inches. All trophy bluegills from any lake.

A fisherman might spend a lifetime on good waters and never run into this situation, but I feel it probably happens much more often than many anglers realize. Never be afraid to troll a fly during summer months; it could lead to some exciting fishing.

I know one fisherman who chums his bluegills as ocean anglers chum in large sharks. The primary difference is that he uses bread or small mealworms instead of ground-up fish and blood. He stands at the end of his dock and begins crumbling up dried slices of white bread, and tosses in the small worms.The bulls lie back and watch the chum until it begins drifting downward in the water.

Then, and only then, will he bait up with a piece of bread or a mealworm on a small hook and "cast his bread upon the waters." If the chum has started a feeding frenzy, which it usually does, he can land several big bluegills before they regain their caution. It's a trick worth remembering when bulls are edgy and reluctant to strike.

One of the finest bull bluegill lures I've found for deep-water fishing is a small Shyster or No. O Mepps Aglia spinner. I remove the treble hook and replace it with a long-shank No. 10 single hook. Add half an angleworm (not a nightcrawler) and allow it to trail out behind the spinner.

When bulls are deep, from 8 to 15 feet in depth, cast out past their suspected holding spot along the deep-water edge of a weed-bed or dropoff and begin the retrieve once it has sunk to the desired level. I generally count to four very slowly and begin the retrieve. If that doesn't work, count to five, and then to six on consecutive casts. Once you locate the proper depth and sinking time needed you'll have to fish the spinner slow. The tiny spinner blade should be barely turning over. The throb of the blade and the dainty morsel on the hook is as deadly as arsenic on big gills.

Another trick you can add to your repertoire is to use one or two tiny white Uncle Josh fly-rod flickers. These wee bits of porkrind can produce scores of strikes when added to a tiny spinner. They waver in the water and have a tantalizing action.

A word of caution: Big bluegills are very wary and difficult to approach. If you're not willing to fish with light line, surely nothing over 4-pound test, you'd best forget about taking trophy gills. They are slow, deliberate feeders in deep water and will follow a lure for some distance before making up their minds to strike. A heavy leader or line will turn them away from any well-presented lure or bait. Keep it light and enjoy the razzle-dazzle fight of a big bream.

When my twin brother George and I were youngsters my parents owned a cottage on a southern Michigan lake. It held massive weedbeds during the summer months and was inhabited by large bluegills. The trick was to catch them, and that was easier said than done for two pre-teenagers.

A local told us that live crickets were the ticket for the big gills. We would have to fish them deep, and our reward would be the "deepwater roach," as the old-timers then called them.

The one thing that sticks in my mind about that fishing thirty years ago was we had to fish in 20 feet of water. The old-timers showed us how to hook the live crickets under the shell on top, which didn't kill them when done cautiously. Cane poles made this fishing slightly simpler, and we set our bobbers near the tip of our poles so we'd be fishing in 16 or 18 feet of water. Our baits were just a couple feet off bottom. A tiny split shot was sufficient to take the cricket down into the domain of bull bluegills.

A small bobber was used to indicate a feeding gill. It took some doing to swing a big bream up from the depths with that much line out, but we'd make sure the fish was hooked well and then bring them in hand over hand. We'd slide our cane poles across the gunwales of the boat until we could reach the line and then put the fetch on them. It may have been crude fishing by today's standards, but it's amazing how many people still enjoy this type of fishing. Oh, the size of those gorgeous beauties! Each would weigh about a pound, and they were absolutely beautiful fish. I still remember those days with vivid clarity, when the fish would bite eagerly and all the problems of the world seemed much smaller and farther away.

There are times during midsummer when bluegills take to the depths and hold near bottom. They often pick flat hard-bottomed areas near weedbeds. I once owned a business and dealt with a fellow named Bill. I never learned his last name, but I learned he knew how to catch bulls during the hot summer months. He practiced a method of fishing called the "bottom crawl." His success with jumbo gills was something that bordered on being unbelievable.

Bill fished big deep-water bluegills the same way some people fish walleyes. The basic difference was his bait. He would rig up with a Lindy rig and a long-shank No. 12 single hook. To this he would add the tail half of an angleworm. He added a tiny cork or Dylite bobber about 12 inches above the hook. Above his swivel he used a ⅛-ounce walking slip sinker. The sinker would take it down and the wee bobber would hold his bait a few inches off the bottom.

Bill's technique was to fish on dead-calm days, cast as far away from his boat as possible, and let the sinker and bait fall to the floor of the lake. He allowed it to sit motionless for two or three minutes after casting and then would slowly inch it back to the boat. He told me that it often took ten to fifteen minutes to fish out each cast. If that was unproductive he'd cast again at a 90-degree angle to his first presentation.

In this manner Bill fanned out casts and worked every inch of the water within casting distance of his boat. "Bottom crawling is an excellent means of locating large concentrations of bulls. Midsummer bluegills often congregate in one small area, and they can be difficult to locate. Once you've found them it isn't difficult to creel a limit of lunker gills, like these," he said, after showing me fifteen hand-sized bluegills he'd just taken.

He also told me that if one area doesn't produce, move up or down the lake and relocate. It may take several moves before the fish are located, but it's one of the deadliest techniques I know of to find and catch platter-sized bluegills.

I know of no other gamefish as difficult to take in trophy sizes as bull bluegills. They represent a distinct challenge to fishermen, and that quality endears them to me.

15 CRAPPIES

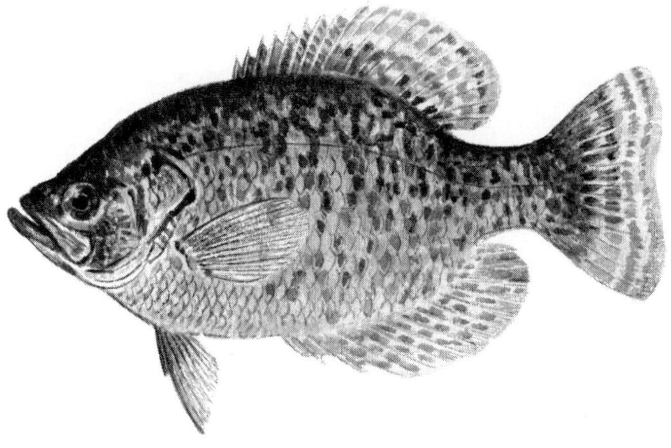

The crappie consists of two subspecies, the white crappie and black crappie. They both provide a wealth of fishing pleasures for young and old fishermen alike. It's probably a toss-up whether the bluegill or the crappie is more instrumental in hooking anglers on fishing.

Crappies are not noted for their fighting abilities nearly as much as other sunfish, but no one can doubt their eating qualities. As a table fish, they are hard to beat.

Black and white crappies are often found in the same waters, but their preferences are notably different. Black crappies are found in clear weedy lakes or rivers and cannot stand as much turbidity as the white crappie. Blacks are more bottom-oriented than whites, and this is an advantage for fishermen. White crappies prefer silty lakes or rivers over cleaner waters, and these gamefish are often found in many Southern reservoirs. Both gamefish feed avidly on smaller fish, especially minnows.

White crappies are silver or silvery-olive on the sides, with an olive-green cast to the back. The white is more elongated than the black and has six spines in the dorsal and anal fins. The spots along the sides are arranged in seven to nine vertical bars, and it has eight or nine vertical dark bands along the sides.

The black crappie has a high-arched back. The sides have dark irregular markings. Because of this mottling, many anglers call it a calico bass. It has a flattened appearance with silvery sides blending into an olive or near-black back. The spots are scattered over the sides and the dorsal, anal, and caudal fins. It has six anal spines and seven or eight dorsal spines, an easy clue to remember when trying to determine its identity.

A characteristic which endears crappies to fishermen is their tendency to school. Whites school in huge pods, while blacks tend to gather in smaller groups, but if you catch one fish of either species, the chances are good others are nearby.

Both species of crappies are widespread in distribution. The white seems more numerous in Southern states, but introduction of both fish has been made in numerous states, including the Northwest.

There is one very important point anglers should realize about crappies: They are never found very far from some type of heavy cover. It seems to be an instinctive need for these gamefish. Cover may be weeds, sunken cribs, brushpiles, clumps of evergreen boughs wired together and sunk when ice goes out, reeds, sunken treetops, or other thick cover.

In sort of a contradictory manner I'll also state that at some periods, especially during midsummer, crappies will forsake their beloved brushy cover and suspend in the middle of a lake, far from any cover. This often happens when the water warms sufficiently to drive minnows to deep water. When baitfish head out, the crappies tag along in order to stay close to their food supply.

There's a small Michigan lake I know of where a since departed fisherman (bless his soul) sank almost one acre of brush the year before his death. Those tree limbs and brushpiles are still there and were sunk for a reason—to attract schools of crappies. They lie in 8 feet of water and extend upward for 3 feet. The lake is clear and cool and the crappies use that area all year.

JIGGING

Although small minnows would probably work on this lake, I hate carting them around and trying to keep 'em alive long enough to use. Instead I have switched to very small jigs, lures in the ⅛- or 1/16-ounce class, and have found them equally effective. When crappies start biting I would rather be catching them than trying to catch minnows and impale them on my hook. It's just too slow, and crappie fishermen have learned to take advantage of hot fish while it lasts.

Crappies have large tender mouths, so I use fairly small lures which have less of a tendency to rip out while I'm playing the fish. Typical of the lures I'll use for jigging over brushpiles are Burke's Wig-Wag Jig, Wig-Wag Jig Spinner, and Wig-Wag Minno-Spins, and Gapen's Ugly Beetle or Pinky jigs. I'm a firm believer in yellow, white, or pink jigs for crappies, although I've taken many fish on black, green, or brown lures. Fishermen are advised to carry plenty of lures when fishing in the brush because the loss ratio is high.

I like to anchor along the edge of a submerged brushpile and jig straight up and down beneath the boat. If the fish are in a good mood they will strike avidly every time the jig is lowered to them. The best technique I've found is to make very short jigs with frequent short pauses. This gives the lure a sharp tantalizing up-and-down movement with plenty of time for the fish to strike.

The jig should be bouncing up and down in the brush to attain its maximum effectiveness. This is the primary reason why so many lures are lost, although a jumbo crappie can pop your line if it is light enough. I generally use a maximum of 4-pound mono for all crappie fishing.

There are many days when the added flash of a spinner blade will up the number of strikes. If the fish are sluggish and reluctant to bite, switch to the Wig-Wag Jig Spinner and ease back away from the brushpile and cast in to it. A swimming lure will occasionally produce better than one jigged up and down.

Crappie jigs are much more versatile than many believe. Several times I've made excellent catches by trolling these lures. It requires some foresight and judicious rod-tip action, but a trolled jig can often turn the trick when other techniques fail, especially when the fish are suspended in midsummer.

If fish cannot be found in the normal locations near some type of cover, and the weather has been very warm, it's worth checking deeper water. Crappies will usually suspend from 12 to 20 feet down, and this calls for trolling tactics to locate them.

Wherever legal, attach two jigs to one line, one on a dropper about 3 feet above the bottom lure. The lower jig should be slightly heavier, about ¼ ounce, while the dropper jig can weigh about 1/16 or ⅛ ounce. Use a very slow forward trolling speed, or backtroll to cut the speed even more. Lower the jigs to 12 to 14 feet and begin trolling. Give the rod tip a sharp upward 6-inch jig every few seconds.

Leonard Thomas works the jig out of a black crappie taken from Georgian Bay. Jigging near a submerged brushpile is productive for big crappies.

This will cause both jigs to dart and dance on the tight line. It may take an hour or two of this strategy but you'll eventually locate the fish. Once they are found, do not troll on by but circle around immediately and make another pass through the crappies. If they stay in the same location and do not spook the fish you can anchor and cast more effectively.

SPINNER-FLY COMBOS

One of the deadliest rigs I know for jumbo crappies is a small silver or brass spinner followed by a No. 6 or No. 8 red, yellow, or white fly. The spinner-fly combination brings out the rough-house antics of the largest crappies in the area. The overall size of this combination is such that only big fish pick on it. The total length may be 3 inches, much larger than many anglers are used to fishing crappie with.

I prefer casting the spinner-fly combination, although it works well for trolling if weighted. The rig should be cast out and allowed to sink slowly with spinner blade flashing. Many times the crappie will pick it up on the downdrift and your only indication of a strike will be more rapid sinking of the line or a switch in the line descent.

The lure should be fished slowly with occasional pauses to allow it to sink again. A crappie will often strike just as you begin the retrieve.

This rig is versatile, and I've taken a number of black and white crappies by jigging it up and down directly beneath the boat.

LANTERN FISHING

One of the methods I've found for taking large numbers of big crappies from Northern and Southern impoundments is lantern fishing. The basic method was discussed in the chapter on rainbow trout, but it also pays off with jumbo crappies. The boat should be rigged out in the same manner, but the lures and baits are different.

Small shiner minnows can be fished on a "crappie spreader," a wire affair with two arms which hold the minnow-baited hooks away from each other. A small bell sinker fastens to the bottom end and takes the minnows down near bottom.

Crappies are indifferent about how minnows are hooked. I've personally had good success hooking them through both lips, but other variations include hooking through both eyes, under the dorsal fin, and back near the vent. The important thing is to use lively minnows; floaters and bloaters are useless for this type of fishing.

After the lanterns are attached to the gunwales it will take several minutes for the minnows to arrive. The crappies are never far from their food source and they feed actively after dark. Once the panfish begin feeding on the light-attracted minnows, they will usually be at depths of less than 10 feet.

Bait up the crappie spreader and lower it over the side, but try to keep it at about 6 or 8 feet. The crappie will spot the wiggling shiner minnows, and you'll probably have two fish on in less time than it takes to tell about it.

Although I really do not like minnow fishing for panfish, I've found this is a relaxing nighttime sport, at least until a crappie school moves in under the boat. And then the action gets as fast-paced as any I've experienced.

Another deadly bait for jumbo crappies is a variation of the throat-latch bait described for walleyes. I'll catch the first crappie, make a small cut through the skin behind the head and another along the dorsal fin, and then peel back the flap of skin. It is easy then to remove a piece of flesh about 1½ to 2 inches in length and half as wide.

Attach a single No. 6 or No. 8 hook to a small June Bug spinner or any other small spinner and you're in business. I prefer fishing this rig very slow and creep it along bottom or over brushpiles. The effect fish flesh has on other crappies is unbelievable. They seem to shoulder one another aside to waylay the spinner and cut bait. It's a trick worth trying whenever crappie action slows down.

One year I was fishing in Georgian Bay, Ontario, for walleyes. This took place at night and left little to do during the day. I checked with the lodge owner and he informed me that large numbers of jumbo crappies had been taken the previous day by two visiting fishermen. He pointed out their general fishing area and I left in search of them.

I found the two busily catching another load of big "specks," as they called the black crappies. Their lure was simple to the extreme but very effective. It was a 1/32-ounce yellow marabou Doll fly fished 2 feet beneath a tiny bobber.

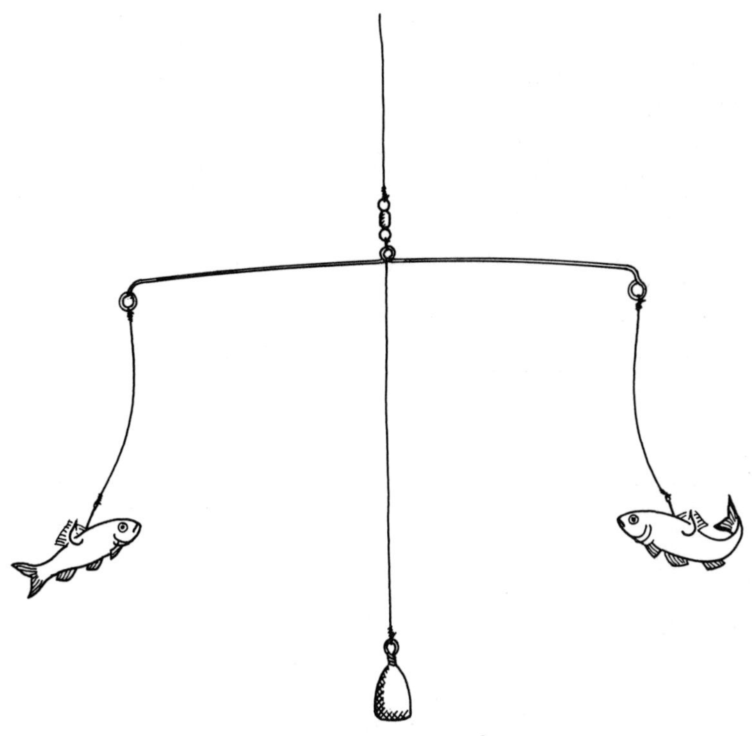

Another method of taking big crappies, especially in impoundments, is to use a "crappie spreader" at night baited with lively minnows.

That portion of Georgian Bay is a maze of shallow water and weeds with tiny avenues of open water little more than 4 feet deep between the weedbeds. They would find an opening in the weeds and cast the bobber and Doll fly into open water and retrieve it slowly with tiny twitches. Each time they gave the Doll fly action a crappie would arrow out from under the weed cover and nail the tiny jig. They had twenty of the largest crappies I've ever seen. Their technique combined a knowledge of crappie habitat (cover) and their willingness to strike small jigs. Some of those specks were in the 2-pound class.

TROLLING

Don Ronn, owner of Bay Shore Resort and Tackle in Gladstone, Mich., once showed me how to take big crappies from Little Bay De

Noc, a fertile bay extending in off northern Lake Michigan. Like most crappie lures, his was simple and very productive.

"Crappie like flashing spinner blades and they move around a great deal in this water, so I prefer trolling over still-fishing, at least until I begin catching fish. Trolling enables me to pinpoint schools of fish. I've learned that a silver No. 0 or No. 1 Mepps Aglia, without bucktail, is the best lure," he said.

He also told me that no weight is needed and the spinner will sink about 2 feet on a slow troll. "Most of our weedbeds or rock-piles are fairly shallow, and the crappies lie just over or alongside this cover. The spinner will usually pass just over their heads."

Don trolls a zigzag pattern over the tops of these weedbeds or rockpiles, and I watched him take several fish that would rate as a trophy in anyone's book. Some of these fish were giant slabs, each weighing well over a pound and some up to 2 pounds. The only way Don varies from this basic trolling pattern is to give his rod tip a yank now and then to vary the action of the spinner. No one who has seen Don's crappie stringers can dispute that this is an effective fish-finding method.

After Don pinpoints a school of crappies he will cut his engine and begin casting with the same lure. He takes almost as many fish in this manner as with trolling.

FLY FISHING

Small yellow or white wet flies tied with generous amounts of tinsel will create havoc among crappies when the fish are near the surface. I've fished several lakes where reeds, weedbeds, or brush-piles are within easy casting distance of shore. During spring months the fish will work in close and a wading flycaster can get in his innings.

I prefer using a WF6F line with a Heddon Graphite rod. A small reel balanced for the rod and a 7½-foot leader tapered down to 4X is sufficient for crappies. Make casts as long as necessary and allow the flies to sink slowly. Twitch them back with vertical jiggles of the rod or by retrieving the line in 1-inch pulls. Frequent pauses will often trigger strikes as the fly sinks slowly.

I carry two types of flies for crappies, weighted and unweighted. The unweighted variety works best much of the time, but there are days when the fish are deeper and weighted flies are more productive. I use a countdown method to judge sinking time by slowly counting "One hundred, two hundred, three hundred," etc. Fish out a cast at one sinking time and if nothing happens, allow slightly more time for the lure to sink. Sooner or later it will pay off with the proper combination. Just remember how long you've counted before the retrieve began.

A big crappie is lipped from the water after it struck a trolled Mepps #2 spinner. The flashing spinner blade gives a good imitation of a minnow.

16

YELLOW PERCH

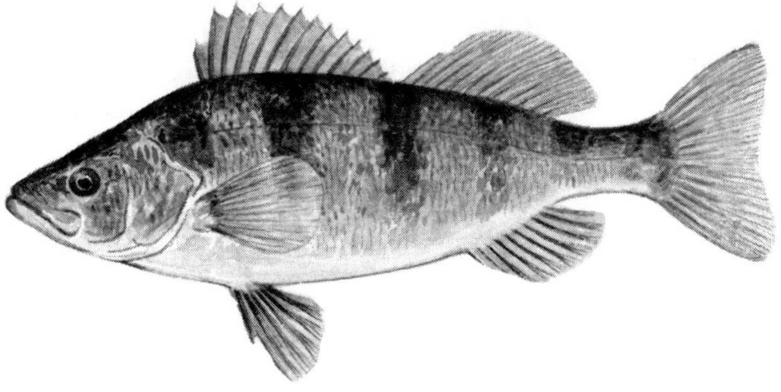

Although the bluegill may be considered a superior fighter on the end of a rod, and more than capable of holding its own as a table fish, the yellow perch attracts millions of anglers yearly when big runs begin simply because they are a schooling fish and are easily caught. This allows anglers to fill large coolers with this fine-eating panfish. In some states, such as Michigan, there is no limit of perch taken from Great Lakes waters and it's possible to catch 300 or more in one day's fishing. Gutted and gilled, or filleted, this represents a tremendous amount of food for any family.

The yellow perch is a rather long fish with a slightly hump-backed look. Both dorsal fins are separated, and it has a slightly forked tail. Color will vary slightly from one area to another, but the belly is usually white and the sides have a golden-yellow color and an olive-colored back. Six to eight dark vertical bands extend from the back down past the lateral line. The forward fins are usually an orangish-red color, while the tail is an olive green. I've seen some Great Lakes perch taken from deep water which were nearly white or pearl-colored. The mouth is fairly large for the size of the fish and it will strike larger lures or minnows than most other panfish, with the exception of crappies.

Perch are primarily lake fish, although they are occasionally found in rivers or streams at times other than during the spawning season. They are abundant throughout the Great Lakes states, in both inland lakes and the Great Lakes, and their range extends from Nova Scotia south to South Carolina and west through Missouri. Plantings of this gamefish have introduced it into many Western states where it has since taken hold and appears to be flourishing.

Yellow perch are wanderers; they will feed actively in one area for up to an hour or two and then move off in search of more food. The key to consistent catches is to keep trying new locations until a school of perch is located. I've seen times when the better part of a day was spent fishing new areas with little success. When the fish were located, it was fast and furious fishing with every man for himself. Perch feed with a passion and then leave with little warning, and the angler must program himself to take advantage of every second. Wasted seconds mean wasted fishing time and fewer fish.

I've seen fishermen get into schools of perch and hook one on every cast. The fish weren't stringered or dropped into a live basket or cooler; the fishermen simply dropped them onto the floor of the boat and began fishing again. They figured that the perch mess could be cleaned up once the fish departed.

CRAYFISH AND MINNOWS

Some of the fastest perch fishing I've encountered was on Captain Donny Nichols' boat out of South Haven, Mich. He fishes southern Lake Michigan during the prime months of July and August when massive schools of perch move in on various nearby rockpiles to feed. The fish work through the rocks in search of crayfish. Nichols figured he'd offer them just what they wanted; he scouted around until he found a load of crayfish, enough to last him through the season.

He keeps his crayfish in a live well and every angler on his charter boat has a nearby supply. They fish with "perch spreaders" similar to those used for crappies, and one crayfish is impaled on each of the two hooks and lowered to the bottom. It's important to keep a tight line and to fish within inches of bottom; yellow perch are bottom-oriented fish. One or two light pecks at the bait is the signal to set the hook and begin the perch's long journey to the frying pan. Two fish at a time are common, and it's a big thrill to hook two jumbos at once.

The first time I tried this sport with Donny, my crayfish had just settled to bottom and I felt a light tap. I set the hook and then waited for a moment. Donny was standing near my elbow, grinning. "You've done this before, I see," he said as I set the hook again and brought up two squirming 12-inch perch. He was referring to my hooking one fish and then waiting an instant before bringing it up. This enables the second crayfish to tempt another perch and allows the fisherman to take his fish two at a time. "Yup," I said, like Gary Cooper, "I've done this before."

The battle of a yellow perch isn't spectacular when compared to larger gamefish, but it is a satisfying sport. When two slab-sided perch take hold and begin pulling in opposite directions, you've got a pint-sized battle for a minute before each can be landed.

Six of us fished that day for four hours and landed just over 500 yellow perch. The largest was a pot-gutted female 15 inches long which would be a trophy yellow perch anywhere.

One thing about perch fishing is that it's difficult to fish just for trophies; there are so many smaller perch in the school that trying to single out just the largest is difficult if not impossible. The only way to catch a trophy perch is to do as we did on Lake Michigan and catch hundreds of these fish for just one wallhanger. It may sound like a waste of fish, but it isn't; the smaller perch are far better eating than trophy specimens (this generally holds true with all gamefish) and every fish taken can be utilized for food. Perch fishing by the numbers is not wasteful but usually an act of conservation, because these fish tend to overpopulate an area in short order.

In open-water areas, minnows can be fished in the same manner as crayfish, and in certain locales a lively 2-inch shiner minnow is more productive. Crayfish are deadly only if the area contains rockpiles where these crustaceans are found.

Perch fishing is a highly contagious fever which spreads like wildfire whenever the word goes out that the perch run is on. Men, women, and children leave school, work, or their homes to cash in on this bonanza of fishing activity. The spawning run is one time when an angler stands his best chance of taking a trophy perch. The females are generally the largest of the species, and they are heavily laden with roe when these runs occur.

Perch runs take place during spring months as the fish head up tributary streams to drop their eggs. It becomes an annual attraction, and large numbers of this prolific gamefish are taken. With luck, one may be a trophy specimen.

When the runs are on, nothing can beat a minnow fished near bottom. The fish often concentrate in deeper holes or near brushpiles just before spawning, and this is where most people fish. It's a gregarious type of sport, and elbow-to-elbow fishing is common at the better locations, but no one takes offense when another angler squirms in nearby. It is just part of the routine and expected from other fishermen.

JIGGING

Some squeamish anglers will dislike the following advice, but one of the best baits for big yellow perch is an eyeball from a smaller member of the tribe. The first time a fisherman showed me this trick I thought I'd heave, but the 10-to-13-inch open-water perch he caught by adding a perch eye to his jig left little room for a queasy feeling. The perch should be killed with a sharp rap behind the eyes before an eye is removed. Insert the eyeball on the point of a lure such as Best's Russian Hook and begin jigging.

Jigging with these thin-metal spoons requires a certain feel, and I know of no better way to practice than to jig next to the boat and see how it reacts to rod movement. Once you've satisfied yourself that the lure is working properly, lower it to bottom and then raise it back up an inch or two. Begin jigging with short 2- or 3-inch upward strokes of the rod tip and allow it to flutter back down on a slack line.

If this doesn't work, try raising it a foot off bottom and repeat the jigging maneuver. The next step is to lower it back to the bottom and slowly jig it upward an inch at a time for 2 or 3 feet before allowing it to shimmy back down. This latter method is one of the best for waylaying big perch. They hit it like a runaway truck and are usually hooked solid.

Another technique that works when all else fails (if there are perch around) is to "shiver" it in one location. Try moving the lure an inch or two sideways without raising it in the water. It's almost impossible to do, but it gives the lure and perch eye a shivering motion that is tempting to yellowbellies.

The thing to remember about jigging for open-water yellow perch is to keep the lure moving at all times. Perch will seldom strike a motionless lure or bait unless it is alive.

The perch eye and Russian Hook combination is an oddball method that produces when other techniques fall on their prat. It's a handy one to consider whenever the action slows down or the fish quit biting.

This brings us to another point: If the perch are hitting well and suddenly the action falls off, the fish have probably either spooked or simply followed their food source to another area. Whenever I hook a perch I try to determine in which direction the hooked fish tries to swim, and that is usually the direction the school has taken. If they leave, move off in that direction 50 or 100 yards and many times they can be relocated. It doesn't always work but it does on enough occasions to make it worthwhile.

SPOONS AND SPINNERS

Some of the nicest perch I've taken have fallen to lures used for smallmouth bass. One time I was fishing the Bass Islands area of Lake Erie near Toledo. We'd made the run in my 20-foot Lund from Port Clinton and arrived in plenty of time to cast the shoals near Middle Bass Island.

Smallmouth bass and walleye were our goals, but it was a pleasant summer day and we were casting small Lau Lures and Jig-a-Do streamers, each an excellent lure for both species. The action was less than spectacular, but seldom did twenty minutes go by without hooking a nice fish.

Kay and I fished on, and suddenly I had a strike totally unlike the solid authoritative strike of a smallie or the stop-right-now take of a husky walleye. The fish was smaller but tussled briefly but well before I led it to the boat. A husky yellowbelly came up and was added to the cooler. Two minutes later Kay added a whopping 14-incher, a big female with a protruding stomach full of small minnows.

We fished that school of perch for an hour and boated nearly fifty jumbo perch; the smallest was a husky 8-incher. Kay's big one took the honors that day, but we lost two fish we felt were larger.

Halfway through that siege with the perch I switched over to an Eppinger Devle Dog, a smaller version of the famous Dardevle. I would cast it out, allow it to sink near bottom along the edge of the shoal, and limp it slowly back to the boat. Those fish didn't seem to care what we threw their way as long as it had action aplenty and some flash.

Another technique that often works for larger perch is to troll a silver willowleaf spinner about 6 inches ahead of a lip-hooked minnow. Slow speeds are needed. This method of fishing can be expanded to casting, although the force needed to cast often tears minnows off the hook.

Use a No. 4 or No. 6 long-shank hook and insert the point through both lips of the minnow and begin trolling. I like to work the edges of weedbeds or dropoffs. Although perch are a bottom-oriented fish they will come up several feet for this combination when it is trolled over their heads.

They are attracted by the fluttering action of the willowleaf spinner, and then they follow up to attack the trailing minnow. This method works best during summer and fall months. After you've taken the first fish, circle and make another quick pass through the same area. Many times you can locate a school of yellow perch and the action will be hectic until the fish spook from the sounds of the boat and motor. Some fishermen row, making less noise, and catch larger numbers of perch.

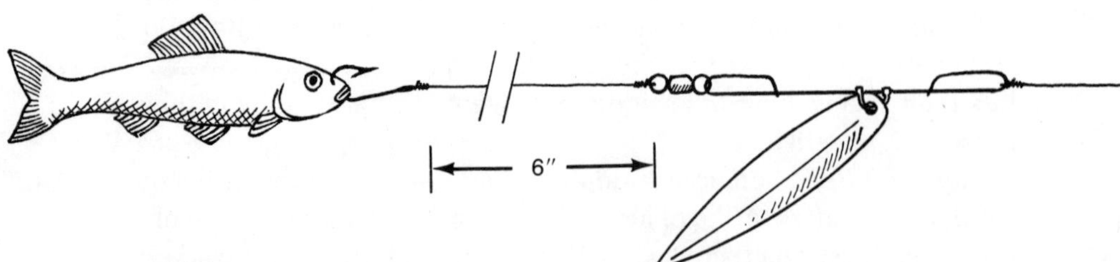

A simple trolling rig that often produces large yellow perch consists of a No. 4 or No. 6 long-shanked hook baited with a minnow behind a willowleaf spinner.

ICEFISHING

Icefishing is the premier way to catch large amounts of yellow perch. The fish seem to travel and feed in more compact schools, and it's possible to take some truly large specimens through the ice.

As with perch fishing during any other season, the ice angler must prospect for his fish. Too many fishermen stay firmly rooted to one spot and hope the perch will come to them, but this seldom happens. Consistency in taking yellowbellies through the ice means going after them and boring numerous holes before a concentration of fish is found.

I use a Jiffy power auger to drill holes, because we often have from 12 to 24 inches of ice during winter months in my neck of the woods, and that means backbreaking labor with a hand auger or a spud. A good place to drill your first holes is within 100 yards of other anglers if they are catching fish.

Bore two or three holes at once, at least 20 yards apart. This should do for about an hour.

Some icefishermen prefer minnows for icefishing, but I've found the action can be faster when Russian Hooks are used. The perch eye or an anise-flavored artificial white grub is plenty of bait for use with jigging spoons. A tiny piece of rubber inner tube is cut and placed onto the hook after the perch eye to hold it firmly in position.

Lower the lure and bait to the bottom and follow the same jigging instructions mentioned earlier in this chapter. The important thing is to keep it moving at all times.

I try to position my ice holes over 6 to 20 feet of water, depending on the season. Early in the icefishing season and again just before ice-out the fish usually are in shallow water. During midwinter they often hole up and feed in 15 to 20 feet of water, and these areas are frequently shared with smelt, a welcome treat with a batch of fresh-cooked perch.

I'll work the entire gamut of jigging movements in one hole and fish hard for fifteen minutes. If by that time I haven't taken any fish I'll move to one of the other nearby holes and repeat the procedure.

If an hour passes and I haven't taken any fish I'll pick up my equipment and move at least 100 yards in an attempt to locate the fish. It may take a series of moves such as this before a perch school is found.

When you locate the fish, and they begin biting, you can take a tip from Michigan's Russian immigrants who once fished for the market. They jig with two lines in one ice hole (if legal in your state). This has to be the deadliest icefishing method I've seen. These expert fishermen hook one perch and then continue jigging with the other rod until another fish is hooked.

Then they lift the first fish out and quickly lower the lure into the water. This lure is jigged until a fish is barbed and then the other fish is landed.

Thc key to this amazing technique is that perch often hover around another hooked fish, and doubles are common. The important thing is to keep that school of fish located directly under you as long as possible. As long as one fish is on and fighting, others will stick around to see what is going on. It sounds farfetched, but anytime you see an angler with two lines in one hole, you're looking at an expert perch fisherman.

The first time I watched this trick performed on yellow perch I wondered how they kept their lines from tangling. One elderly gentleman told me in broken English, "The perch always move away from each other when hooked. If two perch are hooked at once they usually head in opposite directions and very rarely do they tangle my lines.

"Look at this," he said. "Both fish are hooked and tugging in opposite directions." One fish was heading north and the other was southbound and going nowhere. He lifted one out, lowered the line after unhooking the perch, and quickly had another doubleheader. It was the most mystifying technique I've ever seen.

Perch are one of our most prolific gamefish, and it is difficult to seek just trophy specimens. Many times you'll have to catch hundreds of perch for each trophy, but few other angling sports allow a fisherman the opportunity to fill the freezer with tasty fish and still offer him a chance at a lunker. But perch fishing is geared to the lover of fast-paced action, fine-tasting white meat sizzling in a hot pan, and the occasional 12-to-15-inch perch for the wall.

17

OTHER PANFISH

When fishermen think of panfish they automatically think of bluegills, crappies, and yellow perch. Often overlooked are other members of the panfish group such as rock bass, warmouth bass, sunfish, white bass, and yellow bass. Each has its habits and peculiarities, and for each there are specialized fishing techniques that produce best.

ROCK BASS

The rock bass is widespread in North America. It shows a definite trend toward the typical sunfish shape, with a relatively flattened appearance with a large mouth and a jaw hinge extending back past the middle of a large eye; a dark spot on the gill cover; and a greenish-olive color with a tinge of brass or bronze. Small dark spots are located in lines along the body. It has a continuous dorsal fin and a red-colored iris in the eye.

Rockies often frequent the same waters as smallmouth bass. They like clean lakes and streams and prefer hard-bottomed waters. Look for rock bass near shallow waters, rocky dropoffs, shoals, underwater brush, submerged tree stumps, and brushpiles.

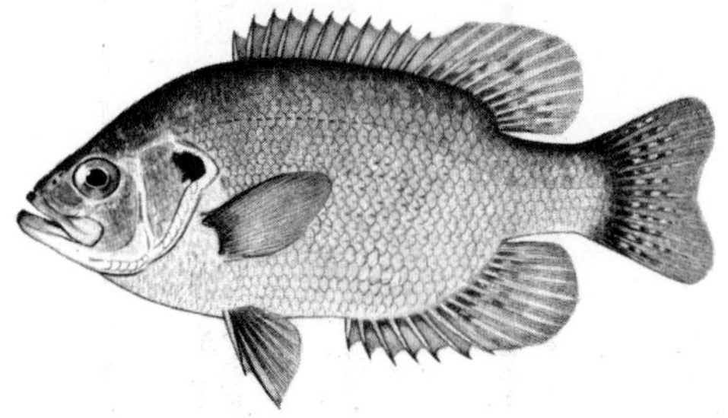

Some of the finest rock bass fishing I've had was after dark when smallmouth bass were my quarry. I would cast a small Creek Chub Plunker or a Heddon River Runt toward areas such as those mentioned above and would consider it a blessing if I managed to creel several rock bass in addition to the smallies.

Areas that provide more cover than I feel necessary for smallmouths often harbor feeding rock bass after dark. One night I was plugging the dropoffs and rocky shoals and had a hefty strike. I set the hook and the fish didn't respond in typical smallmouth fashion—it didn't jump.

"That's no smallmouth. He's not jumping. I'll bet you've got a big rock bass on," my buddy said. He was right; that fish bulldogged in typical sunfish fashion but didn't offer a showy fight. I found the fish tired much easier than a smallmouth, and it was simple to control his rushes because he didn't jump. The most action he provided was a boatside flurry as I gilled him. It was a solid rock bass weighing almost 3 pounds. Although he wasn't a record fish he represented a trophy of the highest class.

One method I've found that pays off with big rock bass after dark is to fish subsurface lures like a Midget Mirrolure or Dardevle Midget. Rock bass feed actively on small minnows after dark, and these lures represent forage fish.

The Mirrolure should be fished without any action other than that which is built into the lure. A silver scale finish should be used to closely match minnows found in the lake.

I've had my best success with the silver-finish Dardevle Midget. An erratic retrieve is best, and I've found it pays to retrieve at a speed that brings out the best wobbling motion and then allow it to flutter down for a foot or so and before reeling again. This gives the lure a start-and-stop motion that rock bass seem to go nuts over.

WARMOUTH BASS

The warmouth bass has a shape basically similar to that of the rock bass but the body is heavy and short, with a single dorsal fin. The warmouth bass does not have the streaks and dark spots of its close cousin. It has four dark color bars on the cheek and gill cover, and it also has teeth on the tongue, unlike any other panfish. The overall color is brassy with dark-brown patches, which gives the sides a mottled effect. It has a red iris like the rock bass.

The warmouth is usually a fish of Southern waters, although it does stray into such Northern states as Minnesota. The other Great Lakes states have very few warmouth bass.

It thrives in both cloudy or clear waters and prefers quiet water over a muddy bottom containing vegetation such as dense weedbeds. This sunfish is more at home in lakes but will frequent slow, turbid streams.

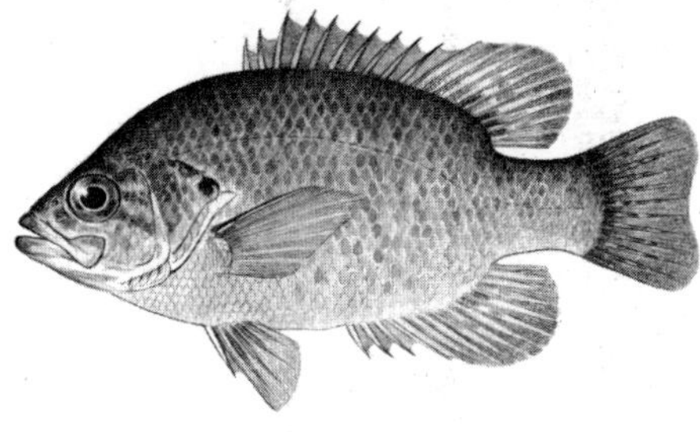

When taken from bayous containing weedbeds or muddy bottoms, these fish are not pleasant to eat because they tend to absorb the taste of their environment. Fish taken from clear water are more tasty.

One clue to making consistent catches of warmouth bass lies in the weather. If it is hot, expect this species to frequent deep underwater weedbeds. If it is cool, warmouth will be found near shallow weedbeds.

I've taken some warmouth bass from Southern waters and found they fight on a par with rock bass. They aren't flashy fighters, but larger ones will give a good account for themselves.

This species, like the rock bass, tends to be a schooling fish, and locating them is the most difficult part of catching them. The same techniques work as for rockies.

SUNFISH

Sunfish belong to a broad family with as many relatives as a man with three wives. Included in the tribe are green sunfish, orange-spotted sunfish, pumpkinseed, redear sunfish, longear sunfish, spotted sunfish, and redbreast sunfish. Some are found only in small areas, so I'll discuss only the more popular species.

The green sunfish is found in a great many states but particularly in the Midwest and certain portions of the South. It has a black spot on the ear flap; it is located in the middle and does not extend out to the margin of the flap.

The body of the green sunfish is greenish, and the dorsal, anal, and tail fins have a yellow edge on the tips. There is a dark area on the dorsal and anal fins.

This gamefish does not thrive in large waters when it must compete with other species. It does well in creeks, streams, and small ponds. It prefers dirtier water than some panfish species and will do well in sluggish creeks.

The green sunfish is a natural for the fly fisherman and responds well to both wet flies and sponge-rubber spiders. It has a fairly large mouth and can gobble down many flies or small ultralight lures.

Crickets are a top choice during summer months. The fisherman may have to fish fairly deep for continued success, but the same basic techniques that work for bluegills will take green sunfish.

The redear sunfish or *shellcracker* is a popular sunfish in many Southern states. My largest specimen was taken from Florida's St. Johns River several years ago; it weighed just over 2 pounds.

Shellcrackers have an olive color with dark-olive spots. This fish has a small mouth which does not extend past the front of the eye.

It obtains its proper name from a spot at the tip of the gill flap, bright-red on the males and orange on the females. The "shell-cracker" nickname comes from its habit of eating snails and other shelled organisms.

The redear has a definite liking for large areas of quiet water and will gather around stumps, logs, or roots. It seldom frequents aquatic vegetation as do other sunfish.

Shellcrackers do not compete with other sunfish for insects, so fly fishing won't work, nor will other common panfishing techniques that depend on an appetite for insects.

Redears spawn in the spring, and the best catches are made when they begin spawning. An angler locates a good bedding area and fishes worms on a cane pole. It's not fancy but is very productive, because male shellcrackers will slam into almost any worm dropped into the redd. Many Southern anglers, especially in Florida, look forward to the shellcracker spawning time just as Northern anglers look forward to the perch run. The excitement sweeps over the land like a swarm of locusts and everyone gets in on the fun of cane-polin' for redears.

The pumpkinseed sunfish is a panfish found primarily in the northern tier of states. It does not grow as large as some of the other sunfish but it holds a special place in the hearts of many fishermen.

This fish is considered the common sunfish by many anglers and authorities and is a popular sport fish for young and old alike. The reason for its popularity is the fact that it normally stays quite close to shore, well within casting distance of most fishermen.

This sporty sunfish is one of the most colorful and has a rigid gill flap with an orange or red spot on the end. The body is a light olive with a great variety of colored spots along the sides. Vivid emerald-blue lines work back from the mouth and eye region to the edges of the gill flaps. The fins are a yellowish color in adults and the tail fin an olive green. The sunfish that could most easily be mistaken for the pumpkinseed is the bluegill, but it has whitish-gray fins and tail.

Pumpkinseeds frequent weedy areas, docks, swimming rafts, and logs for cover and are not inclined to spend much time in open water as bluegills do. They feed heavily on smaller fish, insects, and snails or small mollusks.

A trophy common sunfish will be about 9 inches long, although very few live long enough to attain that size. I've found the best time to fish for big pumpkinseeds is during the spring spawning period, when the larger fish are found protecting their nests.

Little damage can be done by fishing for spawning panfish, because they are so prolific that it is virtually impossible to thin them out of suitable waters.

The same techniques that work for bluegills will work for the common sunfish. The only advice is to fish shallower waters than usual, because pumpkinseeds are often found shoreward of other sunfish and bluegills.

WHITE BASS

The white bass is a popular gamefish and is one of only two true native bass found in freshwater. (The largemouth and smallmouth bass are technically members of the sunfish family.)

The white bass is found from the Great Lakes south, east, and west as far as Utah and Texas and southern Georgia. It works east as far as eastern New York but does not extend farther north in any appreciable numbers.

Whities are a popular gamefish wherever they are found because of their willingness to strike. This fish prefers large clear lakes and very seldom will populate a body of water smaller than 300 acres. Reservoirs, impoundments, and large natural lakes are best for white bass.

This fish has a slightly compressed body with a forked tail, two separate dorsal fins, and teeth on the base of its tongue. It is a silvery-looking fish with a tinge of yellow below. It has about ten dark narrow lines or stripes which run horizontally the length of the body.

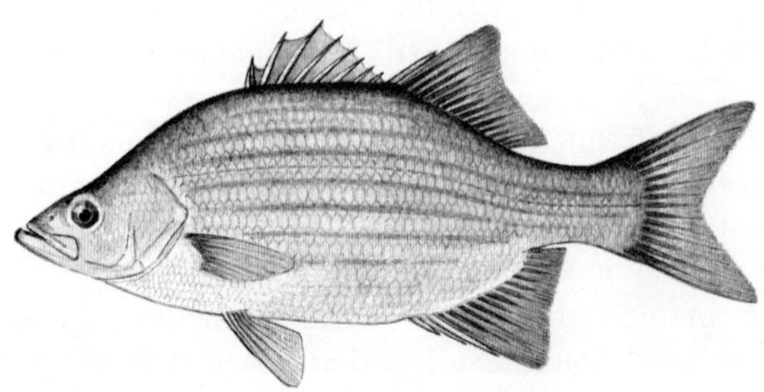

I'll never forget my first experience with white bass on Dale Hollow Reservoir in Tennessee. The time was June and fishermen were anchored all over the lake waiting to hit the fish "on the jump." This occurs when these gamefish work up under a school of gizzard shad and force them to the surface. The baitfish jump through the water while white bass tear them to shreds.

Once this occurs, white bass will be in the area for only a short time, and then the shad flee to another area and the whities follow. The trick is to roar up fairly close to the surface turbulence, cut the engine, and coast within casting distance. With luck and proper judgment of distance you can arrive with enough time to catch a few fish before the school breaks up and goes back down.

Once I was fishing with Jim Little of the Tennessee Wildlife Resources Agency. He is the regional fishery biologist for that area and accustomed to fishing for white bass on the jump. We were watching the flat surface of the lake when a boil occurred 200 yards away. "Hit it!" Jim hollered as I punched the throttle on my twin 70 Evinrudes. We kicked up on step within 10 yards and flew across the lake. "Cut it back!" he ordered when we were 50 yards away. I cut both engines and the boat coasted silently to a stop within 20 yards of the feeding fish.

"Fish the edges of the boil," he instructed as he sent a silver spoon arching alongside the fish. "Reel it fast and give it a couple hard jerks. Hey, I've got one! Look at those fish, look at 'em!" He was dancing around like a youngster with a new toy.

I tried to watch his action, but a white bass yanked hard on my small Dardevle and we battled our fish in silence. Jim lifted his over the gunwale and it flopped off onto the floor. He made his second cast with 4 feet of line hanging off his rod tip. A white bass jump is no place for slow dainty casting. My fish soon followed his and I sent another cast near the seething mass of white bass and gizzard shad.

Jim had two strikes on that cast; he missed the first but nailed the second fish. "C'mon, reel faster. Keep it coming; twitch it, give it a yank. Hey, you've got one, good. Get him in, hurry, hurry." His chatter was contagious as I dropped a 2½-pounder alongside his 3-pounder. It was frenzied fishing with heart-pounding excitement.

We each made one more cast to that jump before the fish sounded. I lost my fish next to the boat, and Jim boated a 2-pounder. Sweat was dripping off his brow as we relaxed a little and placed the fish in the cooler. It is fast, sporty fishing and the competition is keen among other anglers.

I'd just picked up the last fish when Jim hollered, "Hit it!" Three o'clock. Lots of fish. Gawd almighty, look at those fish!" We cranked up the engines and managed to beat another fisherman

When white bass are schooling and striking, a catch like this is easy. A double-jig setup is one of the best rigs for taking this fish in numbers.

who had spotted the school after we began moving. Our first casts into the school resulted in another doubleheader and then the fish went down.

We spent most of the afternoon hitting the jumps, taking fish from some schools but putting others down when I crowded them too close. The cooler was nearly full of 2-to-3-pound white bass when we headed for the barn.

Another time I hit white bass on Lake St. Clair near Detroit. The technique here is totally different, because we'd see very few fish breaking the surface. We were forced to fish much deeper.

I tied a ⅛-ounce Pinky jig on the end of my leader, knotted in a 12-inch dropper 2 feet above, and used a 1/16-ounce Pinky on that line. A yellow jig went on the dropper, and the bottom lure was white.

This rig was cast out and allowed to sink to bottom, and then I would jig it slowly back to my boat. I was anchored off the mouth of the Clinton River. I'd been fishing for two hours and had taken an occasional yellow perch and two freshwater drum, but the white bass were conspicuous by their absence.

Lightning finally struck twice as a school of white bass moved into the area and two fish hit at once. They went tearing off in opposite directions, and I had my hands full trying to tame those fish. It was like trying to quiet a wildcat with a willow switch. I finally boated both fish, and my esteem for white bass rose another notch.

The fishing remained steady for an hour, then suddenly went dead, and three more hours passed before the whites paid another visit to my area. I'd almost always hook two fish at once, but would often lose one or both fish during the battle. I managed to boat twenty-five fish that day with the double-jig setup. This rig is one of the best when white bass are working an area near bottom.

YELLOW BASS

The yellow bass has a more limited range than the white bass and is found primarily from Michigan and Wisconsin south to Texas and Louisiana. This gamefish is found around large rocky reefs or shallow gravel shoals.

The yellow bass is shaped much like the white bass but has silvery to corn-yellow sides and is a dark olive green along the dorsal area. It has six or seven dark horizontal lines running along the sides, three of which are above the lateral line. Those lines lying below the lateral line are broken or irregular toward the tail. This is a key point in determining whether the fish is a white or yellow bass. A 1-pound yellow bass is considered a trophy anywhere in its range.

These gamefish are usually caught near bottom or at middle depths and only rarely on the surface. Trolling is the customary method of locating schools of yellow bass. Once a school has been found, most anglers stop and cast with flies, spoons, spinners, or tiny plugs. This gamefish is noted for vicious strikes and short dogged fights on light tackle.

The world of the lesser-known panfish is indeed large, and the various groups of sunfish and basses can deliver a brand of fishing which ranges from sedentary worm-dunking to the high-voltage excitement of taking white bass on the jump. I wouldn't have it any other way.

V

SALMON

18
ATLANTIC SALMON

The Atlantic salmon is one of the great gamefishes of the world, famed for its long runs and high-jumping acrobatics. Few species are so capable of capturing an angler's heart and soul.

Anyone fortunate enough to catch an Atlantic salmon would be wise to consider his fish a trophy. There are few, if any, techniques that produce just trophy specimens. The same methods take trophy fish or grilse.

Thanks to poor land and timbering practices in the past, and man-made pollution, Atlantic salmon now occupy only a portion of their former range. Indiscriminate netting in rivers and estuaries and on the high seas has reduced their number to a mere handful compared to a century ago.

The Atlantic salmon is capable of growing to huge sizes, although most of the truly large specimens now come from storied streams in Norway and a few other scattered European countries.

On the North American continent, this salmon is at home in unpolluted wilderness streams where anglers fish only with flies. In fact, fly fishing is the only legal method of taking these great gamefish in the streams which will be mentioned in this book.

Salmon are found only in certain streams flowing into the northern Atlantic Ocean and some streams in Ungava Bay in northern Quebec, and evidence shows a few fish stray through Hudson Strait and down into a limited number of streams flowing into Hudson Bay along its eastern shoreline.

One stream may attract Atlantics while another river 10 miles away may not. Down through the ages anglers and biologists have pondered the reasons that make one river acceptable and another nearby stream unsuitable.

It has also been proved that "big fish" rivers exist which attract only the larger specimens while a nearby river will attract only grilse, the smaller and often immature salmon. For all practical purposes, a grilse will weigh up to about 8 pounds and after that is considered a salmon.

The body of an Atlantic salmon is about five times as long as it is deep. These fish have teeth on the vomer, in the middle of the roof of the mouth. Body coloration varies greatly and depends on whether the fish taken is fresh-run, if it has been in the river for some length of time, whether it is male or female, whether it is a pre-spawning or post-spawning fish, and other variables. Sea-run salmon are bright silver on the sides and a bluish-black on the back.

Male fish assume a dark-red color on their flanks while on the long migration to their spawning grounds. Females often attain a very dark or even black flank if the trip is long and arduous.

The average weight of Atlantic salmon taken by North American anglers is about 12 pounds in many rivers, although a handful of 30-to-40-pounders are taken annually.

At present Atlantic salmon are taken in Quebec from streams entering the St. Lawrence River, from frontier or New Quebec (that portion flowing north into Hudson and Ungava bays), New Brunswick, Nova Scotia, Prince Edward Island, Labrador, Newfoundland, Michigan, and Maine. The Connecticut River is receiving a very small and important run of Atlantics as this book goes to press. This is electrifying news, because the Connecticut River was once a major salmon stream in those long-gone days before man made his everlasting imprint on the waters of this continent. If these salmon catch hold and are protected for several years, Eastern anglers may again cast flies to holding salmon in the Connecticut River in the manner of their great-grandfathers who fished before the turn of this century.

Atlantic salmon fishing is called the sport of kings—often in reference to the cost of angling for this species. It is expensive, often to the extreme. A seven-day beat on one of the more famous Canadian salmon streams may cost as much as an Alaskan hunting trip. Fees of $100 to $250 per day are not unheard of when fishing waters are leased to large companies or fishing clubs. This is out of the reach of many anglers, who must be satisfied with lesser-producing rivers where fees are smaller or open water exists.

Some of these waters can be productive when the run begins. Too few of us, however, have the time to wait out a salmon run, so it pays to cultivate the friendship of someone living in that area. I did this one time and formed a lasting friendship with an old guide on New Brunswick's Tobique and St. John rivers. Both streams are now being heavily netted by the Indians of that province and the fishing is just a glimmer of former days. Unfortunately, such is the case in too many waters where Atlantic salmon were once present.

Anyone planning a trip for Atlantic salmon would be well advised to consider venturing to frontier Quebec. Some of the storied streams of that area include the George, Koksoak, Whale, and Tunulik rivers (the last is considered a char stream primarily, although some salmon are taken every year). My choice for fantastic fishing would go to the George, a picturesque stream tumbling north to Ungava Bay through a tortuous route of white-water rapids, smooth dark pools, and gigantic boulders.

Two years ago I fished and hunted from Wedge Hills Lodge, about 60 miles upstream from Ungava Bay. This area during late August is alive with Atlantic salmon. They average 12 to 14 pounds, and an occasional 20-pounder is taken. The stark beauty of the area will capture your heart. Salmon fishermen watch migrating Quebec-Labrador caribou daily while casting flies to this water, some of the finest left on this continent.

Heavy tackle isn't needed. I fished exclusively with an 8-foot rod, a No. 8 floating fly line, and a leader tapered down to 2X. The reel should have a minimum of 100 yards of 20-pound-test braided Dacron backing, because several of the fish I landed took all my fly line in one smooth rush and had me well down into my backing before I could stumble down the rocky shoreline in pursuit. Several

Ben Girard tails a fighting Atlantic salmon in Quebec's George River.

of my fish required 200 yards of rough-and-tumble fighting, causing numerous stumbles and skinned shins, before they could be tailed. Almost every fish hit a No. 2 or No. 4 Muddler Minnow fished just under the surface.

Salmon flies are as colorful as the fish themselves. Down through the years many patterns have evolved that consistently hook Atlantics. Here are some of my favorites and those of other dedicated anglers:

WET FLIES

Black Prince	Moray Downe	Black Dog
Greenwell	Limerick	Bull Dog
Lady Caroline	Black & Gold	Blue Highlander
White Tip	Wilkinson	Duchess
Snow Fly	Blue Charm	Black Ranger
Lady Amherst	Silver Scott	Blue Jock Scott
Silver Rat	Restigouche Rat	Thunder & Lightning
Nicholson	Canary	Blue Doctor
March Brown		

DRY FLIES

Badger Spider	White Wulff	Rat-Faced McDougal
Grizzly Bivisible	Gray Wulff	Brown Wulff
Surface Stone Fly	Black Gnat	Quill Gordon
Irresistible	Pink Lady	Black Wulff

Certain other flies take salmon and do so consistently, but those listed are a good starting point. One other pattern, the Muddler Minnow, should find a spot in an angler's fly box, because this fly has come to be an exciting producer on many streams, especially those of northern Quebec.

Salmon flies are found in all sizes ranging from No. 14, which might make a dandy fly for dimpling brown trout or rising salmon, to the huge 1/0 to 6/0 flies touted on some waters. The angler is well advised to carry a large assortment of these proven patterns in all sizes.

Wet flies are usually tied in "low-water" and "high-water" dressings. The low-water fly is sparsely dressed and generally tied on a lighter hook. It presents a smaller image to the salmon during periods of late summer when water levels are low. The high-water models are used when rivers are high and discolored, and they are tied fuller and on heavier hooks. This enables them to sink deeper in swift, heavy currents.

One facet of fly fishing unknown to many fishermen is that old sorry-looking and worn-out flies often move fish when everything else fails. New flies are often too bulky and present a larger image to the fish. Some of the best wet flies are those with soft hackle feathers which enable them to sink faster.

Down through the years wherever salmon fishermen gather, the never-ending discussion arises as to why salmon take flies. When they leave salt water they have enough stored energy to survive several months in fresh water without feeding. It has been proved conclusively that Atlantic salmon do not feed upon entering fresh water, so why do they strike flies?

Many anglers maintain that salmon strike out of irritation, much the same as a male bluegill will strike something entering its spawning area. But most Atlantic salmon are intercepted on the way to their spawning site; they are not protecting a redd. They may be irritated, but I don't believe this to be the sole reason why they strike a fly.

My theory—and it embraces those held by other anglers and biologists—is that salmon strike from a conditioned reflex. As parr and smolt they fed often on small insects on the river of their birth before heading for the salt. Perhaps this reflex action is triggered in adult fish when they see a fly swing over or near their heads.

Whatever the reason, Atlantic salmon do strike flies and often strike very well if the imitation is to their liking and they are interested. What makes salmon fishing so much fun, and so frustrating, is that the fish very seldom are in an active striking mood and therefore the casting must be repetitious. Many fishermen will work hard for days between strikes.

Whatever means of fly fishing the angler chooses, it behooves him to first locate the fish. Blind fishing is seldom productive, because salmon often hold in areas different from trout. A guide who knows the waters being fished is a genuine asset to beginning salmon fishermen; he can point out productive lies, tell exactly where to cast, and explain how to work that spot to best advantage. Each lie represents a different set of complex problems which must be solved or the angler may never "kill" a salmon. It should be noted that salmon fishermen never "catch" or "keep" Atlantic salmon; the fish is "killed."

Two basic methods of fishing for Atlantic salmon prevail on North American streams—wet-fly and dry-fly fishing. Each is productive at certain times and on certain waters, and a critical look at the most productive methods is needed to learn how to take these fish. Salmon-fishing opportunities are rare for the average angler, so it hardly pays to make a salmon trip without solid advance knowledge.

I do not claim to be an expert on Atlantic salmon and have several times felt totally incompetent when a salmon steadfastly refused my offering. I have fished Atlantics several times, but surely much less often than some anglers reading this book. The advice that follows is based mostly on personal experiences in Quebec, New Brunswick, and Nova Scotia and one cherished but unproductive day on the Little Codroy in Newfoundland. Down through the years I've also had expert advice from some of this continent's best salmon guides, who although otherwise unlettered had the equivalent of a college degree in Atlantic salmon behavior and how they respond to flies and where they hold.

WET-FLY FISHING

The method of fishing wet flies for Atlantic salmon is considered the most orthodox and has been described for countless centuries in angling circles. Wet flies are used because a salmon often strikes what it sees and is therefore attracted to the flash of the wet fly. Many of our standard patterns are brightly colored with varying amounts of tinsel, which reflects light and thereby attracts the salmon.

Some old-time salmon fishermen felt that the fish are attracted to a fly only as long as light is being reflected off it and will reject or call off the strike if the wet fly passes into an area where the light no longer falls heavily on it. A fly then presented from a slightly different angle will often move the fish.

A short strike or miss often is the result of the fly moving from a sunlit area where considerable flash is seen into an area where the fish no longer can see it clearly. Some anglers may disagree with this explanation, but I believe it to be true through my observations of salmon strikes on several rivers.

The wet fly is customarily cast across the current flow and downstream at an angle of about 45 degrees. The current will tighten the line and cause the fly to swing in an arc past suspected lies, and then it will straighten out downstream. The effect of the current on the fly, leader, and line makes it appear alive and swimming. This is best accomplished by fishing with a tight line. A mistake many beginning fishermen make is to produce slack in the line, which decreases the distance the wet fly will swim on each cast.

A wet fly will cover a lot more water than a dry fly and therefore is the method fished by most anglers. It increases the opportunity to move a fish to the fly.

If a fish has not been located and the angler is fishing blind, it pays to work each pool thoroughly. The standard procedure is to fish each cast out thoroughly, take one step downstream, and fish the next cast in the same manner. When the entire pool has been fished through in the cast-step-cast manner, it often pays (if time permits) to fish down through the same water in the same manner with a different fly. Salmon are noted for refusing one fly but striking the next one presented.

Some areas are well known for certain flies, and the fisherman should determine the most productive patterns in every location. It does little good on certain waters to be without the local favorite; guides and local sportsmen keep up on what produces fish and are frequently generous with the knowledge, but the angler must usually ask—they seldom volunteer.

The classic method of fishing a wet fly for salmon is to cast across and downstream at an angle of 45 degrees. The current swings the fly past suspected lies, giving it action. It is important to keep a tight line.

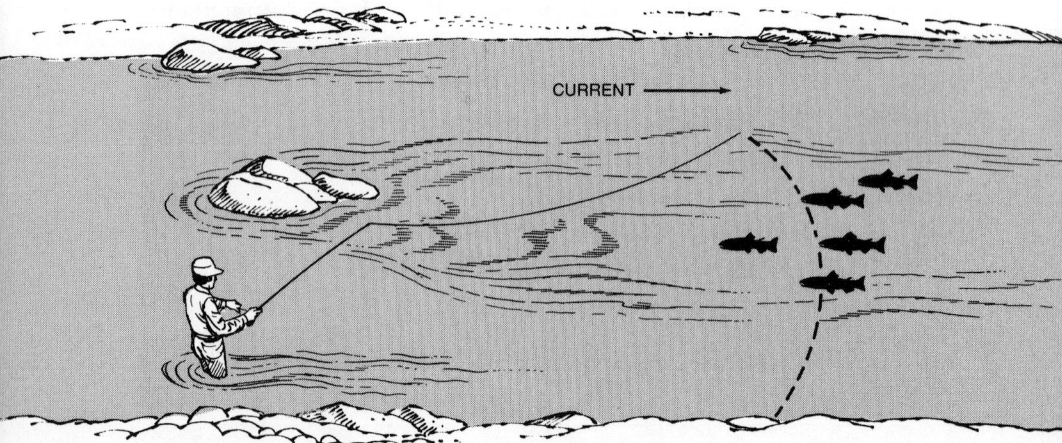

One year, before the Indians gill-netted most of the salmon from New Brunswick's St. John River, I was fishing with Arnold DeMerchant, a guide from Perth. We would anchor at the head of a pool in Arnold's freighter canoe and I would fish down and across. I'd been using a Jock Scott for some time without moving a fish. We'd made several drops and the fish were reluctant to move to it.

The lack of action finally got to Arnold, and he said, "Beggin' your pardon, sir, but some of the local lads have been doing well lately on Restigouche Rat. Now that Jock Scott of yours, he's good, but I'd like you to give my favorite fly a try, eh?" he stated and asked, all at the same time. Many guides will never offer or suggest a fly change and will suffer through a trying day while the angler uses everything except the right thing. Arnold, by stating what the "local lads" used, had aroused my curiosity and I accepted his favorite fly gratefully.

Two casts later a 12-pound salmon came hard to the fly from the depths of the Bath Pool and instantly shot into the air, twisting and turning, before crashing down. Within seconds the fish was into my backing as he headed downstream.

Arnold raised the anchor and poled the canoe downstream through the pool and put me on the beach, where I carried the fight to the fish in traditional manner. Although the temperature was in the 80s, that fish wasn't sluggish—it ran and jumped several times before I led it to the beach. I dislike gaffing intensely, because many of my trophy fish are released, so I played it to a standstill and ultimately tailed the fish in ankle-deep water. Arnold deftly removed the fly and we returned it to the river.

Similar stories are told in salmon circles about guides cautiously suggesting a change of flies, and it often pays off for the angler. Some guides are more reticent than others, but Arnold's knowledge of the water and productive flies made his suggestion a lifesaver that day.

Fishing wet flies from a boat is a slightly different situation from wading. The angler should begin casting about 20 feet from the boat, cover that water thoroughly, and then lengthen each successive cast by about 6 inches until he has covered all the water within reach. The boat is then dropped downstream, repositioned, and held in place by an anchor or pushpole.

A trick some fishermen use, and others never realize, is that there are two sides to each boat and salmon can lie on either side. It pays to fish one side thoroughly and then work the other side in the same manner. Some anglers fish one side on one cast and the other side on the next and keep lengthening line until all available water is covered.

Two trains of thought exist on how the fly should be fished. Some believe the wet fly should travel across and downstream on a tight line without any movement other than what is given it by the current. Another segment feels that it helps to jiggle the fly line with the line hand as the fly swings across and down. I've fished both methods, both wading and from a boat or canoe, and I have taken more Atlantic salmon by jiggling the line every two or three seconds during the drift than when it is fished without motion. On the other hand, I've talked with many more skillful anglers than myself who believe the opposite.

The additional fly movement is a trick that can pay off with healthy strikes from salmon that would not otherwise strike. When the success of any Atlantic salmon trip is gauged by the number of fish moved or hooked and landed, the angler should know every trick in the book to enable him to enjoy his salmon outing.

Spot fishing for salmon usually takes place when the angler or guide can actually see the fish holding in position. There is much to be said for locating fish instead of fishing blind. Polarized sunglasses will enable fishermen to spot fish on bottom that would be overlooked. I am used to spotting fish, since it is commonly done for steelhead in Michigan, where I live. A salmon will often look like a submerged log or a darker-than-normal spot on the bottom. Close examination will often reveal a head or tail movement that enables you to determine its exact location and how to best fish for it.

Once a fish has been located, most anglers stick with the immediate area until they move the fish or decide it will not strike. Many times a certain fly will move a fish where it might lie near bottom and refuse other offerings.

Anglers faced with a fish which has been located will usually try a vast array of flies presented from various angles. If after an hour of steady casting, the fish hasn't moved, it is usually best to rest the pool and that salmon for an hour or so, and then resume casting.

Time of day generally means little to an Atlantic salmon, but the hour or so just before dark has been kind to me in past situations where I've had fish located. Persistent casting is often rewarded in such cases.

There are several tricks one can use when fishing wet flies. One is to allow the fly to hang motionless in the current after it makes its across-and-downstream swing. Many fish, especially those that have been in the river for some time, will often strike as the fly hovers near the surface after completing its swing.

The majority of salmon fishermen use floating fly lines, and this was once called the "greased-line method." This method calls for throwing a loop of line upstream or mending the line. This allows the wet fly a more dragless drift through the holding water and also presents it sideways to holding salmon. Old-timers used to grease their line so it would float, and they could then roll a loop upstream to slow the drift. It's much easier now with the modern floating fly lines which are available. The only caution is to be gentle when mending the line—otherwise you'll lift the wet fly from the water.

Another variation of wet-fly fishing is to lift the rod to a more vertical position. This will speed up the swimming action of the fly. The rod should never be lifted to a full upright position, because if a fish should strike, there will be no room left with which to set the hook. As in everything else, moderation is best.

The angler should learn to evaluate each current flow and determine whether the speed of the fly should be increased or decreased. To decrease the travel speed of the fly, the rod tip can either be lowered near the water or slack line can be fed into the cast. Each will have the desired effect on the speed the fly moves down the current and over the salmon.

Another wet-fly trick is to allow the fly to complete its swing and then pull it upstream toward you. This causes it to swim along the surface in an upstream manner, and it will occasionally produce a showy strike.

Some anglers prefer using the "Portland Creek riffling hitch," a method of tying a half hitch at the side of the fly head instead of directly to the eye of the hook. This causes the fly to swim in a more broadside manner to salmon and can be extremely deadly when the fish are reluctant to move to the fly.

A fish that comes to the fly and doesn't take is one that is interested. The angler should make a quick mental note of how much line he had out and cast that same amount of line again—no more or less. It's important to duplicate the exact cast again and again, because currents vary slightly all the time and if the fly is 2 inches off, you may never move that salmon again. It has to be precise, and this calls for mental discipline and constant awareness of where your fly landed on the last cast and how much line was out. It does little good to raise a fish once and then not be able to move him again because you can't cover him properly.

There seems to be an endless debate among anglers over the relative merits of the single- or double-hook salmon fly. I personally have used both and find the hooking qualities of the two about equal but the holding qualities far superior with single hooks. A hooked salmon is a demon, and his wild gyrations will often work the two barbs back and forth against each other and the end result is surely a lost fish.

I have landed some salmon on double-hook flies, but I've also lost more than my share. My success ratio is much better when I use single-hook flies.

DRY-FLY FISHING

Comparing dry-fly fishing to wet-fly fishing for Atlantic salmon is like comparing a Lincoln with a Chevrolet. Each will do the job for which it was intended, but one supplies more comfort and satisfaction than the other.

In my limited opinion, there is no other method of fishing which places such a high demand on skill as does fishing the dry fly for salmon. The thrills involved in this sport are tremendous, because it gives the angler a great deal of satisfaction to lure a big salmon up from the bowels of a pool for a tiny bit of fluff. The dry fly usually calls for a lighter tippet, and this places an added burden on the fisherman, but when he succeeds, he has reached a lofty plateau in fishing.

One key to dry-fly fishing is when the angler can locate fish that are jumping or breaking the surface in large rolls. This pinpoints their location and indicates the fish are interested to a limited degree in surface activity.

Constant exposure to guides and to other salmon fishermen who prefer fishing on the surface, and my limited experience at the sport, has indicated that seldom will a salmon take a dry fly the first time he shows himself. The fish may move two, three, or more times to a dry fly before finally taking. When they do take, it's often with a classic head-to-tail rise that is a joy to behold.

The dry-fly man should have a generous variety of sizes, colors, and shapes of productive flies. The guides tell me that as a rule, light flies should be used on bright days and dark flies on dark days. Some may dispute this, but the salmon I've been fortunate enough to take on a dry fly have always followed that pattern.

The accepted method of fishing a dry fly is to present it so that it will not drag across the surface of the river. Some anglers contend, and perhaps rightly, that a dragging dry fly will spook many fish. I have seen cases where this is true and others where nothing short of a charge of dynamite would disturb the fish.

If the current is moderate to slow, the angler can cast across and down or across and slightly upstream and mend his line in classic style to obtain the longest possible drag-free drift. This, however, is not always possible in some areas if the water is swift.

If salmon have been located it is possible to cast almost directly upstream. I try to position myself below and to one side of the salmon and make my presentation so the fly will pass over the fish but not my fly line. Some salmon are spooked by a fly line drifting over their heads. This can be avoided by stopping the fly line abruptly so it curves slightly and allows the leader and fly to pass over the fish while the fly line passes to one side.

The best possible position to hold your rod in order to obtain the maximum amount of drag-free float is with the tip near the water. This enables a quick set on a strike and will also allow the dry to travel the maximum distance before drag sets in. Some line can be pulled off the reel and fed into the drift in certain cases to obtain a longer drift.

The ideal method of dry-fly fishing calls for a sinking leader. I carry a small tube of toothpaste for this purpose and apply it liberally before fishing, making certain that is is completely removed before casting. It does wonders for sinking the leader and rendering it less visible to the fish. Several commercial leader-sinks are on the market which serve the same purpose.

One dry-fly trick that works at times when fish are not responding well is to fish a cast in the normal manner and then pull the fly under the surface as it drifts past a located fish. A salmon that passes up a dry fly will often sock one that has been pulled under. It doesn't produce all the time, but it may add a fish to your catch that possibly would never have been taken with other conventional methods.

There is a common mistake many fishermen make when striking

salmon—they strike too soon. I've found it better to allow a second or two after the take before striking. This usually ensures better hook penetration. A strike made too early will often pull the fly from the salmon and it won't be hooked.

Fishing for Atlantic salmon is a sport every angler should indulge himself in at least once during a lifetime of fishing. It is expensive, but so are automobiles and color television sets, and I've found that an Atlantic salmon trip will live in your memories much longer than any other pastime. I've fished for them, caught my share, and they will remain a part of me and what I am as long as I live.

19

LANDLOCKED SALMON

The landlocked salmon and his close cousin, the ouananiche, are direct relatives of the Atlantic salmon. These landlocked fish are descendants of seagoing fish which were trapped in fresh-water lakes and streams when glaciers receded thousands of years ago.

The landlocked salmon is usually a fish of lakes and ponds in upper New England as well as New Brunswick and Quebec. Some of these fish thrive in rivers or streams flowing into large deep lakes.

The ouananiche is also a landlocked salmon but lives in swift-flowing streams of Quebec, Labrador, and Newfoundland. Although in certain instances the ouananiche is capable of making a run down to salt water, it seems to prefer not to and spends it's lifetime making stream fishermen delirious with pleasure.

Landlocked salmon are difficult enough to catch consistently without the added burden of trying to take only trophy specimens. The several times I've tried this sport I've felt that any landlocked salmon unlucky enough to grab my lure is a trophy fish, whether it's a 2-pounder or a 6-pounder. Some species are trophies at any size. This is one of those few.

The landlocked version looks like a smaller version of the Atlantic salmon. The markings are similar in almost every respect, and the fighting qualities are much the same. They do have longer fins and irregular-shaped black double X marks. The eye is often larger in landlocked fish.

Ouananiche are slightly different from Atlantics in both shape and coloration. The fins of this gamefish are larger in proportion to the total girth and length. It tends to be more slender and often darker in color. The sides and upper dorsal areas are heavily speckled with brown or black crosses or spots.

Landlocked salmon have for years provided quality sport for residents of Maine, Vermont, New Hampshire, and New York. Recently stockings have been made in Quabbin Reservoir in Massachusetts.

Landlocked salmon taken today average much smaller than those caught near the turn of this century. Fish were reported to weigh upwards of 20 pounds in those glorious days, but a 6- or 7-pound fish is considered a trophy in these times. Ouananiche run much smaller, and a 4-pounder is considered a big fish.

Fly fishing is considered the appropriate method of catching landlocked salmon and ouananiche. But it should be pointed out that certain other techniques produce on these fish and are entirely legal. Although trolling or fishing with hardware may seem sacrilegious to addicted salmon fishermen, it is perfectly legal in many areas to use bait, spoons, flies, or whatever.

The diet of the landlocked salmon is such forage fish as smelt, alewives, yellow perch, and sticklebacks or other minnows. This menu offers a key to catching them. Ouananiche feed actively on small fish, insects, and trout or other small ouananiche.

The largest percentage of landlocked salmon will be taken from spring ice-out until the tail end of June and again late in the fall before the waters freeze over. At this time they prowl the shorelines in search of smelt, their favorite forage fish.

During warm weather, landlocks will head for deeper water, often to depths of 25 feet. This places an added burden on sportfishermen because it is extremely difficult to place a fly at these depths and still fish effectively. Trolling or still-fishing is the accepted practice during the summer months, while fly fishing gets a big play earlier and later in the season.

TROLLING FLIES

Flies are generally more productive early in the season than any other lure or bait. Landlocked salmon are feeding heavily on smelt, which gather off stream mouths before starting their annual spawning run. Bucktails and streamers are the preferred flies, and the following patterns produce fish consistently: Edson Light Tiger, Edson Dark Tiger, Nine-Three, Green Ghost, Black Ghost, Gray Ghost, Supervisor, Mickey Finn, Warden's Worry, and the Red-and-White Bucktail.

Fast trolling normally produces best when trolling the above flies. I prefer using a light-action fly rod, a well-balanced single-action fly reel with 100 yards of backing, and a 9-foot leader tapered down to a 4-pound-test tippet. I've found a level sinking fly line to be adequate for trolling flies.

If a wind is blowing the angler should troll along the downwind shore of the lake. Landlocked salmon prefer rough water and feed actively when whitecaps are tossing sheets of cold water over the boat. This can be dangerous, and no one should fish when the lake is too rough for comfort, but some wave action can aid the fisherman. It reduces visibility and stimulates feeding activity among salmon.

A zigzag trolling course is much more productive than a straight run. The combination of trolling at speeds just short of pulling the fly from the water and the alternate "chugging" motion of the rod tip is the prime factor in taking these fish during spring months.

Many fishermen believe in fishing the fly a minimum of 50 to 75 yards behind the boat. Short, sudden turns to port or starboard, a trick that can be borrowed from the steelhead or brown trout troller, give the fly a more lifelike appearance.

Areas to troll are near rivermouths, along rocky shorelines, near islands, and over submerged shoals or ledges. The fishing should be done in fairly shallow water, since landlocks are feeding near shore and the surface. They are often taken in 1 to 3 feet of water when the schools of smelt move inshore to spawn.

Some Maine fishermen "double-team" landlocked salmon. One angler will troll a conventional fly on a long line behind the boat, while the man seated in the bow will cast toward shore or rocky areas. His fly should land and be retrieved with quick, short jerks. If this doesn't take fish it may lure them from hiding where they might strike the trolled fly.

FLYCASTING

Fly fishing needn't be limited to trolling or trolling and casting in the manner just described. For many years landlocked salmon fishermen have delighted in casting from a boat or shore and fishing flies in a more conventional manner. The best area for this is below falls on streams which attract runs of salmon or in the rivermouth areas.

If an area is suspected of holding landlocks, the fisherman should fish in a semicircle around the boat. Try different retrieves until the proper combination of retrieval speed, action, and fly has been determined.

Many anglers suggest fishing several casts near the surface with a fast retrieve. If this doesn't produce, allow the fly to sink several feet and try either a slow or fast retrieve. There are times when salmon are in shallow water where they prefer the fly to scuttle along bottom with a jerky action.

There are a few times each season when conditions are suitable for fishing a dry fly—when the lake is mirror-calm, usually at dusk or dawn, and the dimples of feeding fish can be seen.

The technique is to drift slowly along or scull a canoe and cast dry flies to an area where feeding fish have been located. Allow the dry to remain motionless on the surface for several seconds and then begin the retrieve with cautious twitches of the line. The explosive strike of a landlocked salmon at dawn is something that will be forever etched in your memory.

As I have said, landlocked salmon fishing is not all fly fishing, regardless of how some fishermen may feel. Trolling, still-fishing, and the use of hardware or live bait are natural variations of this sport and will probably always be so.

BAITS AND LURES

One of the most productive methods of taking big landlocked salmon is by still-fishing with live smelt in well-known "smelt holes." During summer months smelt often go to various depths to find more comfortable water temperatures. The salmon are close behind as smelt descend. The natives usually know the whereabouts of these holes and have found that still-fishing offers them their best chance for a fine-eating salmon.

Live smelt are used for this type of fishing, and one of the biggest difficulties is obtaining fresh bait. The smelt should be hooked just under the dorsal fin and allowed to swim about in a free manner. If the fish keeps swimming to the surface it is acceptable to attach one small split shot to hold it at the proper level. Give the salmon a bit of slack line when he strikes the minnow, and when you feel him surge away, set the hook hard.

Trolling is another fine way to hook up with a hard-fighting landlocked salmon. Artificial lures which can be used are Rapalas, Mepps spinners, small Dardevles, Mooselook wobblers, small Flatfish, and Colorado spinners, and a host of other lures will work as well.

Although lures are popular with trollers, the smelt is accepted as being the premier bait in landlock waters. A double-hook rig can be used, with the hooks spaced about 3 inches apart. One hook should be placed through the lips, while the tail hook can be inserted near the vent. The smelt should be curved slightly to give it a revolving or wobbling action.

Cowbells are often used as an attractor. The rigging should be the same as described in the brown trout chapter. The cowbell-smelt arrangement should be trolled at a slow speed which brings out the throbbing action and the flash of the cowbell blades. This is an exceptional producer when landlocked salmon are holding in deep water.

Another trolling trick that few anglers have tried is to combine a cowbell with a 24-to-36-inch leader and a streamer fly instead of a lure or smelt. This combination works well when the angler "chugs" his rod tip to give action to the fly. The chugging motion allows it to breathe or pulsate like a live fish, and the strikes are hard, jarring affairs with the end result being a big landlock crashing from the water in a classic jump.

OUANANICHE

Ouananiche or "little salmon" are dwellers of primitive rivers and streams, principally in Quebec, although some fish are thought to reside in Ontario. They are also found in Labrador and Newfoundland and provide heady sport in any area.

I'll never forget my first exposure to ouananiche. I was fishing Quebec's Kaniapiskau River about 200 miles north of Gagnon, a frontier mining town. The purpose of my trip was big brook trout, but once I'd hooked my first salmon, all thoughts of brookies disappeared.

My guide, a Cree, ran the freighter canoe downstream through rapids like a New York cab driver entering the Midtown Tunnel. He was confident of his ability to dodge barely submerged boulders, and we soon coasted into a fairly quiet stretch of water. It looked rather slow and quiet for brook trout, but he pointed near a ledge of rock against the far bank. "Cast," he said. I did.

The ¼-ounce Dardevle made a dainty splash and hadn't traveled more than 3 feet when a fish struck—actually, it exploded on my spoon. My arm shook from the force of the strike, and that fish slammed from the water, pinwheeled like a fireworks display going out of control, and then parted the water as neatly as a cleaver. My jaw dropped open as the silvery fish completed another twisting, rolling leap so characteristic of the salmon family. I didn't know what I had on but I knew enough to enjoy it while it lasted.

The fish fought well, although briefly, and I led it to the canoe. My guide dipped it from the water and I had my first opportunity to admire the sleek lines and raw power packed into that 3-pound frame. "What is it?" I asked Joe. "Ouananiche," he replied. "Plenty of 'em here this pool. Fun?" he asked, noting the grin spreading across my face.

We played tag with ouananiche for three hours in that pool and found they were an accommodating gamefish. I seldom went more than ten minutes without hooking another high-jumping fish. I kept one fish, a 4-pounder, and released the others. I was able to hook, play, and land almost twenty fish in that period, although my guide shook his head whenever I released a salmon.

We returned the following day to the same pool, and I was armed with a fly rod and a wallet full of small Atlantic salmon patterns. I fished a floating line with a 7½-foot leader tapered to 4X. The fish would strike whenever the fly completed its downstream swing and hold momentarily in the current. They would occasionally come heavily to a wet fly as it was making its swing. These were the hardest strikes of all.

I landed eight fish that day. The size and the fly pattern made little difference as long as it was bright. I'm sure the fish had been feeding to some degree on brook trout fry, and any pattern that closely imitated these tiny gamefish would work.

Several ouananiche were taken from the edge of fast water where they held in a cushion of quiet water behind or alongside a boulder that broke the force of the current. If the fish could be located, they would strike almost every time a fly curled around their rock and entered the holding water. It was premier fly fishing of the finest kind and one I regretted leaving.

The landlocked salmon and ouananiche are two gamefish that deliver a powerhouse of fishing excitement wherever they are found. They strike hard and sure, jump often, and represent some of the finest trophies this continent can offer.

20

CHINOOK SALMON

The Chinook salmon is the largest of the five breeds of Pacific salmon. Nicknames such as "king" and "tyee" suggest an awesome size and king-size fighting abilities, and the Chinook lives up to both reputations.

Chinook and coho salmon have been planted in the Great Lakes and have made a valuable contribution to the fisheries in those areas. To date, they haven't grown to the gigantic sizes found along the Pacific Coast, but fish of 20 to slightly over 40 pounds are taken yearly from the Midwest, most notably from Lake Michigan and Lake Huron.

The West Coast Chinook often grows to 60 pounds, with some recorded hook-and-line catches weighing over 90 pounds. The world record weighed 93 pounds and was caught in 1977 from Kelp Bay, Alaska. The average Chinook taken from California waters north to Alaska weighs between 20 and 30 pounds, but this is a hefty package of action-packed dynamite on the end of a line.

The Chinook salmon by choice is a lover of big rivers and waters. Some spawning migrations have taken kings as far as 1,200 miles before they find a gravel bar of their choice. A classic example is the runs of tyees ascending Washington's Columbia River and finally ending their spawning run in Idaho waters. Some of these fish will cover 1,000 miles in less than sixty days.

Spawning runs occur during spring, summer, and fall. The timing depends partly on how far the fish must travel to reach their natal spawning bars. Typical of all Pacific salmon, the Chinook dies after spawning. Someone once said that Pacific salmon are "born an orphan and die childless." Chinook salmon from the Great Lakes also spawn and die from the spawning bouts.

Pacific Chinook salmon and those found in Great Lakes waters have the same coloration. There is no difference between the two except their geography, and fishing methods are the same.

Chinook salmon are unbelievably handsome. The sides are silvery from tail to head, provided the fish are not preparing to ascend a stream to spawn. As the pre-spawning urge strikes, they assume a dusky greenish-brown appearance with a dark belly. An open-water fish has a dark greenish-blue dorsal area with numerous black spots covering the entire tail and dorsal fin. The tail is broad and thick, with a thick caudal peduncle. The insides of the mouth are black or dusky, which helps distinguish Chinooks from coho salmon.

Once Chinooks enter spawning streams the males develop a hooked jaw and a vast array of body colorations ranging from cherry red to a dirty gray-brown. I've seen a few male fish with flaming sides the color of orange pineapple ice cream. The females often turn a yellowish-gold or greenish-yellow color, and the black spots shine like small pieces of black coal in clear water.

Coho salmon often ascend a river in large schools, but Chinooks tend to be more individualistic in nature. They either run alone to the spawning waters or travel in very loose schools.

Some states protect spawning salmon, although the Great Lakes states do not because their fishery is maintained by constant stocking and not by natural reproduction. Although catching Chinooks in a stream can be a test of skill, endurance, and the strength of your tackle, the best fishing is always found in open water of the Pacific Ocean or in the Great Lakes.

I'll never forget one of my most fascinating experiences with Chinook salmon. Dr. Ned Hether, a dear friend of mine, called and wanted to fish Chinooks. We trailered the boat from my home to

Harrisville, Mich., on Lake Huron, during the peak of the Chinook run. We arrived at dawn and saw hundreds of slick-sided salmon rolling through the surface film.

Ned and I lowered our lures to the proper depth indicated by my Garcia OTP (oxygen temperature probe) to find the 54° water in the area indicated on my chart recording graph as containing huge fish. We trolled for thirty minutes, making short bursts of speed and turns to port or starboard.

One of the downrigger rods suddenly sprang to attention with a rattle that shook the stern of my boat. "Fish on! Grab it, Ned. Reel hard, take up that slack." I was issuing orders like a harried desk clerk at a busy hotel.

Ned grabbed the rod as it bucked in his hands. Thirty yards off the stern a silvery shape shot into the air, twisted once, and fell back only to pinwheel from the water again. "It's the biggest fish I've ever seen," Ned said. "I can't do anything with him. Turn this boat around," he hollered, as the fish headed down the lake with line streaming out behind. The fish was getting dangerously close to another boat.

"Hold him back, Ned. If he gets into those other downrigger wires, he's gone. Lean on him!" I barked. Ned's a big man, and he leaned on the rod and reel so hard I was afraid it would snap. The fish wallowed to the surface not 6 feet from the other boat. He had stymied that run, but more action followed.

The fish sounded, and I backed the boat near the point where the line cleaved the surface and Ned leaned on the king again. "He's coming up!" he hollered, his hands spinning as he crowded badly needed line back on the reel.

The words had just left his mouth when the Chinook vaulted into the air, 10 feet off our stern. It hung briefly in the early-morning sunlight before splashing back down. It took off away from the boat on a scorching run that made the star-drag reel whine. I was afraid it would explode from the pressure.

The fish covered 50 yards in less than ten seconds and slammed out of the water in another startling leap, the bright-colored Flatfish sticking from his mouth like the glowing stub of a cigar. That jump took most of the fight from the fish, and the battle settled down to a pump-and-reel battle, gaining a foot and losing 6 inches, until Ned was able to pressure the fish within reach of my tailer.

I slipped the wire noose around the broad wrist of the fish's tail and pulled the trigger. It was all I could do to hold on as the

Chinook lashed back and forth hard enough to break 30-pound monofilament. We lifted the prize into the boat and Ned admired his first Chinook salmon, a silvery 31-pounder.

A half-hour later Ned locked horns with an evil-tempered 28-pound king that led us all over that portion of Lake Huron before we could boat it. We finished up the day with three Chinook—not a fantastic catch for the fish-rich Lake Huron waters, but one that was immensely satisfying to both of us. I'd gotten a great deal of pleasure from watching my friend tangle with big Chinooks.

Trolling is the number-one method of taking Chinook salmon wherever they are found. Kings are considered less of a nomad than cohos and are often found closer to shore, especially just before spawning. This is a prime period for taking trophy fish because they often go on feeding sprees that would make a Roman banquet look like a midnight snack. They feed actively and put on pounds of steel-girded muscles capable of taxing an angler's strength and his tackle to the utmost. Landing these fish can be difficult, but not impossible; the most important thing is to be able to hook them. Chinooks are among the wariest fish found in open water.

A vastly different set of ground rules exist for Chinook salmon than for other gamefish. Certain times of the year and certain times of day are more productive. In the Great Lakes area, September and the first of October are best, while West Coast anglers catch their largest Chinooks from July through September.

Chinooks are extremely light-sensitive, and early-morning, late-afternoon, and after-dark hours produce more jarring strikes than any other period. Bright sunlit days usually produce slow fishing. My fishing for king salmon has taken me to Washington, Oregon, and throughout the Great Lakes, and wherever I've gone, I've noticed a tendency for these fish to strike best early in the morning before the sun is full on the water. I've been able to take a limit of 20-to-35-pound salmon many times in the two hours from full dark through that period just after dawn. It means getting out of bed earlier and being on the water before the sun comes up, but it also means taking the best shot of the day at a trophy king salmon.

The fisherman geared up mentally to fish coho salmon will generally fail miserably on Chinooks because these fish react, feed, and migrate differently. They seldom mass together in huge schools where competitive feeding takes place. Kings will gather together in loose schools just before they ascend a spawning stream. More often than not they are loners compared to coho salmon. Fishermen will seldom locate immense schools of Chinooks, and my opinion therefore is that the best time to fish this heavyweight salmon is just before spawning runs occur.

Some of the best Chinook fishing occurs on stormy days when the boat skipper has his hands full handling his craft. There is something about rough water and overcast, stormy skies that gets kings charged up and biting well. Turbulent water with gray-flecked waves mean difficult and somewhat dangerous fishing but also increased feeding.

Any fish the size of Chinook salmon is as difficult to stop when hooked as a runaway steamroller. The initial strike is awesome; the rod tip snaps down and line melts off the reel. If the drag is set too tight the result will be a broken rod. I know of no other fish with the Charles Atlas strength of a fresh-hooked king salmon. They

Paul Harvey, a top-notch Oregon guide, shows off a big Chinook he caught from his surf dory. Note the downriggers mounted on the gunwales. *Tom Opre photo.*

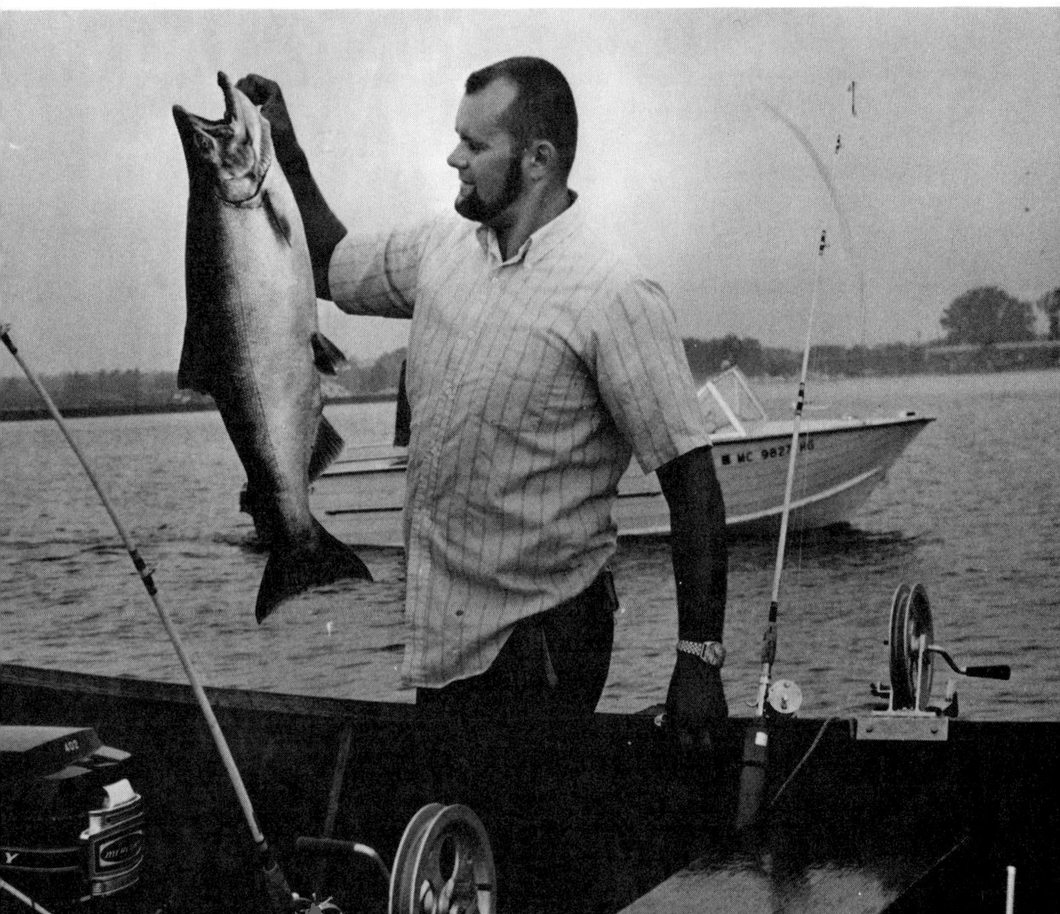

fight until their heart is gone in a series of long runs, head-standing jumps, and savage boatside explosions. Hooks are straightened out, lines broken, fiberglass rods shattered like a lightning-splintered dead elm tree, and they can make a frazzle out of a fisherman's nerves.

TROLLING

Trolling is the best method of open-water fishing. I believe in slow speeds, the slower the better. I select lures that work well at these lower speeds. Large plugs generally produce better action at slow speeds than spoons do, and they provide better hook penetration.

My choice for lures would be an M2 or T4 Flatfish in chrome or orange, red, and black; J-Plugs in green, blue, or khaki colors; and Ping-a-T's in Golden Greenie, white fleck, or white fleck with pink spots. These three lures have accounted for over 1,000 big Chinook salmon for me during my travels, and they work as well along the West Coast as in the Great Lakes. The most important thing about these plugs is that they work with an exciting wiggle at slow speeds. The Ping-a-T will dive to nearly 20 feet without weight at my normal putt-putt trolling speeds.

The J-Plugs work best off downriggers that hold them at the proper depth. Flatfish can be fished on flat lines (not on downriggers) with a 1-ounce RubberCor sinker attached 2 feet ahead of the lure.

I'll generally have enough fishermen on my boat to fish four or six lines. Before setting lines my initial step is to determine the proper water temperature. If 54-degree water is at 20 feet I'll fish lures or set my downriggers so all lures will be between 15 and 19 feet, just above the major concentration of salmon.

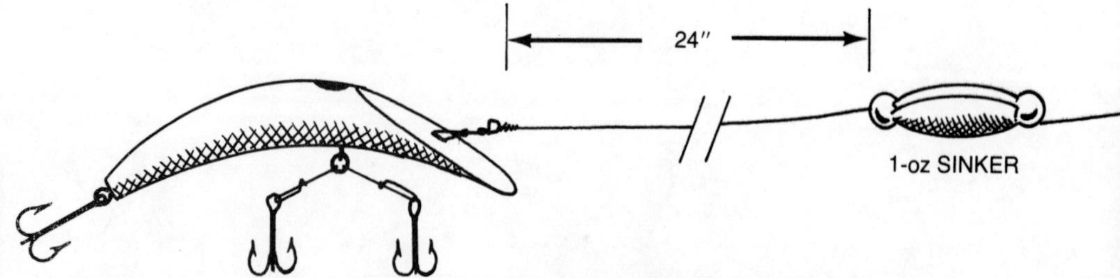

Best rig for fishing a Flatfish on a flat line (no downrigger) is shown here.

The two stern downriggers will usually be fished deepest, at 19 feet, and each will be rigged with a J-Plug, usually one green and one blue or khaki. The lure should be run about 50 feet behind the cannonball for maximum productivity.

One gunwale-mounted out-downrigger will be set at 15 feet with a silver Flatfish, and the other out-downrigger will be set at 17 feet with an RYF colored Flatfish. This will cover most depths with four proven colors and lures. The out-downrigger lures should run about 4 or 6 feet behind the cannonball.

I'll then fish two flatlines with Ping-a-T's on each, a golden greenie and a white flecked with pink spots. If the trolling pressure from other boats isn't heavy I'll run these lures about 100 feet behind the boat without weight. They should be fished on long rods held at right angles to the boat, which enables them to work out past the downrigger lines without tangling.

The only problem with this trolling trick is that all lines should be raised when a big Chinook is hooked, or he is likely to tangle them in one quick rush toward the boat. If the boat operator can keep the fish away from the boat until he's too tired to fight any longer (which is often difficult to do) the other lines can stay down.

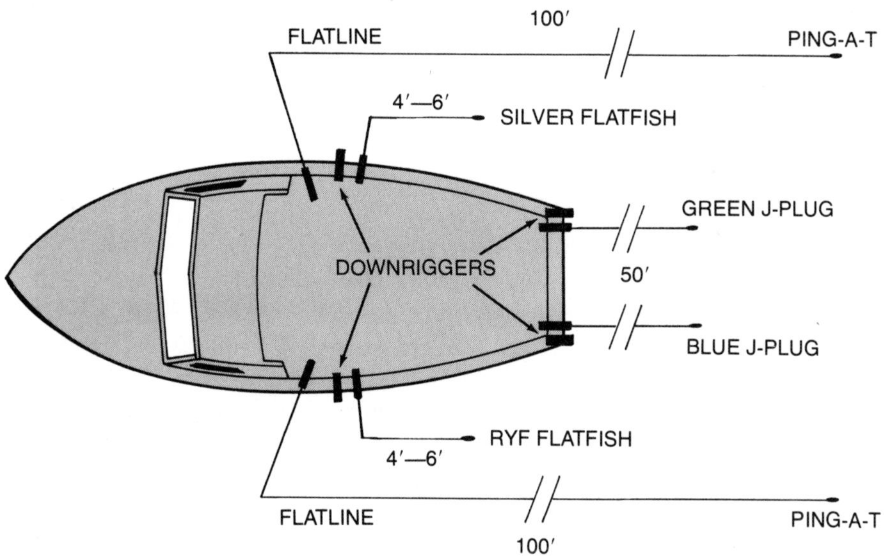

System for trolling six lines for Chinooks. The first two lines are fished flat, the four others off downriggers.

Great Lakes fishermen often continue trolling while one fish is being fought, and this enables the other lines to remain in operation.

Although I've had my best success while trolling slow, I'll have to admit that an occasional speed-up can often trigger strikes. Use a short burst of speed with no more than 10 feet of boat travel, and then throttle back down to the normal speed. A speed-up is relative; I don't mean full-throttle takeoff but a quick burst at half-throttle before easing off on the gas. This will cause the lures to increase their wiggle and start heading for the surface, and this change of vibration will often produce a strike.

Whenever Chinooks mob into an area in any numbers it usually signals the beginning of heavy fishing pressure with large numbers of boats. Invariably, all boats will begin trolling a circular pattern or one that goes in and out. I've noticed that Chinook salmon will often strike a lure more readily if it travels a pattern different from other lures.

A friend of mine, Chuck Lunn, a fantastic salmon fisherman, once decided to try trolling across the grain, so to speak. If the traffic is such that a boat can troll at opposite angles to the flow of other fishermen, that boat will often hook more fish. I've seen Lunn make limit catches by trolling across the grain while other anglers were boating only the occasional fish by following the established pattern.

The above trick won't work when too many fishing boats are concentrated in a small area, because it would result in tangled lines and flared tempers.

Another trolling trick I've learned is that when salmon are concentrated in one area, and a pack of fishing vessels are after them, they will often clear out and head in close to shore. I've taken numerous fish by trolling inshore waters, often as shallow as 6 feet, when the going gets too heavy outside. The fish seem to feel safer when they aren't surrounded by boats and lures.

There will be days when the above-mentioned plugs will not produce. This often occurs several days after the fish work into an area and have been pounded hard from daylight to dark by fishermen. When this happens the fish will often respond only to lures or attractors throwing off more flash, such as a Herring Dodger or string of cowbells ahead of a lure or baitfish.

When plugs fail I never hesitate to bring them in and attach a Jensen Dodger and lure. I prefer No. 0 or No. 1 Dodgers in Kelly

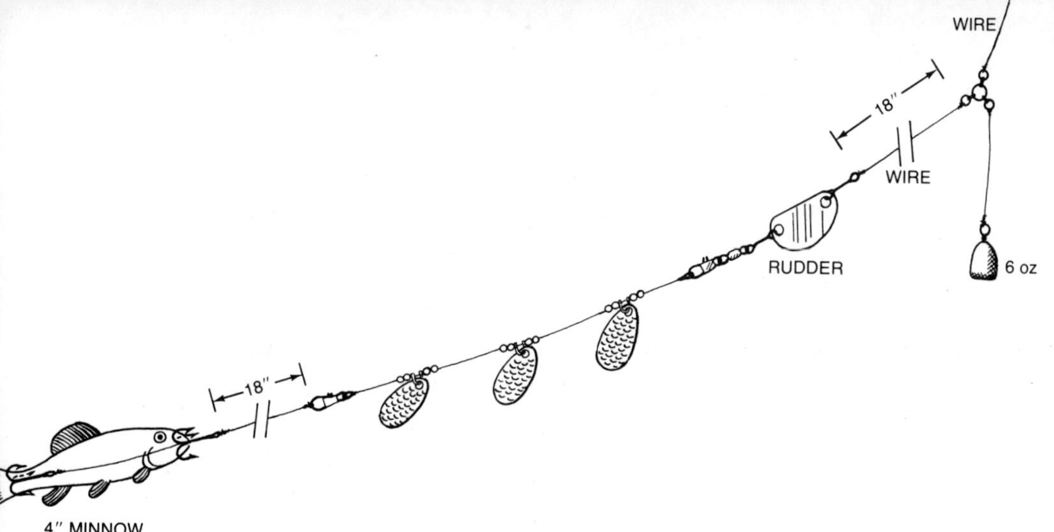

Baitfish-and-cowbell rig is effective for trolling when Chinooks have been pounded hard by fishermen and respond only to flash.

green, pink, chartreuse, or half chartreuse and half white. I'll usually attach a green or blue Michigan Squid fly on an 8-inch leader behind the Dodger and fish them on a short 4-foot line behind my stern cannonballs. Various-colored Dodgers should be used on the out-downriggers, and I'll use either a FirePlug or Johnson spoon on a short leader. These should be fished close to the cannonball, because Dodgers are productive only if they have something fairly heavy to pull against. The cannonball provides this leverage.

If Dodgers are used, use just one size; never pull two size 0 and two size 1. Keep them all the same size, because it requires different trolling speeds to bring out the action of various-sized Dodgers. I lower them over the sides to watch the action and adjust my trolling speed until I obtain a sharp, whippy action. They can be lowered to the proper depth once you've adjusted the speed to the action.

One facet of Chinook salmon fishing which is overlooked by many anglers is downrigger release tension. The release should be set tight to ensure adequate hook penetration when a big king strikes. If the release is set too light, many briefly hooked fish will get away. I set my releases so the fish must pull hard two or three times before it releases the line. The fish will almost always be firmly hooked.

Art Dengler, a first-class trout and salmon fisherman, once showed me how he takes big Chinooks. The fish were holding deep, at 90 feet. Hundreds of other boats were trolling circles around fish which were being marked on the Vexilar chart recording graphs, but the Dodger and lure fishermen weren't catching any fish.

Art decided he'd fish Chinook like lake trout, a sport he's become famous for. He rigged up his wire-line trolling rig with 6 ounces of lead weight 2 feet ahead of a set of chrome Six-Pak Cowbells. He then fastened an 18-inch leader of 30-pound monofilament and tied in two No. 2 treble hooks, one about 3 inches ahead of the tail hook.

He sewed a 4-inch shiner minnow onto the leader, with the rear hook inside the minnow's vent and the front hook through both lips. This is the typical trolling cowbell-minnow rig that was described in the brown trout chapter.

A hard-fighting Chinook gives these two anglers in a small boat a hardy workout. Overcast skies and choppy water are best conditions for taking these salmon.

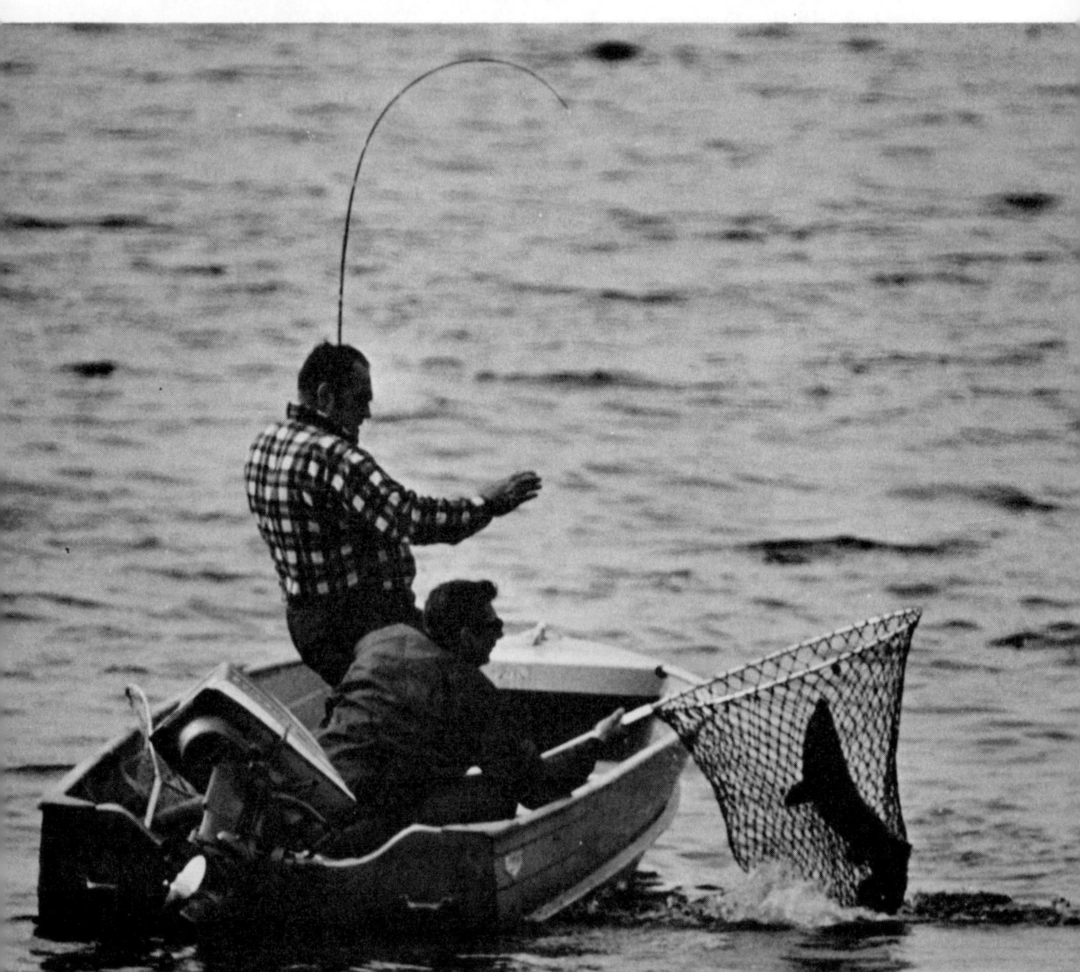

He slowly lowered the wire line, weight, cowbell, and minnow to the bottom at a very slow trolling speed. Once the weight was scratching bottom, he raised it slightly and began trolling. Every ten seconds Art would raise the rod tip to a vertical position and then quickly lower it in the classic chugging manner.

His graph was reading hundreds of Chinook salmon. The chart had just quit marking fish when his lure, working about 200 feet behind the boat, stopped with a jerk. He set the hook and a big Chinook pulled again, this time hard enough to nearly sprain his wrist. Wire line sizzled off the oversized reel as the king headed for distant parts. He tried applying pressure, but the fish was too strong and line continued to peel off. He spun the boat around and moved slowly down on the fish as it grubbed along bottom, trying to rub the hooks from its jaw. When Art had regained some sorely needed line and was positioned directly over the fish, he began applying pressure. The fish made another 50-yard run before stopping. Art later told me that this fish was the strongest one he'd ever hooked.

High-voltage excitement rippled through the boat as Art began applying more pressure, and he could feel the fish slowly allowing itself to be worked toward the surface. The fish came up meekly until it was on the surface and then it clattered from the water, the cowbells twisting and flashing in the sunlight. It looked well over 30 pounds.

Other boats hovered nearby watching the battle as Art bore down in earnest. After a forty-five-minute struggle Art's partner slid the net under a vinegar-fresh Chinook salmon, bright silver with a broad spotted tail. It later weighed 36 pounds, a fine testimonial to a little-known method of fishing Chinook salmon when they go deep.

MOOCHING

West Coast fishermen practice a method called "mooching." It sounds like something done by a freeloading guy that's always out of cigarettes, but it is a highly productive technique. Several variations of this method are practiced in widely scattered locations.

The most productive method involves using fresh anchovy and two large 1/0 single salmon hooks. The head of the baitfish is cut off at a 45-degree angle near the gills, and one hook is attached near the tail and one through the flesh near the gills. Some fishermen use a commercially produced rig that allows the use of the entire fish, with the head inserted into a narrow beveled plastic holder. This sharp angle of either the fresh-cut bait or the anchovy rig gives it an erratic wounded-fish action.

Concentrations of Chinook salmon are located and the fisherman will move into the area and stop his boat. The mooching rig is lowered to the proper depth, and then the boat moves forward for about 10 feet and stops. The rig twists and darts upward in the water as the motor is gunned and then flutters back down like a wounded minnow when the boat slows down. This is mooching in its classic form, and it is a deadly producer of big Chinook salmon.

A variation on the mooching technique can be accomplished with lures such as large Dardevles, Johnson spoons, Williams Wablers, or anything else that represents a wounded anchovy or other marine baitfish that Chinooks feed on.

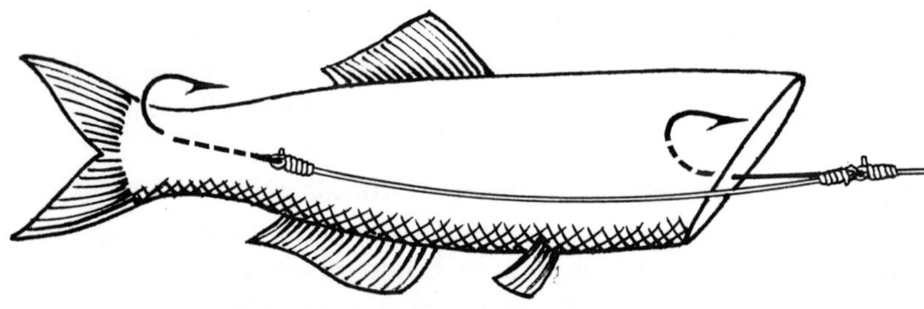

Mooching rig of two hooks baited with a fresh anchovy is favorite of West Coast anglers. Note how baitfish is cut at an angle.

The fishing technique is accomplished with the same stop-start-stop method of boat and lure control. The lure will dart upward, with a heavy wobble, and then flutter down on its flat surface. This imitates a wounded fish that a salmon has disabled, and it produces arm-wrenching strikes. In fact, I'd wager that mooching produces some of the most jarring strikes possible from a Chinook, especially when it strikes just as the boat begins moving forward. Stout fiberglass or all-glass rods are commonly used with heavy mono or braided Dacron.

BAITFISHING

A baitfishing technique has evolved in several Michigan areas where Chinooks move into quiet inland lakes or harbors before spawning runs begin. Enterprising anglers have found that Chinooks strike well after dark on bait, and certain locations are gunwale to gunwale with boats for a chance at this exciting fishery. It pays off with plenty of hooked fish in the 30-to-40-pound class, although many of the largest fish are lost when a rampaging king tangles with someone else's fishing line or anchor rope.

This baitfishing rig is very simple, inexpensive, and productive. Attach a No. 2 treble hook to the bottom of the fishing line after threading it through a ¼-ounce egg sinker. Pinch a split shot onto the line 12 inches above the hook, with the egg sinker above the split shot. This prevents the larger sinker from sliding down onto the bait.

A large gob of nightcrawlers is threaded onto the hook, or a large spawn bag tied from fresh Chinook eggs can be used for bait. The important thing is to offer the feeding fish a last chance for a healthy mouthful. Small baits will catch the odd trophy Chinook, but larger ones will produce more strikes.

The egg sinker, split shot, and bait are tossed out near the boat and allowed to sit on bottom without motion on a tight line. The bait will float up off bottom several inches where cruising kings can spot it. The first indication of a strike will generally be a tap-tap-tap at the bait. Allow a few inches of slack line to spool off, which gives the fish a chance to take the bait deep in his mouth. When the fish begins moving off and the line pulls tight, set the hooks and hang on, because the fish will often slam out of the water on the strike. I've seen 30-pound kings jump right into a boat in their first frenzied attempt to get away.

These bait fishermen generally use heavy line, because they can't afford to give the fish running room. The hooked Chinooks are snubbed tightly and the sounds of popping rods are common every night because the tackle isn't strong enough to withstand such abuse. But the fishermen simply go out the next day, buy another stiff pool-cue rod, and return the following evening for another slugging match with big salmon on short lines.

The best baitfishing usually takes place at rivermouths where the fish congregate before heading upstream to spawn. Sharp dropoffs, river channels, and flat muddy-bottomed water 6 to 10 feet deep are

Dick Rudzinski shows off a big Chinook he took within sight of Chicago's skyscrapers. Plantings of these salmon in the Great Lakes have been successful and fish up to 40 pounds are taken annually.

ideal for this fishing. Dark evenings, with drizzling rain, usually produces the hottest fishing, and the hours around midnight seem to generate the most interest among fishermen and the salmon.

STREAM FISHING

In the West, certain streams attract hordes of salmon and equal numbers of fishermen. The heaviest fishing pressure takes place in tidal estuaries or just upriver from salt water. The kings are bright from the sea and will often provide an action-packed battle that will rattle your teeth from the strike until the fish is firmly packed on ice in the cooler.

Many fishermen prefer using 12-foot prams or small aluminum boats, and they troll large wiggling plugs like the Flatfish. They attach 1 to 3 ounces of lead keel sinker 2 or 3 feet ahead of their lures and then troll upstream. Some fish are taken trolling downstream, but it is not as productive.

The first time I tried this method a Chinook grabbed my lure with a mighty surge of power that straightened me up in my boat seat. The king progressed downstream in a raw demonstration of power generated from a hefty seafood diet. It streaked down away from the boat, arrowed into the air, and landed in a shower of spray. The fish was 100 yards away before I could swing my pram around and head after it.

I finally was able to boat the 37-pound hook-jawed king after a thrilling thirty-minute battle which included a series of nonstop jumps that covered the width of the estuary. That fighting Chinook salmon hooked me on the sport of estuary trolling.

Once Chinook salmon move upstream from the brackish-water estuaries or from the Great Lakes, they are just as susceptible to fishing practices as ever. Anglers must realize that salmon, once they leave open water, do not feed but will strike an accurately placed lure, fly, or bait. Many Western states do not allow fishing for salmon, although certain streams such as California's Smith River have exceptional fly fishing for huge trophy king salmon.

Many Great Lakes tributaries, particularly in Michigan, host huge runs of Chinook salmon, and these fish provide exciting angling during fall months.

A West Coast fly fisherman battles a Chinook fresh from the sea in one of the rivers the salmon enter on their upstream spawning migration. Anglers use lead-core lines to take their flies down.

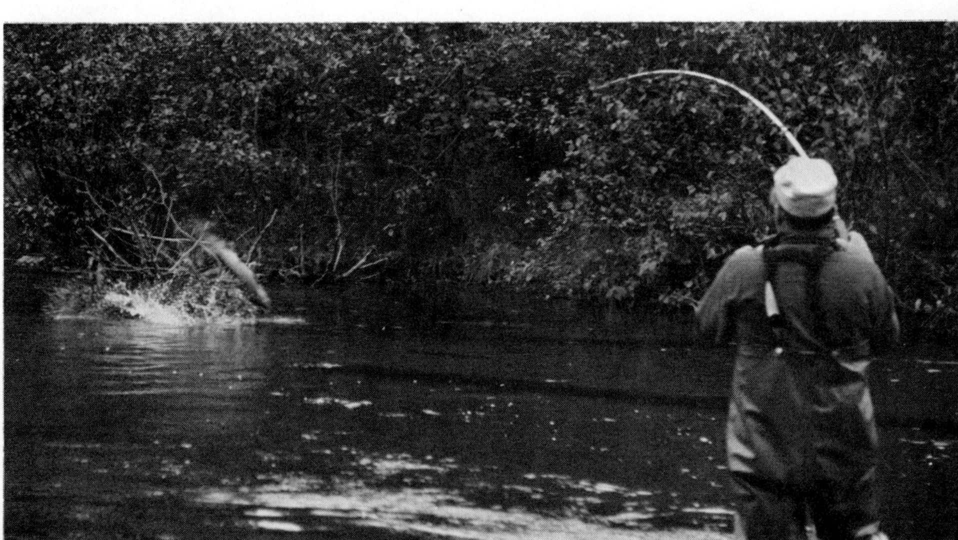

Fishermen intent on taking big fly-caught river Chinook salmon from the Smith River should take note of the methods used. These anglers use lead-core shooting heads to take their flies down into the depths of large holes where tightly packed schools of salmon hold.

This is heavyweight fishing for extra-large fish, some weighing well over 40 pounds. Leaders are usually tapered down to about 10-to-15-pound test and a variety of flies are used. Many are of bright colors and are tied on weighted or unweighted hooks in sizes 6 up to 1/0. As always, local patterns are usually more productive and often change from season to season. Learn what is producing and buy accordingly.

These fishermen cast across and downstream with a typical wet-fly technique, but the weight of the lead-core shooting head enables casts of 100 feet plus faster sinking times. The line is allowed to sweep the fly directly in front of the holding fish. A strike is often soft and difficult to detect. Once the hook is set the angler tries to work his fish from the pool so others can fish. A cadre of dedicated fishermen work the lower pools of the Smith River every fall when fresh salmon move upstream, and these anglers are poetry in motion. Many of these fishermen are on the river from daylight to dark. Fly fishing for Smith River kings is almost a cult with many Western anglers.

Fly fishing for Chinook salmon also has a following in Michigan, where several streams harbor large numbers of Chinook salmon every fall. One of my most exciting salmon trips took place several years ago when my brother and I hooked, landed, and released over thirty kings in one day. The largest weighed an even 37 pounds and the smallest, a runt, scaled only 18½ pounds. The average fish weight was 24 pounds, and every fish was taken on flies.

A silvery female Chinook, fresh from Lake Michigan, was holding deep under the protective branches of a toppled cedar on the Père Marquette River. The fish was in an impossible location; every fly would either hang up in the protective branches or pass far over its head.

I finally decided to shoot my weighted fly across stream and slightly up, feed it several coils of slack line to obtain a quick sink, and then work it in front of the fish's nose. It sounded easy but appeared hopeless.

The first several casts lodged in the tangled cedar branches, and I

George Richey, the author's brother, unhooks and releases a 34-pound Chinook salmon he fought on a slender fly rod. It took thirty minutes to land this giant.

broke them off to avoid spooking the fish. I finally managed a perfect cast, and the hen salmon moved out, intercepted the fly, and swirled heavily in the current as the hook buried itself in a huge black maw. "Fish on!" I hollered to George, who was downstream working another big Chinook.

My fly line rattled through the guides like sleet off a window as the fish headed downstream. I was able to turn her into a narrow opening between two stumps, and she piled through the chute of open water like a tailback making a broken-field end run. "You'd better get moving," George mentioned as he headed downstream with the net. I caught up to the fish in the next pool and she exploded downstream on another run, jumped once, landed in a logjam, fell back into the water, and churned away again. That crash landing would have knocked the wind out of me but it didn't seem to bother the fish any; she kept ripping more line off my reel and was 50 yards down into my backing.

We caught up again as she rested in another pool, her tail beating a lively tattoo against my leader. As I waded closer she somersaulted from the water and bolted downstream on another 100-yard run. This was one of the most powerful gamefish I've had the pleasure of hooking.

George finally worked into position downstream from the fish as she began wallowing on the surface, still fighting angrily but rapidly tiring. He held the net motionless, I dropped her head over the hoop, and we claimed a 28-pounder. The battle covered over a quarter-mile of river.

Fishing in Great Lakes spawning streams for Chinook salmon places a demand on the angler to use utmost caution, learning how to spot the fish before they spot you, and a knowledge of how and where to cast the fly so it will sweep by directly in front ot the salmon's nose. It sounds easy, but only a handful of salmon fishermen ever learn to do it right; many fumble around and spook more fish than they hook. This spoils the fishing for others and decreases everyone's chances of taking a trophy Chinook.

Polarized sunglasses are necessary; in fact, I'd rather take to the river without waders than leave my glasses home. They enable you to see through the surface glare and spot resting salmon. Without sunglasses a hulking big Chinook will appear as a log or a dark spot on the bottom, if you can see it at all.

Once a fish is spotted you must determine the best approach to use in order to cast accurately to the fish. I heartily advise anglers to work in to the river downstream from the fish and cast about 6 or 8 feet upstream from the salmon. Allow the fly to sink to bottom and gauge the current flow so the fly will work directly past its nose and along bottom. It takes repeated casting of this nature to "tease" a salmon into a strike.

Be advised of one thing: Chinook salmon will not strike a fly hard. It simply stops for an instant and then continues on. Anglers used to the jarring, vicious strike of an open-water king will be disappointed by this soft take. If you wait for a 35-pound king to rip a fly hard, you'll probably have 100 strikes, never know it, and fail to enjoy the back-alley scrap of a big fish.

I caution people to fish for the Chinook's head. If the fly is nearby, and the head moves—even an inch or two—set the hook. This telltale head movement is the only clue you'll have to a strike. This, of course, means you must be able to see the fish. In areas where fish are not visible, set the hook whenever the fly stops moving.

Most of the Chinook salmon hooked with this method will be barbed in the upper jaw, just inside the mouth. They simply go wild when hooked in this location.

Another fly-fishing technique for visible fish is to wade cautiously into the river upstream from the fish. Lengthen line and lay the fly across and slightly upstream from the salmon and allow it to swing around in the classic Atlantic salmon wet-fly technique. The fly must pass within an inch or so of the fish's nose to bring about a strike. If the head moves, set the hook. Strikes are more visible when fishing from above than when standing below the fish.

Almost any brightly colored fly will produce. I like vivid colors because they are easier to spot while fishing to visible salmon and they enable me to guide the fly to the fish by lengthening line or taking in a coil or two of fly line. If the fly can be seen, it can be worked directly to the fish, and this increases the possibilities of a strike.

Anglers intent on taking a big Chinook with this method are advised to walk the riverbanks and look for fish. Do not wade the river, because many Chinooks will be spooked by the noise and motion of wading. They get pretty owly at times, and to be productive, the game of stalking and casting to visible king salmon must be played according to the rules.

I've learned that the occasional twitching of the line as the fly swings in front of the fish will produce a solid take. It doesn't work all the time, and I normally rely on the current to provide the fly with all the action it needs to be productive.

There is a certain excitement found in stalking streams which hold 20-to 40-pound fish that grabs hold of me and won't let go. I have experienced many thrills in nearly thirty-five years of fishing, but I can't think of anything that delivers such fast-paced action with big fish as does Chinook salmon fishing. This gamefish is common in both the Midwest and West Coast areas and wherever he's found, he treats all anglers to the same type of fight. Kings are just as mean as they are big, and that suits me just fine. I think they are one of the finest trophy fish an angler could ever hope to hook.

21

COHO SALMON

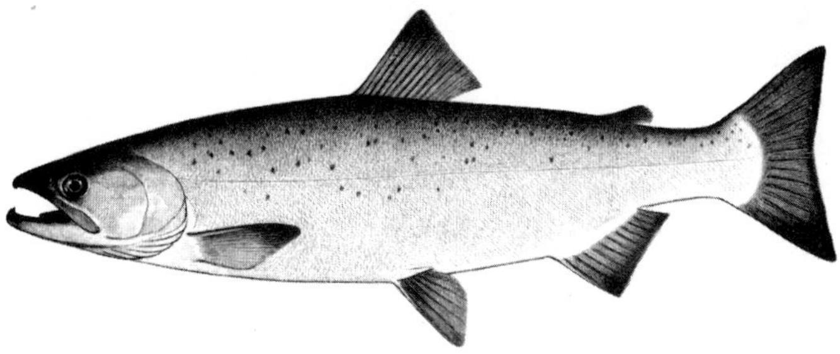

The coho or silver salmon has long been a favorite gamefish with Pacific Coast fishermen. In 1966, the Michigan Department of Natural Resources brought this species to the Midwest, and fishing success on the Great Lakes has grown at a fantastic rate. The value of this gamefish, in both areas, is extremely high as a rod-caught trophy.

Cohos strike with the force of a piledriver and make acrobatic leaps that would make a sailfish blush, and they also provide some of the finest eating of any gamefish. Fortunately they grow to large enough sizes to be considered trophy fish.

In open-water areas of the Pacific Ocean or the Great Lakes, the coho is very similar in appearance to a Chinook salmon. I've noted a tendency for the small silvery scales to fall off a coho easier than off a Chinook, especially when netting a fish. The lateral area of a coho is as silvery as a newly minted dime, and the dorsal area is a greenish blue which gradually lightens to the silver sides. The upper lobe of the caudal fin is sparsely dotted with dark spots, and the lower lobe is not spotted. Spots do not occur on the dorsal fin as with Chinook salmon. The inside of the mouth, around the gumline, is a dusky gray color, which helps differentiate the coho from the Chinook.

Once the fish begin ascending spawning streams, both male and female undergo bodily chemical changes which cause a distinct color change. Males often become cherry-red along the sides, with black lower jaws and an enormous hook or kype on the tip of the lower jaw. Females turn a dusky-green or burnt-olive color. The flesh of both fish is definitely inferior as table fare once these body changes occur.

Although certain techniques are local, used only in certain areas, the methods discussed here will produce silver salmon from the Great Lakes area or the Pacific Northwest. Sport fishing for cohos has taken hold in the Midwest, and innovative anglers have learned how to catch these fish. According to some estimates, the sport-caught total is higher for the Great Lakes states than for the states of California, Oregon, Washington, Alaska, and the Province of British Columbia, but I'll leave that argument to those who enjoy working with figures. I'd rather work hard at catching fish, and the following are some of my proven big-fish techniques.

SPRING FISHING

Spring fishing offers some of the finest angling of the year. The cohos are fairly small, although an occasional trophy fish is taken. The thing I enjoy most about spring coho fishing is it takes place within a few feet of the surface; the salmon are feeding on top. Early-in-the-year cohos often congregate near rivermouths and warm-water discharges, and since they are right on the surface the angler doesn't need heavy weights to take his offering down.

I prefer using small lures and light monofilament. Use lures such as the Tiny Tad (Tadpolly), small FirePlug, Herring Dodgers, and Michigan Squid or Rattlure flies, Bayou Special spoons, Johnson spoons, Little Digs, or other small salmon plugs or lures. The trend is to darker lures at this period than in summer or fall.

Trolling a flatline (no weight) is the preferred method of fishing. Occasionally a fisherman working the "color line," that mixture of dirty stream water and clean ocean or lake water, will take a trophy coho during the spring months. I've found it best to troll slightly faster during spring months than during summer or fall, particularly when working the color line.

One productive springtime fishing method is the "meat line." This is a series of three or four No. 0 Jensen Dodgers hooked head to tail with a small spoon trailing behind on a 12-inch 20-pound-mono leader. Two or 3 feet ahead of the first Dodger is 4 ounces of lead weight to take it below the surface. This unlikely combination is lowered over the stern and trolled in the prop wash, about 20 feet behind the boat. The violent action of the Dodgers and the turbulent prop wash will give this attractor-lure combination an exciting flash that spring cohos can't resist. It requires a stout line to handle a strike on this short line; I'd suggest at least 30-pound mono or braided Dacron.

SUMMER AND FALL

Summer and fall fishing is most productive in terms of trophy coho salmon. These fish often add a pound or more of weight each week during heavy feeding sprees. Unfortunately, these fish are often found in deeper water at this period, and there can be a lot of barren water around a school of salmon feeding in the Pacific Ocean or one of the Great Lakes. Locating these fish is the biggest problem, although this has been solved, in part, by the use of chart-recording Sona-Grafs, electronic water thermometers, and the constant parade of fishing chatter between boats equipped with VHF-FM marine radios. I've found that any coho fisherman who wishes to catch trophy open-water cohos should invest in a marine radio, learn which channels are used for ship-to-ship conversations, and monitor those channels. The information can help catch more and bigger fish.

A trick that can be used when fishing unfamiliar waters is to tag along behind a charter boat that specializes in catching coho salmon. I'd suggest trolling at least a quarter of a mile behind the boat, but follow the same route and try to determine at which depth and on which lures the anglers are taking salmon. This can shortcut the time needed to catch fish. The average charter-boat skipper is accustomed to smaller boats tagging along, provided they do not crowd him or get in his way when a fish is being fought.

Although downrigger fishing isn't as popular on the West Coast as it is in Great Lakes waters, where this controlled-depth fishing aid was developed, more ocean fishermen are now using downriggers and have found they up their catches of coho salmon.

A downrigger is merely a means unto an end; it allows the fisherman to pinpoint the exact depth he wishes to fish and to hold his lures or attractors and lures at that specified depth. It has been a boon to sport fishermen for many species, but shows its true value when salmon fishing. I use Luhr Jensen Auto-Trac downriggers, two on the stern and one on each gunwale, and have often had three fish on at once. Three trophy coho salmon, each in the 12-to-18-pound class, can provide long-remembered excitement.

Almost any lure or attractor-lure combination will catch midsummer or fall coho salmon, although I strongly suggest that bright fluorescent colors be used. The hot pinks, reds, oranges, blues, greens, chartreuse, chrome, or half-and-half green and silver or blue and silver work exceptionally well. If the coho schools have been hit hard by fleets of fishermen, a trick well worth trying is to switch to black lures. Few salmon lures are produced in black, but with a can of quick-drying spray paint you can paint your own. This has worked for me several times.

Research made by several knowledgeable fishermen jibes with my finding: We feel that salmon strike best early in the morning, particularly when they are beginning to school together before the spawning run begins. It pays to be on the water and trolling long before the sun pops over the eastern horizon.

Coho salmon will often congregate along the edge of a sharp dropoff and attack almost any lure that follows the lip of the ledge. This can be frustrating fishing, because many times the fish cannot be seen on a chart-recording graph and it becomes a hunt for the exact depth and areas which hold these fish.

Jack Duffy, a well-known fisherman and charter-boat skipper, is one of the finest salmon anglers I know. He advocates working on and off a dropoff and feels salmon will often strike a lure as it falls over the edge of an underwater bank. He fishes Herring Dodgers and flies early in the day until the boat traffic gets thick, and then switches to "clean lures." He prefers clean lures (no attractors) during the middle of the day because he feels too many attractors will spook big cohos once other boats begin trolling. His lures, usually spoons or plugs, are often run about 30 feet behind the cannonballs, and he enjoys tremendous success with big fish.

David Richey displays a trophy coho salmon caught in Lake Michigan while trolling off a downrigger. Coho offer superb sport in the Great Lakes, where they were stocked in 1966, and on the West Coast.

I remember a trip I made with Jack two years ago on Michigan's Platte Bay, considered by some fishermen the greatest concentration of coho salmon in the world. We made the 15-mile run from Frankfort in record time and were setting our lines before the sun began bulging the dawn sky. The third line was just settling in place when one of the out-downrigger rods popped up, the sign of a strike. I grabbed the rod and a well-hooked trophy coho slithered into the air, tailwalked briefly, and smashed back down. Jack was just lowering the fourth downrigger when another went off. "Fish on," I hollered. "Grab that rod." It was bucking in its rodholder by the time Jack got to it.

My coho vaulted out of the water again, with the body of my green J-Plug sliding up the line toward the boat. Jack was fighting his coho and yelling like a wild man. "Look at my fish go! Dave, look at my fish!" Jack was hollering. He's caught thousands of big coho salmon, but each one brings a first-timer's reaction from him. His fish was skipping across the surface as though its tail were on fire.

Jack's mate was wheeling the boat, and two other lines were still down. I pressured my fish close to the boat and made a lucky swipe that resulted in the coho sliding into the net. I was just bringing it over the gunwale when a third downrigger rod snapped up with a loud pop. Far astern a silvery 16-pound coho was lashing the water to a froth. I dropped the net, grabbed that rod, and began fighting another coho.

Jack finally got his big coho, a 17-pounder, up to the boat, and one-handed the large landing net around his prize and dumped it into the fish cooler. He scrambled around, raised the three downriggers, attached the fishing line to the release systems, and sent them back down to the depths. We were racing the sun and the other boats that were beginning to come into the area.

He lowered the three lines while I fought my fish, and we managed to team up and land a silvery male before another coho struck. The action went on like that for two hours. We had just landed the last fish of our coho limit when they stopped feeding heavily. As we made a leisurely cruise back to Frankfort with a bulging fish box, Jack said, "You know, coho fishing has to provide some of the most spectacular sport any angler would ever hope to have. These fish are hard to stay hooked up with. Man, my arm is sore from all the fish we hooked." We'd lost about six fish besides the ones that were boated.

TRICKS FOR COHOS

Coho fishing can be spectacular, but it still requires knowledge of the fish and their feeding habits. Certain tricks that work well are often overlooked by sport fishermen.

One little-known trick is to add strips of Prism Tape to the backs of lures. This tape comes in green, blue, silver, gold, and rainbow colors and will reflect a tremendous amount of light in deep water. A piece half an inch wide and 2 inches long will suffice. It pays to experiment with various colors. Some days it produces best when attached to the top of lures, and other times it works better when placed on the bottom side.

Something that few anglers are aware of is that coho salmon, especially the bigger fish, are picky feeders. They might strike well one day on a certain lure in a special color and the following day they will hit a different-colored lure. Size can also be an important factor; big salmon prefer a larger lure during the summer or fall than during spring months. I've taken trophy coho salmon on 4-inch plugs and 5-inch spoons during the latter part of the season.

One of the deadliest coho tricks I've learned is to fish two lines off one downrigger. An easy method to do this is to crimp a three-way swivel 4 feet above the downrigger release. One line, the bottom line off the regular release, is attached, and the cannonball is lowered slightly. A lightweight rubber band is looped through one eye of the three-way swivel and is attached to a barrel swivel about 4 feet up the line from the lure on that line.

Both lures are lowered to the proper depth, and the downrigger is locked into place. If a fish strikes the upper line, with the rubber band, the band breaks and the fish is hooked on a weight-free line. It increases the chances of taking a trophy coho but is legal only in states which allow the use of two lines per angler.

A fisherman once told me of a trick that can be very productive late in the season when schools of cohos are being pounded hard. "When the fishing slows down, look around for open pockets of water where other boats aren't trolling. Many times the fish will be found in those seldom-fished areas," he said.

An Oregon guide, a man who knew what he was talking about, once told me, "If the cohos have been holding at one depth and biting well, and they suddenly disappear, they have usually headed for deeper water. Schools of fish are often pushed to greater depths because of the heavy fishing pressure."

The above technique once saved the day for me on Lake Michigan near Manistee, Mich. The weather had been beastly hot with the temperature hovering in the 90s. Hundreds of boats were trolling in 80 feet of water, but the fish were sluggish in the warm water and reluctant to strike. Finally, the fish just disappeared and not a salmon was caught.

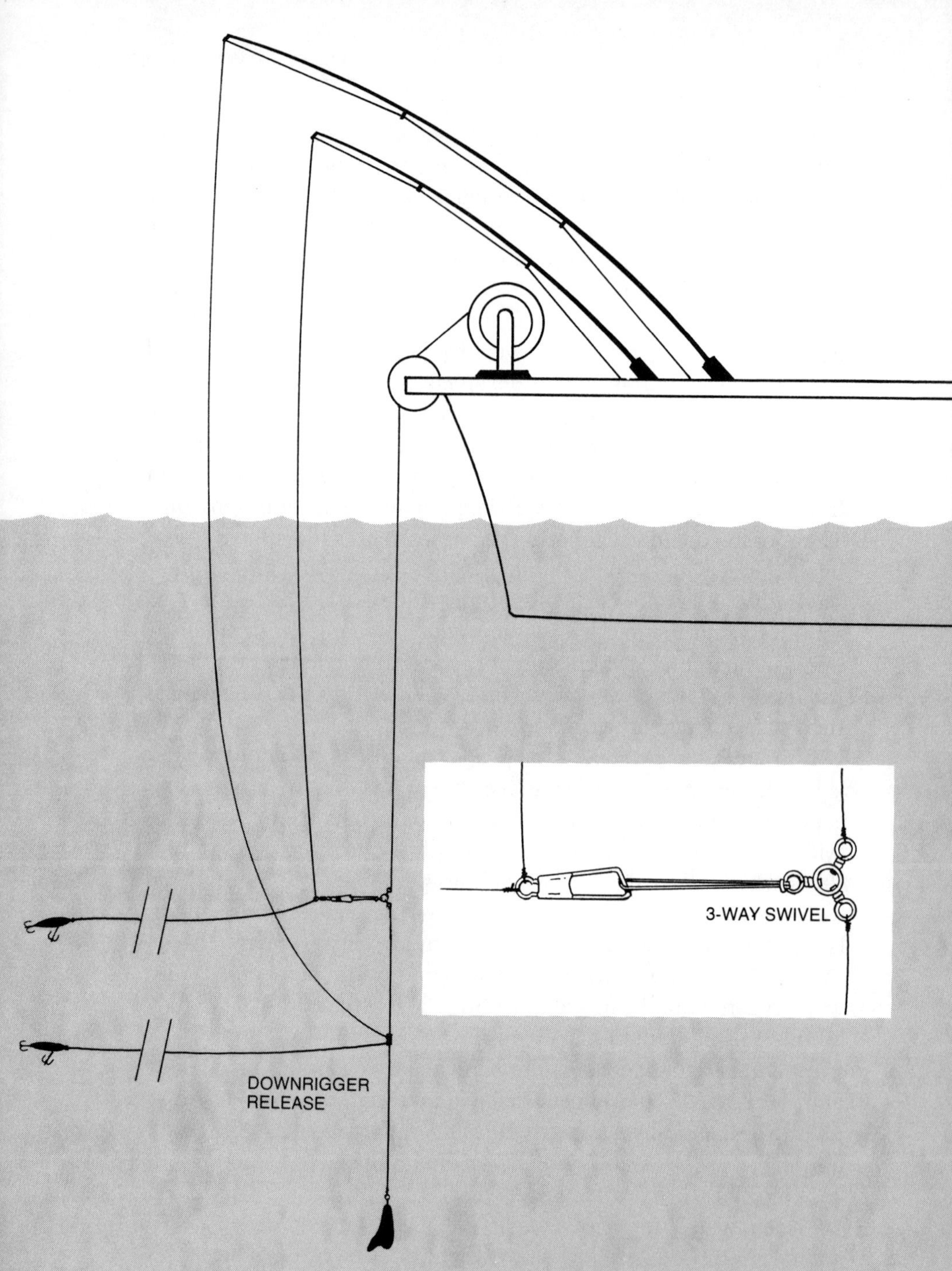

Method of fishing two lines off a downrigger. The bottom line is attached to the downrigger line with a conventional release; the top line to a three-way swivel on the downrigger line with a rubber band.

Several boats teamed up and we began searching the depths. We finally found the coho holed up in 130 feet of water. This is deepwater fishing at its toughest, but the fish would strike almost every time we lowered our downrigger lures into their midst. One fish, a 22-pounder, provided me with thirty minutes of the hardest tug-of-war battle I've ever encountered from a coho. Trophy fish never come easy, but fishing for coho salmon at depths of 100 or more feet is commonplace in the Great Lakes. After you've battled a big coho up from those depths he'll burp for ten minutes from the compressed nitrogen in his blood. They react much the same as a diver suffering the bends from ascending too quickly.

Many of the same techniques that produce for lake trout, brown trout, and Chinook salmon will also work well on coho salmon. The mooching method discussed in the previous chapter is a good one to try when all else fails.

Late in the season, coho fishermen often use sewn minnows rigged as discussed in the brown trout and Chinook salmon chapters. It can be a deadly producer when other fishermen are using hardware. The trolling speeds must be kept slower for this type of fishing.

One technique that produces well when coho salmon prepare to

When coho salmon are preparing to ascend a spawning stream, they gather near the rivermouth. A good way to take them is to anchor a boat near the rivermouth and cast to the fish.

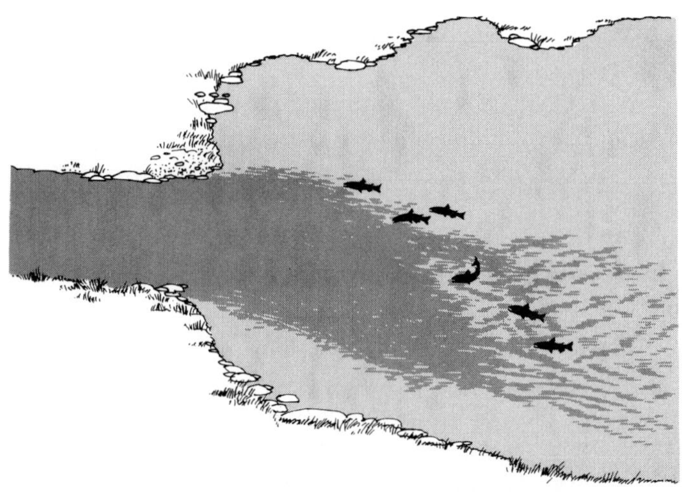

hit the spawning streams is to anchor a boat near the rivermouth and cast. Two years ago I tried this, and it was far more productive than trolling. I personally enjoy downrigger fishing, but you're unable to feel the strike when the rod is fastened to a downrigger release and a rodholder. This isn't the case when you cast off a rivermouth.

The strikes are hard and sure and often within 20 yards of the boat. I prefer Kelly-green lures such as Mepps spinners in a No. 4 or No. 5 size, light-green Dardevles, green-and-silver Little Cleos, green Tadpollys, or a variety of other lures. I've had some success with other colors at this time but have found that green often produces when all other colors fail. The lures can be fished with a variety of retrieves, but a steady retrieve that brings out the best action of the lure is best.

RIVER FISHING

I'm a river fisherman at heart. I like the sounds of a stream chuckling through hardwoods and evergreens, the feel of the current pulling at my legs, and I thrive on the excitement generated by fishing for pre-spawning or spawning cohos in a river.

As I've stated before, and it bears repeating here, fishing for spawning salmon in certain waters of the Great Lakes *does not* affect the future runs of these gamefish. This is an accepted and sporting method of fishing, although some Western fishermen feel differently because spawning salmon are protected in waters along the Pacific coast.

There are five basic river-fishing techniques which produce once cohos work upstream, and they are geared to the trophy fisherman, although each will take smaller specimens. Two or three of these techniques have been discussed in previous chapters on steelhead and Chinook fishing and will not be repeated except for a brief description of each method with certain differences noted for coho salmon.

Coho often work upstream in large schools. I've seen upwards of 300 fish moving together through a river system. The fish will concentrate in a hole until other fish pile in behind them so heavily that the fish on the upstream end of the pool are forced to swim up the river. I've seen certain holes which were black with fish from top to bottom.

One of the finest methods of taking big cohos from deep rivers is to cast deep-diving lures like Heddon's River Runt Spook. This technique was described in an earlier chapter but it also produces big coho. The fish will usually be found very close to heavy underwater brushpiles. The tail ends of deep pools will also produce fish when the lure is cast quartering across and upstream and allowed to dive near bottom and retrieved with a fast, tight wiggle.

Fly fishing is my favorite sport, and fly-caught coho salmon are easy. I mean that; these fish are so easy to catch in shallow rivers on flies that a competent angler could easily catch thirty or forty fish daily. I've done this countless times, and at one time I guided fishermen during fall months and never had a client go home without a sore arm and his limit of coho salmon. We would often catch and release our limits daily. I've taken poor fishermen, anglers that couldn't cast a fly accurately, and under direct supervision, they would land a limit of five coho salmon in less than two hours. This points out my contention that spawning cohos are almost too easy to catch.

The fly-fishing techniques described for steelhead and Chinook salmon will work here, provided the fisherman can place his cast so the fly will pass just in front of the salmon's nose. A novice will often miss the take; as I guide I'd have to tell them to strike. The most puzzled look would come over their faces when they hooked a fish and didn't feel it take the fly. Suffice it to say that coho salmon will seldom strike hard, although they will chase a fly for long distances. I've watched big male cohos chase a fly 6 feet before taking it.

One of the deadliest methods of taking super-big coho salmon is to approach the river and the fish in much the same manner as in fly fishing. I prefer a fly rod for this method but substitute a No. 2 or No. 3 brass, copper, or silver Mepps spinner for the fly.

The fish is stalked in the same manner, but a spinner is used to tease the fish. Casting a spinner, even a small one, calls for a good sense of timing to avoid a hook in the ear. The cast is made with the rod held nearly horizontal, and a soft lob cast can be laid out without spooking the fish. Avoid a heavy lure splashdown because this will scare every fish in the area. I try to achieve a delicate plop by halting the flight of the spinner just before it strikes the water. It will enter the water softly.

The spinner should be allowed to tumble downstream at the same speed as the current until it is close to the salmon. The rod tip is then lifted slightly and pulled toward the angler, and this will cause the spinner blade to revolve. The blade must be turning over when it approaches the fish. This works best when the fisherman stands downstream from the fish and casts up past it.

Once the spinner passes the fish, lift it quickly from the water and make another cast to the same spot. A coho will either strike or spook out of the area on the second or third cast.

The spinner technique also works well if the angler is positioned upstream from the fish. The spinner is cast across and down and allowed to flutter past just upstream from the fish's nose. Many times you'll be able to see the strike, although you'll seldom feel it. The spinner will stop, just as with a fly, and the fish will quickly carry it to one side and drop it. The entire process takes about a second, so the fisherman must set the hook whenever he sees the fish move.

I've found that big coho salmon, particularly large males, will strike a spinner if it is cast downstream from their holding position and then brought upstream past the side of the head. It often takes two or three husky split shot to keep the spinner near bottom, but the fish will strike as the lure approaches its head. These strikes may be vicious, but the salmon will generally just turn its head sideways, inhale the spinner, and then drop it. It pays to watch the fish's head and set the hook whenever it moves.

Although coho salmon do not feed once they move upstream to spawn, they will still take bait off the bottom. They do not swallow it but I suspect it represents a threat to their eggs and they pick it up to move it away in much the same manner as they move a spinner or fly.

Some of the largest coho salmon are taken on nightcrawlers or spawn bags fished on the bottom. As proof of this occurrence, Paul Lewandowski of Rochester, N. Y., managed to land Michigan's state-record coho on a spawn bag while fishing the Platte River for steelhead. That fish was caught in October 1976 and weighed 30 pounds 9 ounces, only seven ounces short of a new world record.

Spawn bags or nightcrawlers are allowed to bounce naturally downstream through good holding water. Deep holes, runs, and pockets of deep water above or just below a shallow gravel spawning bar are ideal locations to fish bait.

I hold my rod tip at a 10 o'clock position and keep a tight line, and this gives me a superb feel of the bait and split shot bouncing downstream. Whenever it stops, I'll set the hook, although some

Eddie Long unhooks a big river coho for Lawrence Richey, the author's father, on the Platte River in Michigan. The fish struck a fly teased in front of it.

big coho will mouth the bait for varying lengths of time before moving off with it. This often feels like a dainty fish pecking at the bait. Whenever this sensation is felt, lower the rod tip for an instant, and then set the hook. You might be rewarded with a heavyweight scrap in fast water, and the end result will be worth the effort of learning this sport.

Baitfishing is a good method of taking trophy cohos once they enter a spawning stream, but it is overlooked by far too many anglers. A fisherman who excels at bouncing spawn bags for steelhead will have little trouble catching a coho with this method.

Coho fishing is big business wherever this gamefish is found. There is something about trophy fishing that brings salmon fishermen into productive areas from far away. I've witnessed this lemminglike migration of anglers on both the West Coast and in the salmon-rich Great Lakes states. The attraction fishermen feel for the silver salmon is one that must be seen to be appreciated.

The sport of coho fishing means tourism, and tourism means dollars in good fishing areas. But these areas do not remain popular for long if they do not produce exciting fishing for big silvers. Trophy salmon fishermen are looking for exciting angling and big fish, and luckily the coho is capable of furnishing great sport in many areas. I would hope it shall always remain so, because the coho salmon is a superb gamefish worthy of a trophy classification in anyone's book.

VI

OTHER FISH

22

GRAYLING

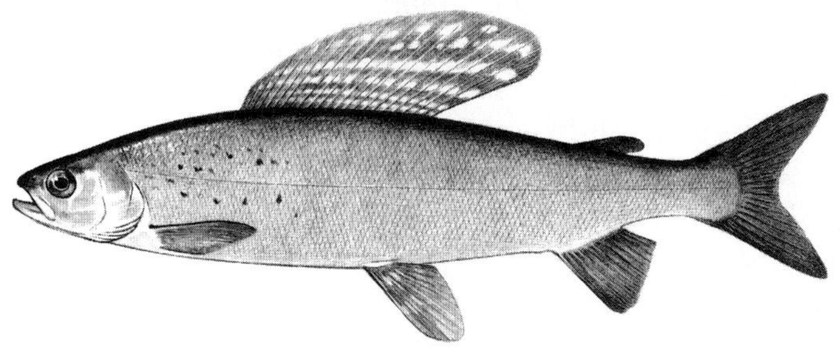

The Arctic grayling and the Montana grayling are considered to be two of the most highly prized gamefish available in North America. A good bit of the popularity accorded these fish stems from their relative scarcity; nowhere except in certain remote sections of northwestern Canada are grayling plentiful. All too many streams and lakes in the western continental United States are now barren of grayling where they were once found in large numbers.

Another reason for the widespread popularity of this gamefish is its superb beauty and hard-fighting qualities. Hook a grayling on a fly and light tippet, or on a small lure and light line, and it will deliver a dogged and flashy fight.

Grayling are found in both lakes and streams, and some of the largest fish are taken from huge lakes like Great Bear in the Northwest Territories.

The story of the grayling in the United States, especially in the lower forty-eight states, sounds like a litany of despair. Man's greed and his ruthless timbering practices resulted in heavy siltation and the ruin of many streams; the warming of the waters resulted in a loss of both tree and stream cover; and the relentless fishing practices in the latter half of the nineteenth century combined to force a drastic overkill of this splendid gamefish. Michigan once harbored beautiful grayling in many streams of the Upper and Lower Peninsulas. By the early 1900s, grayling were gone from these rivers, and the last recorded fish was caught in a small Upper Peninsula stream in the 1930s.

The story reads the same wherever this gamefish was found. Alaska now offers some of the finest grayling fishing left in the United States. Only a remnant population is still found in Montana, Wyoming, and Utah, and efforts at transplanting these fish have usually met with failure.

Prime habitat for grayling, other than in Alaska, now rests in northern portions of Saskatchewan, the Yukon, and Northwest Territories, and to a lesser extent in British Columbia.

The grayling is well known for its sail-like dorsal fin. These fish vary greatly in color even when taken in the same lake or watershed. I've seen brownish-colored fish, gray-colored ones, and others with a silvery back and a small amount of V- or X-shaped spots just behind the gills and horizontal wavy lines between the rows of scales. These lines, like the spots, may be distinct or barely noticeable. The skin of these fish often gives off a silvery or brassy glow, depending upon which way the light strikes them, and it is often noticeable underwater when the angler fights a fish.

The dorsal fin is a thing of beauty. It is larger in male fish, starting low in front and sweeping higher in back. It is just the opposite in females. This large fin has irregular rows of light and dark spots, and the upper edge is a blush of color ranging from pink, white, or violet to a very pale blue. Many times the upper portion of the dorsal fin will have long wavy light-colored lines. The pelvic fins are often streaked with the same vivid colors displayed on the dorsal fin. This gorgeous bannerlike dorsal fin is often spread wide while the fish is fighting the rod, and it throws off a rainbow of colors during a battle.

The biggest trick to catching grayling is to find an area where they are abundant. This often necessitates a lengthy journey by air to a major western Canadian city and then further air travel to a remote lake or stream where grayling dimple in quiet water. It is not an easy fish to get to, nor is the fishing cheap. A trophy fisherman looking for a big male grayling may spend $1,000 or more in his search for this fish.

A low-budget fisherman traveling west on a family vacation might do well to consider trying for this species in the three continental states that offer some fishing. This fishing is never fast and often entails a high-country hike to work into remote lakes or the headwaters of certain streams. Another possibility is that the fish may not be striking well during your visit and you'll wind up skunked. This has happened to me several times while pursuing graylings in Glacier National Park in Montana and Yellowstone National Park in Wyoming. But there are those memorable occasions when the fish can be easily caught.

Conditions change periodically in these high mountain lakes, and a body of water may contain grayling for a period of years and then the fishing goes downhill when other species are introduced, either naturally or by periodic fish plantings. It would do little good in this book to pinpoint the grayling lakes I fished years ago because by the time this book has been published, the fish may well have disappeared.

My suggestion is to contact the various fish and game offices in Montana, Wyoming, and Utah and determine which lakes currently have grayling of catchable size. Another trick is to contact the National Park Service offices in Glacier or Yellowstone parks and determine where to go in those areas. This is how I used to locate good grayling lakes.

In the lower states, grayling seldom weigh over 1½ pounds, and fish much smaller will compose the major portion of a catch. The average grayling taken from a remote wilderness area of northern Canada will probably average nearly 2 pounds, and I consider a trophy Arctic grayling to be anything over 3 pounds. I've personally taken fish, large males with huge sweeping dorsal fins, that have weighed 4 pounds, but they are extremely scarce in most areas.

I'm primarily a fly fisherman, but some of my largest trophy fish have struck small Panther Martin or Mepps spinners. One of my most memorable grayling trips was on the Camsell River, just below White Eagle Falls, a major tributary of Great Bear Lake. Kay and I were fishing with Charley Hamelin, a Cree guide for Branson's Lodge. He is a superior fishing guide whom I've often fished with in that area.

Like many Crees, Charley didn't talk much until we'd gotten to know each other. He had to learn my likes and dislikes, and I had to learn to accept his stoic behavior. Once we became friends, he opened up and made suggestions any trophy fisherman likes to hear. One day he said, "Let's go and catch grayling on the Camsell. I know an area where the river empties into the lake where you can catch big fish." When Charley talks trophy fishing, I listen, because I know him well enough to realize that he seldom offers a suggestion unless it's been proved time and again.

We nosed the boat up into a fast-water riffle where the Camsell flows into a bay on this massive lake. The river at this point was about 30 yards across and 5 feet deep, and so swift that Charley had to keep the outboard going at half-throttle to hold us in position so we could cast.

"Look! There's several big grayling. Cast the spinner far upstream and allow it to tumble down with the current and work it past their nose," Charley offered. The current made it difficult to spot the fish; the grayling blended in with the bottom and they were holding behind small boulders. It was difficult to work the tiny spinners down to the bottom unless you made a cast at least 40 feet above the fish and allowed it to sink on a slack line before starting the retrieve.

My first two casts were off the mark—I hadn't read the current speed and depth accurately and the spinners passed over the heads of the fish. The third cast was fine, and the spinner twinkled down past the largest grayling. He rose off the bottom, his dorsal fin glittering in the sunlight, and followed the lure without striking. "You've got him interested. Keep throwing to that fish," Charley coached from the stern. He was as anxious for us to score as we were.

My next cast was met by the solid take of a grayling, and it tore off downstream, into the large hole formed by the current at the junction of the lake. We bulldogged back and forth for several minutes. The fish boiled out of the hole once in a classic head-to-tail leap, its dorsal fin spread like a banner. That jump settled the affair, and the fish rolled over on its side and came to the boat, a beautifully colored male weighing almost 4 pounds.

Kay and I took turns catching grayling from that riffle for two hours. We could see almost every fish holding against the light-colored bottom. They would move away from the protection of a small boulder, make a pass at our spinners, and then scurry back. Every fish we caught could be seen and fished for with tiny spinners. Charley was satisfied with our success, and Kay and I were ecstatic.

My wife made one cast into the large deep hole at the rivermouth and had a heavy strike. She set the hooks and the fish bored away from the boat. For a minute she thought she had on a giant grayling, but was greatly disappointed when the green shape of a 10-pound northern pike hove into view. Pike of this size are fun to catch, but not when one is geared up mentally for trophy grayling.

Kay's largest grayling topped 3 pounds and jumped several times with shimmering leaps that completely cleared the surface. Some writers have claimed that a grayling offers little battle, but I haven't found it so. On light line (the only way you should fish) these gamefish offer a spirited battle comparable to any other species of the same size. The dorsal fin acts as a means of leverage, and grayling often present the broad dorsal to the pull of the line. It becomes a test of skill to subdue a trophy fish.

Many old-time writers contend that a grayling has a soft mouth and hooks are easily torn out if too much pressure is exerted while fighting the fish. This is an old wives' tale; grayling have very small mouths but the lips are tough and leathery. It takes small lures or flies to hook these fish, but once hooked, they seldom get away, and I've never lost one when a hook ripped out.

One of the best means of taking big grayling is to prowl the borders of a lake and cast small wet or dry flies to surfacing fish. This method is usually productive early in the day and again just before dusk, which in subarctic lakes may be from 10:00 p.m. until 2:00 a.m. One year I fished Great Bear Lake at 2:00 a.m. and caught grayling on wee dry flies until every pattern I had was chewed ragged by the fish.

Some lakes lend themselves well to wading, although I've had my best fishing from either a canoe or a small boat. Grayling in shoreline shallows are wary fish and will head for deep water at any hint of noise. I've found it best to coast or paddle within casting distance of shore. Roar in under power and every fish in the area will be gone within seconds.

Grayling roam the shallows of northern lakes in schools. I've found as many as 100 fish dimpling a quiet bay, and every fish will be feeding within a 50-yard radius. The taking of a big grayling under these conditions necessitates catching and releasing numerous smaller fish for every trophy. However, it can be done, and this increases the enjoyment of taking that one very special fish. In my opinion any grayling is a trophy, regardless of size. The only question is what constitutes a trophy for other anglers. I've seen fishermen claim and mount a 12-inch grayling that would weigh

Kay Richey gills a grayling from the mouth of the Camsell River where it flows into Great Bear Lake in the Northwest Territories. This fish struck a small Panther Martin spinner fished in fast water.

less than a pound. Serious fishermen strive for a fish weighing at least 3 pounds.

A trick I learned long ago is that grayling are curious and will follow anything if they feel it represents food. This can be advantageous to a fly fisherman, because if they steadfastly refuse one fly after following it, they may come back and strike a similar pattern in a larger or smaller size. It takes some experimentation to catch big grayling consistently, but they are not hard to fool.

Grayling are not seemingly wary of fishermen, but light tippets and silent wading or boat movement is necessary. I strongly suggest fly fishermen use nothing heavier than a 3X tippet. If the fish seem easily spooked by a cast I'd add a length of 6X tippet. This will usually fool even the wariest grayling, although each fish hooked will provide an epic struggle.

The fly choice isn't a matter of great concern, although I generally use flies tied on No. 10 to No. 14 hooks. Some of the more productive patterns are dark: a Black Gnat, Black Ant, Stone Fly, March Brown, Brown Hackle, Black Hackle, Gray Hackle, Dark Cahill, and Quill Gordon. There are times when grayling are picky feeders, and the angler is well advised to carry a selection of the above flies tied on No. 18 or No. 20 hooks. A small fly will occasionally take fish when larger patterns fail.

Fly-fishing the lakes consists of making a soft accurate presentation over fish rising to the surface. Allow the fly to remain motionless for several seconds and then begin inching it back very slowly. A high-riding dry fly that sits well up on its hackles will skate across the surface and kick up tiny ripples. I've watched grayling hover just inches below a dry fly until it is moved, and then they arch out of the water and will often take the fly on the way down. This is an exciting rise form and quite common with grayling.

Some fish will merely pluck such an imitation off the surface with a barely audible sound. One second the fly is floating high and dry, and the next instant it has disappeared.

A mistake many fly fishermen make is to strike immediately after the grayling hits, and this usually results in the fish being lightly hooked in the lip. It is better to allow a very brief pause after the take before setting to insure that the fish will take the fly deeper in its mouth and be well hooked.

Wet flies can be fished on a floating fly line as long as the leader sinks. The most productive technique I've found, although it doesn't offer the classic head-to-tail surface rise, is to inch it along fairly rapidly. A brief one-second pause will suffice every 2 or 3 feet. Grayling will move to the fly as the retrieve slows down, and these strikes are sure and hard.

Fly fishing on the swift streams characteristic of grayling waters is an entirely different ballgame. Anglers used to fishing swift waters for trout will probably have little trouble taking grayling.

These fish often hold behind large boulders or shelves of granite that break the current flow. It's not uncommon to look into a cushion of pocket water behind a boulder and spot 15 or 20 grayling holding in each spot. But seeing them and catching them are two entirely different matters.

River grayling feed in one of three styles. They will either leap from the water and take the fly on the way down, slash upward and take it off the surface with a hefty splash, or ease up to it, drift downstream with the fly for a few feet, and strike with a tiny dimple.

A characteristic of river fish is that they often take a fly *downstream* from their holding position. They will seldom move upstream to make the strike. More often than not, grayling will drift down with the fly and suck it under several feet behind where they were holding in the current.

Downstream casting is much more productive in heavily fished rivers. Make a slack-line cast quartering across and downstream and the fly will travel down a feeding lane ahead of the fly line. The dry fly should be presented to feeding fish without drag, although I've seen the odd time when grayling will pursue and strike a fly dragging across the surface.

I've taken several grayling over 3 pounds which struck a wet fly or nymph. The proper procedure is to cast across and down and mend the line as necessary to obtain a longer, deeper drift. A few of these fish have struck as the fly straightened out below me, and I feel they had probably followed it for some distance. The strikes often come just as you prepare to lift the line from the water to make another cast. In this respect, it pays to fish each cast out as though a trophy fish were following it.

The upper Madison River and upper Gallatin River, as well as the headwater lakes, offer fair to excellent fishing for Montana grayling. In Wyoming some good grayling fishing used to be found in Johnson Lake in the southwest portion of the state and Upper Clay

Butte Lake in the north-central section. Many grayling lakes are available only to fishermen willing to hike or ride in on horseback. The fish rarely measure over 14 inches, and much more common are 10-inchers.

The grayling is a relatively rare gamefish that needs the protection of dedicated fishermen. No one can argue with an angler taking an occasional trophy for a mount, but it's very easy to denounce the fish hog who catches and keeps his limit of smaller fish on a consistent basis.

With proper protection in the remaining continental waters which still hold graylings, and the fixing of low creel limits in Canadian waters, there is every reason to assume that future generations of fishermen will be able to go after this sporty fish with the strikingly beautiful dorsal fin. Like the wolf, grizzly bear, and mountain lion, the grayling is a living symbol of the wild places left in North America.

If the sportsmen of this continent are capable of benefiting from the mistakes of previous generations, and can learn something of how to manage this valuable species, we will be able to fish for graylings in some waters long after the turn of the next century.

23 STURGEON

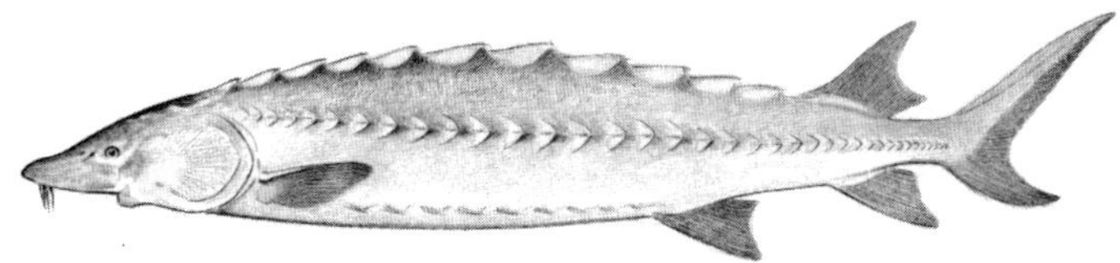

In certain portions of the United States, sturgeon fishing is one of the most exciting forms of trophy fishing available to freshwater fishermen. The sturgeon is one of the largest fish commonly encountered in sweet water. It rates a notch or two above the alligator gar in size in certain areas.

Fishermen who tangle with this primitive gamefish must possess a certain type of death wish. Once an angler has gotten hold of a big sturgeon, it becomes a contest as to whether the fish will haul the fisherman into the water or vice versa. More than one fisherman has been rendered unconscious or had an arm or leg broken by a powerful bottom-feeding sturgeon.

Sturgeons are ancient fish, with ancestors that can be traced back to the days of sabertooth tigers and dinosaurs. The waters they now frequent are the same ones that previous generations swam through when man was a stoop-shouldered hulk with only a spear for survival. That sturgeons have survived thousands of years of predatory attack, advancing and receding glaciers, and modern pollutants is testimony to their adaptability.

There are several species of North American sturgeon, but only three figure significantly in the sport-caught catch of these fish: white sturgeon, Atlantic sturgeon, and lake sturgeon. The white is also known as the Pacific sturgeon; it is frequently fished for in certain large rivers and bays which form the Pacific watershed. They are quite common in the massive Columbia River and in California's Sacramento River and San Francisco Bay, where there is a thriving fishery.

The Atlantic sturgeon is an anadromous species that enters rivers along the Eastern Seaboard from Florida north to Newfoundland.

The lake sturgeon is a freshwater fish that seldom ventures into salt water. The lake sturgeon's range is from Saskatchewan east to Quebec, including all the Great Lakes, certain inland lakes in Michigan and Wisconsin, and down through the Mississippi River valley and into the Ohio and Missouri rivers. It is also found in the St. Lawrence River in New York State.

These three sturgeons are the heavyweights of their family. It's not uncommon to hook or spear sturgeon weighing upwards of 100 pounds, although the average sport-caught fish will usually weigh slightly less. The world-record white sturgeon, the only one on which records are kept, is 360 pounds, a monster fish taken from Idaho's Snake River. Lake sturgeons also belong in the king-size class. Michigan's state record weighed a whopping 193 pounds and was speared through the ice.

The sturgeon—and I'm lumping the three species together in this classification—is among the homeliest brutes I've laid eyes on. Even a mother sturgeon must find them repulsive to look at. It looks like a prehistoric monster—which is what it is. It has no body scales like other fish but possesses numerous lengthwise rows of bony shields or humps along the dorsal, lateral, and ventral areas.

The head is long and narrowly tapered, almost to a point. The mouth is underslung, toothless, and situated well back from the snout. Four barbels are located in front of the mouth, and they serve as food detecting sensory organs. All sturgeons are bottom feeders, feeding on mollusks, crustaceans, and minute bottom-dwelling morsels.

The upper caudal lobe is longer than the lower lobe on all

sturgeons. These fish also possess a white tubular column, called a notochord, instead of a true backbone. Little difference exists between male and female sturgeons except the obvious one of sperm or roe in spawning fish. The roe is considered a delicacy, as is the flesh of all sturgeons.

Certain Western states have detailed regulations governing fishing for white sturgeons. Wherever white sturgeons are found—and they are never plentiful in any one area—they are not something which an angler should set aside a two-week vacation to try fishing for. There are certain periods of time when an angler stands a better chance of catching fish than others. Spring or early summer is the best time to take these fish on hook and line.

A spectacular white sturgeon fishery has evolved in California's San Francisco Bay near Sausalito in recent years. The peak of this fishery develops about mid-March and continues for some time. Anglers in that area have learned to pinpoint the locations of spawning herring by circling sea gulls. These silvery fish spawn by the millions and drop their eggs on rocks and kelp. When the tides go out, gulls sail in on locked wings and squabble over the exposed eggs. This collection of herring eggs also attracts bottom-snuffling white sturgeons.

Once the big whites find a fresh batch of spawn, they leap into the air in seeming jubilation. The gulls, herring, and leaping sturgeon are fine for locating a good concentration of fish, but it does little good unless the fisherman has the necessary bait—fresh herring roe.

Fishermen use small boats and anchor in the swift current of the outgoing tide. A large 8-ounce lead weight is used in the fast water to hold the bait, and a single 7/0 hook is baited generously with fresh herring roe. There is no need to cast; the bait and sinker can be lowered almost directly beneath the boat. The line should be kept tight in order to feel the sucking strike of a big sturgeon.

Many anglers use 30-to-60-pound-test monofilament line for this fishing, and some battles take on epic proportions. Fish up to 200 pounds have been taken in battles which last several hours. The average weight of diamondbacks, as they are called in California, will be close to 100 pounds. At this writing, the limit is one fish per day. A 100-pounder is a whale of a fish guaranteed to leave the person wishing he'd stayed with tossing No. 12 dry flies to rising brown trout.

A similar form of sturgeon fishing takes place in certain large rivers like the Columbia or Snake. This fishing is also bottom fishing, but large balls of worms or nightcrawlers can be used to fish the deep holes. It isn't fast fishing; only the San Francisco Bay fishing can be termed fast, and it lasts only as long as the herring spawn. Try to catch one at other times and you'd probably have more fun watching grass grow.

The one technique that seems to work in rivers is to select a large pool where sturgeons have been seen jumping. This type of fishing is sedentary; once the bait is tossed out into the hole, the line is kept tight, and the angler sits back with the patience of Job for a strike. It may take a day, a week, or a month of fishing before a vacuum-nosed sturgeon wanders through the area and takes notice of the bait.

A similar method of river fishing takes place every June on the St. Clair River, between Michigan and Ontario, and just north of Detroit. These are lake sturgeons moving upstream to spawn, and fishermen anchor in the swift currents in much the same manner as the anglers in San Francisco Bay. The primary difference is that this fishing takes place at night.

After the boat is anchored in the swift current the anglers bait up with a 1/0 treble hook liberally adorned with nightcrawlers. It takes from 6 to 10 ounces of lead to hold the bait down on bottom in this fast water.

If the angler picks the right spot he will often be rewarded with a tapping strike and then solid resistance. Anglers that fish from small boats, such as in the St. Clair River or in San Francisco Bay, take their lives in their hands, because a fresh-hooked sturgeon is an evil-tempered ugly brute. Jumps commonly take the fish nearly 6 feet in the air and one jump can cover 30 or 40 feet of water. If a boatload of fishermen happen to be under a tail-lashing sturgeon when it comes down, the anglers are liable to go to the bottom along with the fish. It's like sitting on a keg of dynamite with a short sputtering fuse. One fisherman told me, "Fishing for trophy sturgeon is like playing Russian roulette with five chambers loaded. Those fish can kill you."

A similar river fishery takes place on the Menominee River between Michigan's Upper Peninsula and northeastern Wisconsin. This fishing is usually done from small boats or from sand and gravel bars along the river. Again, this is bottom fishing, and large gobs of nightcrawlers are the preferred bait.

SPEARING

Although open-water fishing for sturgeon is fun, it is child's play compared to sturgeon spearing through the ice. Certain states, such as Michigan and Wisconsin, have spearing seasons during winter months, and the odds are definitely stacked against the fisherman.

For instance, Michigan has spearing on three island lakes (Burt, Mullet, and Black). It is also done on Wisconsin's Lake Winnebago. In Michigan, between thirty and forty sturgeons are speared yearly, which averages out to about 33 man-days expended for each fish taken. These are odds of the largest sort.

A spearer sets up a lightproof shanty over 16 to 18 feet of water. A five- or six-tined spear is used, weighted with about 20 pounds of lead just above the tines. It takes considerable weight to drive the tines through the hide of a large sturgeon.

Some spearers sprinkle white beans onto the floor of the lake beneath their spearing hole in order to spot the cruising fish.

A 12-inch wooden decoy is lowered near bottom and continuously twirled back and forth or around in circles. Although sturgeons are not predatory fish they seem to be attracted to the motion of the fish decoy.

After the fisherman has balanced his spear just above the hole, and the decoy begins moving about, he has nothing to do but sit, wait, and watch. And that wait, for some, could take an eternity. Some fishermen have tried every day of the season for twenty years and have never seen a sturgeon. They are scarce.

There is a certain method to spearing which should be observed. The spear, once a sturgeon works beneath the shanty hole, is never thrown—it is dropped. Light refraction works underwater during winter months the same as during open-water periods, and if the spear is literally thrown at the fish, the chance of making a successful hit is very small. If the spear is dropped straight down onto the fish the angler has a better chance for good penetration.

One man I talked with rates as close to being an expert on sturgeon spearing as anyone. "Big sturgeons actually scare me. They are so big and so powerful that I often wonder why I go after them. One fish broke my arm trying to get it out the shanty door. Since that time I've been afraid of them, but I keep going back to prove something to myself." That is dedication to a sport.

There are two schools of thought on fighting a speared sturgeon. One is to wrestle him from the water and through the shanty door as quickly as possible and try to keep the fish from knocking hell out of you and the shanty in the process. This can be extremely difficult when a 100-pound-plus sturgeon is doing his best to remove the spear sticking out of his back. I've known spearers that have had their shanty demolished in less time than it takes to tell about it. More than one spearer has been knocked unconscious during a last-minute duel with a speared sturgeon.

A spear fisherman waits above a hole in the ice for a big sturgeon to cruise into range. A decoy baitfish suspended near bottom seems to attract sturgeon, which ordinarily are not predatory fish.

Patience rewarded the spearman with a fine lake sturgeon. A fish this size, with a spear imbedded in its body, can cause considerable damage thrashing about in an ice shanty. *Courtesy Michigan Travel Bureau.*

Another school of thought is to bury the first spear in the fish and let him fight against the spear and spear rope until he weakens. Some spearers then sink another spear into the fish before bringing it through the spearing hole.

I've talked with several spearers and many agree that the longer a sturgeon fights the spear, the greater the chances will be of losing the prize. They advocate hauling the fish up as quickly as possible and getting him out the shanty door before he knows what is happening. This is easier said than done.

I've tried sturgeon spearing several times and find it extremely boring. I get almost hypnotized by staring into the greenish water for long periods of time. The wooden decoy starts looking like a 150-pound sturgeon until I shake my head and clear away the cobwebs. I've sat for a week at a time in a shanty and have yet to see my first sturgeon, although I've seen spearers 50 yards away take fish.

Sturgeon fishing isn't for me. I've tried it and I don't like the sport, but that doesn't mean that some readers might not enjoy the long odds and danger involved with this pastime.

But if you are personally willing to sacrifice your time in pursuit of a prehistoric relic that is capable of thrashing you within an inch of your life, and you enjoy sitting and waiting for long days or nights for an exciting tug on your line, then sturgeon fishing might be for you.

24
CATFISH

Catfish are found worldwide in nearly 1,000 various subspecies, but only a few are of importance to North American sport fishermen. Among these are the blue catfish, flathead cat, channel cat, white catfish, and the smaller members, the bullheads. This chapter will deal only with the larger catfish.

An endearing quality of the catfish is their ability to live and thrive in turbid or clear waters, thus offering a specialized brand of fishing in streams or heavily fished muddy lakes. Streams which may be unsuitable for other sport fish are often home to one or another of the catfish clan. Another excellent feature is that all catfish provide fine eating. Moreover, they are capable of growing to large sizes, and the battle often ends with the angler feeling he's tangled with a caged tiger. The strike may be soft, but the action that follows can be spectacular.

Big catfish are by no means rare. Several of these species, other than bullheads, can weigh in at 20 to 60 pounds, and fish much larger have been taken.

It's unfortunate, but down through the years many fishermen have viewed catfish with scorn; they consider the fish repulsive because of its skin color, its lack of scales, the hideous barbels located near the mouth, and the waters where they are caught.

Only recently have anglers learned to accept the fish for what it is, a willing biter that can provide a scrap which will be long remembered. I know of no angler who has slugged it out with a 15- or 20-pound catfish and who has anything but praise for its fighting abilities. They seldom jump, but provide a dogged underwater battle that leaves the fisherman shaking a sore arm and his head for not having tried catfishing earlier.

All catfish look the same, superficially. The various identifying marks are an adipose fin, a short but high dorsal fin, and a long anal fin. Every catfish carries a set of barbels or "whiskers" which act as sensory taste buds which allow these fish to locate food in dirty water. Short, stiff poisonous spines are found on the forward portion of the dorsal and pectoral fins; they can inflict painful injuries to a careless angler.

This chapter will cover the various catfish tribes as a whole, because a technique that will work for one member will take others. As a whole, catfish are omnivorous and will eat anything, including dead fish or other decaying matter, nightcrawlers, live fish, crayfish, fish eggs, mollusks, water-borne seeds, aquatic vegetation, chunks of meat, commercially prepared stink baits, doughballs, and other things. Many catfish can be taken on flies, leadhead jigs, small metal lures, spinners, and other lures normally associated with other fish.

One thing fishermen have going for them is that this species is always hungry and will feed at any time of day or night. Catfish are one continuous gut looking for something to put in it.

Angling tactics are many and varied for trophy catfish. The thing to remember is that big fish like big meals, within reason. One should also fish in areas known to produce big cats. Many states have lists of rivers or lakes which consistently produce lunker catfish, and it pays to search out these areas.

I'd suggest that catfishermen ply their trade in the South or Midwest where these fish are appreciated. Few Eastern anglers, their minds intent on trout, care for catfish, and many despise them.

The channel catfish is a widespread fish with avid followers north from Florida throughout the Great Lakes states. This fish is a streamlined fighter given to feeding in channels or swift river currents, although it is commonly found in many lakes. I've taken several from the Intercoastal Waterway along Florida's east coast. Wherever they are found, the channel cat provides heart-warming angling action and superb eating from the frying pan.

I've caught channel cats by rolling live shrimp along the bottoms of Southern rivers. The presentation must be slow and deliberate, but they feed heavily on freshwater shrimp in these waters. One of my favorite places to fish is near a bridge piling or abutment. The current swirls around these structures and spills food into the mouths of waiting catfish.

Channel cats tend to be bottom-oriented most of the time, but I've also taken a large number by casting small plugs or spoons in rivers. One time I was fishing near the mouth of Michigan's Au Sable River where it empties into Lake Huron. A few steelhead were being taken on spawn bags, but I didn't have any so I began casting small spoons quartering across and upstream and allowing the lure to bounce downstream with the current. I'd reel just enough to bring out the wiggling action of the lure.

After about ten casts the spoon stopped and I set the hook, fully expecting to see an acrobatic steelhead climb into the air. The fish stayed deep, bulldogged back and forth, and occasionally took out line against my drag. A nearby fisherman walked over to watch. "Steelhead?" he asked.

"It sure doesn't fight like a steelie, but it's a strong and powerful fish," I told him. The fish was rampaging hard and deep and it slugged heavily against my rod.

It took over five minutes to wear that fish down on 6-pound mono before I could finally lead it to the net. A deeply forked tail, numerous spots, and a bewhiskered head broke the surface. "It's a channel catfish!" I yelped. My day had suddenly taken on a new appeal as I strung the first of a dozen 4-to-7-pound cats.

The key to taking channel cats on artificials is to fish them very slow. This species of catfish will often attack live bait, and smaller gamefish make up a large portion of their diet.

Another excellent stream-fishing technique for channel cats is to tail-hook small crayfish, softshells if you can find them. They are weighted down with a tiny split shot and drifted through holes, pools, runs, and pocket water or riffles in much the same manner as one would stream-fish for trout or smallmouth bass. Light line and a limber rod are important for sensitive bait control.

Blue catfish can be the giants of the catfish species. Ol' Blue is found throughout the Midwest and South as far as Mississippi. Some of the largest specimens are taken from the Minnesota, Mississippi, Ohio, and Missouri rivers. Very large fish have been caught from some Southern impoundments such as Kentucky Lake. Big means just that; some blue catfish have been reported to weigh well over 100 pounds, and 15-to-20-pounders are not considered rare in any area.

This catfish is considerably less fond of turbid water than others of its clan and will often frequent swift, clear streams. Good hotspots to look for this species include streams with hard bottom such as bedrock, gravel, sand, or small boulders. It will often feed in water fast enough to be considered ideal trout habitat.

Blue cats are a steady producer in farm ponds which have been stocked with catfish or other species. Some of the larger catfish will be taken from deep river holes, but the farm-pond blue is no slouch; he'll tax your tackle to the limit.

One of my favorite tricks for farm-pond blue cats is to catch a dozen tiny bluegills. Separate males from females and remove the ovaries from the immature female panfish. These tiny sacks of roe will be just right for bait if they are about the size of a half-smoked cigarette. Use just enough weight, usually one tiny BB split shot 12 inches above the hook, to sink the bait in quiet waters. Too much weight will create a telltale drag that alerts cautious feeding blues. If they feel a drag they will drop the bait.

Insert the point of a No. 4 or No. 6 Eagle Claw hook into the skein of immature eggs and cast it out. Allow it to lie on bottom with a very loose drag or several coils of slack line. A catfish will pick it up off bottom and move away slowly as he swallows the eggs. Give the fish several feet of slack line and then allow the line to come tight before setting the hook.

Blue catfish are strong fighters with plenty of power to spare. I've tussled with several fish over 15 pounds, and they are capable of making a grown man wince before they can be led into the net. They fight with strong underwater surges and often head for submerged brush or other debris during the last stages of the battle. A last-minute flurry of activity often takes place on the surface as the blue lashes out with his tail in an attempt to get away.

The flathead catfish is another popular species. Average weight is 3 or 4 pounds. Certain areas provide heavyweight fish that can scale up to 100 pounds, but they are considered rare.

Trotlines are an effective method of taking both flatheads and blue catfish. The flathead seems to enjoy a fish diet more than other catfish species, and therein lies a clue to taking this fish.

Various states have regulations listing the length of trotlines, the numbers of hooks used, whether the line has to have the owner's name attached, and other rules. Anglers should determine the local ruling in each area before setting a trotline.

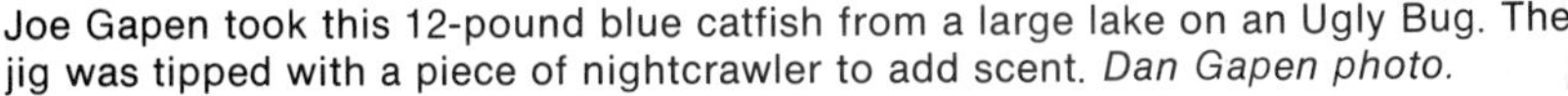

Joe Gapen took this 12-pound blue catfish from a large lake on an Ugly Bug. The jig was tipped with a piece of nightcrawler to add scent. *Dan Gapen photo.*

A trotline is a length of heavy line which can be attached either to both banks of a river or to floats or buoys in the middle of a lake. A series of short dropper lines 3 to 6 feet long are spaced along the entire length of the main trotline. For flatheads, many fishermen bait the dropper hooks (usually 1/0 single hooks) with small chunks of fish. The common carp makes a fine bait for large catfish, and it can be hooked through the back, near the tail, through the vent, or through the mouth. Flatheads couldn't care less as long as it represents a decent meal. If the carp is dead it should be fished on or very near the bottom.

Live carp are a superb bait. I've watched trotliners take 30-to-40-pound blue and flathead cats on carp large enough to produce a respectable battle on a spinning outfit. Hook a large live carp through the mouth and allow it to swim on the end of a trotline dropper.

Some fishermen prefer using homemade or commercially prepared cheese, blood, or stink baits. Some of these concoctions are so vile they would gag a maggot, but the strong odor and taste seem to appeal to catfish.

The bait is attached to each of the dropper hooks and lowered into the water. Trotlines are usually tended several times during the day or night.

Locating catfish hotspots is a skill learned from long experience. A deep hole lined with brush or logs on many streams is home for big catfish. There was once a reckless breed of men who would wade a stream and locate underwater holes in the bank or in brushpiles and would reach in slowly to feel for a big flathead or blue catfish. Once they located a fish, it would normally remain motionless while the "tickler" ran his hands back and forth along its belly or sides. They would keep working forward until the gills were located. They would then reach in quickly, take a firm hold of the gills, and do their best to wrestle the fish from the hole or brush.

More than one of these fishermen had arms or fingers broken or were pulled underwater when a too-big catfish took offense to their actions. Twenty years ago this method produced cats in the 40-to-50-pound class, but it took a strong man and one with more than his share of nerve to practice this dying sport.

The same waters were often shared with water moccasins, huge snapping turtles, and catfish large enough to drown a man. More than one old-time tickler has a finger or two missing from a surprise encounter with a large snapping turtle.

These trotline fishermen struggle to hold up six trophy flathead catfish taken from Ohio's Piedmont Lake. *Erwin Bauer photo.*

I can't say I recommend this sport to anyone, and I'm not sure it's legal now in any state. I tried to research it for accuracy according to today's rules but could find no records of it anywhere. It may still be legal, but aspirants are advised to check it out thoroughly in each area. I'd advise giving second thoughts to practicing this sport anyway. It can be a widowmaker.

BAITS FOR CATFISH

Much has been made of preparing your own catfish bait rather than buying commercial baits. Both produce well but some of the better catfish fishermen have so-called secret baits that have been handed down from one generation to another. I'm a firm believer in using home-brewed baits that produce. There are as many different recipes as there are catfish, but here are some I've used, and they produce—if you can stand fishing with them.

Mix equal parts of Limburger cheese, flour, and raw hamburger in a bowl and add just enough water to produce a thick mixture. Set this mess in a jar and place it outside in the sunshine for two or three days, preferably far from the house. The riper the meat and cheese, the better it produces.

Another bait with a wide following is made from chicken blood. Drain the blood through an old heavy wool garment or cloth bag to remove the excess moisture. The remains of the blood will filter through and coagulate into a thickened state. It can be left in the sun for a day to ripen further. Once it becomes thick enough to cut, the blood should be sliced into chunks for bait. If your wife will let you, keep the blood bait in the refrigerator in a tightly sealed glass jar. This type of bait is not very tough and is best used with a slightly smaller treble hook than is commonly used for baitfishing.

For a stink bait that really produces, place minnows, chunks of fish, or pieces of raw meat in a jar and allow it to sit in the sun for several days. The juices from the decaying fish or meat will produce the awfullest smell that humans have ever been exposed to. When this mixture gets so high you can't stand it, dip 2-inch chunks of common kitchen scouring sponges into the liquid. Keep the sponge baits in a sealed jar with extra juice in the bottom. This makes a durable bait that can be recharged simply by dipping the sponge back into the liquid.

An old Tennessee fisherman told me, "Son, if you want to catch big catfish, don't mess around with those stink baits. The finest bait in the world is field mice." I blinked at this advice as my mind conjured up thoughts of trying to catch enough mice for bait.

"Buy a dozen mousetraps, bait them with peanut butter, and set them around an open weedfield. The next morning you'll have enough bait to last for a day of fishing," he said.

He showed me dusty photographs of big catfish he'd taken by still-fishing field mice in deep holes. He would hook a mouse under the back skin and use enough weight to take it to the bottom. "Sit and wait 'em out," he said. "Them mice draw big cats like stink baits draw flies." As I examined photos of 20-to-40-pound catfish I decided he might be right, in his area at least.

Catfish may prefer smelly baits, and they may look like the devil, but I know of no other species that can provide such a spirited struggle and provide such good eating. Thoughts of hush puppies and deep-fried catfish make my mouth water and enable me to recall long-drawn-out fights with members of this clan.

These gamefish have a ho-hum reputation that is not deserved. I feel anglers should give this sport a try and then decide whether the catfish deserves the flak it has taken over the years. In my book, it's a gamefish that merits more attention.

25 WHITEFISH

The whitefish is a member of a large group of fish which frequent northern waters. The members of this family are seldom considered trophy fish simply because few anglers have mastered the specialized techniques needed to take these fish on anything more than an occasional basis.

Whitefish are rugged gamefish that fight extremely well for their size. They can be taken by trolling, jigging, dry-fly fishing, and bait-fishing. Once hooked, whitefish give a good account of themselves with strong lunges and frequent bouts of head shaking. They have a relatively tender mouth, and many are hooked and lost when the angler applies too much pressure.

Whitefish differ greatly from trout, although they belong to the char-trout family. These spunky gamefish have the adipose fin and soft-rayed dorsal fins of their close relatives. They are a large schooling fish and travel in compact groups at the depths. The head and mouth of a whitefish are smaller than those of a trout or char, and it also has a deeply forked tail. They are generally silvery in color and the scales are large.

The whitefish commonly pursued by sportsmen rate as some of the finest eating fish in the world. The unfortunate thing is very few anglers are aware that whitefish can be caught on hook and line year-round. To catch them requires specialized riggings and some knowledge of their feeding habits.

This chapter will cover the lake whitefish, round whitefish or Menominee, and mountain whitefish. The first two are common to the Great Lakes, while the third is confined to many free-flowing mountain streams and lakes of the West.

LAKE WHITEFISH

Icefishing for lake whitefish is one of the fastest-growing winter sports in the Great Lakes. It can be difficult fishing, because whitefish are delicate feeders and the strike can be hard to detect when heavy winter winds are blowing.

Whitefish angling usually takes place in 20 to 100 feet of water, depending on the lake or area. In the Great Lakes many whitefish are taken from depths of 40 to 75 feet, while Ontario anglers fishing Lake Simcoe, near Toronto, often take these fish from 20 feet of water.

Pre-baiting or chumming is an important method of drawing lake whitefish into the fishing area. Some fishermen use small salted minnows, but the trend in recent times is to use whole kernel corn or several tablespoons of chub roe beneath the icefishing hole. The whitefish will congregate around the free smorgasbord table and dine on chum. One session of chumming will usually draw whitefish in for an entire day.

A small gold No. 8 or No. 10 single hook is baited with a small chunk of chub spawn. If the eggs of the chub are loose, fishermen tie them to the hook with several turns of red thread. A split shot or two is fastened 12 inches above the hook and lowered until the weight hits bottom. Bring it up about 16 inches and the spawn-baited hook will be just inches off bottom. Whitefish are commonly bottom feeders, especially during winter months.

The same method of fishing may be used but the angler can switch from chub roe to small 1-to-2-inch shiner minnows. These are fished alive; a small hook is inserted just under the dorsal fin and then the minnow is lowered down near bottom. Live minnows will outproduce chub roe on some days.

A point should be made about striking whitefish. It is best to wait out the first tentative nibbles of the fish and set the hook only after the gamefish has pulled the line tight and is moving away to digest the meal. If the strike is made too soon, you'll often miss the fish entirely or lose it during the fight because it wasn't hooked firmly.

Another productive method of winter fishing for this species is jigging. Anglers use small Swedish Pimples in silver or white and bait the treble hook with chunks of raw fish eggs. The lure is lowered to bottom and jigged up and down with short 6-inch movements of the rod tip. Whitefish often strike very hard, and this method often produces the largest fish. A 5- or 6-pound whitefish produces a formidable battle when hooked in deep water through the ice.

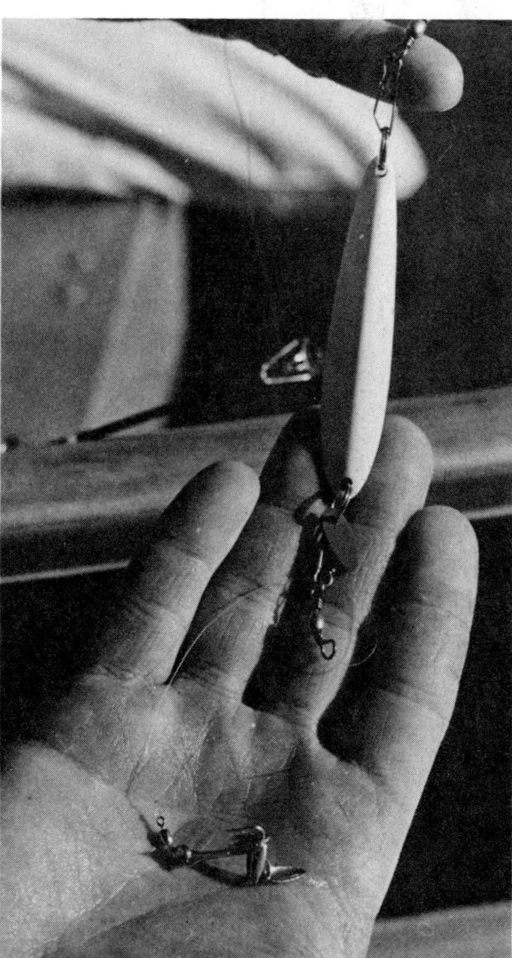

This whitefish chugging rig consists of a Swedish Pimple, a short leader, and a baited treble hook with tiny flippers.

Anglers learned a few years ago that another technique works well during winter months. They use tiny Swedish Pimples and remove the treble hooks and replace them with pink, white, pearl, or green plastic flippers. A 12-inch length of leader then goes down to a No. 8 single hook. A minnow or marble of chub spawn is attached to the hook.

When this lure is jigged up and down, the lure flashes and the flickers flick, and the combination attracts whitefish in from afar. Hard strikes may be felt on the lure itself, but it is the short, tapping strikes on the bait which will result in hooked fish.

The previous method can also be used during spring, summer, and fall months when jigging from an open boat. It is usually easy to locate good areas, because during warm-weather months many people turn out to fish for lake whitefish. Move in, lower an anchor quietly, and begin jigging. Large catches of whitefish are common once a school is located, and these fish often average between 3 and 8 pounds and provide fine eating. Shoals waters are best for springtime fish.

Another little-known fishing technique is to troll very small spoons or plugs during spring months. Many whitefish are caught in the Great Lakes during the spring lake trout run. Whitefish often mingle with lake trout and will strike a trolled lure if it is presented at the proper depth. I've had my best success trolling with tiny silver FirePlugs at this time.

The average lake trout fisherman loses a good many of the whitefish he hooks simply because he thinks they are lakers and not whitefish. He knows that lake trout have a fairly tough mouth and therefore tends to horse the fish in. Try this with a whitefish and the fish will be lost when the hooks tear out of his tender mouth.

Several years ago a good friend of mine, Emil Dean, a charterboat skipper from Bear Lake, Mich., made angling history in that state when he caught a 12½-pound lake whitefish while trolling on Lake Michigan. I've since talked with a commercial fisherman who specializes in whitefish and has taken 13-to-15-pound whitefish from the northern portion of Lake Michigan. The world record is only 13 pounds, so it's obvious that fishermen are missing a good bet for trophy whitefish by not concentrating their efforts in this area.

In northern Canada, lake whitefish have the ability to turn on countless anglers every summer when they begin rising for small mayflies. A lightweight fly rod and line with a 9-to-12-foot tapered leader is used. These surfacing fish are leader-shy and a sloppy cast will put them down.

I've hit this sport on several Ontario lakes, and Kabinakagami Lake north of Wawa is a good choice. Early morning and just before dark, while the lake is calm, are the best times to get in on this action.

The ideal method to fish for rising whitefish is to watch for a rise. Within a few seconds another rise will occur a few feet away, usually caused by the same fish. You can then determine the direction the fish is traveling and cast the fly ahead to the proper area. It doesn't pay to cast to rising fish, because they feed while moving and a fly dropped on a rise will often be several feet behind the fish.

Small mayfly or caddis fly patterns tied in sizes 10 to 14 are about right for rising whitefish. If a fish rises to your fly, delay the

This whitefish was taken through the ice from a shanty by jigging a small chunk of egg spawn. It's best to ignore the first nibbles of whitefish and wait until the fish has pulled the line taut as it moves away with the bait.

strike for about a second to allow the fish to take the imitation into its mouth. Because of the underslung nature of its mouth it will usually roll under the fly or come half out of the water when it takes the fly. If you attempt to set the hook at this time you will generally lose the fish.

ROUND WHITEFISH

The round whitefish is a smaller member of this family, and only recently has it become a highly desired gamefish. Its range is from Labrador to British Columbia, but it reaches its greatest abundance in all the Great Lakes except Lake Erie.

It is also called a Menominee whitefish. It is a prolific scavenger of all types of fish eggs, a quality that doesn't make it very popular with some fishermen.

Official records are seldom kept on this species, although Michigan waters hold an abundance of these fish, especially in the northern portion of Lake Michigan. The record in that state is about 3 pounds.

The vast numbers of this fish remind me of yellow perch schools and how difficult it is to catch a trophy fish simply because of the abundance of smaller fish. I've anchored in one location in Michigan's Platte Bay, about 35 miles from my home, and have caught over a hundred Menominee in two hours.

They move into the shallow water over sandbars during the salmon spawning season and eat eggs drifting down the river. Bait up with single salmon eggs and a No. 12 or No. 14 gold short-shank hook and you can literally fill the boat on certain days. Ninety-nine out of a hundred will be about 12 inches in length, but the odd fish will scale upwards of 2 pounds and provide a thrilling if short battle on light line.

Many anglers fish for the round or Menominee whitefish with two hooks rigged on a spreader or dropper system. They feel a tiny tug and set the hooks and will often take fish two at a time. Single eggs, small pieces of worms, or artificial salmon eggs like Burl's Golden Nuggets will produce all the action a fisherman could want.

Smoked, the Menominee is one of the finest-eating gamefish found in North American waters. They are very oily when eaten in a fresh state. Pickled briefly in salt brine and smoked over an applewood fire for two or three hours, the round whitefish will make a gourmet drool in anticipation.

MOUNTAIN WHITEFISH

The mountain whitefish is a Western species that often shares the same waters with rainbows, cutthroats, browns, and Montana grayling. The average fish weighs less than a pound, but fish up to 5 pounds are occasionally taken. The range of this species is through the cold-water streams (and occasionally lakes) of the mountainous West as well as certain rivers and lakes of Alberta and British Columbia.

It feeds predominantly on insects in free-flowing rivers, and this makes it a natural for feather tossers. The rise of this whitefish is often similar to that of trout, and many anglers are disappointed when their catch is landed. Montana biologists once stated that mountain whitefish were the most abundant sport fish taken in that state.

Both dry and wet flies are productive. Anglers are advised to use dry flies when insects are emerging and wet flies or nymphs at other times.

Winter is a prime time for taking this whitefish, because angling often palls for trout when rivers begin freezing and the snow starts to fall. There are winter days when anglers can fish nymphs on a light tippet and take these fish on nearly every cast. Fish the main channels of the river for top sport.

Single salmon eggs or tiny bits of earthworms are also good baits for the spinfisherman during winter months. The bait should bounce naturally along bottom. The take is generally soft, as with other whitefish, and the action begins after the hook is set.

Although they seldom jump, they do provide an excellent gamy battle for a brief time before coming to the net. Remember that they have soft mouths and don't play them with too heavy a hand.

The group of whitefish has never been fully accepted as a top-drawer sport fish in this country. Many anglers continue to think of them as trash fish, just one step ahead of carp or suckers. But this is not the case; they are part of sport fishing because of their willingness to strike flies, lures, or bait; because they produce a short but hard fight; and because they often rank as superior table fare for anglers.

Whitefish are here to stay, and I'd advise fishermen to make their acquaintance. They may very well learn that something has been missing from their lives—and it would be the whitefish.

APPENDIX

HOW TO PREPARE YOUR TROPHY

The trip to Quebec's Ungava Bay had been long and arduous, and once the Air Canada flight settled into Montreal, it was a short four-hour flight north to Fort Chimo—the jumping-off place for Arctic char.

I'd dreamed for years of taking a trophy char. The fishing tales and photos I'd seen of char with flaming red sides and bellies, the no-quarter fight they produced in streams rushing as fast as a race horse to join the salt waters of Ungava Bay, had urged me on. I stepped off the Quebec Air flight in Fort Chimo and immediately boarded a bush plane bound for the Tunulik River Camp, a lodge run by Eskimos strictly for char fishing.

The float plane soon nestled down on the oil-slick surface of the Tunulik River estuary, and several Eskimo-driven boats came out to meet us. The anticipation of tangling with a big char had my blood boiling. Someone had once said that anticipation is better than participation, but I hoped to prove that theory false.

Minutes later I uncased my rods and reels, grabbed a handful of Dardevles, and followed my young Eskimo guide down to the boat. Soon we were stationed near the Tunulik River Falls, a short distance upstream from camp.

"Big fish," he indicated, his hands widespread in the classic language of fishermen. The char he pointed to was nestled snugly behind a rock with torrents of white water pouring over his head. The fish was visible only when the foam subsided for an instant, but I'd seen enough to recharge my batteries. I wanted that fish like nothing else from previous fishing trips.

My first cast sailed upstream, the current swept it downstream fast and deep, and I steered it into the holding pocket. The lure stopped briefly, in much the same manner as it would if lodged between two rocks, and I set the hook out of pure reflex. No one knows whether I was more startled than the char, but the fish headed out into the heavy current with the drag on my reel whining in a high-pitched shriek.

The char, a long slender male fresh from salt water, caught the edge of the white water and turned downstream, riding the current like a beach bum on a rolling Hawaiian surf. The water rumbled over huge boulders that tossed white-water haystacks 10 feet in the air. The char was bouncing from crest to crest as the line continued to peel out in a madcap race down the river.

My guide tugged at my elbow and began a downstream race over slick ledges of algae-covered granite. I lost my balance once and toppled into the river, but the race was still on and I was as determined to win as a decathlon star. The guide pulled me to my feet and we continued downstream, although I was wet to my waist.

The wind sprint lasted for 200 yards, with the char well ahead by the time we arrived at the estuary. My fish was bulldogging in the current 75 yards away. I'd gain a foot and the fish would take it back, and this tug of war continued for fifteen minutes before it began to tire. My arm and wrist were beginning to complain from the effort.

I worked the fish twice within 20 yards of the net, and both times it managed to gather enough reserve strength to head out into the river current. I finally moved down the estuary shoreline as far as possible and laid heavily on the rod, determined to either turn the fish back to me or break off trying. The combination of fighting the rod and the current flow slowly took its toll and the char came my way, still fighting every inch of the way.

The fish made a last-second bid for survival by cleanly jumping from the water. I slowly pumped it in, and my guide expertly tucked its head into the net. The fish I'd dreamed of and traveled so far to catch was mine.

I relaxed for a moment and soaked up the beauty of the situation. The fish had taken me nearly a quarter of a mile downstream from the falls; it had fought a superb battle and given me everything I'd hoped to obtain from that trip. I studied the male fish, its white-edged fins looking remarkably like those of a brook trout, the sleek cream-colored spots along the lateral lines, and the silver and olive-green back. The belly was just beginning to turn to a blush of orangish pink. It was a truly beautiful fish, and my thoughts were to have it mounted. I quickly snapped several close-up shots with my Minolta 35mm camera to capture the delicate colorations so that my 13-pound char could be painted up in similar colors by the taxidermist. I could clearly picture the mounted fish in my office.

This is where my daydreaming and planning went astray. I wanted the fish frozen to ensure that it would retain its freshness and not spoil during the next six days and on my trip home. The owner of the lodge told me they didn't have a freezer or any method of keeping fish. We'd either have to eat the fish, skin it and salt the skin, or I could hope to catch a trophy on the last day of the trip. None of these alternatives pleased me, but I elected to have one of the guides skin the char and salt it down.

I watched the operation as he made a fine-line slit along the lateral line on the side which would be toward the wall. A dull teaspoon was used to separate the flesh from the skin. The Eskimo guide did a masterful job. Once the skin was completely removed, except for the head and tail areas, the spine was severed and salt was copiously rubbed into the flesh side of the skin.

Two days later the skin still looked good, and I rubbed more salt into the flesh side and hoped for the best. The fishing was super and I continuously had fish on, but none topped my 13-pounder.

The trip soon drew to a close. We flew back to Fort Chimo and were promptly weathered in. We rented a room from a local Eskimo and toughed out the weather, a mixture of fog and rain. Two days later it cleared and I flew on to Montreal. I'd missed my earlier flight connection because of the delay and was forced to go on standby for an opening on other flights. It was almost two days before I could fly from Montreal, and I was sorely troubled about my char; it was the only one I'd kept.

On arrival at home I took the salted skin directly to Jim Freisser, a semi-retired fish taxidermist. Jim used to do all the fish mounts for the Museum of Science and Industry and the Musem of Natural History in Chicago. He'd done several of my fish mounts before, and I trusted his expertise in mounting gamefish. He's a pro.

He tagged my fish and placed it in his freezer. "Dave, never allow someone to salt down a fish before it goes to a taxidermist. Although the skin along the back, belly, and sides is often preserved, the area around the head has not been cared for and will usually present problems for any taxidermist. The flesh decomposes along the cheeks and gill covers, and inside the skull, and it can often ruin a mount," he told me.

I crossed my fingers and waited for a year. Jim has so much business he no longer wishes to attract more, which is why his address isn't mentioned in this chapter. I mention his name not to give him any more business, which he doesn't really want, but to illustrate the problems of a good fish taxidermist and what fishermen can do to help preserve their trophy for mounting.

My fish was finally done, and when I picked it up from Jim I took one look at my trophy and was instantly taken back to the Tunulik River. A good mount enables an angler to achieve a total recall of his fish and the surroundings. Jim later told me that he'd had trouble with the head area, just as he'd predicted, but he was able to salvage the fish and produce an exceptional mount.

There are many do's and don'ts involved in selecting a fish for a full-size trophy mount. Some are obvious and many are not, such as not salting down a trophy skin.

Any fish worthy of being considered a trophy should be treated with tender loving care. Many fish are ruined, or at least marked badly, during the landing process. A struggling fish in a landing net will fray the fins and knock off loose scales. It's nearly impossible for a *qualified* taxidermist to repair mangled fins.

You'll note I've stressed the word "qualified" in the previous paragraph. There are exceptional taxidermists who specialize in fish, and there are butchers who have no conception of what a trophy fish should look like. It requires an artist's touch to bring out the subtle color variations and blendings in a fish, and very few have acquired an eye for true fish colors. I've seen hideous jobs that look as though the fish were sprayed with aluminum or red barn paint. These jokers ask $1 to $2 per inch and are robbing their clients.

A good taxidermist will display his wares just like any salesman. If your local man displays only pheasants, deer heads, or squirrels, I'd suggest looking elsewhere. Too many trophies are a once-in-a-lifetime fish for many anglers, and it won't make you feel good to have someone botch up that trophy fish you hoped to show off to friends.

Another thing to avoid at all costs is a still-lively fish that flops around in the boat. This thrashing around loosens or removes scales, creates bruises on the skin and flesh, and may even break the skin. Any skin cuts will create problems for the taxidermist and increase his charge.

I recommend that a trophy fish be netted and left in the water, where a sharp blow between the eyes will kill it instantly. Fish seldom thrash until they are lifted from the water. This will prevent the fish from bruising the skin, splitting fins, or knocking off scales, and it increases the chances of a pleasing mount.

As soon as the fish is dead, wrap it in a wet cloth or towel and arrange the fins so that they will not be bent or broken during freezing. The caudal (tail) fin should be laid flat, and care must be taken to prevent any curling. This can usually be accomplished by keeping the wrapping wet until it is placed in the freezer.

Saran Wrap is good for wrapping around the moist covering. Make at least two full wraps around all parts of the wet towel to ensure that air doesn't get to the fish and cause freezer burn. The fish can then be wrapped in freezer wrapping paper.

Fish that cannot be frozen, such as my Arctic char, can still be preserved. Before your trip, visit your local pharmacist and obtain a pint or two of formalin or phenol. Formalin can be used as a preservative just as it comes from the bottle; phenol should be diluted half and half with water.

Immerse the fish completely without skinning or cleaning and allow it to remain submerged until the day you head home. Then soak several towels in either formalin or phenol and completely wrap the fish in the saturated towels. Cover the towels with several wrappings of Saran Wrap. The plastic wrap will hold in some of the odor, but be alert for strange looks from other passengers. The stuff smells like a devil's brew pot.

Once you've gotten the fish home, it should be packaged while still frozen and shipped air freight to the taxidermist or delivered personally. It is best to ship perishable items like frozen fish on a Monday so the fish won't spend a weekend in a warm warehouse. The taxidermist should be alerted that the fish is on its way so he can pick it up when it arrives. Ship in dry ice and in an insulated container.

One of the common complaints taxidermists make is that customers insist on gutting their fish. A vent-to-gill cut along the belly creates tremendous problems, and even an exceptional mount cannot hide the fact that the fisherman gutted his trophy. If possible, freeze the fish whole and let the taxidermist worry about removing entrails and gills.

There are several marks of a good fish taxidermist, but few anglers know what to look for. The key point is to ask yourself, "Does this mount look alive?" If it looks like a dead fish hanging on a board, it's a poor mount. The mount should look alive, wet, and vibrant with vivid colors. Beware of the taxidermist who cannot expertly blend his colors.

There has much been made lately of fiberglass mounts, but I still prefer a skin mount done by a professional. Unfortunately, very few taxidermists nowadays know how to skin-mount a fish. Many belong to the fiberglass or papier-mâché group, and these people are not offering the angler his real fish, just a replica.

One of the signs of a good skin mount is a smooth finish without any signs of cracking or shrinkage. I have some of Jim Freisser's mounted fish which were done fifteen years ago and they look just as alive now as they did the day I received them. Poor skin mounts will show signs of shrinkage around the head or base of the tail within a year.

A bad mount will have bumpy features and appear listless or static. Some taxidermists still mount fish on boards or plaques, a practice no longer common among experts in the field of fish taxidermy.

A good taxidermist is more than just an artist with camel's-hair brush or airbrush; he's capable of making the fish appear alive. One method by which this is accomplished is to use a curved mount. The fish can be arching upward, such as a brown trout rising for a dry fly. The tail can be flared outward or inward, or the body can be curved slightly to the right or left. Any curvature of the mount will make it appear lifelike even when hanging on your den wall.

An open gill cover is another good sign of an excellent mount. A good taxidermist uses lifelike materials to simulate the gills in a fish, and this added touch makes it look alive and fresh from the water.

This mounted smallmouth bass has a lifelike appearance owing to the naturally curved body and open mouth.

Close-up of head shows open gill cover and simulated gills underneath—another mark of a realistically mounted fish.

These two close-ups, of the eye and the area around the dorsal fin, show hand-painted dots applied by the taxidermist that blend in with the natural coloring of the fish.

Some taxidermists mount a fish with jaws so widespread it resembles the fake white shark in *Jaws*. A slightly open mouth is acceptable and preferred over a closed-mouth mount, but beware of the man whose work shows a preference for gaping jaws. This looks phony. The insides of the mouth, the tongue, and the gum lines should be realistically painted.

Fins are another point to check when shopping around for taxidermy work. The top men use thin plastic behind the fins to keep them slightly flexible. A stiff, rigid fin will become brittle with age and break if handled.

A series of color photographs in clear, sharp detail is an asset when delivering fish to be mounted. Include two or three pictures of each side, a couple of the back, one or two of the head and gill covers, and one of the tail and belly areas. These enable the taxidermist, if he's a good one, to reproduce the exact coloring. I once watched Jim Freisser match up a muted purple undertone of a Quebec brook trout for a friend. It matched perfectly with the photo that Tom took, and he was vastly proud of his trophy speck. Film is cheap insurance when you wish to have a professional fish mount made.

The difference between the men and the boys in fish taxidermy is in how the fish is painted. I've seen some excellent airbrush work, but many old-timers still use a hand-held brush and meticulously paint in each dot, vermiculation, stripe, and varied blending of

Reverse side of smallmouth mount is equipped with a hanger that permits the fish to be displayed on the wall.

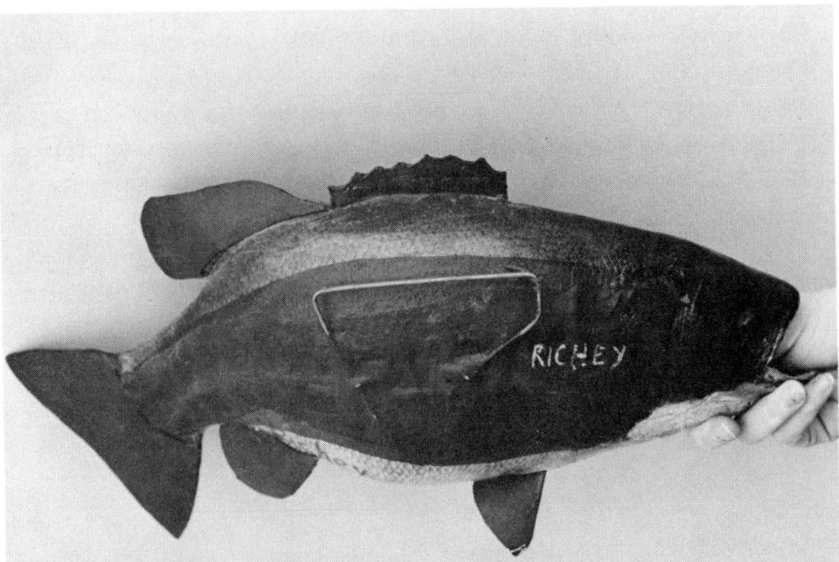

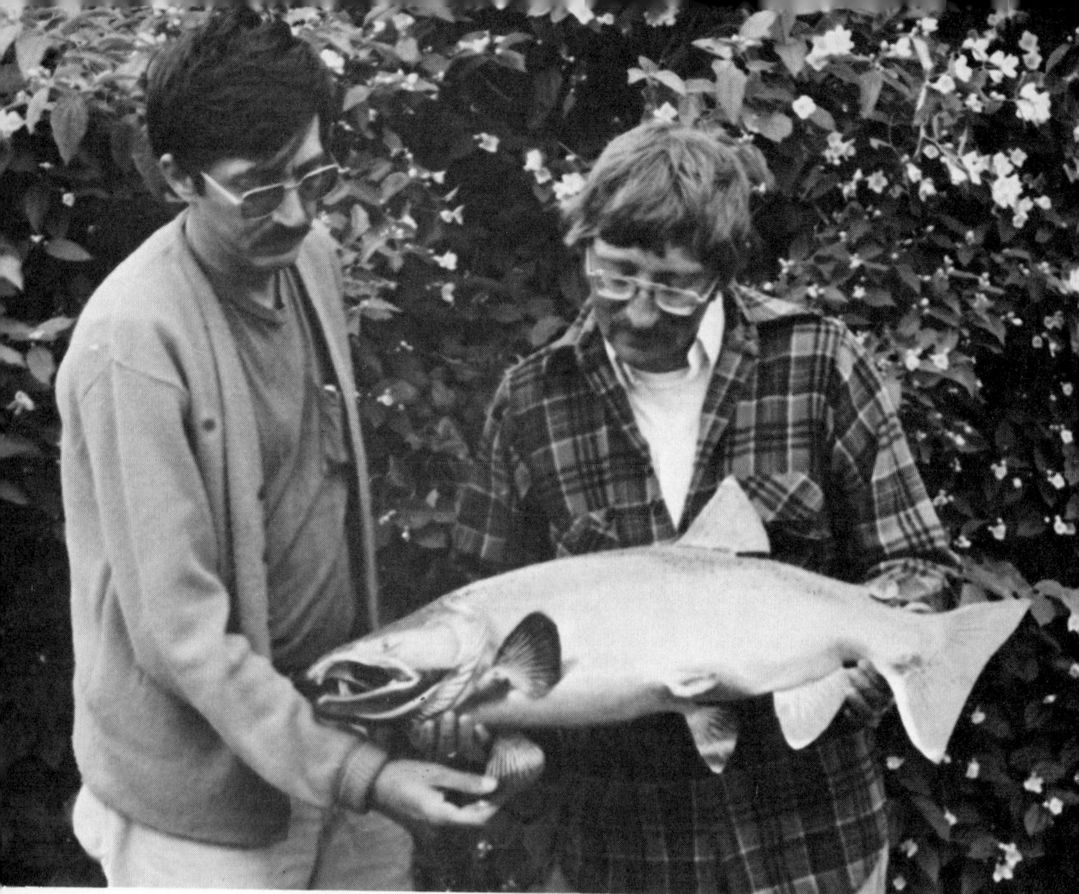

This coho salmon was mounted by an expert taxidermist who retained the flexibility of the fins with a thin plastic backing. A rigid fin is more apt to break as it becomes brittle with age.

color. The experts hand-paint each and every speckle of color in a finished mount. Few taxidermists do this because it is time-consuming and many simply do not have the talent.

A good fish mount by a professional taxidermist is not cheap. The going rate, as this is written, is between $3 and $4 per inch, and the trend is toward the higher figure. It is not uncommon to spend between $100 and $150 for a trophy salmon or brown trout. Smaller freshwater fish, of course, are priced less, but the beginning rate for almost any fish will be about $60. If a taxidermist quotes you a figure of $35 to $50 for a 20-inch trout, you are well advised to decline with thanks and look elsewhere. Cheap rates often beget cheap mounts, which is known as "Richey's law."

Few top-quality taxidermists today can deliver a topnotch fish mount in less than a year. Jim Freisser often has people waiting three years for one of his mounts.

Absence makes the heart grow fonder, and this is doubly true of a well-mounted trophy fish. A good mount will allow you to recall the thrilling battle all over again without leaving the comfort of your favorite chair. And, if you're like me, one glimpse of your trophy will bring about a treasured moment when you relive the day and the moment of capture. And that is what trophy fishing is all about.

WHERE TO GO FOR TROPHY FISH

Like the changing seasons, a fishing hotspot for trophy gamefish may be fantastic one year and a dud the next. This chapter is the result of painstaking research, countless letters and personal phone calls, and plenty of on-the-spot fishing by myself. This state-by-state update on the hottest locations is based on how well an area produces, how long it has produced respectable numbers of trophy fish, and whether the odds are in your favor of its producing lunkers again.

Pinpointing fishing hotspots for trophy freshwater gamefish is almost as hazardous as prejudging your mother-in-law. It can be done but is subject to a bit of error. Some readers may disagree with my choices, while others may feel I've overlooked their favorite fishing hole. So be it. But I hope you will all find trophy fish waiting in the following locations.

ALABAMA

Largemouth bass
Guntersville Reservoir, Wheeler Reservoir, Pickwick Reservoir, Wilson Reservoir, Bartlett's Ferry Lake, Goat Rock Lake, Lake George, Martin Lake, Weiss Lake, Blackburn Fork, Mulberry River, Tombigbee River, Alabama River

Smallmouth bass
Tennessee River, Wheeler Lake, Alabama River, Wilson Lake, Pickwick Reservoir

Spotted bass
Tallapoosa River, Martin Reservoir, Yates Reservoir, Coosa River, Weiss Lake, Mitchell Lake, Black Warrior River, Blackburn Fork, Sipsey River, Tombigbee River, Cahaba River

Trout
None in Alabama

Northern pike
None in Alabama

Muskellunge
Tennessee River

Pickerel
Cahaba River, Little River, Conecuh River

Walleye
Coosa River, Tennessee River, Alabama River, Cahaba River, Ten Saw River, Weiss Lake, Mitchell Lake, Tombigbee River, Black Warrior River

Sauger
Black Warrior River and tributaries, Blackburn River, Sipsey Lake, Tennessee River, Mulberry River, Pickwick Reservoir, Guntersville Reservoir, Wheeler Reservoir

Bluegill
Pickwick Reservoir, Wheeler Reservoir, Guntersville Reservoir, Tallapoosa River, Coosa River, Weiss Lake, Mobile River Delta, Alabama River, Cahaba River, Little River, Conecuh River

Crappie
Chattahoochee River, Tallapoosa River, Coosa River, Black Warrior River, Tombigbee River, Mobile Bay, Grand Bay, Bon Secour Bay, Blackburn Fork, Mulberry Fork, Weiss Lake

Yellow perch
None in Alabama

Other panfish
Yellow bass—most lakes & streams; white bass—Tombigbee River, Black Warrior River, Blackburn Fork, Coosa River, Weiss Lake,Tallapoosa River, Tennessee River, Guntersville Reservoir, Wheeler Reservoir, Pickwick Reservoir

Salmon, grayling, sturgeon, whitefish
None in Alabama

Catfish
Channel and blue catfish—Coosa River, Weiss Lake, Tallapoosa River, Chattahoochee River, Bartlett's Ferry Lake, Goat Rock Lake, Tennessee River, Guntersville Reservoir, Sipsey Lake, Alabama River, Mobile Bay, Cahaba River, Black Warrior River, Martin Reservoir

ALASKA

Largemouth, smallmouth and spotted bass
None in Alaska

Rainbow trout
Strubel Lake, Chickako Lake, Star Lake, Reesor Lake, Bow River, Two Lakes, Oldman River, Brooks River, Tikchik Lake, Agulawak River, Kvichak River, Wildhorse Lake, Henderson Lake, Chikuminuk Lake, Tyrrell Lake

Steelhead
Naha River, Karta River, Situk River, Eagle Creek, Snake Creek, Petersburg Creek, Anchor River, Deep Creek, Karluk River, Naknek River, Sitkoh Creek, Ninilchik River

Brown trout
Raven River, Stauffer Creek, Fallen Timber Creek, Dog Pound Creek, Athabasca River, Peace River, Beaver Creek

Brook trout
Upper Stony Creek, Prairie Creek, Alford Creek, Lookout Creek, Blue Lake, Elbow Lake, Muskiki Lake, Rat Lake

Dolly Varden
Berland River, Wildhay River, Muskeg River, Kvichak River, Cardinal River

Lake trout
Cold Lake, Grist Lake, Namur Lake, Margaret Lake, Peerless Lake, Swan Lake, Rock Lake, Wentzel Lake, Ghost Reservoir, Summit Lake, Tangle Lake

Northern pike
Kvichak River, Pinehurst Lake, Moose Lake, Fort Lake, Skeleton Lake, Beaver Lake, Calling Lake, Sturgeon Lake, Cold Lake, Buck Lake, Lake McGregor, Park Lake, Wilson Lake, Chestermere Lake

Walleye
Fawcett Lake, Sturgeon Lake, Smoke Lake, Buck Lake, Siebert Lake, Moose Lake, Wolf Lake, Helena Lake

Yellow perch
Sturgeon Lake, Moose Lake, Beaver Lake, Elkwater Lake, Kehiwin Lake

Coho salmon
Yukon River, Charley River, Colville River, Bristol Bay, Kenai River, most coastal areas

Chinook salmon
Bristol Bay, Brooks River, Coville Lake, Grosvenor Lake, most coastal areas

Arctic grayling
Kuskokwim River, Tanana River, Yukon River, Charley River, Nation River, Clear Creek, Birch Creek, Steese Creek, Kandik Creek, many lakes and streams

Whitefish
Lake Wabamum, Pigeon Lake, Buck Lake, Moose Lake, Hanmore Lake

ARIZONA

Largemouth bass
Lake Powell, Lake Mead, Colorado River, Lake Mohave, Lake Havasu, Apache Lake, Roosevelt Lake, Lake Carl Pleasant, San Carlos Reservoir, Bartlett Lake, Salt River

Smallmouth bass
Verde River

Brown trout
Oak Creek, Tonto Creek

Rainbow trout
Luna Lake, Becker Lake, Big Lake, Nelson Reservoir, Rainbow Lake, White River, Black River, Little Colorado River, Lyman Reservoir, Tonto Creek, Grand Canyon Area, Glen Canyon Dam, Lake Powell, Lake Mohave

Brook trout
Lee Valley Lake

Northern pike
Cholla Lake, Stoneman Lake, Lyman Lake, Upper and Lower Mary Lake, Canyon Lake, Lake Pleasant, Apache Lake

Walleye
Apache Lake, Saguaro Lake, Lake Powell, Colorado River, Canyon Lake

Crappie
Lake Mead, Lake Mohave, Lake Havasu, Roosevelt Lake, Bartlett Lake, Pena Blanca Lake

Bluegill
Salt River, Lake Carlos Pleasant, Lake Mead

Yellow perch
McClelland Lake, Puk's Lake

Redear sunfish
Colorado River

White bass
Glen Canyon Dam

Yellow bass
Salt River, Saguaro Lake

Catfish
Lake Mohave, Verde River, Lake Mead, Pena Blanca Lake, Bartlett Lake, Apache Lake, Saguaro Lake

ARKANSAS

Largemouth bass
Lake Conway, White River, Black River, Nimrod Reservoir, Ouachita River, Atkins Lake, Mississippi River, Arkansas River, Cache River

Brown and rainbow trout
Spring River, Bull Shoals Dam, White River, Ouachita River below Blakely Dam, Little Missouri River below Narrows Dam

Northern pike
Norfolk Lake, DeGray Reservoir

Walleye
Norfolk Reservoir, Greers Ferry Reservoir, Bull Shoals Reservoir, Beaver Lake, Ozark Lake, Ouachita Lake, DeGray Lake, Greeson Lake, White River, Ouachita River, Hamilton Lake, Saline River

Bluegill
Lake Ouachita, Sugarloaf Lake, Conway Lake, Crooked Creek

Crappie
Lake Nimrod, Lake Chicot, Grand Lake, Maumelle Lake, Norfolk Lake, Lake Ouachita, Atkins Lake, Cache River, Arkansas River, Ouachita River, Black River, Mississippi River, Lake Conway

Rock bass
Buffalo River, Spring River, Upper White River, War Eagle River

Warmouth bass
Many lakes and streams in eastern Arkansas

Redear sunfish
Bear Creek Lake, Wilmot Lake, Crystal Lake

Longear and green sunfish
Streams in northwest Arkansas

White bass
Lake Hamilton, Bull Shoals Lake, Lake Norfolk, Ouachita Lake

Catfish
Sugar Loaf Lake, Crystal Lake, Mississippi River, Nimrod Reservoir, White River, Buffalo River, Arkansas River, Cache River

CALIFORNIA

Largemouth bass
Colorado River, Clear Lake, Shasta Lake, Lake Miramar, Upper Otay Lake, Lower Otay Lake, El Capitan Lake, Lake Sutherland, Lake Murray

Rainbow trout
Truckee River, Hot Creek, Lake Tahoe, Shasta Lake, Folsum Lake, Pine Flat Reservoir, Isabella Reservoir, Cachuma Reservoir, Millerton Lake, Twitchell Reservoir, Colorado River

Steelhead
Klamath River, Eel River, Scott River, Mattole River, Smith River, Trinity River, Mad River, Russian River, Garcia River

Lake trout
Lake Tahoe

Cutthroat trout
Eel River, Klamath River, Redwood Creek, Mad River

Brown trout
Truckee River, Colorado River, Donners Lake, Cachuma Reservoir, Twitchell Reservoir, Isabella Reservoir, Shasta Lake, Folsum Lake

Golden trout
Golden Trout Creek, Upper Little Kern, Kern River

Bluegill
Shasta Lake, Clear Lake, Millerton Lake, Lake Berryessa, Sacramento River (delta area)

Crappie
Clear Lake, Lake Berryessa, Folsum Lake, Pineflat Reservoir, Isabella Reservoir, Cachuma Reservoir

Walleye
Casitas Reservoir, El Capitan Reservoir, Cachuma Reservoir

Chinook salmon
San Francisco Bay, Mad River, Scott River, Salmon River, Van Duzen River, Smith River, Klamath River, and many places along the coast

Coho salmon
Ten Mile Stream, Noyo River, Navarro River, Russian River, and many places along the coast

Sturgeon
San Francisco Bay near Sausalito

Catfish
Clear Lake, Lake Berryessa, Twitchell Reservoir, Cachuma Reservoir, Folsum Lake

COLORADO

Largemouth bass
Jumbo Reservoir, Bonny Dam, Lone Tree Reservoir, Boyd Reservoir, Horseshoe Reservoir, Loveland Reservoir, North Sterling Reservoir

Brown trout
Arkansas River, S. Platte River, Big Thompson River, Laramie River, White River, Frying Pan River, Roaring Fork River, and many of the same lakes and reservoirs holding rainbow trout

Rainbow trout
S. Platte River, White River, Frying Pan River, Arkansas River, Yampa River, Roaring Fork River, Dowdy Lake, Colorado River, Gunnison River, Seaman Lake, Jefferson Lake, Rio Grande River, Vega Reservoir, Monument Lake, Eleven Mile Lake, Taylor Reservoir, Tarryall Lake, Upper Conejos River, Shadow Mountain Reservoir

Cutthroat trout
Gunnison River and many remote timberline or alpine lakes

Brook trout
Dowdy Lake, Parvin Lake, Seaman Lake, Jefferson Lake, Tarryall Lake, Eleven Mile Lake, San Cristobal Lake, Monument Lake, Roaring River, Frying Pan River, Gunnison River, Granby Reservoir, Twin Lakes Reservoir, Vallecito Reservoir

Bluegill
Bonny Reservoir, Smith Reservoir, Lonetree Reservoir, Two Buttes Reservoir, Halbrook Lake

Crappie
Sterling Reservoir, Jumbo Reservoir, Summit Reservoir, Lonetree Reservoir, Horsecreek Reservoir, Bonny Dam, Loveland Reservoir, Horseshoe Reservoir

Yellow perch
Lonetree Reservoir, Boyd Reservoir, Loveland Reservoir, Horseshoe Reservoir, Sterling Reservoir, Jackson Reservoir

Rock bass
Bonny Reservoir, Karval Reservoir, Two Buttes Reservoir

Pumpkinseed sunfish
Hasty Lake, Sloans Lake, Thorston Lake, Bonny Reservoir, Queens Reservoir

White bass
Bonny Reservoir, Sterling Reservoir, Cherry Creek Reservoir, Julesberg Reservoir, Adobe Creek Reservoir, Blue Lake, Boyd Lake

Northern pike
Bonny Reservoir, Boyd Reservoir, Queens Reservoir, Two Buttes Reservoir, Holbrook Lake

Walleye
Julesberg Reservoir, Bonny Dam, Adobe Creek Reservoir, Horsecreek Reservoir, Horsetooth Reservoir, Boyd Reservoir, Jumbo Reservoir, Two Buttes Reservoir, Jackson Lake

Channel catfish
Jumbo Reservoir, Adobe Creek Reservoir, Horsecreek Reservoir

CONNECTICUT

Largemouth bass
East Twin Lake, Bantam Lake, Lake Lillinonah, Wood Creek Pond, Pachaug Pond, Mashapaug Lake, Black Pond, Moodus Reservoir

Smallmouth bass
Lake Lillinonah, Waumgumbaug Lake, Mashapaug Lake

Rainbow trout
Ball Pond, Highland Lake, West Hill Pond, Mashapaug Lake, Wononskopomuc Lake

Brown trout
Natchaug River, Crystal Lake, Gardner Lake, Mashapaug Lake, East Twin Lake, Highland Lake, West Hill Pond, Housatonic River, West Branch Farmington River, East Branch Salmon River, Fenton River, Bigelow Brook, Mt. Hope River

Brook trout
Ball Pond, Mohawk Pond

Northern pike
Connecticut River, Bantam River

Chain pickerel
Lake Waramaug, Lake Wononskopomuc, Rainbow Reservoir

Walleye
Lake Zoar, Lake Lillinonah

Bluegill
East Twin Lake, Lake Lillinonah, Moodus Reservoir, Waumgumbaug Lake

Crappie
Lake Pocotopaug, Highland Lake, Lake Saltonstall, Pataganset Lake, Lake Lillinonah, Gorton's Pond, Lake Zoar

Yellow perch
East Twin Lake, Lake Zoar, Rogers Lake, Bashan Lake, Candlewood Lake, Crystal Lake, Bantam Lake, Wood Creek Pond, Black Pond, Moodus Reservoir, Squantz Pond

Pumpkinseed sunfish
Pachaug Pond, Lake Saltonstall, Candlewood Lake, Bantam Lake, Lake Waramaug

Catfish
Connecticut River

DELAWARE

Largemouth bass
Noxonton Millpond, Concord Pond, Trussem Pond, Silver Lake, Burton Pond, Lake Como, and various other freshwater ponds

Trout
White Clay Creek, Pike Creek, Mill Creek; trout fishing is very limited

Yellow perch
Rehoboth Bay, Indian River Bay

Pickerel
Concord Pond

FLORIDA

Largemouth bass
Lake Jackson, Kississimmee Lake, Talquin Lake, Lake George, Tsala Apopka Lake, Panasoffkee Lake, Lake Okeechobee, Eustis Lake, Harris Lake, Lake Hell 'N Blazes, Tohopekaliga Lake, Lake Oklawaha, Lake Kerr, St. Johns River, Oklawaha River, Suwanee River, Homosassa River, Crystal River, Apalachicola River

Bluegill
Lake Istokpogo, Lake Martin, Lake Seminole, Blue Cypress Lake, Lake Lena, Lake Trafford, Apalachicola River

Crappie
Lake Istokpogo, Lake Martin, Lake Lena, Lake Seminole, Blue Cypress Lake, Lake Marianna, Lake Trafford, Apalachicola River, Lake Okeechobee, Lake Apopka, Orange Lake, St. Johns River

Redear sunfish
Lake Griffin, Lake Panasoffkee, Withlacoochee Backwaters, Dead Lake, Lake George, Yale Lake, Harris Lake, Puzzle Lake

Warmouth bass
Withlacoochee River, Peace River, St. Johns River, Kissimmee River, Suwanee River

Pickerel
Kissimmee Lake, Talquin Lake, Lake George, Tohopekaliga Lake, Lake Harris, Lake Kerr, St. Johns River, Eustis Lake

Sturgeon
Apalachicola River and other northern Florida rivers

GEORGIA

Largemouth bass
Lanier Reservoir, Allatoona Reservoir, Hartwell Reservoir, Montgomery Lake, Lake Jackson, Lake Sinclaire, Clark Hill Reservoir, Lake Worth, Lake Blackshear, Lake Fort Gaines, Lake Seminole, Flint River, Canoochee River, Ogeechee River, Suwanee River

Smallmouth bass
Blue Ridge Lake

Rainbow trout
Burton Reservoir, Seed Reservoir, Rabun Reservoir, Lake Lanier tailwaters, and some streams in northeast Georgia

Walleye
Blue Ridge Lake, Burton Lake, Lake Lanier, Hartwell Lake, Lake Allatoona, Chatuge Lake

Pickerel
Lake Blackshear, Lake Worth, Satilla River, Okefenokee Swamp, Seminole Lake, Fort Gaines Lake, Flint River, Alapaha River, Ocmulgee River, Canoochee River, Suwanee River, Ogeechee River

Bluegill
Lake Fort Gaines, Lake Worth, Lake Blackshear, Lake Seminole, Highfalls Lake, Satilla River, Ocmulgee River, Altamaha River, Ogeechee River

Crappie
Lanier Reservoir, Allatoona Reservoir, Hartwell Reservoir, Lake Worth, Clark Hill Reservoir, Lake Sinclaire, Lake Jackson

Yellow perch
Lake Burton, Lake Clark Hill, Lake Lanier, Lake Rabon, Seed Lake

White bass
Bartlett's Ferry Lake, Goat Rock Lake, Lake Oliver, Clark Hill Reservoir, Lake Blackshear, Lake Jackson, Lake Sinclaire, Lake Sidney Lanier

Warmouth bass
Okefenokee Swamp

Longear sunfish
Satilla River, Oconee River, Ocmulgee River

Catfish
Lake Sidney Lanier, Allatoona Reservoir, Hartwell Reservoir, Lake Jackson, Clark Hill Reservoir, Lake Blackshear, Lake Worth, Lake Seminole

HAWAII

Largemouth bass
Can be found in various streams and reservoirs on the islands of Oahu, Kauai, Maui

Rainbow trout
Kauaikinana, Kawaikoi, Waiakoali, Mohihi, Koaie, and Waialae streams on the island of Kauai

IDAHO

Largemouth bass
Swan Falls Dam

Smallmouth bass
Brownlee Reservoir, Swan Falls Dam

Rainbow trout
Lake Pend Oreille, Coeur d'Alene Lake, Lochsa River, Clearwater River, Selway River, Salmon River, South Fork Salmon River, Middle Fork Salmon River, Boise River, Little Salmon River

Steelhead
Snake River, Waha Lake, Blue Lake, Salmon River, Clearwater River, Brownlee Dam

Dolly Varden trout
Pend Oreille Lake, Priest Lake, Salmon River

Brook trout
Moyie River

Lake trout
Priest Lake

Cutthroat trout
Moyie River, Priest Lake, Lake Pend Oreille, Coeur d'Alene Lake, Salmon River and tributaries

Walleye
Lake Pend Oreille

Crappie
Shepherd Lake, Brownlee Reservoir, Strike Reservoir, Fernan Lake

Yellow perch
Lake Lowell, Cascade Reservoir, Chatcolet Lake, Fernan Lake, Hauser Lake

Chinook salmon
Salmon River, Clearwater River, Brownlee Dam

Channel catfish
Swan Falls Dam

White sturgeon
Snake River, Waha Lake, Manns Lake, Blue Lake, Spring Valley Reservoir, Brownlee Dam

ILLINOIS

Largemouth bass
Mississippi River, Crab Orchard Lake, Horseshoe Lake, Lake Murphysboro, Devil's Kitchen Lake, Baldwin Lake, Benton City Lake, Sangchris Lake

Smallmouth bass
Kishwaukee River, Iroquois River, DuPage River, Plum River, Wabash River

Rainbow trout
Apple River

Steelhead
Lake Michigan shoreline

Brown trout
Apple River, Lake Michigan shoreline and Waukegan, Diversey, and Jackson harbors

Lake trout
Lake Michigan shoreline

Northern pike
Fox Lake, Rend Lake, Catherine Lake, Channel Lake, Lake Marie, East Leon Lake, Bluff Lake, Homer Lake, Grass Lake, Petite Lake, Nippersink Lake, Pistakee Lake, Spring Lake, Mississippi River (Pool 13), Potter's Slough, Millers Lake, Kinkaid Lake

Muskellunge
Spring Lake, Shabana Lake, Chain of Lakes

Walleye
Mississippi River (Pool 18), Ohio River, Wabash River, Kankakee River, Rock River, Fox Chain of Lakes, Cedar Lake, Lake Marie

Bluegill
Lincoln Trail State Lake, Rend Lake, Deep Lake, Waldon Springs Lake, Shabbona Lake, Cedar Lake, Crab Orchard Lake, Devil's Kitchen Lake, Horseshoe Lake

Crappie
Mississippi River (Pool 16), Beaver Dam Lake, Carlyle Lake, Kinkaid Lake, Sam Parr Lake, Stump Lake area

White bass
Fox Lake, Catherine Lake, Lake Marie, Channel Lake, Bluff Lake, Grass Lake, Petite Lake, Carlyle Lake, Crab Orchard Lake, Sangchris Lake, Mississippi River (Sylvan Slough), Rend Lake

Sauger
Mississippi River

Yellow perch
Lake Michigan

Redear sunfish
Lake Argyle, Lake Murphysboro, Horseshoe Lake, Lincoln Trail State Lake, Walnut Point State Lake, Washington County Lake

Catfish
Flatheads—Lake Springfield, Rock River, and Little Wabash River; blue catfish—Wabash River

INDIANA

Largemouth bass
Indiana River, Tippecanoe River, Kankakee River, Wabash River, Ohio River

Smallmouth bass
St. Joseph River, West Fork White River, East Fork White River

Brown trout
Lake Michigan shoreline

Steelhead
Little Calumet River, Trail Creek, Lake Michigan shoreline

Lake trout
Lake Michigan shoreline

Northern pike
Tippecanoe River, Kankakee River, Lake Wawasee, Kootz Lake, Wabee Lake, Troxall Lake, Fawn River, Pigeon River, Hudson Lake

Walleye
Kankakee River, Quick Creek River, Cataract Lake

Muskellunge
Brookville Reservoir, Whitewater River and tributaries

Bluegill
Sylvan Lake, Lake Wawasee, Willow Slough, Grist Reservoir, Lake Manitou

Crappie
Wabash River, West Fork White River, East Fork White River, Muscatatuck River

Yellow perch
Lake Michigan, Tippecanoe River, Lake George, Lake Wawasee, Clear Lake, Lake James, Crooked Lake

Rock bass
Indiana River, Tippecanoe River

Channel catfish
Indiana River, Tippecanoe River, Ohio River, Muscatatuck River, Kankakee River, Wabash River, St. Joseph River

Blue catfish
Indiana River, St. Joseph River, Kankakee River, Wabash River, West Fork White River, East Fork White River

IOWA

Largemouth bass
Spirit Lake, Clear Lake, Coraville Dam, Mississippi River backwaters

Smallmouth bass
Spirit Lake, Clear Lake, Iowa River, Maquoketa River, Cedar River

Northern pike
Spirit Lake, Lost Island Lake, Clear Lake, Lake Okoboji, Storm Lake, Trumbel Lake, Mississippi River

Sauger
Mississippi River

Walleye
Storm Lake, Spirit Lake, East Okoboji Lake, Clear Lake, Des Moines River, West Okoboji Lake, Raccoon River, Mississippi River

Muskellunge
West Okoboji Lake

Crappie
Spirit Lake, East Okoboji Lake, Clear Lake, Mississippi River backwaters

Bluegill
Spirit Lake, Clear Lake, Coraville Dam

Yellow perch
Spirit Lake, Clear Lake, Mississippi River

White bass
Spirit Lake, Clear Lake

Channel catfish
Clear Lake

KANSAS

Largemouth bass
Neosho River, Marais River, Fall River, Verdigris River, Elk River, Kanopolis Lake, Kirwin Reservoir, Webster Reservoir

Smallmouth bass
Very rare—try Shoal Creek, Spring River

Spotted bass
Neosho River, Cottonwood River, Marais River, des Cygnes River, Elk River, Caney River, Walnut River, Fall River

Northern pike
Tuttle Creek Reservoir, Council Grove Reservoir, Milford Reservoir, Perry Reservoir, Cedar Bluff Reservoir, Norton Reservoir, Elk City Reservoir, Melvern Reservoir

Walleye
Wilson Reservoir, Pomono Reservoir, Cheney Reservoir, Milford Reservoir, Norton Reservoir, Solomon River, Saline River, Kanopolis Lake, Kirwin Reservoir, Tuttle Creek Reservoir, Smokey Hill River, Verdigris River

Bluegill
Verdigris River, Leavenworth County State Lake, Woodson County State Lake, Crawford County State Lake # 2, Lone Star Lake, Pomonia Reservoir, Kanopolis Lake

Crappie
Solomon River, Pomonia Reservoir, Tuttle Creek Reservoir, Kirwin Reservoir, Kanopolis Lake, Fall River, Verdigris River, Saline River, Smokey Hill River

Yellow perch
Lake Wabaunsee, Cedar Bluff Reservoir

Warmouth bass
Found in several stripmining lakes in the southeast

White bass
Smokey Hill River, Kanopolis Lake, Lovewell Reservoir, Cedar Bluff Reservoir, Saline River, Fall River

Catfish
Arkansas River, Dawnee River, Medicine Lodge River, Rattlesnake Creek, Fall River, Verdigris River, Lovewell Reservoir, Kirwin Reservoir, Tuttle Creek Reservoir, Pomonia Reservoir

KENTUCKY

Largemouth bass
Kentucky Lake, Cumberland Lake, Dewey Lake, Herrington Lake, Rough River Reservoir, Barren River Reservoir

Smallmouth bass
Slate Creek, Elkhorn Creek, Ohio River, Kentucky River, Tennessee River, Cumberland River, Nolin Reservoir, Licking River, Nolin River, Green River, Dale Hollow Reservoir, Buckhorn Reservoir

Rainbow trout
Cumberland Lake, Rough River Reservoir

Walleye
Harrington Lake, Lake Cumberland, Barren Lake, Dale Hollow Reservoir, Rough River Lake, Kentucky River, Green River, Licking River

Muskellunge
Barren River, Barren River Reservoir, Dale Hollow Reservoir, Nolin Reservoir, Ohio River, Green River, Licking River

Northern pike
Harrington Lake

Sauger
Kentucky River, Kentucky Lake

Bluegill
Kentucky Lake, Kentucky River, Harrington Lake, Dewey Lake, Dale Hollow Reservoir, Rough River Reservoir, Buckhorn Reservoir, Nolin Reservoir, Barren Lake

Crappie
Kentucky River, Kentucky Lake, Cumberland Lake, Dale Hollow Reservoir, Harrington Lake, Dewey Lake, Barren Lake, Buckhorn Reservoir

White bass
Kentucky River, Dale Hollow Reservoir, Harrington Lake, Nolin Reservoir

Catfish
Kentucky River, Kentucky Lake, Nolin Reservoir, Barren Lake

LOUISIANA

Largemouth bass
Spring Bayou Reservoir, Pearl River backwaters, Vermilion River, Mermentau River, Caddo Lake, Cross Lake, Sabine Lake, Lake Verrett

Spotted bass
Many of the small rivers or streams

Chain pickerel
Almost all waters

Bluegill
Spring Bayou backwaters, Lake Verrett, Lake Providence, Black Lake, Bruin Lake, Cane River Lake

Crappie
Vermilion River, Mermentau River, Lake Verrett

White bass
Ouachita River, Pearl River backwater, Spring Bayou backwater

Warmouth bass
Pearl River, Chicot Lake, Bruin Lake

Redear sunfish
Bruin Lake, St. John Lake, Davis Lake, Anacoco Lake

MAINE

Largemouth bass
Sebago Lake, China Lake, Big Lake, Moose Pond, Spednic Lake, Belgrade Lake

Smallmouth bass
Fish River Lake, Kennebec River, Moose River, Penobscot River, Kennebago River, Spencer River, Allagash River, Belgrade Lake, China Lake, Branch Lake, Spednic Lake

Rainbow trout
Kennebec River

Brook trout
Allagash River, Spencer River, Kennebago River, Penobscot River, Moose River, Kennebec River, Fish River Lake, Long Lake, Pushineer Pond, Rangeley Lake, Gardner Lake, Chesuncook Lake, Moosehead Lake, Brassua Lake, Kennebago Lake, Seven Ponds streams, Sebago Lake, Massalonskee Lake, Branch Lake, Phillips Lake, St. Croix River

Brown trout
Alamasook Lake, Sebago Lake, Winthrop-Belgrade Lakes, China Lake, Branch Lake

Lake trout
Allagash River, Spencer River, Kennebago River, Penobscot River, Moose River, Kennebec River, Fish River Lake, China Lake, East Grand Lake, West Grand Lake, West Musquash Lake, Pleasant Lake

Black crappie
Sebago Lake, Virginia Lake

Whitefish
Long Lake, Chesuncook Lake

Atlantic salmon
Narraguagus River, Machias River, Pleasant River, Dennys River, Sheepscot River, Aroostook River, St. Croix River

Landlocked salmon
Allagash River, Spencer River, Kennebago River, Penobscot River, Moose River, Kennebec River, Fish River Lake, Chesuncook Lake, Moosehead Lake, Gravel Banks Pool,

Rangeley Lakes, Sebago Lake, Green Lake, Lower Patten Pond, Branch Lake, Beech Hill Pond, Phillips Lake, Hopkins Pond, Alligator Lake, Upper Lead Mountain Pond, Molasses Pond, Upper Middle Branch Pond, Floods Pond, East and West Grand Lakes

MARYLAND

Smallmouth bass
Potomac River

Rainbow trout
Gunpowder River, Bear Creek, Beaver Creek, Hunting Creek, Savage River, Principio Creek, Rock Creek

Brown trout
Gunpowder River, Rock Creek, Bear Creek, Beaver Creek, Principio Creek, Savage River

Brook trout
Savage River, Principio Creek, Gunpowder River, Bear Creek, Hunting Creek, Rock Creek, Beaver River

Northern pike
Deep Creek Lake, Loch Raven Reservoir, Conowingo Reservoir, Susquehanna River

Walleye
Susquehanna River, Conowingo Reservoir, Loch Raven Reservoir, Deep Creek Lake

Yellow perch
Severn River, South River, West River, Rhodes River, Wye River, Miles River, Chesapeake Bay, Choptank River

Channel catfish
Potomac River

MASSACHUSETTS

Largemouth bass
Onota Lake, Pontoosac Lake, Lake Buel, Lake Garfield, Quabbin Reservoir, Long Pond, Whitehall Reservoir, Norton Reservoir, Connecticut River backwaters

Smallmouth bass
Long Pond, Swady Pond, Watuppa Pond, Lake Quaboag, Lake Lashaway, Lake Wickaboag, Lake Quinsigamond, Whitehall Reservoir, Quabbin Reservoir, Lake Garfield, Lake Buel, Pontoosac Lake, Onota Lake

Rainbow trout
Deerfield River, Farmington River, Green River, Quabbin Reservoir, Comet Pond, Lake Quinsigamond, Lake Mattawa, Lake Cochituate, Lake Quacumquasit, Ware River, Quinapoxet River

Brown trout
Lake Onota, Deerfield River, Konkapot River, Farmington River, Green River, Quabbin Reservoir, Cliff Pond

Brook trout
Deerfield River, Konkapot River, Farmington River, Green River

Lake trout
Quabbin Reservoir

Walleye
Connecticut River

Chain pickerel
Stockbridge Bowl, Onota Lake, Pontoosac Lake, Lake Garfield, Quabbin Reservoir, Lake Quannapowitt, Spy Pond, Long Pond, Concord River, Sudbury River, Furnace Pond, Monposett Pond

Bluegill
Norton Reservoir, Stockbridge Bowl, Cheshire Reservoir, Pontoosuc Lake, Concord River

Crappie
South Pond, Norton Reservoir, East Bromfield Reservoir, Indian Lake, Subbatia Lake

Yellow perch
Quabbin Reservoir, Norton Reservoir, Long Pond, Lake Chequaquet, Pleasant Lake, Depot Pond, Lawrence Pond, Mystic Pond, Middle Pond

Pumpkinseed sunfish
Lake Quannopowitt, Lake Nippensicket, Norton Reservoir, Niponsit Reservoir

Channel catfish
Connecticut River oxbows

MICHIGAN

Largemouth bass
Saginaw Bay, North Lake, Lake Fenton, Grand River bayous, Muskegon Lake, Martiny Lakes, Pigeon Lake, Cusino Lake, Brevort Lake, Winnewana Lake, Four Mile Lake, Wamplers Lake, Cass Lake, Pontiac Lake, Manistee Lake

Smallmouth bass
St. Mary's River, Big Bay De Noc, Little Bay De Noc, Whitefish River, Escanaba River, Sylvania Lakes, Lake Huron near Les Cheneaux Islands, Waugoshance Point, Manistee Lake, Bear Lake, Portage Lake, Grand Traverse Bay, Lake St. Clair, Skegemog (Round) Lake, Bear Lake, Starvation Lake, Missaukee Lake, Shiawassee River, Cass River, Misery Bay, Eagle Bay, Huron Bay, Cass Lake

Rainbow trout and steelhead
Rainbows—Union Lake, Proud Lake, Maceday Lake, Burt Lake, Horseshoe Lake, Holloway Reservoir, Cedar Lake, Lake Ann, Walloon Lake, Sunrise Lake, County Line Lake, Ackerman Lake; steelhead closest to the Great Lakes and resident rainbows farther upstream—St. Joseph River, Black River, Grand River, Muskegon River, Sauble River, Little Manistee River, Pentwater River, Big Manistee River, Bear Creek, Betsie River, Platte River, Elk River, Boardman River, Bear River, Sturgeon River, Rifle River, East Branch AuGres River, Tawas River, Au Sable River, Thunder Bay River, Ocqueoc River, Chocolay River, Carp River, Middle Branch Ontonogan River, Mosquito River, Two Hearted River, Misery River, Laughing Whitefish River, Whitefish River, Escanaba River, Ford River, Menominee River

Brown trout
Green Lake, Lime Lake, Lake Leelanau, Higgins Lake, Starvation Lake, Chub Lake; Lake Michigan near Frankfort, Traverse City, South Haven, Muskegon, Manistee, Thompson Creek, Manistique, Little Bay De Noc; Lake Huron near Alpena, Tawas City, Hessel, Cedarville, Alabaster, Grindstone City, Harbor Beach; Lake Superior near Marquette, Munising, L'Anse, Baraga; Platte River, Betsie River, Pere Marquette River, Big Manistee River, Little Manistee River, Muskegon River, St. Joseph River, Sturgeon River, Au Sable River, Carp River, Rifle River, Thunder Bay River, Middle Branch of the Ontonogan, Paint River, Menominee River, Net River, and hundreds of smaller streams

Lake trout
All of Lakes Michigan, Huron, and Superior, Higgins Lake, Duck Lake, Gull Lake, Crystal Lake, Mullet Lake, Maceday Lake, Torch Lake, Cass Lake, Elk Lake, Lake Charlevoix, Walloon Lake, Big Glen Lake, North Lake Leelanau, Chicagon Lake, Banana Lake, Clear Lake, Dodge Lake, Island Lake

Brook trout
Upper Pine River, North Branch Ford River, Black River, upper Au

Sable River, upper Manistee River, Clam River, West Branch Sturgeon River, Little Sturgeon River, Teaspoon Creek, Fox River, Cedar Creek, Maple River, Silver Creek, West Branch Escanaba River, West Branch Sturgeon River (Upper Peninsula), Big Castle Lake, Union Springs Pond, Spree Lake, Iron River, Moon Lake, Paulding Pond, Haywire Lake

Splake
Harrisville, Grand Sable Lake, Imp Lake, Wintergreen Lake, Beaton's Lake, Finger Lake, Chicagon Lake, Copper Harbor, Pretty Lake, Paulding Pond, Dutch Fred Lake, Lake Bellaire, Lake Ann, Big Glen Lake, Higgins Lake, Mullet Lake, Union Lake

Northern pike
Keweenaw Bay, Isle Royale bays, Huron Bay, Little Bay De Noc, Green Bay, Potagannissing Bay, Munuscong Bay, Portage Lake, Au Train Lake, Milakokia Lake, Douglas Lake, Tittabawassee River, Bad River, Cass Lake, Saginaw Bay, Manistee Lake, Muskegon Lake, and hundreds of smaller lakes

Muskellunge
Lake St. Clair, Detroit River, St. Clair River, St. Mary's River, Hamlin Lake, Bass Lake, Elk Lake, Skegemog (Round) Lake, Indian River, Lac Vieux Desert, Chicagon Lake, Iron Lake, Tahquamenon River, Munuscong Bay, Stuart Lake, Kaks Lake, Thornapple Lake, Lincoln Lake, Budd Lake, Bankson Lake, Lake Lansing, Michigan Center Chain, Lake Nepessing, Big Bear Lake, Murphy Lake, Pontiac Lake, Heron Lake, Tipsico Lake, Silver Lake, Huron River Ponds, Whitmore Lake

Walleye
Lake Gogebic, Munuscong Bay, Manistique Lake, Indian Lake, Burt Lake, Lake Cadillac, Lake Mitchell, Houghton Lake, Lake St. Clair, Detroit River, St. Clair River, Huron River, Muskegon Lake, Muskegon River, Manistee River, Manistee Lake, Bear Lake, Portage Lake, Little Bay De Noc, Hubbard Lake, Black Lake, St. Mary's River, Potagannissing Bay, Saginaw Bay, Lakes Huron, Superior, Michigan, Erie

Sauger
Torch Lake, Portage Lake, Little Bay De Noc, Escanaba River

Bluegill
Gun Lake, Coldwater Lake, Chemung Lake, Houghton Lake, Manistee Lake, Ponemah Lake, Lobdell Lake, Fenton Lake, Squaw Lake, Pratt's Lake, Wiggins Lake, Blue Lake, Long Lake, Duck Lake, Graham Lake, Painter Lake, Martiny Lakes, White Lake

Crappie
Saginaw Bay, Thornapple Lake, Robinson Lake, Fremont Lake, Hart Lake, Lake Macatawa, Flint River, Wixom Lake, Houghton Lake

Yellow perch
Lake Michigan near the port cities of Benton Harbor–St. Joseph, South Haven, Saugatuck, Ludington, Manistee, Onekama, Frankfort; Lake Huron near the port cities of Detroit, Mt. Clemens, Port Huron, Caseville, Bayport, Sebewaing, Quanicassee, Linwood, Standish, Tawas City, Oscoda, Alpena, Cedarville-Hessel; Long Lake, Portage Lake, Huron Bay

Sunfish
Au Train Basin, Hermansville Lake, Quanicassee, Shiawassee River, Swan Creek, Cass River, Lake Lansing, Huron River

Atlantic salmon
Lake Charlevoix, Boyne River, Gull Lake

Chinook salmon
Nearly every port city along Lakes Michigan, Huron, with emphasis on

Chinook salmon *(continued)*
South Haven, Muskegon, Ludington, Manistee, Traverse City, Alpena, Rogers City, Cheboygan, Harrisville, Oscoda, Tawas City, Detroit; Marquette Harbor, Manistique Harbor, Little Bay De Noc, Big Manistee River, St. Joseph River, Au Sable River, Boardman River, Thunder Bay River, Betsie River, Rifle River, Detroit River, Ocqueoc River

Coho salmon
Nearly every city along Lakes Michigan and Huron with emphasis on the ones mentioned for chinook salmon; St. Joseph River, Black River, Grand River, Platte River, Betsie River, Tawas River, East Branch AuGres River, Rifle River, Cass River

Sturgeon
Burt Lake, Mullet Lake, Black Lake, St. Clair River, Menominee River

Whitefish
Huron Bay, St. Mary's River, Higgins Lake, Torch Lake, Crystal Lake, Grand Traverse Bay, Lake Michigan (northern portion), Keweenaw Bay, Lake Superior, Munising Harbor

Catfish
Muskegon River, Grand River, St. Joseph River, Kalamazoo River, Raisin River, Cass River, Shiawassee River, Tittabawassee River, Bad River, Au Sable River, Saginaw Bay, Lake St. Clair, Lake Erie, Wixom Lake, Smallwood Lake, Maple River, Union Lake, Skegemog (Round) Lake, Thornapple River, Grand River–Pettys Bayou, Houghton Lake, Holloway Reservoir

MINNESOTA

Largemouth bass
Many of the major lakes in the southern portion of the state; Mississippi River bayous

Smallmouth bass
St. Croix River, Rainy Lake, Brule Lake, Saganaga Lake, Greenwood Lake, Little Vermilion Lake, Basswood Lake, Miltona Lake, Ida Lake, Lake Kabetogama, Lake of the Woods, Winnibigoshish Lake

Steelhead
Baptism River, Brule (Arrowhead) River, Knife River, Sucker River, Root River, Whitewater River

Brown trout
Root River, Whitewater River, Straight River

Brook trout
Many streams which headwater and flow down to Lake Superior have good numbers of brook trout. Some "coasters" taken at widely scattered points along Lake Superior. Contact the DNR for an updated list of reclaimed brook trout lakes

Lake trout
Mountain Lake, Clearwater Lake, Seagull Lake, Gunflint Lake, Snowbank Lake, West Pike Lake

Northern pike
Lake of the Woods, Red Lake, Leech Lake, Lake Winnibigoshish, Lake Traverse, Mille Lacs, Otter Trail Lake, Birch Lake, Vermilion Lake, Basswood Lake, White Iron Lake, Rainy Lake, Saganaga Lake, Bemidji Lake, Pelican Lake, Gull Lake, Cormorant Lake, Lida Lake, Rush Lake, Minnetonka Lake, St. Croix River, Rainy River, St. Louis River

Walleye
Lake Kabetogama, Rainy Lake, Crane Lake, Pelican Lake, Namakan Lake, Leech Lake, Winnibigoshish Lake, Red Lake, Vermilion Lake, Lake of the Woods, Ottertail Lake, Round Lake, Washkish Lake, Shetek Lake, Lake Minnewaska, Lake Minnetonka, Spring Lake, Lake Traverse

Muskellunge
Kitchi Lake, Woman Lake, Boy Lake, Andrusia Lake, Leech Lake, Minnetonka Lake, Cass Lake, Winnibigoshish Lake, Bottle Lake, Moose Lake, Spider Lake, Lake of the Woods, Bad Axe Lake

Panfish
Bluegills, crappies, yellow perch common in almost every warmwater lake; some good fishing along the Mississippi River

Coho salmon
Minnesota is phasing out their salmon program but some fish still turn up from Duluth north along the Lake Superior shoreline

Atlantic salmon
Some stocking on an experimental basis along the North Shore of Lake Superior

Catfish
St. Louis River, Mississippi River, St. Croix River

MISSISSIPPI

Largemouth bass
Pickwick Reservoir, Mississippi Delta area, Limestone Creek, Strong River, Chunky River, Bowie River, Pearl River, Yucatan Lake, Mary Lake, Rodney Lake, Big Lake, Mary Walker Bayou

Smallmouth bass
Pickwick Reservoir

Walleye
Tombigbee River, Buttahatchie River

Sauger
Pickwick Reservoir

Bluegill
Sardis Reservoir, Enid Reservoir, Moon Lake, Eagle Lake, Strong River, Mossy Lake, Limestone Creek, Pearl River, Bowie River, Chunky River

Crappie
Pickwick Reservoir, Moon Lake, Tunica Cut-Off Lake, Eagle Lake, Mossy Lake

Warmouth bass
Wolf Lake, Mossy Lake, Lake George, Big Black Lake, Sunflower Lake

White bass
Pickwick Reservoir

Sunfish
Eagle Lake, Sardi Reservoir, Enid Reservoir, Grenada Reservoir, Arkabutta Reservoir, Bogue Homa Lake

Catfish
Pickwick Reservoir

MISSOURI

Largemouth bass
Table Rock Lake, Norfolk Lake, Clearwater Lake, Lake of the Ozarks, Spring Lake

Smallmouth bass
Pomme de Terre Lake, Gasconade River, Bourbeuse River, Big River, Black River, Meramec River, Upper St. Francis River, Current River, Huzzah River, Elk River, James River

White bass
Lake Taneycomo, Bull Shoals Lake, Table Rock Lake, Norfork Lake, Clearwater Lake, Lake of the Ozarks, Pomme de Terre Lake, Osage River, Fox River, Salt River

Walleye
Mississippi River, Current River, Osage River, Lake Taneycomo

Muskellunge
Pomme de Terre Lake, Stockton Lake, Pony Express Lake, Binder Lake, Trimble Lake (Smithville Reservoir), Nodaway Lake

Bluegill
Lake Taneycomo, Bull Shoals Lake, Table Rock Lake, Norfork Lake, Lake of the Ozarks, Osage River, Platte River, Nodaway River, Lamine River, South Grand River

Crappie
Lake Taneycomo, Bull Shoals Lake, Table Rock Lake, Norfork Lake, Clearwater Lake, Wappapello Lake, Lake of the Ozarks, Montrose Lake, Gasconade River, Fox River, North River, Missouri River, Mississippi River

White bass
Clearwater Lake, Norfork Lake, Bull Shoals Lake, Lake Taneycomo, Table Rock Lake, Pomme de Terre Lake, Lake of the Ozarks, Osage River, Fox River, Cuivar River

Rock bass
Gasconade River, Meramec River, Bourbeuse River, Big River, Upper St. Francis River, Eleven Point River, Jacks Fork River, Huzzah River, Elk River, James River

Channel catfish
Wappapello Lake, Lake of the Ozarks, Montrose Lake, Lake Taneycomo, Clearwater Lake, Swan Lake, Osage River, Moreau River, Chariton River, Platte River, Nodaway River, Fox River, Wyaconda River, Cuivar River, Missouri River, Mississippi River

Rainbow trout
Lake Taneycomo, Bull Shoals Lake, Bennett Spring River, Montauk River, Roaring River, Capps Creek, Niangua River, Roubidoux Creek, Eleven Point River

MONTANA

Largemouth bass
Flathead Lake, Long Pine Lake, Echo Lake, Kicking Horse Lake, Nine Pipe Lake

Rainbow trout
Spring Creek, Smith River, Cut Bank River, Sun River, Missouri River, Canyon Ferry Lake, Gallatin River, Madison River, Ruby River, Big Hole River, Yellowstone River, Stillwater River, Flathead River, McDonald River, Flathead Lake, Clark's Fork, Swan River, Blackfoot River, Rock Creek, Georgetown Lake, Bear Paw Lake, Gartside Lake, Barnum Pond

Brown trout
Spring Creek, Smith River, Missouri River, Gallatin River, Madison River, Jefferson River, Beaverhead River, Ruby River, Big Hole River, Yellowstone River, Flathead River, Rock Creek, McDonald River, Clark's Fork, Wolf Creek

Brook trout
Big Hole River, Stillwater River, Boulder River, Georgetown Lake, and many alpine lakes

Cutthroat trout
Stillwater River, Salmon Lake, Flathead Lake, Flathead River, Clark's Fork, Blackfoot River, South Fork Flathead River, St. Mary's Lake, Yellowstone River, many alpine meadow streams and lakes

Lake trout
Whitefish Lake, Flathead Lake

Dolly Varden trout
Flathead Lake, Flathead River, Lake McDonald

Northern pike
Fort Peck Reservoir, lower Missouri River

Walleye
Nelson Reservoir, Yellowtail Reservoir, Holter Reservoir, Hauser Reservoir, Fort Peck Reservoir

Sauger
Fort Peck Reservoir, Missouri River, a few other eastern lakes and streams

Grayling
Big Hole River and some high mountain lakes in Glacier National Park

Whitefish
Abundant in many streams and often considered a nuisance; very common on the east slope of the Rockies

NEBRASKA

Largemouth bass
Medicine Creek Reservoir, Ravenna Lake, Hayes Center Lake, Smith Lake, Burchard Lake, Verdon Lake, Louisville Lake, Grove Lake, Maloney Reservoir, Swanson Reservoir, Grove Lake

Smallmouth bass
Lake McConaughy, Medicine Creek Reservoir, Maloney Reservoir

Rainbow trout
Otter Creek, South Loup River, North Platte River, Hot Creek, White River, Lake McConaughy, Chadron Water Supply Reservoir, Long Pine Creek, Snake River, Dismal River

Brown trout
Otter Creek, Hot Creek, North Platte River, White River, Niobara River, Pine Creek, Deer Creek, Snake River

Northern pike
Pelican Lake, Rockford Lake, Twin Lake, Military Lake, Lake Ericson, Missouri River, Cedar River, Cottonwood Lake, Wellfleet Lake, Lake McConaughy, Ballards Marsh, Maloney Reservoir, Smith Lake, Watts Lake, Island Lake, Lewis & Clark Reservoir, Grove Lake, Burchard Lake, Decatur Lake, Gallagher Canyon Reservoir, Merritt Reservoir, Medicine Creek Reservoir

Walleye
Lake McConaughy, Maloney Reservoir, Island Lake, Whitney Reservoir, Ballards Marsh, Decatur Lake, Lake Babcock, South Loup River, Watts Lake

Bluegill
Maloney Reservoir, Swanson Reservoir, Rock Creek, Grove Lake, Crystal Lake, Beaver Creek, Burchard Lake, Verdon Lake, Louisville Lake, Smith Lake, Ravenna Lake, Hayes Center Lake, Ballards Marsh, Clear L.

Crappie
Medicine Creek Reservoir, Swanson Reservoir, Enders Reservoir, Johnson Reservoir, Jeffery Reservoir, Southerland Reservoir, Smith Lake, Island Lake, Hay Springs Lake, Whitney Reservoir, Decatur Lake, Verdon Lake, Louisville Lake, Lewis & Clark Reservoir, Dead Timber Lake

Yellow perch
Maloney Reservoir, Johnson Reservoir, Enders Reservoir, Medicine Creek Reservoir, Smith Lake, Kimbell Irrigation Reservoir, Clear Lake, Willow Lake

White bass
Lake McConaughy, Harlen Reservoir, Medicine Creek Reservoir, Maloney Reservoir, Johnson Reservoir, Southerland Reservoir

Sauger
Lewis & Clark Reservoir, Lake Babcock, Beaver Creek

Channel catfish
Swanson Reservoir, Morman Lake, Lake McConaughy, Enders Reser-

Channel catfish *(continued)*
voir, Jeffery Reservoir, Southerland Reservoir, Ravenna Lake, Hayes Center Lake, Smith Lake, Island Lake, Whitney Reservoir, Lewis & Clark Reservoir, Grove Lake, Dead Timber Lake, Decatur Lake, Burchard Lake, Cedar River

NEVADA

Largemouth bass
Lake Mead

Rainbow trout
Truckee River, Walker Lake, Topaz Lake, Lake Mead, Humboldt River

Brown trout
Lake Tahoe, Truckee River, Walker Lake, Topaz Lake

Cutthroat trout
Lake Tahoe, Pyramid Lake, Bridgeport Lake, Walker Lake, Topaz Lake

Lake trout
Lake Tahoe

Bluegill
Lake Mead, Lake Mohave, Stillwater Marsh

Crappie
Lake Mead, Rye Patch Reservoir

Yellow perch
Lahontan Reservoir

Walleye
Humboldt River, Rye Patch Reservoir

NEW HAMPSHIRE

Largemouth bass
Nothing notable

Smallmouth bass
Approximately 1,200 warmwater lakes in the southern portion; Sunapee Lake

Rainbow trout
Lake Francis, First Lake, Second Lake, Third Lake, Stratford Bog, Munn Pond, Big Diamond Pond, Little Diamond Pond, Big Brook Bog, Scott's Bog, Connecticut River, Androscoggin River

Brown trout
Connecticut River, Cones Siding Run, Mascoma River, Ashuelot Pond

Brook trout
Sunapee Lake, Cold River, Sugar River, Big Diamond Pond, Little Diamond Pond, Connecticut River, Androscoggin River, Saco River, Dead Diamond River, Munn Pond

Lake trout
Lake Francis, First Lake, Second Lake, Third Lake, Scott's Bog, Big Brook Bog, Munn Pond, Lake Winnipesaukee, Squam Lake, Sunapee Lake, Winnisquam Lake

Northern pike
Connecticut River

Walleye
Merrimack River, Connecticut River

Landlocked salmon
Lake Francis, Scott's Bog, Munn Pond, Big Brook Bog, First Lake, Second Lake, Third Lake, Big Diamond Pond, Little Diamond Pond, Connecticut River, Stratford Bog, Lake Winnipesaukee, Squam Lake, Winnisquam Lake, Newfound Lake, Sunapee Lake, Androscoggin River

NEW JERSEY

Rainbow trout
Big Flat Brook, Musconetcong River, Wanaque River, Paulinskill River, Manasquan River, Upper Raritan River, Pequest River

Brown trout
Wanaque River, Musconetcong River, Big Flat Brook, Pequest River,

Upper Raritan River, Manasquan River, Paulinskill River

Brook trout
Upper Raritan River, Pequest River, Big Flat Brook, Wanaque River, Musconetcong River, Manasquan River

Northern pike
Spruce Run Reservoir, Lake Hopatcong

Walleye
Delaware River, Warren county shore, Sussex county shore

Muskellunge
Delaware River

Catfish
Delaware River, Rancocas River, Cohansey River, Salem River

Largemouth bass
Union Lake, Imlaystown Lake, Collier's Mill, Delaware Canal, Raritan Canal, Budd Lake, Shadow Lake, Tinton Reservoir, Big Swartzwood Lake, Hopatcong Lake

Smallmouth bass
Delaware River, Steenykill Lake, Big Swartswood Lake, Hopatcong Lake

Chain pickerel
Rancocas River, Salem River, Cohansey River, Tuckahoe Lake, Union Lake, Hopatcong Lake

NEW MEXICO

Largemouth bass
Elephant Butte Lake, Caballo Lake, Conchas Dam

Rainbow trout
Costilla Creek, Latir Creek, Rio Grande River, Red River, Hondo Lake, Cabresto Lake, Rio Pueblo River, Santa Barbara River, Lake Maloya, Eagle Nest Lake, Clayton Lake, Vermejo River, Costilla River, Ricardo River, Charette Lake, Storie Reservoir, McAlister Lake, Mora River, Spirit Lake, Baldy Lake, Hazel Lake, Elephant Butte Lake, Animas River, Lost Bear Lake, Santiago Lake

Brown trout
Mora River, Pecos River, Costilla River, Vermejo River, Eagle Nest Lake, Santa Barbara River, Hondo Creek, Cabresto Lake, Red River, Latir Creek, Rio Grande River

Brook trout
Pecos River, Mora River

Cutthroat trout
Mora River, Pecos River, and many small streams and lakes

Bluegill
Conchas Lake, Elephant Butte Lake, Caballo Lake, Alamagordo Lake, Lake McMillan

Crappie
Elephant Butte Lake, Conchas Lake, Caballo Lake, Alamagordo Lake, Lake McMillan

Yellow perch
Elephant Butte Lake

Sunfish
Conchas Lake, Elephant Butte Lake, Alamagordo Lake

White bass
Caballo Lake

Catfish
Elephant Butte Lake, Caballo Lake, Conchas Lake

Walleye
Alamagordo Reservoir, Elephant Butte Lake, Conchas Lake, Ute Reservoir, Caballo Lake

NEW YORK

Largemouth bass
Waneta Lake, Lamoka Lake, Chau-

Largemouth bass (*continued*)
tauqua Lake, Conesus Lake, Braddock's Bay, Irondequoit Bay, Blind Sodus Bay, Sodus Bay, East Bay, Little Sodus Bay, Long Lake, Port Bay, Saratoga Lake

Smallmouth bass
Lake Erie, Niagara River, Cayuga Lake, Canandaigua Lake, Seventh Lake, Lake Champlain, Raquette Lake, Seneca Lake, Otsego Lake, Lake Ontario, St. Lawrence River, Braddock's Bay, Sodus Bay, Black Lake, Little Sodus Bay, Port Bay

Rainbow trout and steelhead
Seneca Lake, Canandaigua Lake, Keuka Lake, Catherine Creek, Grout Brook Run, Mettawee River, Salmon River, Chateaugay River, North Branch Chazy River, West Branch Ausable, Delaware River, and many others

Brown trout
Battenkill River, Mettawee River, East Branch Delaware River, Ausable River, Willowemoc, Kinderhook River, Saranac River, Salmon River, Chateaugay River, North Branch Chazy River, Beaverkill River, Owasco Lake, and many ponds on Long Island

Brook trout
Long Lake, South Pond, and many ponds on Long Island

Lake trout
Cayuga Lake, Canandaigua Lake, Keuka Lake, Lake George, Indian Lake, Lewey Lake, Raquette Lake, Otsego Lake

Northern pike
Sacandaga Reservoir, Cayuga Lake, Little Sodus Bay, Lake Champlain, Niagara River, Eagle Lake, St. Lawrence River, Silver Lake, Crane Pond, Fern Lake, Franklin Falls Flowage, Union Falls Flowage, Saratoga Lake

Muskellunge
St. Lawrence River, Susquehanna River, Niagara River, Conewango River, Allegheny River, Chautauqua Lake, Canadarago Lake, Middle Cassadaga Lake

Pickerel
Skaneateles Lake, Cayuga Lake, Owasco Lake, Seneca Lake, Keuka Lake, Lamoka Lake, Waneta Lake, Canandaigua Lake, Lake Champlain, Canadarago Lake

Walleye
Lake Champlain, Canandaigua Lake, Oneida Lake, Lake Erie, Lake Ontario, Sacandaga Reservoir, Red Lake, Niagara River, Hudson River, Susquehanna River, Allegheny River

Bluegill
Chautauqua Lake, Round Lake, Mohawk Lake, Lake Champlain, Back Lake

Crappie
Chautauqua Lake, Lake Champlain, Sodus Bay, Lake Ontario

Yellow perch
Lake Erie, Lake Ontario, Niagara River, Grand River, Skaneateles Lake, Keuka Lake, Seneca Lake, Canandaigua Lake, Owasco Lake, Cayuga Lake

Other panfish
Lake Erie, Lake Ontario, Oneida Lake, Lake Champlain, Chautauqua Lake, Cayuga Lake, Lake George, Grand River, and other lakes

Whitefish
Lake Champlain, Indian Lake, Saranac Lake, Otsego Lake, Lake Eaton, Lewey Lake, South Pond

Coho and chinook salmon
Lake Erie and Lake Ontario (these fish have been judged to contain high levels of contaminants and

regulations change from year to year)

Sturgeon
Lake Champlain

NORTH CAROLINA

Largemouth bass
Lake Norman, Rhodhiss Lake, Lake Wylie, Currituck Sound, Buggs Island Lake, Lake Gaston, Lake Catawba

Smallmouth bass
Fontana Reservoir, Nantahala Reservoir, Chatuge Reservoir, Hiwassee Reservoir, Glenville Reservoir, New River

Bluegill
Hiwassee Reservoir, Chatuge Reservoir, Glenville Reservoir

Crappie
Catawba River, Rhodhiss Lake, Lake Hickory

Yellow perch
Beard Creek, Currituck Sound, Lake Rhodhiss, Apalachia Lake, Roaring Gap Lake

Other panfish
Currituck Sound, Lake Waccamau, Lake Rhodhiss, Lake Hickory, Tillery Reservoir, Hiwasse Reservoir, Chatuge Reservoir, Glenville Reservoir, Lookout Shoals Reservoir, Lake Wylie, Yadkin River

Rainbow trout
Upper Dan River, Nantahala Reservoir, Cheoah Reservoir, Fontana Reservoir, Santeelah Reservoir

Brook trout
Upper Dan River

Walleye
Santeelah Reservoir, Hiwassee Reservoir, Fontana Reservoir, Roanoke River

Sauger
Lake Norman

Pickerel
Gaston Reservoir

Muskellunge
Lower French Broad River, Little Tennessee River, Hiwassee River, Fontana Lake, Hiwassee Lake, Santeelah Lake

Flathead catfish
New River

NORTH DAKOTA

Northern pike
Lake Sakakawea, Jamestown Reservoir, Garrison Reservoir, Devils Lake, Crooked Lake, Ashtabula Lake, Turtle Lake, Harvey Dam, Buffalo Lake, Coldwater Lake, Battle Lake, Lake Darling, Little Missouri River, Tobacco Garden Creek

Walleye
Lake Sakakawea, Oahe Reservoir, Jamestown Reservoir, Heart Butte Reservoir, Lake Ashtabula, Lake Darling, Snake Creek, Spiritwood Lake, Garrison Reservoir, Garrison tailrace

Sauger
Oahe Reservoir, Lake Sakakawea, Garrison Reservoir, Missouri River

Muskellunge
Spiritwood Lake, Lake Williams

Bluegill
Jamestown Reservoir, Danzig Reservoir, Van Oosting Dam, Cedar Lake

Crappie
Mahato Bay, Little Missouri River, Douglas Creek, Lake Ashtabula, Heart Butte Reservoir

Yellow perch
Lake Ashtabula, Lake Darling, Jamestown Reservoir, Garrison Reservoir

White bass
Lake Ashtabula, Heart Butte Reservoir

Channel catfish
Mahato Bay, Little Missouri River, Douglas Creek, Heart Butte Reservoir

OHIO

Largemouth bass
Pymatuning Lake, Portage Lake, Lake Atwood, Lake Charles Mill, Lake Leesville, Grand Lake, Lake Beach City, St. Mary's Lake

Smallmouth bass
Lake Erie near South Bass Island, North Bass Island, Middle Bass Island, Kelleys Island; Huron River, Vermilion River, Muskingum River

Rainbow trout
Chagrin River, Conneaut Creek, Punderson Lake, Mad River, Rocky River, Turkey Creek Lake, Wolf Run Lake, Barnesville Reservoir, Belmont Lake, Dow Lake, Fork Run Lake, Jackson City Reservoir, Monroe Lake, Rose Lake

Steelhead
Chagrin River, Conneaut River, Arcola Creek, Turkey Creek, Rocky River, Lake Erie

Brown trout
Mad River; a few fish taken from Lake Erie

Lake trout
A few fish taken from Lake Erie

Northern pike
Sandusky Bay, Delta Reservoir, Charles Miller Reservoir, Oxbow Lake, Findley Lake, Atwood Lake, Nimisila Reservoir, Logan Lake

Walleye
Lake Erie Islands, Bellevue Reservoir, Maumee River, Sandusky River, Belin Reservoir, Pymatuning Lake, Seneca Reservoir, Indian Lake, Portage Lake, Mosquito Lake

Pickerel
Long Lake

Muskellunge
Hargus Lake, Knox Lake, Leesville Reservoir, North Reservoir, Clendening Reservoir, Deer Creek, Grand River, Pymatuning Lake, Rocky Fork Lake, Little Miama River, Lake Erie, Mogadore Reservoir, Piedmont Lake

Bluegill
Burr Oak Lake, Buckeye Lake, Rocky Fork Lake

Crappie
Buckeye Lake, Grand Lake St. Mary's

Yellow perch
Lake Erie near the islands, Sandusky Bay

White bass
Lake Erie, Pymatuning Lake, Sandusky River

Catfish
Lake Erie, Sandusky Bay, Pymatuning Lake, Grand Lake St. Mary's, Muskingum River, Piedmont Lake

Coho and chinook salmon
Lake Erie, Chagrin River, Conneaut Creek, Grand River, Huron River, Lower Cold Creek

Sturgeon
Lake Erie

OKLAHOMA

Largemouth bass
Lake Texoma, Eufaula Reservoir, Fort Cobb Reservoir, Fort Supply Reservoir, Foss Reservoir, Heyburn Reservoir, Hulah Lake, Tenkiller Lake, Lake Winster, Lake Humphreys

Spotted bass
Markham Ferry Reservoir

Northern pike
Bluestem Lake, Clayton Lake, Arbuckle Lake

Walleye
Canton Lake, Altus Lugert Reservoir, Tenkiller Lake

White bass
Lake Texoma, Eufaula Reservoir, Foss Reservoir, Fort Supply Reservoir, Heyburn Reservoir, Hulah Lake, Tenkiller Lake, Lake Winster

Catfish
Tenkiller Lake, Lake Winster, Hulah Lake, Heyburn Reservoir, Fort Supply Reservoir, Fort Cobb Reservoir, Foss Reservoir, Eufaula Reservoir, Lake Texoma

OREGON

Rainbow trout
Paulina Lake, Diamond Lake, East Lake, Davis Lake, South Twin, Elk Lake, Lake of the Woods, Morgan Lake, Klamath Lake, Wickiup Reservoir, Ochoco Reservoir, Detroit Reservoir, Haystack Reservoir, Beulah Reservoir, Clackamas River, Santiam River, Rogue River, Umpqua River, Molalla River

Steelhead
Chetco River, Cooes River, Deschutes River, Nestucca River, Nehalem River, Rogue River, Siletz River, Sixes River, Smiths River, Suislaw River, Umpqua River

Brown trout
Upper Umpqua River, Rogue River, Deschutes River

Brook trout
Diamond Lake, Paulina Lake, Crane Prairie Reservoir, Big Lava Lake, Klamath Lake, Malheur Reservoir, Wickiup Reservoir

Lake trout
Crescent Lake, Odell Lake, Big Cultus Lake, Wallowa Lake

Cutthroat trout
Clackamas River, Molalla River, Santiam River, Tualatin River, Yamhill River, Luckiamute River

Golden trout
Several lakes in the Wallowa Mountains and Cascade Mountains; Deschutes River

Bluegill
Colorado Lake, Savvie Island Sloughs, Withy Lake, Tahkenitch Lake, Triangle Lake

Crappie
Gerber Reservoir

Yellow perch
Siltcoos Lake, Tahkenitch Lake, Tenmile Lake, Mercer Lake, Savvie Island Sloughs

Catfish
Snake River

Chinook and coho salmon
The entire length of the Pacific Ocean shoreline; Columbia River, Rogue River, Umpqua River, Nestucca River

Sturgeon
Willamette River, Columbia River, Snake River

PENNSYLVANIA

Largemouth bass
Pecks Pond, Promised Land Lake, Fairview Lake, Gouldsboro Lake, Elk Lake, Duck Harbor Pond, Lower Woods Lake, Lake Quinsigamond, Green Lane Reservoir, Gordon Lake, Koon Lake, Shawnee State Park, Youghiogheny Reservoir

Smallmouth bass
Delaware River, Big Pine Creek, Sinnemahoning Creek, Hunters Lake, Conneaut Lake, Allegheny River, Holtwood Dam, Green Lane Reservoir, Susquehanna River, Dutch Fork Lake, Juniata River

Rainbow trout
Lackawaxen River, Shohola Creek, Equinunk Creek, Big Bushkill Creek, Brodheads Creek, upper Delaware River, Poncho Creek

Steelhead
Elk Creek, Twenty Mile Creek, Walnut Creek, Trout Run, Crooked Creek, Raccoon Creek, Six Mile Creek, Seven Mile Creek, Eight Mile Creek, Twelve Mile Creek, Sixteen Mile Creek

Brown trout
Allegheny River, Big Pine Creek, Big Fishing Creek, Loyalsock Creek, East Licking Creek, Yellow Breeches Creek, upper Delaware River, Slate Run

Brook trout
Mountain Creek, Honey Creek, Big Fishing Creek

Northern pike
Lake Wilhelm, Shenango River Lake, Presque Isle Bay, Lake Marburg, Kyle Lake, Conneaut Lake, Conewango Creek, Canadohta Lake

Pickerel
Pecks Pond, Fairview Lake, Elk Lake, Promised Land Lake, lower Promised Land Lake, Gouldsboro Lake, Duck Harbor Pond, Lake Quinsigamond, Belmont Lake, Miller Pond, White Oak Pond, Black Moshannon Lake

Muskellunge
Allegheny River, Susquehanna River, Delaware River, Pymatuning Lake, Gordon Lake, Shawnee Lake, Belzville Lake, Conneaut Lake, Youghiogheny Reservoir, Canadohta Lake, Somerset Lake, Lake LeBoeuf

Walleye
Pymatuning Lake, Lake Wallenpaupack, Lake Erie, Allegheny River, Susquehanna River, Holtwood Dam, Sweet Arrow Lake, Juniata River, Somerset Lake

Bluegill
Conneaut Lake, Gordon Lake

Yellow perch
Black Moshannon Lake, Walnut Creek

RHODE ISLAND

Largemouth bass
Wordens Pond, Watchaug Pond, Brickyard Pond, Warwick Pond, Bowdish Pond, Johnson's Pond

Brown trout
Wood River, Falls River, Breakheart Brook, Roaring Brook, Flat River, Paris Brook, Beach Pond, Wallum Lake, Stafford's Pond

Bluegill
Bowdish Reservoir, Browning Mill Pond, Gorton Pond, Mishnock Pond, Chapman Pond

Yellow perch
Watchaug Pond, Wordens Pond, Locustville Pond, Gorton Pond, Tucker Pond

Sunfish
Yawgoog Pond, Beach Pond, Watchaug Pond, Wordens Pond, Locustville Pond, Gorton Pond, Tucker Pond

SOUTH CAROLINA

Largemouth bass
Lake Greenwood, Lake Murray, Catawba Lake, Lake Marion, Lake Moultrie, Clark Hill Reservoir, Santee-Cooper Reservoir

Rainbow trout
Saluda River

Brown trout
Saluda River

Walleye
Lake Hartwell, Clark Hill Reservoir, Murray Lake

Sauger
Clark Hill Reservoir

Chain pickerel
Lake Greenwood, Lake Murray, Santee-Cooper Reservoir

Bluegill
Lake Greenwood, Lake Murray

Crappie
Lake Murray, Lake Greenwood, Wateree Reservoir, Catawba River, Lake Marion, Lake Moultrie, Santee-Cooper Reservoir

White bass
Lake Greenwood, Santee-Cooper Reservoir, Wateree Reservoir, Lake Murray

Other panfish
Edicto River, Little Peedee River, Big Peedee River, Coosawahatchie River, Salkehatchie River

Catfish
Wateree Reservoir, Catawba River, Lake Moultrie

SOUTH DAKOTA

Largemouth bass
Sheridan Lake, West River Prairie, Big Stone Lake

Rainbow and brown trout
Rapid Creek, Sheridan Lake, Sylvan Lake, Center Lake, Deerfield Reservoir, Spearfish Creek

Northern pike
Roy Lake, Oahe Reservoir, Fort Randall Reservoir, Clear Lake, Big Stone Lake, Enemy Swim Lake, Buffalo Lake, Cottonwood Lake, Pickerel Lake, Okoboji Creek

Walleye
Pickerel Lake, Clear Lake, Roy Lake, Poinsett Lake, Missouri River, Oahe Reservoir, Sharpe Reservoir, Big Stone Lake, Enemy Swim Lake, Francis Case Reservoir, Fort Randall Reservoir

Sauger
Oahe Reservoir, Fort Randall Reservoir

Bluegill
West River Prairie, Big Stone Lake, Roy Lake, Enemy Swim Lake

Crappie
Sheridan Lake, West River Prairie, Fort Randall Reservoir, Oahe Reservoir, Big Stone Lake, Lake Traverse, Lake Poinsett

Yellow perch
Big Stone Lake, Clear Lake, Roy Lake, Cottonwood Lake, Pickerel Lake, Enemy Swim Lake

Catfish
Fort Randall Reservoir, Oahe Reservoir

TENNESSEE

Largemouth bass
Reelfoot Lake, Kentucky Lake, Dale Hollow Reservoir, Center Hill Reservoir, Old Hickory Lake, Cheatam Lake, Daniel Boone Lake, Wautauga Reservoir, Fort Patrick Henry Reservoir, Cherokee Lake, Norris Lake, Fort Loudon Reservoir, Watts Bar Reservoir, Pickwick Lake, Bedford Lake

Smallmouth bass
Dale Hollow Reservoir, Elk River, Center Hill Reservoir, Cherokee Lake, Norris Lake, Watts Bar Reservoir, Chickamauga Lake, Kentucky Lake, Caney Fork River

Spotted bass
Obion River, Hatchie River, Loosahatchie River, Wolf River, Kentucky Lake, Chickamauga Lake

Rainbow trout
Watauga Reservoir, Wilbur Reservoir, Doe Creek

Brown trout
Elk River, Watuaga Lake tailwater, South Holston tailwater, Little Tennessee River, Hiwassee River

Northern pike
Emory River, Daddys Creek, streams in the Catoosa Wildlife Area

Walleye
Dale Hollow Reservoir, Center Hill Reservoir, Norris Lake, Wautauga Reservoir, Old Hickory Lake, Percy Priest Lake, Woods Lake

Sauger
Holston River, Norris Lake, Watts Bar Reservoir, Chickamauga Lake, Kentucky Lake

Chain pickerel
Garrett Lake, Laurel Hill Lake

Muskellunge
Dale Hollow Reservoir, Woods Reservoir, Norris Reservoir, Fort Patrick Henry Reservoir

Bluegill
Fort Patrick Henry Reservoir, Davy Crockett Reservoir, Reelfoot Lake, Laurel Hill Lake, Garrett Lake, Whiteville Lake

Crappie
Center Hill Reservoir, Old Hickory Lake, Cheatam Lake, Daniel Boone Lake, Fort Loudon Reservoir, Dale Hollow Reservoir, Watts Bar Reservoir, Chickamauga Lake, Pickwick Lake, Kentucky Lake, Reelfoot Lake

White bass
Cherokee Lake, Douglas Reservoir, Norris Lake, Fort Loudon Reservoir, Watts Bar Reservoir, Hales Bar Reservoir, Pickwick Lake, Kentucky Lake

Catfish
Cheatam Lake, Douglas Reservoir, Garret Lake, Kentucky Lake, Humboldt Lake, Laurel Hill Lake, Dale Hollow Reservoir

TEXAS

Largemouth bass
Lake Texoma, Caddo Lake, Lake Travis, Falcon Lake, Toledo Bend Reservoir, Sam Rayburn Reservoir, Lake Tawakoni

Northern pike
Greenbelt Lake

Walleye
Lake Meredith, Lake Diversion, San Angelo Lake, Lake Cypress Springs

Panfish
Caddo Lake, Falcon Lake, Lake Texoma, Sam Rayburn Reservoir, Toledo Ben Reservoir, Lake Tawakoni, Lake Travis

Catfish
Caddo Lake, Lake Tawakoni, Lake

Travis, Sabine River, Colorado River, Rio Grande River

UTAH

Largemouth bass
Glen Canyon Reservoir, Flaming Gorge Reservoir

Rainbow trout
Bear Lake, Fish Lake, Flaming Gorge Reservoir, Glen Canyon Reservoir, Logan River, Weber River, Provo River, Scofield Reservoir

Brown trout
Flaming Gorge Reservoir, Glen Canyon Reservoir, Logan River, Weber River

Brook trout
Uinta Lake, Provo River

Lake trout
Bear Lake, Flaming Gorge Reservoir, Fish Lake.

Golden trout
Uinta Lake

Cutthroat trout
Flaming Gorge Reservoir, Bear Lake, Strawberry Reservoir, Logan River, Weber River

Walleye
Utah River, Provo River, Willard Bay Reservoir, Lake Powell

Channel catfish
Utah Lake, Green River, San Juan River, Colorado River

VERMONT

Largemouth bass
Connecticut River, Lake Champlain

Smallmouth bass
Lake Champlain

Rainbow trout
Otter Creek, upper Connecticut River, Lake Champlain, Lake Memphremagog, Willoughby Lake, Echo Lake, Northern Lake, White River, Black River, Williams River, Saxton's River, West River

Brown trout
Battenkill River, Otter Creek, Lake Memphremagog, Well's River, White River, West River, Black River

Brook trout
Battenkill River, Connecticut River, Lake Champlain

Northern pike
Lake Champlain, lower Connecticut River

Muskellunge
North Lake Champlain

Walleye
Lake Champlain, Lake Memphremagog, Lake Bomoseen, Waterbury Reservoir, White River, Connecticut River, Claytor Lake, Clinch River

Crappie
Lake Champlain

Yellow perch
Lake Champlain, Lake Memphremagog, Lake Dunmore, Shelburne Pond

Landlocked salmon
Lake Memphremagog, Averill Lake, Lake Seymour, Salem Lake, Caspian Lake, Lake Dunmore, Crystal Lake, Echo Lake, Willoughby Lake, Maidstone Lake

VIRGINIA

Largemouth bass
Currituck Sound, Lake Prince, Lake Meade, Smith Lake, Philpott Reservoir, John Kerr Reservoir, Lake Gaston, Lake Anna, Lake Brittle

Smallmouth bass
Nottaway River, Philpott Reservoir, James River, Tye River, New River, Holston River, South Fork Shenandoah River

Rainbow and brown trout
Philpott Reservoir, Big Run River, Broad Run River, Rush River, Hughes River, Thornton River, upper Rapidan River, St. Mary's River, Garth Run River, Moormans River, Smith Creek

Northern pike
Gaston Reservoir

Pickerel
Cowpasture River, Big Back Creek

Walleye
New River, Clayton River, Clinch River, Kerr Reservoir, Buggs Island Lake, Smith Mountain Lake, Nottoway River, James River, Round River

Muskellunge
Smith Mountain Lake, Claytor Lake, Burke Lake, Carvin's Cove Lake, Shenandoah River, Clinch River, James River

Bluegill
Lee Hall Reservoir, Harwood Mill Pond, Burnt Mill Reservoir, Dan River, Staunton River, Lake Brittle, Lake Shenandoah

Crappie
Lee Hall Reservoir, Harwood Mill Pond Reservoir, Burnt Mill Reservoir, Philpott Reservoir, Lake Brittle

White bass
Pound Lake, Levisa River

Rock bass
Nottoway River, Pound Lake, Levisa River

Channel catfish
South Fork Shenandoah River

WASHINGTON

Largemouth bass
Silver Lake, Banks Lake

Rainbow trout
Green Lake, Merrill Lake, Merwin Lake, Spirit Lake, Silver Lake, Spencer Lake, Diablo Reservoir, Banks Lake, Jamestown Lake, Clear Lake, Curlew Lake

Steelhead
Cowlitz River, Duckabush River, Green River, Hoh River, Humptulips River, Kalama River, Puyallup River, Queets River, Quinault River, Skagit River, Skykomish River, Stillaguamish River, Washougal River

Brook trout
Merrill Lake, Pierre Lake, Deed Lake

Cutthroat trout
Grandy Lake, Whatlom Lake, Icicle Creek, Nason Creek, Chiwaw Creek, Sutherland Lake, Deed Lake, Pierre Lake, Browns Lake, Columbia River, Nasell River, Toutle River, Kalama River, East Fork Lewis River, North Fork Lewis River, Elochoman River

Dolly Varden trout
Icicle Creek, Nason Creek, Chiwaw Creek, Diablo Reservoir

Walleye
Long Lake, Banks Lake, Columbia River

Crappie
Silver Lake, Banks Lake, Potholes Reservoir, Eloika Lake, McNary Reservoir

Yellow perch
Silver Lake, Campbell Lake, Banks Lake, McNary Reservoir, Potholes Reservoir

Sunfish
Banks Lake, Potholes Reservoir, Tanwax Lake, McNary Reservoir

Chinook and coho salmon
Westport, Neah Bay, Laposh, Puget Sound, Hope Island, Columbia River, Grays Harbor area, Strait of Juan de Fuca, and along the entire shoreline of the Pacific Ocean

WEST VIRGINIA

Largemouth bass
Bluestone Reservoir, Sutton Reservoir, Lake Sherwood, Plum Orchard Lake, East Lynn Lake, Tygert Lake, Summersville Lake

Smallmouth bass
Bluestone Reservoir, Sutton Reservoir, New River, Greenbrier River, Potomac River, Elk River

Rainbow trout
Cranberry River, Shaver's Fork River, Williams River, Seneca Creek, Anthony Creek, Seneca Impoundment, Teter Creek Lake, Edwards Run Pond, Spruce Knob Lake, Summit Lake

Northern pike
Sutton Reservoir, Elk River, Ohio River

Walleye
Summersville Reservoir, Sutton Reservoir, Elk River, New River, Greenbrier River

Muskellunge
Bluestone Reservoir, Sutton Reservoir, Little Kanawha River, Elk River

Bluegill
Bluestone Reservoir, Sutton Reservoir, Bear Rocks Lake, Cedar Lake, Mountain View Lake, Horse Creek Lake

Crappie
Bluestone Resrvoir, Sutton Reservoir, Kanawha River

Rock bass
Greenbrier River

Catfish
Bluestone Reservoir, New River, Little Kanawha River

WISCONSIN

Smallmouth bass
Bad River, Chippewa River, Mississippi River, Namekagon River, St. Croix River, Totogatic River, Eau Claire River, Wisconsin River, Fox River, Flambeau River, Manitowish River, Pestigo River, Menominee River, Couderay River, Lac Vieux Desert, Tomahawk Lake, and hundreds of others

Rainbow trout
Lake Michigan, Neenah Creek, Bad River, Butternut Creek, Trout Brook, Bark River, Brule River, Fish Creek, Reiboldt's Creek, Hibbards Creek, Sioux River, Siskowitt River, Little Brule River, Pokegama Creek, Nebagamon Creek

Steelhead
Rieboldt's Creek, Heins Creek, Hibbards Creek, Whitefish Bay Creek, Ahnapee River, Kewaunee River, Manitowac River, Cranberry River, Fish Creek, Brule River, Lake Michigan, Lake Superior

Brown trout
Lake Michigan, Lake Superior, Green Bay, Brule River, Rieboldt's Creek, Cave Point, Kewaunee River, Moonlight Bay, Jacksonport, Bailey's Harbor, North Bay, Rowley Bay, Sister Bay, Sturgeon Bay

Northern pike
Chequamegon Bay, Green Bay, Shell Lake, Big Round Lake, Yellow Lake, Lac Vieux Desert, Butternut Lake, Pelican Lake, Shawano Lake, Lake Poygan, Lake Winnebago, Winne-

Northern pike (*continued*)
conne Lake, Mississippi River, Fox River, Wolf River, Wisconsin River, Chetek Lake

Walleye
Lake Winnebago, Wolf River, Fox River, Mississippi River, Lac Vieux Desert, Pelican Lake, Lake Poygan, and hundreds of other lakes

Muskellunge
Chippewa Flowage, Flambeau Flowage, Bone Lake, Grindstone Lake, Teal Lake, Round Lake, Spider Lake, Court Oreille Lake, Manitowish River, Lac Vieux Desert, Tomahawk Lake, Alder Lake, Big Muskellunge Lake, Trout Lake

Bluegill
Mississippi River and bayous, Carroll Lake, Pewsukee Lake, Powers Lake, Shawano Lake, Long Lake, and hundreds of others

Crappie
Mississippi River, Chippewa Flowage, Lake Koshkonong, Lake Wissota

Yellow perch
Lake Michigan, Lake Superior, Lake Mendota, Arbor Vitae Lake, Lake Geneva, Lake Winnebago, Curtis Lake, Green Bay

Sauger
Lake Winnebago

Sturgeon
Lake Winnebago, Lake Poygan, Lake Winneconne, Buttes des Mortes Lake, Fox River, Wolf River

WYOMING

Rainbow trout
Pathfinder Reservoir, Powder River, LAK Reservoir, Lake DeSmet, Seminoe Reservoir, Cloud Peak Reservoir, Cook Lake, Green River, Little Popo Agie River, Hamm's Fork Reservoir, North Platte River, Sweetwater River, Ross Lake, Snake River, Shoshone Reservoir

Brown trout
Powder River, Lake DeSmet, Seminow Reservoir, North Platte River, Big Hole River, Madison River, Gardiner River, Lewis River, Yellowstone River, Gros Ventre River, Firehole River, Shell Creek

Brook trout
Shoshone Lake, Sweetwater River, Soda Lake, Cook Lake, Cottonwood Reservoir

Lake trout
Middle Piney Lake, Fremont Lake, Jackson Lake, Jenny Lake, Buffalo Bill Reservoir

Cutthroat trout
Long Lake, Jenny Lake, North Piney Lake, Smith's Fork, Atlantic Lake, Lonesome Lake, Hidden Lake, Gros Ventre River, Jackson Lake, Copper Lake, Yellowstone Lake, Bridger Lake, Shoshone River, Upper Ross Lake, Tomahawk Lake, North Fork Shoshone River, Yellowstone River

Golden trout
Cook Lake, Buffalo Fork, South Fork Little Wind River, Valentine Lake, Grave Lake, Deep Creek Lake, Lonesome Lake

Bluegill
Ocean Lake, Festo Lake

Grayling
Johnson Lake, Upper Clay Butte Lake

Whitefish
Wind River

Other panfish
Ocean Lake, Festo Lake, Lake DeSmet, Lake Hattie, Beck Lake

CANADA

ALBERTA

Rainbow trout
Athabasca River, Strubel Lake, Mitchell Lake, Star Lake, Chickako Lake, Two Lakes, Bow River

Brook trout
Prairie Creek, Upper Stony Creek, Williams Creek, Alford Creek, Lookout Creek, Bouin Lake, Elbow Lake, Rat Lake, Muskiki Lake

Brown trout
Raven River, Beaver River, Stauffer Creek, Fallen Timber Creek, Alford Creek, Dogpond Creek, Shunda Creek, Athabasca River, Peace River

Cutthroat trout
Ram River, Castle River, Daisy Creek, Vicary Creek, Dutch Creek, Racehorse Creek, Oldman River, Livingstone River

Lake trout
Cold Lake, Grist Lake, Namur Lake, Margaret Lake, Wentzel Lake, Peerless Lake, Swan Lake, Rock Lake

Dolly Varden trout
Peace River, Berland River, Wildhay River, Muskeg River, Cardinal River

Golden trout
South Fork Lakes

Northern pike
Lake Athabasca, Lesser Slave Lake, Hay Lake, Utikuma Lake, Peerless Lake, Gods Lake, Siebert Lake, Namur Lake, Winifred Lake, Loon Lake, Bistcho Lake, Zama Lake

Walleye
Sturgeon Lake, Ironwood Lake, Smoke Lake, Wolf Lake, Touchwood Lake, Athabasca River, Peace River, Red Deer River, South Saskatchewan River

Yellow perch
Sturgeon Lake, Kehiwin Lake, Moose Lake, Beaver Lake, Elk Water Lake

Whitefish
Castle River, Crowsnest River, Oldman River, Upper Bow River, Red Deer River, Athabasca River, Lake Wabamun, Pigeon Lake, Hanmore Lake, Buck Lake, Moose Lake

Grayling
Athabasca River, Peace River, Swan River, Wapiti River, Kakwa River, Cutbank River

BRITISH COLUMBIA

Largemouth bass
Columbia River drainage

Smallmouth bass
Christina Lake, Boldue Lake, Kettle River

Steelhead
Nitinat River, China River, Toquart River, Heber River, Stamp River, Ash River, Gold River, Nimpkish River, Fraser River, Dean River, Sechelt Creek, Skeena River, Kispiox River, Bulkley River, Babine River, Morice River, Sustut River

Brown trout
Cowichan River, Little Qualicum River, Niagara Creek

Brook trout
Cowichan River, Spectacle Lake, Round Lake, Semenos Lake

Dolly Varden trout
Campbell River, Comox Lake, Cowichan Lake, Kootenay Lake, Columbia River drainage

Cutthroat trout
Nicomekl River, Campbell River, Serpentine River, Fraser River, Butzen Lake, Dean River, Tlell River, Nimpkish River

Lake trout
Shuswap Lake

Walleye
Peace River, Beatton River, Muskwa River, Fort Nelson River

Chinook and coho salmon
Strait of Juan de Fuca, Queen Charlotte Strait, Rivers Inlet, Strait of Georgia, Knight Inlet, Skeena River, Port Alberni, Howe Sound, Phillips Arm, Bella Coola, and thousands of streams and small bays along the mainland and Vancouver Island

MANITOBA

Smallmouth bass
Winnipeg River, Falcon Lake

Rainbow trout
Katherine Lake, Lake William, Whiteshell Park

Brook trout
Katherine Lake, Gods Lake, Gods River, Churchill River, Nelson River, Limestone River, Weir River

Lake trout
West Hawk Lake, High Lake, Aikens Lake, Moar Lake, Lake Athapapuskow, Gods Lake, Gods River, Kississing Lake, Clearwater Lake, Rocky Lake

Northern pike
High Rock Lake, Winnipeg River, Bird River, Lake St. Martin, Cross Lake, St. George Lake, Aikens Lake, Moar Lake, Lake Athapapuskow, Dogskin Lake, Fishing Lake, Moar Lake, Harrop Lake, Gods Lake, Reed Lake

Walleye
Churchill River, High Rock Lake, Dauphin River, Assiniboine River, Winnipeg River, Manitoba Lake, Saskatchewan River, St. George Lake, Aikens Lake, Moar Lake, Red Deer River, Overflowing River, Clearwater Lake, Kississing Lake

Sturgeon
Winnipeg River

Arctic grayling
Churchill River, Owl River, Deer River, Silcox River

NEW BRUNSWICK

Smallmouth bass
St. Croix River, St. John River, Magaguadavic River, Spednik Lake, Magaguadavic Lake, Digdeguash Lake, Wheaton Lake, Utopia Lake

Brook trout
This species is found in almost every lake or pond in the province

Landlocked salmon
A large number of small ponds or lakes contain landlocks

Atlantic salmon
Salmon River, Big Tracadie, Northwest Miramichi River, Renous River, Tabusintac River, Southwest Miramichi River, Sevogle River, Nashwaak River, Restigouche River, Kedgwick River, Cains River, Upsalquitch River

NEWFOUNDLAND

Atlantic salmon
Little Codroy River, Grand Codroy

River, Crabbs River, Flat Bay Brook, Humber River, Serpentine River, Southwest Brook, Highlands River, Harry's River, River of Ponds, Portland Creek, East River, Torrent River, Baker's Brook, St. John's River, Salmonier River, Colinet River, Trecassie River, Gander River, Northwest Gander River, Southwest Gander River

Brook trout
Steal Cove, Swift Current, Witles Bay, Bascay Bay, Bottom Brook, Harry's River, Humber River

NORTHWEST TERRITORIES

Lake trout
Mackenzie River, Great Slave Lake, Great Bear Lake, hundreds of other lakes, some of which have not been explored for fishing possibilities

Northern pike
Great Slave Lake, Great Bear Lake, Mackenzie River, Anderson River, Dubawnt Lake, and hundreds of smaller lakes

Walleye
Lac St. Theres, Great Slave Lake, Great Bear Lake, Hay River

Arctic grayling
Mackenzie River, Coppermine River, Anderson River, Thelon River, Black River, Great Bear Lake, Great Slave Lake, Dubawnt Lake, Dismal Lake, and hundreds of other lakes and streams; Camsell River

Arctic char
Coppermine area, Tree River, Bathurst Inlet, and many of the offshore islands and tributaries; this fishery has yet to be explored to its fullest

NOVA SCOTIA

Smallmouth bass
Elliott Lake, Dartmouth Lake, Halifax Lake, Clair Lake, Lily Lake, Victoria Lake

Rainbow trout
Giants Lake, Ramsey Lake, Lavers Lake, Clearwater Lake, Sunken Lake

Brown trout
Milford Haven River, Salmon River, Conwallis River, East River, Mersey River, Kilkenny Lake, Sheet Harbor

Landlocked salmon
Grand Lake, Shubenacadie Lake

Atlantic salmon
Medway River, LaHave River, St. Mary's River, Musquodoboit River, Moser River, Ecum-Secum River, Margaree River, East River, Ingram River, Quoddy River

ONTARIO

Largemouth bass
Rideau Lakes, Kawartha Lakes, Bay of Quinte, Lake Simcoe, Lake Erie, Lake Ontario

Smallmouth bass
Lake Erie, Lake Simcoe, Lake Huron, Georgian Bay, Perry Sound, Lingham Lake, North Bay, Batchawana River, Batchawana Bay, Savant Lake, Kabinakagami Lake, Montreal Lake

Steelhead
Agawa River, Baldhead River, Coldwater River, Michipicoten River, Old Woman River, University River, Bighead River, Blue Jay Creek, Nottawasaga River, Manitou River, Saugeen River, Big Otter Creek, Venison Creek, Clear Creek, Dedrick Creek, Young Creek, Wilmot Stream, Ganaraska Stream, Shelter Valley Stream, Bowmanville Creek, Soper Creek

Brown trout
Lake Erie, Lake Huron, Georgian Bay, Lake Simcoe, Tweed Lake, Lindsay Lake, Young Creek, Wilmot Stream, Ganaraska Stream

Brook trout
Severn River, Wakwayokastic River, Groundhog River, Albany River, Winisk River, Black Duck River, Nipigon River, Lake Nipigon, Sutton River, Kabinakagami River, Mettagami River, Attawapiskat River, Kesagami River, Detroit Lake; lakes in Algonquin Park—Scott, Faya, Harry, Jake, Welcome, Dickson, Stinger, Hogan, Tim, Lavielle

Lake trout
Lake Simcoe, Lake Erie, Lake Ontario, Hay Lake, Lake Nipigon, Kawartha Lakes, some Rideau Lakes; many other lakes

Northern pike
Lake of the Woods, Kesagami Lake, Kabinakagami Lake, Nipigon Lake, Rainy Lake, Red Lake, Eagle Lake, Lake Nipissing, Lake Simcoe, Lac la Croix, Savant Lake, Little Vermilion Lake, Timagami Lake, and thousands of others

Walleye
Kabinakagami Lake, Kesagami Lake, St. Clair River, Lake St. Clair, Lake of the Woods, Lake Erie, Moon River, Georgian Bay, Lake Huron, Lake Ontario, Savant Lake, Batchawana River, Rainy Lake, Kawartha Lakes, Lake Nipissing, and hundreds of other lakes and streams

Muskellunge
Lake of the Woods, Lake St. Clair, Georgian Bay, St. Lawrence River, Lake Nipissing, Eagle Lake, Kawartha Lakes, Vermilion Lake

Crappie
Rainy Lake, Bay of Quinte, Georgian Bay

White bass
Lake Nipissing, Bay of Quinte

Whitefish
Lake Simcoe

PRINCE EDWARD ISLAND

Rainbow and brook trout
Cardigan River, Seal River, Keefe's Lake, Glenfinnan Lake, Scales Pond, Mitchell River

QUEBEC

Brook trout
Many private leased lakes along the Ottawa River (permission is necessary and often difficult to obtain), St. Maurice River, George River and many nearby lakes in frontier Quebec; Lake Berard, Lake Spatford, Lake Elliott, Lake Arthur, Lake Simone, Lake Turnback—all on the Haltaparche Club near LaTuque

Landlocked salmon and ouananiche
Peribonca River, Kaniapiskau River, Mistassini River, Ashapumuchuan River, Manouan River

Atlantic salmon
George River, Whale River, Koksoak River, Leaf River, Payne River, Natashquan River, Romaine River, Saint-Jean River, Moisie River, Matane River, Godbout River, Saguenay River, Bonaventure River, Little Cascapedia River, Grand Cascapedia River, Matapedia River, Restigouche River

Northern pike
Mistassini Lake, Gouin Reservoir, and thousands of other lakes

Walleye
St. Lawrence River, Gouin Reservoir, Mistassini Lake, and thousands of other lakes

SASKATCHEWAN

Brook trout
Cypress Lake, Red Deer River, Fir River

Lake trout
Athabasca Lake, Wollaston Lake, Cree Lake, Reindeer Lake, Kingsmere Lake

Northern pike
Lac La Ronge, Reindeer Lake, Cree Lake, Deschambault Lake, Namew Lake, Tobin Lake, Black Lake, Amisk Lake, Scott Lake, Tazin Lake, Careen Lake, Athabasca Lake, Hatchet Lake, Waterbury Lake, Wollaston Lake, Otter Lake

Walleye
Churchill River, Saskatchewan River, Lake Athabasca, Chitek Lake, Fishing Lake, hundreds of other lakes

Whitefish
Lac La Ronge, Peter Pond, Ile à la Crosse

Grayling
Athabasca Lake, Black Lake, Careen Lake, Cree Lake, Cree River, Reindeer Lake, Tazin Lake, Hatchet Lake, Waterbury Lake, Wollaston Lake, Clearwater River

YUKON TERRITORIES

Lake trout
Teslin Lake, Little Atlin Lake, Lake Kluane, Lake Aishihik, Quiet Lake

Northern pike
Nisutlin River, Teslin Lake, and many other locations

Walleye
Liard River, Gusty Lake

Arctic grayling
Rancheria River, Lake Kluane, Swift River, hundreds of lakes and streams

INDEX